the cinema of RICHARD LINKLATER

DIRECTORS' CUTS

Other select titles in the Directors' Cuts series:

the cinema of
RICHARD LINKLATER

walk, don't run

Rob Stone

 **WALLFLOWER PRESS** LONDON & NEW YORK

A Wallflower Press Book
Published by
Columbia University Press
Publishers Since 1893
New York • Chichester, West Sussex
cup.columbia.edu

A complete CIP record is available from the Library of Congress

ISBN 978-0-231-16552-5 (cloth : alk. paper)
ISBN 978-0-231-16553-2 (pbk. : alk. paper)
ISBN 978-0-231-85040-7 (e-book)

Series design by Rob Bowden Design

Cover image of Richard Linklater courtesy of the Kobal Collection

Columbia University Press books are printed on permanent
and durable acid-free paper.
This book is printed on paper with recycled content.
Printed in the United States of America

c 10 9 8 7 6 5 4 3 2 1
p 10 9 8 7 6 5 4 3 2 1

CONTENTS

para Esther, mi Céline

ACKNOWLEDGEMENTS

I would like to thank Swansea University for research leave and the British Academy for the award of a research grant that enabled me to spend invaluable time in Austin, Texas in July and August 2009. In the course of writing this book, I was assisted by several generous and talented individuals. Firstly, thanks are due to Yoram Allon, Jodie Taylor and the dedicated team at Wallflower Press for their support and collaboration. Grateful thanks are also due to Paul Cooke, who first invited me to write on Linklater for his edited book *World Cinema's 'Dialogues' with Hollywood* and who did his best to rid this book of nonsense and errors, as did my friends and colleagues, Elaine Canning, Joanna Rydzewska and Jimmy Hay. Thanks too to all the film students past and present at Swansea University, especially the gang who keep in touch via Facebook, for their interest in the project, which was more important than they know.

Thanks also to colleagues who helped in a variety of ways: Chris Homewood for information on German cinema, Kate Griffiths for help with a few translations, Peter Jones for kitting me out with the equipment I needed for Austin, and Mostyn Jones for invaluable technical assistance. Thanks to Lesley Speed, who graciously provided me with copies of her excellent articles on Linklater, to Josh Steuer, who generously allowed me to have a copy of the workprint of *Dazed and Confused*, and to Andrew Richards, who kindly sent me a copy of the documentary *Linklater: St. Richard of Austin*. Thanks are also due to Nick James, who commissioned my interview with Linklater, which appeared as 'Ambition's Debt' in *Sight & Sound* 20, no. 1 (January 2010), 34–6.

At Detour Filmproduction in Austin, Texas, many thanks to Kirsten McMurray for her assistance and kindness, and at the Austin Film Studios, Chale Nafus and Martin Parrington for the guided tour.

And, of course, a huge thank you to Richard Linklater, who graciously provided the time for lengthy interviews and chocolate cake on his 49th birthday no less! It was a pleasure to meet you.

Finally and always, my thanks and love to Esther Santamaría Iglesias, whose intuition is far superior to my intellect and whose time is my eternal present.

INTRODUCTION

Walk, Don't Run: The Cinema of Richard Linklater

Is it the place or is it the time in which nothing is happening? In the films directed by Richard Linklater there is often a sense that life (as preternaturally prescribed by social pressures, familial expectations and the economic imperative to deploy one's education profitably) is elsewhere. Indeed, the most enduring criticism of Linklater remains that of the passer-by in his debut film *Slacker* (1991), who spots him shooting apparently aimless twenty-somethings on a sidewalk and pointedly proclaims: 'Ain't no film in that shit!' However, this accusation is ignorant of all that has made Linklater one of the most consistent, versatile and contradictory figures in contemporary cinema.

Born in 1960 and a self-taught filmmaker, Linklater's cine-literacy and philo-sophical erudition has often seen him classified as the most European-minded of the American filmmakers who came to prominence with low-budget features in the 1990s and, partly for this reason, he remains one of those most critical of contemporary America. He made the emblematic *Slacker* for just $23,000, with which he conjured a richly atmospheric espousal of slacking not as laziness but as a refusal to engage with the fast-track consumerism and aggressive foreign policy of Presidents Ronald Reagan and George Bush Senior. Subsequent films, including *Dazed and Confused* (1993), *Before Sunrise* (1995) and *SubUrbia* (1996), explored this voluntary internal exile from Republicanism in their advocacy of aimlessness in form and content, offering imagi-nation and reflection as alternative priorities to competition and profit. Derided as a selfish waster, the slacker-protagonist was nothing of the sort. Feigned ambivalence to the tail end of the recession of the late 1980s was just a means of protection so that privately nurtured romantic ideas of the self could be safeguarded instead of surren-dered to social and political expectations. It is precisely because slackers cannot afford to be idle that their deliberate and cultivated appearance of idleness is tantamount to a political stance. Hence a prime contradiction: the committed slacker, which remains the dominant theme in Linklater's cinema.

Richard Linklater in front of his prized original Italian poster for *Citizen Kane* at his home in Austin, Texas

Linklater's characters often inhabit unique time-frames, where their experiences of the here-and-now struggle to match hand-me-down nostalgia for the been-and-gone. These time-frames can be one night or one day or even the duration of the films themselves in which private revolutionaries shape their worlds to the time available. In them, characters exist in a suspended state of contemplation and possibility, moving tentatively if at all and always on their own terms, walking not running from a state of disconnection with the world to one of acquaintance with the like-minded and similarly endangered. The locations that fill these time-frames – Austin, Vienna, Austin, Paris and Austin again – are both authentic places and metaphorical spaces signifying metaphysical potential. In Linklater's speculative travelogues his passengers are saved the claustrophobia of charter flights and gifted instead the widescreen windows of buses and trains or, as in *Dazed and Confused*, cars so cool that their unlikelihood almost betrays the fantasy. Yet these interior journeys are inevitably so informed by philosophy, music and movies that what passes for banality is actually the vibrant inner life of unrecognised heroes in their own downtimes, for whom just tuning the radio to the right station or, better yet, lucking into the perfect song for that instant, is a challenge and a holy moment in the making. Communication with what passes for the real world is therefore maintained by a meta-language made up of secondary sources, of lyrics, guitar licks, quotations, scenes from great films and icons as varied but defiantly equal as Dostoevsky, Welles, the Smurfs, Nietzsche, Buñuel, Scooby-Doo, Joyce, *Gilligan's Island*, Kafka, Godard, Aerosmith, Dylan Thomas and Nina Simone.

The youthful protagonists of Linklater's films include those who subscribe to a pickled memory of youthfulness, like Dewey Finn (Jack Black) in *The School of Rock* (2003) and Morris Buttermaker (Billy Bob Thornton) in *Bad News Bears* (2005). All of them build identities based on literary, philosophical and pop culture references, classic tracks, friendships and the ache of romantic possibilities. They shun hackneyed histories of nationhood and dubious parental traditions in favour of learning from music, movies and the urban legends of their generation. Their travelling, trivia and experiences of other people inspire a sense of parallel lives, in one of which surely, somewhere, sometime, something must be happening. Alongside the simultaneous realities of the novelist Douglas Coupland and Nirvana frontman Kurt Cobain in the early 1990s, Linklater was equally uncomfortable with being hailed as the voice of this generation, even as he expressed similar preoccupations with second-hand values in films that, like Coupland's *Generation X* (1991) and Nirvana's *Nevermind* (1991) riff on the generational shifts in volume and dynamics to be found on the B-side of Americana.

To date, Linklater's Nixon-to-Obama thematic matrix and belief system has been presented in what might be best understood as a synthetic Cubist manner that is far more politicised than has previously been recognised. His long takes, for example, express reflection, digression and patient observation as rejoinders to narrative or generic expectations of conformity and are roughly equivalent to the multi-angled measurements and recreations of objects seen in the work of Pablo Picasso and Georges Braque. Like Linklater, Cubism rejects a single viewpoint, preferring to fragment a three-dimensional subject and redefine it in a temporal collage made up of several points of view, as if seeing it in a shattered mirror. Its synthetic phase (1913–1920) involved a way of seeing what became of a subject when traditional rules of perspective, linearity and foreshortening were abandoned. Although the structuring of Linklater's similarly maverick films from *Slacker* to *Dazed and Confused*, *Before Sunrise*, *Waking Life* (2001) and *Fast Food Nation* (2006) is often described as non-linear or non-existent, their underlying structure is not chaos but a correlative collage. Because their subject is often a specific time-frame, so their form is a variegated composition of the characters, viewpoints, references and events (some parallel, some consecutive) that add up to an exploration of the visual and aural textures found within it. His loose-limbed films may thus offer more shading than conventional linear narratives and in approaching them as Cubist works it becomes possible to appreciate how the times they explore are broken up and re-assembled in a form more appropriate to an audience that sees the world in a much more fragmented manner than mainstream politics and entertainment ever countenance.

In addition to Linklater's long takes, the quotations, characters and music he orchestrates also correspond to Cubist surfaces that intersect at seemingly random angles, thereby replacing a coherent and comforting sense of depth with an existential context that develops intertextually between his films. His cinema may therefore be appreciated for its intersections of textual surfaces, alternative realities and points of view, but unlike sorting the truth from the various untruths described in Akira Kurosawa's *Rashomon* (1950) all of these surfaces, realities and viewpoints are valid. The key to their making and their meaning is a collaborative methodology that problematises theories of film authorship, while the planes of the objects, characters, backgrounds, times and spaces interpenetrate one another to create a shallow ambiguous space that is one of the most distinctive characteristics of Cubism and the cinema of Linklater. These collages take representational imagery beyond the merely mechanically photographic and away from any reality created by the boundaries of traditional single-point perspectives and redirect it towards the metaphysical. To this end, moreover, it is important to appreciate Linklater's deployment of rotoscoping, which involves the tracing and animating of live action footage, in order to explicitly represent metaphysical enquiry in *Waking Life* and *A Scanner Darkly* (2006).

However, perhaps ironically, Linklater's universe is not very big. For example, the Austin-based songwriter Daniel Johnston who proffers Linklater a cassette in *Woodshock* (1985) is back in *It's Impossible to Learn to Plow by Reading Books* (1988) to discover that the writing on Linklater's t-shirt is actually the film's title in Russian, while Mitch (Wiley Wiggins) moves from the *Bildungsroman* of *Dazed and Confused* to the *in media res* of *Waking Life* in which Jesse (Ethan Hawke) and Céline (Julie Delpy) from *Before Sunrise* appear in an alternative reality to their real-time reunion in *Before Sunset* (2004). Another indication that Linklater's universe is not so big is that the events of several films (*Slacker*, *Tape* [2001], *Live from Shiva's Dance Floor* [2003] and *Before Sunset*) take place within the real-time duration of the films themselves. Consequently, attention must be paid to Linklater's films as vehicles for what may be understood in relation to the theorist and philosopher Gilles Deleuze's concept of the time-image. The time-image enables the suspension of the protagonist in time and space in the face of pressure to conform and deliver a narrative. The time-image can thus be seen as a slacker that rebels by inaction, offering instead digressions that entail confrontation with narrative and generic conventions that may be subsequently extrapolated to reach wider targets such as political propaganda and prevailing philosophies. Slacking stalls the narrative and loosens the sensory-motor schema, thereby allowing 'a little time in the pure state' (Deleuze 2005b: xii) to rise up to the surface of the screen. Rarely glimpsed in contemporary American cinema, the time-image in the films of Linklater allows many questions to be asked and their answers pondered.

Limitations of time, of course, also entail mutually determinant restrictions on space. The Russian philosopher and semiotician Mikhail M. Bakhtin categorised spatial and temporal limitations in the novel as chronotopes and Linklater's contrived cinematic equivalents include the single motel room of *Tape*, in which 'time, as it were, thickens, takes on flesh, becomes artistically visible; likewise, space becomes charged and responsive to the movements of time, plot and history' (Bakhtin 2006c: 84). Other such chronotopes include the streets of Austin in *Slacker* and *Dazed and Confused* and those of Vienna in *Before Sunrise*, in which popular culture, as idealised by Bakhtin in the hubbub of the carnival square, opposes the remote official hegemony by an alternative focus on imagination and reflection that expresses a state of becoming and empowerment. An obvious reason why Linklater's universe is limited, although productively so, is that he has resolutely remained in the carnival-town of Austin, Texas, shunning Hollywood to some extent and contributing to the community-based film industry in his state capital. The importance of Austin in the work of the filmmaker is that it is not just a location, but a representation of an alternative state of mind and lifestyle to that of the country that encloses it. The university city of Austin is commonly known as the capital of green, live music and weirdness, being a proudly liberal community within a right-leaning state and nation, which translates directly into the cinema of Linklater and serves as a symbol of its politics and philosophy. Other film locations such as Vienna and Paris are partly metaphors for what Linklater found and founded in Austin, albeit with a dressing of old European cinephilia. At the same time, however, Linklater's universe is also limited in being almost exclusively white, heterosexual, well-fed and at least high-school educated; his characters are not folk who cannot get jobs but those who choose not to. This has made Linklater a reluctant and recalcitrant figurehead of a rather self-indulgent revolution, to the extent that when explicit moral indignation seems imminent, as in *Fast Food Nation*, he delivers a shrug of helplessness that may, in turn, indicate his own mature criticism of the slackers that he inadvertently inspired.

Despite occasional marketing to the contrary, his is not an obvious outsider cinema like that of his Queer or Black contemporaries such as Todd Haynes, Rose Troche and Gregg Araki, or Spike Lee and John Singleton. Nevertheless, he does carry the same burden of being expected to speak for his generation and has suffered the consequent commercial dismissal of his period films *The Newton Boys* (1998) and *Me and Orson Welles* (2008), perhaps because using Depression-era America as a metaphor for the present day was either too precious or too obscure. To be fair, the attitudinous cinema of this new breed of independent-minded American filmmakers was not a coherent movement. It drew up no manifesto, but rather buttressed the integrity of its hard-edged quirkiness with a spirit of independence that made the involvement of the major studios in matters of production and distribution problematic but never wholly irrelevant. Nevertheless, the extent to which a contemporary filmmaker is enabled, entitled or obliged to comment on contemporary society and its values is determined by other contradictions prevalent in the 'high-concept indie' cinema of Linklater, including the very notion that he is an independent filmmaker. Because his films have mostly involved production and distribution deals with major studios he is an ideal case study for an examination of the distortion and dissolution of the supposed tensions and differences between the two sectors.

Also contradictory is the fact that, although he often dismisses linear narrative and its beats, he has explored a wide range of genres, including the black comedy *Bernie* (2012), the teen comedy, western, science fiction and romance, as well as a remake (*Bad News Bears*), two animated features (*Waking Life, A Scanner Darkly*), adaptations of plays (*SubUrbia, Tape*) and the fictionalisation of a work of investigative journalism (*Fast Food Nation*). In crafting these films, as well as his long-term project *Boyhood*, which is being filmed over a twelve-year period for a possible release date of 2015, Linklater is commonly thought to favour on-set improvisation, but although this plays a part his films are based on rehearsed fidelity to the collaboratively nurtured script and their editing is often tied to pre-ordained music cues. Shooting, he has stated, is just 'the final three per cent of filmmaking',[1] which demands an emphasis on his working practice in pre-production when negotiating the obligatory but complex and disruptive concept of auteurism in relation to his work. His films may appear rudimentary in technique, but they are often informed by new technologies, while his left-wing, anti-authoritarian, independent persona and espousal of such causes as vegetarianism, immigrant rights, use of soft drugs, and nostalgia for the counter-culture of the Reagan and Bush years is both a beacon to a particular fan base and a warning light to the majority of voters/cinemagoers. *Dazed and Confused, Before Sunrise, The Newton Boys, Waking Life, Tape, The School of Rock, Before Sunset, Fast Food Nation* and *A Scanner Darkly* have each explored amongst much else the widely misunderstood slacker philosophy as an alternative lifestyle, campaign and ambition. *The School of Rock*, for example, is ostensibly a conventional crowd-pleasing comedy and the single big hit of his career, but it remains remarkably faithful to the slacker ethos and, it will be argued, is one of the most subversive films in recent American cinema.

In approaching the cinema of Richard Linklater, including his little-known documentaries *Live from Shiva's Dance Foor* and *Inning by Inning: A Portrait of a Coach* (2008), attention must be paid to the distribution and reception of his films, the domestic and international critical response, the cult fan base attached to several of them, and their relatively poor (sometimes disastrous) commercial trajectory. Thus, this book aspires to drift, to walk and talk with his films and, in excerpts from lengthy interviews, with Linklater himself. Exploring this cinema in the specific context of Austin, Texas, for example, and within recent and contemporary American society and cultures reveals not just the connections between Linklater and European filmmakers and philosophers, but also the ambiguous and emotive nature of so-called 'independent' American cinema in relation to Hollywood, European art-house cinema, and the traditions of regional cinema in America. Connecting the influence of Robert Bresson, Max Ophüls, Carl Theodor Dreyer, Jean-Luc Godard and Eric Rohmer is just one genealogical aspect of his work, while comparisons of Linklater to Robert Bresson, Krzysztof Kieslowski and Julio Medem reveals him as a metaphysician and, in his own modest and introspective way, one of very few spiritual filmmakers in America. However, Linklater does not subscribe to a regressive binary face-off with the rest of the world against Hollywood, for his work also reveals the legacy of American filmmakers. Moreover, his own influence endures in the films of Kevin Smith, Andrew Bujalski, Aaron Katz, Hans Weingartner and a plethora of up-and-coming-and-struggling American and European filmmakers. Most importantly, for all the literary, philosophical and cinematic influences that Linklater wears on his sleeve, his is a rather regional cinema, as bound to an idea of Austin as any intra-national cinema in Europe such as the Welsh or the Basque.

In sum, in Linklater's cinema it is time, talk and the spaces in between that convey thought and communicate experience. Thematically, his films betray adherence to the celebration of the mundane in early Godard accompanied by Rohmer's ear for tentatively neurotic dialogue and Buñuel's eye for the incongruity of the everyday, but his indebtedness to the aesthetics of other masters is also crucial. For example, whereas the long takes of Bresson invoke predestination and the eloquent trajectories of Ophüls describe an inescapable grand design, those of Linklater are loose and buffeted like his beloved pinball from one incident or idea to another until the film runs out. Thus, his cinema is less about origin and destination than it is about the moment, less about running from A to Z than walking in the spaces in between and wondering just who and why it was decided that the alphabet should be in that order anyway.

Notes

1   All quotations from Richard Linklater, unless otherwise attributed, are from interviews with the author in Austin, Texas, 30 July–1 August 2009.

CHAPTER ONE

Locating Linklater

Independent cinema feels right at home in Austin. Born of a revolution, Texas resisted the union of its Lone Star state with the rest of America for almost a decade, and even then and ever since its capital city of Austin has symbolised resistance to exploitation by the incursive forces that surround it. Americans come from all over the world they say, but Texans come from Texas. Its capital city was named after Stephen F. Austin, a cautious and peaceful sort who led the colonisation of the region by settlers. Fortunes from steers, cotton and oil sponsored the construction of the Texas State Capitol, the University of Texas at Austin and the damming of the Colorado River to make the downtown Lady Bird Lake that blooms as much as any symbolic oasis should. Urban legend has it that the city's slacker community was formed when rednecks and hippies hybridised over marijuana at a concert by fellow Austinite Willie Nelson, the leader of the 'outlaw' country movement of the 1970s. Today left-leaning Austin is a blue dot in a red state, still peopled with folk whose slacking is a charming distraction from the city's modernity, although lately the area has challenged San Francisco's Silicon Valley for high-tech industries that are largely manned by those who came to Austin to drop out but could not stand the pressure of doing nothing. Locating Linklater in Austin is vital, for his films not only emerged from the slacker culture of the mid-1980s but enunciate its undermining of the ideologies of late capitalist materialism via their form, content, style and themes. In this, Linklater applied the techniques associated with representations of alienation in post-war European cinema to a specifically regional concept of American cinema that was also informed by existentialist and Marxist undercurrents. Consequently, his films associated slacker culture with the deliberate wider critical project of communal estrangement from political and national hegemonies and reterritorialised a part of America that would find common identity and cause in the development of independent cinema.

The notion of independence in American cinema had existed since the mid-1910s as an industrial demarcation of films made by small production companies unrelated to the major studios. It also described films by such illustrious figures as Samuel Goldwyn and David O. Selznick, who produced films independently but negotiated their distribution with the majors. Subsequently, poverty row studios of the 1930s and 1940s such as Monogram and First National produced low-budget westerns and thrillers, while exploitation companies such as James H. Nicholson and Samuel Z. Arkoff's American International Pictures (AIP) began producing B-films for double-bills in the 1950s. In 1970 Roger Corman, who had directed a notable series of adaptations of the work of Edgar Allan Poe for AIP, established New World Pictures as a small, independent production and distribution studio whose films paid attention to marginalised, rebellious, adolescent characters and were an influence on Linklater. By the 1980s, however, the term independent 'started to signify films that ventured into themes largely untouched by Hollywood, that assimilated the influence of the experimental and art traditions, and that voiced minority perspectives' (Suárez 2007: 40). Even so, from *Easy Rider* (Dennis Hopper, 1969) to *Slumdog Millionaire* (Danny Boyle, 2009) the majors have always been willing to distribute independently produced films, reasoning that potential profit makes a good choice of 'indie' a safe investment because the risk is limited to its distribution.[1] The major studios are also keen to poach aesthetics, themes and filmmakers from the independent sector as exemplified by Geoff King's apt description of *Traffic* (Steven Soderbergh, 2000) as 'a $50 million Dogme movie' (2009: 158). The independent sector also provides market research on the changing tastes and demographics of its audience, which has been revealed as high-spending, 'educated adults who [are] interested in film as an aesthetic object' (Suárez 2007: 46) and whose idea of creativity is sympathetic to theories of auteurism. In the 2000s the term 'independent' shifted to describe what King identifies as:

> Indiewood, an area in which Hollywood and the independent sector merge or overlap. [...] From one perspective [films produced in this area] offer an attractive blend of creativity and commerce, a source of some of the more innovative and interesting work produced in close proximity to the commercial mainstream. From another, this is an area of duplicity and compromise, in which the 'true' heritage of the independent sector is sold out, betrayed and/or co-opted into an offshoot of Hollywood. (2009: 1)

Mike Atkinson concludes that 'any consideration of the indie climate in the U.S. must begin with this identity crisis' (2007: 18) that is perhaps exemplified in the manner by which the populist brand of independent cinema has become a non-threatening badge of quirkiness that *Juno* (Jason Reitman, 2007), for example, uses to make palatable a parable of anti-abortionist conservatism. Even an oddly-shaped movement such as Mumblecore, whose digitised disciples or 'Slackavetes' of Linklater and Cassavetes have churned out no-budget variations on *Before Sunrise* using digital cameras, twenty-something amateur casts and improvisation, has failed to offer much of an update on the cinematic declarations of its prophets.[2]

However, back in the 1970s, films made by enthusiastic amateurs from far-flung places like Texas were not called independent but regional cinema. Their independence was not an ethical, financial or creative choice but a consequence of localism. Regional cinema could be identified as such for its authentic locations, characters, themes and *mise-en-scène*, its home-based cast and crew, its accent and languages as well as its mostly localised financing, modest ambitions and particularly regional sensibilities, themes and characters. Regional filmmakers lacked the critical support of a *Cahiers du cinéma*, a *cinémathèque* or anything like access to distribution, but they did have the lightweight cameras and sound recording equipment that had enabled the French New Wave. For example, fifteen years before Linklater's *Slacker* was erroneously acclaimed as a new breed of film from Nowheresville, another Austinite named Eagle Pennell had marshalled talented amateurs to make films featuring ordinary folk whose culture was absent from what passed for Texas in Hollywood. Film such as *Giant* (George Stevens, 1956) and countless westerns offered grand vistas and remembered the Alamo; but only *Hud* (Martin Ritt, 1963) and *The Last Picture Show* (Peter Bogdanovich, 1971), which were both adapted from novels by Texan Larry McMurtry, had come anywhere near to genuine street level tensions and smalltown mores.[3] The borderland novels of Cormac McCarthy had not yet impacted,[4] nor had contemporary Tex-Mex film dramas such as *Lone Star* (John Sayles, 1996), *The Three Burials of Melquiades Estrada* (Tommy Lee Jones, 2005) and the adaptation of McCarthy's *No Country for Old Men* (Ethan & Joel Coen, 2007). But forget the Alamo, it was the resolutely un-mythical, working-class Austinite, red of neck and blue of collar, that was the subject of Eagle Pennell's *A Hell of a Note* (1977), *The Whole Shootin' Match* (1978) and *Last Night at the Alamo* (1983). These warm but downcast features reveal a people so rooted in a time and place that a collective identity is discernible in the gait of the films themselves. Long, loose takes of bullshitting urban cowboys are imbued with 'a kind of deeply pessimistic Southern fundamentalist Protestant view of humanity' (Odintz 2009: 19). But there is humour here too. All the opportunistic failures, bar-room *braggadocio*, defeatist advances on weary females and everyday chores of Pennell's characters reveal them as a generation lost between the tenant farmers of the 1950s and the untethered Wooderson (Matthew McConaughey) of Linklater's *Dazed and Confused*. If he had been able to free himself from the alcoholism that blighted his working relationships and killed him in 2002, Pennell might have served as a trailblazer for Linklater instead of the brief flare and fade that still made for an influential legend.

As Pennell discovered, there was only a ragged circuit of film festivals in the 1970s. Instead, films like his were predestined for limited runs in sympathetic local cinemas that occasionally inspired word of mouth. In turn this encouraged filmmakers to apply and submit to festivals, where critics might be open to seeing regional films as genuine American cinema. Hollywood's contemporaneous attempts to attract audiences by employing independent filmmakers had resulted in what Robin Wood called 'the incoherent narrative' of 1970s cinema, in which 'the drive towards the ordering of experience [was] visibly defeated' (1986: 47). Yet genuine empirical disorder was the natural subject of regional cinema like Pennell's, which reflected smalltown life as it was, made up as it went along. Whether by lack of training, disdain for formulaic narrative, a piecemeal production schedule or simply an unhurried experimentation with film-making that did not broker any realistic possibility of ever reaching an audience, the regional cinema of mavericks such as Pennell flirted with Modernism in responding to its own criteria and limitations. This was not the obscure, experimental cinema of Stan Brakhage (*Dog Star Man*, 1961–64), though it was no less unconventional; nor was it the militantly Queer, underground cinema of Kenneth Anger (*Lucifer Rising*, 1972), although its cultural identity was no less specific. Pennell lacked the work ethic of John Cassavetes, whose performance of independent auteurism contributed to the purist, romantic tenet of opposition to Hollywood, but like Cassavetes and Linklater he was one of the few who quit talking about something and did it. His collaborative cohort of Austinite cast and crew made *The Whole Shootin' Match* for about $20,000 and watched it at the Dobie, Austin's off-campus movie theatre on Guadalupe Street. Thereafter, popular response prompted a screening at the USA Film Festival in Dallas in April 1978 and a new festival held in Salt Lake City in Utah in September of that year, where it featured in the sidebar Regional Cinema: The New Bright Hope alongside the New York-based *Girlfriends* (Claudia Weill, 1978) and *Martin* (George A. Romero, 1977) from Pittsburgh. The suggestion was that the regionalism of these films was alternative and inseparable from their meaning. Robert Redford's viewing of *The Whole Shootin' Match* in the Utah festival so inspired him to want to nurture 'strays like this' (Cullum 2009: 23) that he moved the festival to Park City and changed its name to one of association with his Sundance Institute, whose precise aim was to encourage new breeds of regional filmmaking. This objective would be realised when the Pennell-inspired *Slacker* was nominated for the Sundance Grand Jury Prize for Dramatic Film in 1991.

Before Sundance, regional filmmaking in America was not a movement or a revolution but a homemade adventure that meant its parochialism was sometimes the punchline for a rare audience from elsewhere. Only occasionally might a regional filmmaker such as Austinite Tobe Hooper manage to transcend the stereotypes of Texans by turning them on their leather-faced heads in *The Texas Chain Saw Massacre* (1974), whose associate producer (Kim Henkel), sound technician (Wayne Bell), and assistant cameraman (Lou Perryman) had each learnt their skills as part of Pennell's crew. Yet Hooper's success was not just generic; it was also a terrifying response to what most audiences, festivals and critics disdained about rural America and, as such, was a particularly subversive example of regional cinema. Other regional filmmakers who escaped the fate of obscurity were mostly urbanites by comparison: Baltimore had John Waters (*Desperate Living*, 1977), New York had John Sayles (*The Return of the Secaucus Seven*, 1980) and Los Angeles had Alan Rudolph (*Welcome to LA*, 1976), while New York was sufficiently multi-cultural as to foster films featuring the streetwise but lost souls of John Cassavetes, the immigrants and nomads of Jim Jarmusch and the black working class of Charles Burnett. The catch-all title of 'independent' cinema did such regional filmmakers a disservice by dislocating them from their cultural specificity and grouping them in opposition to one place called Hollywood instead. As Marsha Kinder explains, the notion of regional cinema may be situated within a local and global interface but it is also an ideological construct and a 'relativistic concept' that is fluid and problematic because 'like a linguistic shifter, "regional" means "marginal" in relation to some kind of geographic center or dominant cultural practice, and in the case of cinema, that frequently means Hollywood' (1993: 388).

The eternally problematic term 'independent' has endured, however, while the notion of regional cinema has not. Competing ideas of independence in American cinema by Emanuel Levy (1999), King (2005, 2009), Yannis Tzioumakis (2006) and John Berra (2008) amongst others have each wrestled with the criteria. Tzioumakis sees:

> American independent cinema as a discourse that expands and contracts when socially authorised institutions (filmmakers, industry practitioners, trade publications, academics, film critics, and so on) contribute towards its definition at different periods in the history of American cinema. (2006: 11)

King is more practical and empirical in demanding an industrial location, formal and aesthetic strategies based upon 'a highly stylised minimalism that draws attention to itself as a formal-artistic device' (2005: 82) and a relationship to a 'broader social, cultural, political or ideological landscape' (2005: 2). His correlated observation that 'independent' cinema stakes 'a claim to the status of something more closely approximating the reality of the lives of most people' (2005: 67) suits regional cinema too. Nevertheless, the term 'regional' still fails to resonate in America, unlike in Europe, where provincial television broadcasters have played a vital role in the funding and dissemination of their respective regional cinemas. In the absence of any similar, coherent funding, the independent spirit that may be identified in some American filmmakers of the 1970s and onwards was arguably coincidental. Their financing was haphazard, being mostly a particularistic collage of savings, loans, inheritances, local government and federal grants, public service broadcasting and, more recently, maxed-out credit cards. It was not until the success of Steven Soderbergh's *sex, lies and videotape* (1989) at the Sundance and Cannes film festivals in 1989 that 'the existence of significant available institutional support' (Tzioumakis 2006: 254) and the potential commercial and critical viability of independent cinema outside America became apparent. This new awareness of funds and markets for a small-scale, intimate, character-based American cinema led to 'questions of aesthetics [assuming] an increasingly prominent position in the discourse of American independent cinema' (Tzioumakis 2006: 266). In turn, this contributed to a criteria for the discrimination of 'indies' from studio films, which included marketable similarities to the kind of European cinema that based itself on expression of thought and the negotiation of identities as opposed to a more mainstream deployment of physical expression in the negotiation of obstacles. Linked to this was the increasingly auteurist approach of many critics and a cine-literate audience, who identified the supposed autonomy of filmmakers like Soderbergh as a riposte to the perception of a blockbuster mentality and its concomitant 'dumbing down' of audiences by the major studios. Soderbergh, who appears as himself (albeit rotoscoped) in Linklater's *Waking Life*, was briefly acclaimed alongside Jarmusch (see Suárez 2007) and Sayles (see Bould 2009) as the inheritor of Cassavetes's noble cause (see Charity 2001), but even in Robin Hood mode or Kafkaesque conflict with the major studios most American filmmakers were unable to conquer the geographical impracticality of adopting any collective identity that was much more than a media construct to which they occasionally re-subscribed at festivals.

Linklater's *Slacker* evoked an altogether different collective identity, one that rejected competition. Somewhat ironically therefore, the film was itself initially rejected by Sundance because of festival director Alberto García's demurral, as well as the festivals of Telluride and Toronto. It was, however, shown as a work-in-progress at the Independent Feature Film Market in New York in October 1989, where it inspired a $35,000 advance from the Cologne-based WDR (Pierson 1996: 185). WDR (Westdeutscher Rundfunk/West German Broadcasting) was one of the German networks that pioneered the film and television synergy later adopted by the UK's Channel Four and the deal was possibly due to some vestiges of empathy with the ethos of slacking that resonates in modern German cinema. This is evident from Wim Wenders' road movies *Alice in den Städten* (*Alice in the Cities*, 1974), *Falsche Bewegung* (*Wrong Move*, 1975) and *Im Lauf der Zeit* (*Kings of the Road*, 1976) to the recent *Die fetten Jahre sind vorbei* (*The Edukators*, 2004) directed by Hans Weingartner, who was production assistant on Linklater's *Before Sunrise* in which he also appears in a blue shirt chatting at a table in the café scene.[5] However, the virginal notion of 'independent' cinema that is attached to *Slacker* does not survive in the career of Linklater, who has always drifted in response to the sort of collaboration that he could count on in Austin or could negotiate with the major studios. Following Pierre Bourdieu, Berra claims that 'independence' is only valid in terms of 'the field of restricted production, an artistically heightened, if economically subservient, means of artistic expression' (2008: 71). Yet, although valid, this rather ignores the complex negotiations between production and distribution throughout Linklater's career that dooms any attempt to determine the degree of his independence to inexactitude.

The Hollywood studios have a reach that makes global distribution as easy as 'pushing at an open door' (Cooke 2007: 4), whereas a regional filmmaker will struggle to get picked for a festival. Between these extremes Linklater's career has demonstrated that the production and distribution sectors are rarely cleanly aligned and that a wide range of strategies are possible, if not always successful. For example, his first full-length feature *It's Impossible to Learn to Plow by Reading Books* was made for $3,000 from savings and not distributed, whereas *Slacker* was made for $23,000 with loans and small grants and reached audiences via its successful resubmission to Sundance and a specialist independent distributor. However, the same strategy proved problematic with *Me and Orson Welles*, which was made with a large grant from the Isle of Man Media Development Fund (MDF) and a co-production deal between several companies including Linklater's own Detour Filmproduction. It may have charmed audiences at the 2008 Toronto International Film Festival but hesitant distributors meant that its release was delayed a full year outside Canada (Anon. 2008). *Dazed and Confused* was different: a production deal with Universal that turned sour when the nonplussed studio dumped its distribution on its own subsidiary Gramercy, which had been formed that same year to distribute PolyGram pictures in the USA and Canada.[6]

Learning from this, Linklater made *Before Sunrise* and *SubUrbia* as part of a 'hands-off' deal with Castle Rock Entertainment, which had been established as an independent production company in 1987 by filmmaker Rob Reiner amongst others, but with the financial backing of Columbia Pictures and Nelson Entertainment. Its independence lasted as long as Columbia could afford to let its losses accrue and in 1994 Castle Rock was bought by Warner Brothers Entertainment, which assumed domestic distribution rights while Universal handled the foreign.[7] Like *Slacker*, *Before Sunrise* screened at Sundance, but with major distributor Columbia already attached.

In contrast, *The Newton Boys* was a Twentieth Century Fox production that bombed despite wide distribution. In 2001, a slyer Fox placed *Waking Life,* which it co-produced with the Independent Film Channel (IFC), with its own Fox Searchlight Pictures, which had been formed to handle films with difficult or challenging subject matter such as this. Another tack taken was that for Linklater's *Tape*, which resulted from a collective whose semi-acronym InDigEnt made a badge of verifiable poverty out of the more prosaic Independent Digital Entertainment. *Tape's* distribution was fragmentary with the IFC again stepping in alongside Lions Gate, Metrodome and Palace. At the other extreme, *The School of Rock* was made for Paramount Pictures with most international distribution going to United International Pictures (UIP), whereas *Bad News Bears* was green-lit on the profits from *The School of Rock* and always locked in to a safe pre-production distribution deal with Paramount and UIP. By 2003 Warner Brothers had taken over worldwide distribution of films produced under the Castle Rock label and done so as either Warner Brothers (domestic) or Warner Brothers International (foreign) or Warner Independent Pictures (oxymoronic). Nevertheless, what was left of Castle Rock as a tiny production unit in Time Warner Incorporated (the third largest media and entertainment conglomeration in the world) still managed to ensure for Linklater a modicum of independence for the tiny $10 million budget production of *Before Sunset* in 2004 and also collaborated with a dozen or more producers and executive producers for *Bernie* in 2010, which emulated Linklater's mixing and matching of independent financing for *Fast Food Nation* from BBC Films, HanWay and Participant Productions. Distribution of *Fast Food Nation* was even more of a collage, with rights going to Fox Searchlight Pictures in the USA, Focus Films in Hong Kong, Tartan in the UK and a wide variety of bidding and favourited domestic distributors in other countries. Finally, muddying the mix even further was *A Scanner Darkly*, which was a co-production between Section Eight Productions and Warner Brothers under the aegis of Warner Independent Pictures that, like Fox Searchlight Pictures, was formed to distribute domestic and foreign films that did not fit easily alongside *Harry Potter* and the major's other main attractions.[8] The involvement of Section Eight Productions, meanwhile, brings this obstacle race full circle with Linklater once again making use of Steven Soderbergh's tail wind. Founded in 2000 by Soderbergh and George Clooney in order to gain some semblance of independence for the films that mostly they themselves wished to make, Section Eight Productions operated on a 'one for us, one for the studio' production and distribution balancing act with Warner Brothers.[9]

All things considered, purists might well argue that the only truly independent American film is one that is never seen outside of the filmmaker's immediate family, close friends and festivals; in which case (at least until its inclusion as an extra feature on the Criterion Collection DVD of *Slacker*) the only film of Linklater's that qualifies is *It's Impossible to Learn to Plow by Reading Books*. Yet, despite the huge hillside sign, Hollywood should not be seen as a sovereign state or centralised government within the USA but as a collusion of competing international conglomerates that market the brand name Hollywood as the product of a specific, perpetually sun-blessed place, unchanged since the heyday of the moguls. Moreover, 'the majority of the major studios themselves only have limited ties to the Hollywood area of Los Angeles' (Cooke 2007: 6), which reveals Hollywood as an illusory opponent for supporters of 'independent' cinema. In truth, this idea of 'Hollywood' (which therefore warrants inverted commas too) is more globalised than globalising. Its generic formulas may seem as easily trans-ferable to international markets as the gimmick of the latest game show, but it is actu-ally 'Hollywood' that has been formed and flavoured by such global demands for its product that multiplexes worldwide have become pantheons of its pastiche. Since the decline of the western (perhaps the only true American genre), 'Hollywood' films have been gaily unmasking themselves as faceless investments in universality with recent colours being Bollywood, Marvel and Manga. Nevertheless, as Paul Cooke observes, the extant perception of a division between 'Hollywood' and the rest of the world is 'generally seen in terms of a cultural hierarchy, with Hollywood producing expensive, populist "low culture", while the rest of the world offers spectators lower-budget, more demanding "high cultural" fare aimed at a discerning "art house" audience' (2007: 3). He also observes that 'it is by Hollywood's standards that we define what we mean by mainstream film-making' (2007: 5) and that, consequently, what is left is defined as 'independent' American cinema too. Berra notes a somewhat idealist response from audiences in the 1970s and 1980s that took independence to mean 'both a mode of production and a mode of thinking relating to the financing, filming, distribution and cultural appreciation of modern film' (2008: 9). Since then, however, he argues that:

> The stranglehold which the Hollywood studios have over the film business has contributed to the 'commercialization' of American 'independent' cinema, the gradual erosion of its values, the restraint of its cultural impulse, and the labelling of a 'movement' that has become an invaluable aspect of Hollywood's industry of mass production. (2008: 13)

Finally, Emanuel Levy diagnoses a highly selective mode of reception for 'independent' cinema by audiences in the 1990s that are 'so eager to accept the existence of a form of "alternative" media, that [they] will largely ignore the corporate origins of such films' (2001: 202). 'Hollywood', 'independent', 'low culture', 'art house', 'commercializa-tion', 'movement', 'alternative': is anyone else fed up with all these inverted commas? At least, by definition, you know exactly where you are with regional cinema.

The success on tiny budgets of Sayles' *The Return of the Secaucus Seven* (1980; $60,000), Spike Lee's *She's Gotta Have It* (1986: $22,700), Linklater's *Slacker* (1991: $23,000), Nick Gómez's *Laws of Gravity* (1992: $32,000), Gregg Araki's *The Living End* (1992: $22,700) and Rose Troche's *Go Fish* (1994; approximately $15,000) was because each captured and communicated a realism that resulted from their innate regionalism and consequent social authenticity. They connected with empathetic audiences whose own realities had not (at least not yet) been deemed worthy of colonisation by the major studios. Although the distribution of these films was limited, their influence and reputation has endured by means of word of mouth, academic and critical interest, cult status, intertextuality, special edition DVDs from enterprising distributors and, most importantly, a connection with new generations able to empathise with the groups and individuals that these films portray. They may have had limited production resources and little hope of wide distribution, but each filmmaker shared what Linklater identified and empathised with in the films of Eagle Pennell: 'He was kind of a folk artist who liked doing things in his own backyard. [...] Here's a guy who saw something unique about what was right in front of him' (2009: 15). Analysis of the negotiation of independence in the career of Linklater must accept that definitions of the term are in constant flux, thereby obscuring a complete portrait of the filmmaker. Yet, despite the connotations of parochialism that mean Linklater himself 'doesn't like to be labelled a regional filmmaker' (Pierson 1996: 185), the regionalism of his enterprise remains steadfast and hereditary.

Following the screening of Pennell's *The Whole Shootin' Match* at the 1980 Telluride Film Festival, Roger Ebert of the *Chicago Sun-Times* described it as:

> One of the best examples of a new regional American cinema (I call it the Wood-Burning Cinema) that's been creating itself in the last few years. It was financed and made totally in Texas by Texans. [...] It won't turn up in neighbourhood theatres and may never be on TV, but it creates characters that are such ornery, dreaming, hopeless and precious failures that you can't help sort of loving them. (1980)

The Whole Shootin' Match never did play any neighbourhoods beyond Austin and was thought lost until 2009 when Watchmaker Films released a special edition DVD of a copy found in its co-writer's shed. Then, the thirty years of mythicisation based on nostalgia, Ebert's review and academic interest was found to be well-deserved, while the film's intertextual relationship with *Slacker* and *Dazed and Confused* offered flavoursome corroborative evidence of a tradition of regional cinema in Austin. There had been other home-based Texan filmmakers besides Pennell and Hooper, such as David Schmoeller, who directed *Tourist Trap* (1979), another notable horror film with a 'special thanks to' credit for Albert Band, who directed the western *She Came to the Valley* (1979 aka *Texas in Flames*), and Douglas Holloway, associate producer of *The Whole Shootin' Match*, who made the stoner-comedy *Fast Money* (1980) with Pennell as his cinematographer. Direct links to Linklater also duly appear with Wayne Bell, composer on *Last Night at the Alamo* and sound recordist on *The Texas Chain Saw Massacre*, *The Whole Shootin' Match* and *Fast Money*, who worked as sound editor on *Before Sunrise*, *SubUrbia*, *Waking Life*, *Before Sunset* and *A Scanner Darkly*. The collaborative nature of regional filmmaking clearly depends upon this versatility of local enthusiasts and is a tradition that the cinema of Linklater maintains. On the list of collaborators with whom he has frequently worked are found numerous actors (especially Austinite Ethan Hawke) as well as Kim Krizan (actress in *Slacker*, *Dazed and Confused* and *Waking Life* and co-writer of *Before Sunrise*) and Tommy Pallotta who played Looking for Missing Friend in *Slacker* and produced *Waking Life* and *A Scanner Darkly*. In addition, there are long-time collaborators cinematographer Lee Daniel and editor Sandra Adair, as well as Anne Walker McBay, who cast *Slacker* and went on to produce most of Linklater's films, as well as *Infamous* (Douglas McGrath, 2006) and the *Before*-like *In Search of a Midnight Kiss* (Alex Holdridge, 2007). They are joined by John Frick, who was production designer on *Dazed and Confused* and art director of *The Newton Boys* and the television series *Friday Night Lights* (2006–) that is filmed in Austin. Dig a little deeper and one finds Texan Catherine Hardwicke, writer-director of *Thirteen* (2003) and director of *Twilight* (2008), working as production designer and second unit director on *SubUrbia* and production designer on *The Newton Boys*. In addition, Linklater often returns favours to fellow Austinite filmmakers with fun cameos such as the tour bus driver in Mike Judge's *Beavis and Butthead Do America* (1996), Cool Spy in Robert Rodríguez's *Spy Kids* (2001), Crony 2 in Ethan Hawke's *Chelsea Walls* (2001) and the self-deprecating John Wayne Enthusiast in Hawke's adaptation of his own novel, *The Hottest State* (2006). In this and in a far greater sense, Linklater's endeavours have been crucial to the emergence of a film-literate community in Austin and the establishment of a robust industry.

Perhaps surprisingly, Linklater was not born in Austin but in Houston on 30 July 1960. The son of an insurance agent and a speech pathologist, his parents divorced when he was seven years old and he moved with his mother to Huntsville, Texas, seven miles south-east of Houston, where he would spend weekends with his father. He studied English and played baseball at the Sam Houston State University, but admits, 'I was just drifting [.] I was just taking classes that interested me. At some point I realised I was probably never going to graduate' (in Lowenstein 2009: 5). In his sophomore year in 1982 he took acting classes, wrote several one-act plays and read French and Russian literature on film. Dropping out at the end of that year, he took a job as an oil rigger in the Gulf of Mexico, which enabled him to save $18,000 and read all he could about film. He spent much of his shore leave at repertory cinemas in Houston and spent his savings on a Super-8 camera and editing equipment before moving to Austin in 1984:

> It was a very specific decision based on, 'Where can I live cheap, watch a lot of movies and be around cool people?' I'd had my eyes on Austin since high school. There were lots of cute girls around and Austin's always had this tolerant, hippy vibe. What made it tolerant for me, unlike Dallas, Houston and some of the bigger cities, was the fact that I knew all my friends were artists, painters, writers, musicians. No one asked you, 'What do you do for money?' The rest of the world is, 'Are you in school? Are you going to get your Masters? Your MBA?' It was all about your economic interests, but here it was just about your artistic desires. And that's the world I chose, a more nurturing environment, where no one judged you if you didn't have a job.[10]

Thereafter, Linklater's adopted slacker lifestyle led to the making of short films (or 'film attempts' as he calls them): 'I took the pressure off by admitting that it wasn't going to be meaningful in any way other than as a technical exercise' (in Lowenstein 2009: 9). The supportive environment of Austin had already fostered a regional group of Super-8 enthusiasts led by Austin Jernigan and Ray Farmer, calling themselves the Heart of Texas Filmmakers, who gathered at Esther's Pool on Sixth Street. Vaguely in the style of groups such as Maya Deren's Creative Film Foundation (est. 1955) and Jonas Mekas's Filmmakers' Cooperative (est. 1962), the Heart of Texas Filmmakers revived the Ritz as a cinema but their group was all but extinct as a creative entity when Linklater met Lee Daniel at its last meeting (Daniel 2000). Desperate to see films when the campus cinema stopped providing, they began an experimental film series at the off-campus Dobie cinema in the autumn of 1985 with crucial support from the cinema manager and Louis Black, editor of *The Austin Chronicle*, who granted free advertising space to their endeavour. Linklater and Daniel called themselves the Austin Film Society (AFS) and went on to run screenings at nightclubs, galleries, local community colleges and concerts by the band Texas Instruments. In a laid-back music town, Linklater and Daniel were the film guys.

Meanwhile, Linklater put together his 'film attempts' at his flat-turned-editing room in the West Campus area of the city. His seven-minute *Woodshock* (1985) was an impressionistic record of a music festival staged in Austin's Waterloo Park, during which fourteen bands had played to an audience of skinheads, goths, proto-grunge adolescents and fearless frats whose kegs, bongs and joints were shared quite freely. Shot on Super-8 and with a Nagra tape recorder, *Woodshock* looks and sounds rough, but there is a wry intelligence at work in its delusional aspiration of referencing the Woodstock festival, which means it plays like a pocket-sized satire of Michael Wadleigh's documentary *Woodstock* (1970). Imitating that film's pastoral psychedelia, Linklater lets the sun flare directly into the lens, adds a distortionately loud soundtrack of birdsong, and employs woozy dissolves between revellers and waterfalls. There is much toking, chugging and mugging to camera as Linklater captures quick sketches of an event that will be recreated in the Moon Tower party scene of the 1986-set *Dazed and Confused*. Austinite Daniel Johnston, the songwriter and musician whose music and bipolarity was the subject of the documentary *The Devil and Daniel Johnston* (Jeff Feuerzeig, 2006) also makes an appearance handing out tapes of his music as was his habit. Stepping into Linklater's view he exhorts the filmmaker to ask him a question. 'Where do you work?' is Linklater's inapposite gambit. 'I work at McDonalds,' Johnston grins holding up a cassette tape: 'And this is my new album "Hi, How Are You?".' Far from self-promotion, his gesture is symbolic of a mid-1980s Austin where songwriters would hand out tapes, bands would gig in public parks and filmmakers would stage public screenings. Only the passerby caught in the film's open ending expects some greater purpose from Linklater's filming: 'All right, what are you gonna use this for?'

For? In the spring of 1987 Linklater and Daniel were giving little thought to anything grander than how to cover the costs of renting and watching films: 'If there was a director I liked and wanted to see more films by, we'd do a retrospective' (in

Lowenstein 2009: 12). They renovated a room above Captain Quackenbush's Intergalactic Café on Guadalupe Street and installed a screening facility that provided a venue for film shows, debates and filmmakers to cultivate 'that idler dropout mentality' (Lowenstein 2009: 14). Quackenbush's (which no longer exists but would serve as location for the Pixel vision sequence in *Slacker*) was also the hub of the Austin Media Arts organisation established by Denise Montgomery, who would appear in *It's Impossible to Learn to Plow by Reading Books* and play Having a Breakthrough Day in *Slacker*. Her additional work as sound recordist on *Slacker* and as assistant art director on *Dazed and Confused* provides yet another example of the non-competitive, collective, creative energy of the poets, playwrights, novelists, performance artists, musicians, songwriters and filmmakers who came together in Austin. Linklater was a garage-filmmaker whose *Woodshock*, *It's Impossible to Learn to Plow by Reading Books* and *Slacker* were so pro-Austin that they were only coincidentally anti-Hollywood.

The AFS showed its commitment to amateurism by screening the films of Kenneth Anger, Stan Brakhage, Michael Snow, Jon Jost and James Benning in influential sessions dedicated to the avant-garde that looked to Europe but also proclaimed and celebrated the existence of such a thing in America. There was also Psychedelic Cinema, hailed on the home-made flyers as 'a mind-bending retinal circus!' to patrons who needed little encouragement to go interactive. The Russian Avant-Garde, Beat Cinema ('Two Bucks!') and Gay and Lesbian Experimental Film all performed well, as did late shows of cult favourites such as *Carmen Jones* (Otto Preminger, 1954), *Porcile* (*Pigpen*, Pier Paolo Pasolini, 1969), *Caged Heat* (Jonathan Demme, 1974) and *Ai no korîda* (*In the Realm of the Senses*, Nagisa Oshima, 1976). The two dollar entry fee was sufficient to fund a double-bill of films by Luis Buñuel entitled The Subversive in the Studio and pair Vincente Minnelli's *Two Weeks in Another Town* (1962) with *The Clock* (1945), an obvious influence on *Before Sunrise* in which Corporal Joe Allen (Robert Walker) meets Alice (Judy Garland) while on leave in New York and they spend the day together, walking and talking, seeing the sights and falling in love. As the AFS developed there were also triple bills of films by Dreyer, Godard, Sam Fuller and Robert Aldrich, septuple bills by Bresson, octuple bills by Yasujiro Ozu, and a decuple bill by Rainer Werner Fassbinder. The society tried to scandalise with a screening of Pasolini's *Saló o le 120 giornate di Sodoma* (*Saló or the 120 Days of Sodom*, 1975) and even manufactured flyers on the occasion of its return that heralded, 'a call to all Republicans and Christians and members of the White Race and PTA affiliates and Citizens Against Pornography to unite against these forces. Infidels and blasphemes are plotting the return of *Saló*,' followed by the venue, time and price of admission.[11]

Although playful, such provocation does allude to the divisive legacy of Watergate (1972–74), the Vietnam War (1950–73), and the period of isolationist Republicanism led by the two tenures of President Reagan (1980–88) as well as the corporate-minded foreign policy of President George Bush Senior (1988–92). However, as an Oblique Strategy card in *Slacker* states: 'Withdrawal in disgust is not the same thing as apathy.'[12] Instead, those who participated in this collective withdrawal in Austin claimed reflection, imagination and creativity as the aims of a plethora of non-profit endeavours that facilitated and signified an internal exile from Reaganomics, the rather less oblique strategy of a government intent on economic deregulation, the reduction of government spending, isolationist economic policies and a concurrent interventionism in countries not far south of Austin in Central America. Their communal disgust with the political system found special inspiration in the city's links to the Civil Rights legislation of the late 1960s that had been passed by Austinite President Lyndon Johnson. In contrast, the consequent decline in white Southern American support for the Democrat Party had also contributed to the political ambitions of the West Texas-based Bush family, whose George Junior, says Linklater, 'wasn't the artistic slacker but the money-grubbing slacker, the hedonistic kind, into beer and coke, and then this desperate "Born Again". [...] Where he's from is not Austin, it's an oil-rich town with a Rolls Royce dealership' (in Peary 2004). The isolationism of the slacker community (even within Austin) is easily romanticised but the collective alienation that was a microcosm of the isolation fostered by Reaganomics nurtured an identity that was defiantly liberal in its expression.

The slacker boom in mid-1980s Austin and Linklater's role in it may be usefully compared to that of the contemporary cultural movement known as *La Movida* in Madrid from which the filmmaker Pedro Almodóvar emerged. Spain was barely ten years on from a Fascist dictatorship when *La Movida* offered a platform for previously forbidden lifestyles, sexualities and cathartic artistic expression. This made of Madrid a melting pot that Almodóvar captured and communicated in his own extravagant 'film attempts' such as *Pepi, Luci, Bom y otras chicas del montón* (*Pepi, Luci, Bom and Other Girls Like Mom*, 1980) and *Laberinto de pasiones* (*Labyrinth of Passion*, 1982) that embodied the reckless and imaginative spirit of a collective that had much in common with slackers. Almodóvar's films were never explicitly political but they were so rooted in a specific time and place that their own temporalised regionalism created an enduring aesthetic and association of the city with the writer-director. Almodóvar's Madrid invoked the sometimes desperate wish of its nocturnal inhabitants to make up for lost time by having a good one. His films insisted on gaudy fashions and gender-bent affectations as the strident performance of Postmodern identity in a country that had just escaped totalitarianism. Linklater's Austin, meanwhile, was a flat canvas of wide avenues for slackers whose possession of its sidewalks was cat-like in a pose of indifference best captured in the walking and talking of *Slacker*: 'Who's ever written a great work about the immense effort required in order not to create?' What Madrid and Austin shared was a sense of potential found in the inconsistencies of life beyond a work routine or a familiar family structure, one that contrasted with the uncertainty towards change of the country and state that they respectively capitalised. In contrast, the New German Cinema that lasted until the mid-1980s had been a structured reaction against creative stagnation that had ambitious objectives for an industrially viable, internationally profitable cinema of artistic excellence that sought funding and synergies with television companies instead. The films of Rainer Werner Fassbinder and Wim Wenders were also markedly divergent from the identification with a place that defines Linklater and Almodóvar because they expressed a contrary estrangement from post-war Germany. Their protagonists were rootless rather than communitarian. Yet, although their influence on American cinema is clearest in those who are at odds with their surroundings in the films of Jim Jarmusch (whose collaborations with Wenders' long-time cinematographer Robby Müller effectively transposed the bleak aesthetics of displacement and dislocation to contemporary America), theirs was also the approach that Linklater tried in *It's Impossible to Learn to Plow by Reading Books*, his first full length 'film attempt' in which the filmmaker becomes a nomadic subject before returning to the adopted homeland of Austin.

Although *It's Impossible to Learn to Plow by Reading Books* is a film by a college drop-out and self-taught filmmaker, its aphoristic title does not exclusively favour experience over education, but it does suggest the two should be combined. Shot on a Super-8 camera with a ten-second timer, it was, says Linklater, 'sort of designed around its limitations' (in Lowenstein 2009: 16) and thus has an unmixed, omnidirectional soundtrack that communicates the mindset of travel from all sides and initiates the hypothesis of a Cubist aesthetic in Linklater's films. This minimalist film consists mostly of long and medium shots lasting several minutes of Linklater (who would set the camera's timer before entering the frame) as he travels by Amtrak from Austin to Montana, San Francisco and Houston and back by car to Austin. 'What I had in mind was these long, elegant camera moves [;] this I saw as flowing,' he recalls (ibid.). There are no jump cuts here as the film is less concerned with departures and arrivals than it is with the in-between times and spaces and the minutiae of being alone but not lonely. Linklater snacks, naps and interacts with a variety of coin-operated machines. He reads, shoots hoops, tunes radios and televisions and meets up with old friends and girlfriends, family and like-minded travellers who help each other at the no-money level. But any dramatic interaction with these people is so frustratingly distant that it negates intimacy and suggests flawed human communication. The assemblage of long takes and long shots suggests an endless series of CCTV cameras has tracked Linklater on his travels. Yet the film's objectivity is dismissed by the knowledge that Linklater must have topped and tailed the shots to create this eighty-five minute feature. Somewhere there is a reel of offcuts showing Linklater repeatedly racing back to the camera at the end of every shot to save film, time and money.

It's Impossible to Learn to Plow by Reading Books prefigures *Waking Life* in its individualised search for transcendence promised by the experience of travel, which Linklater aspires to convert into a metaphysical journey that will cure some existential malaise. However, its assemblage resembles a collage of memory fragments of an uneventful journey rather than an incident-filled voyage of discovery. The sequence in San Francisco suggests a revision of that in Chris Marker's *Sans soleil* (*Sunless*, 1983), a visual essay composed of a collage by association of film and memory in which Marker (who unlike Linklater remains behind the camera) retraces the wanderings of John 'Scottie' Ferguson (James Stewart) in the Bay Area in *Vertigo* (Alfred Hitchcock, 1958). Certain narrative Macguffins do betray the collage, however, such as the shot in which Linklater fires a rifle out of his apartment window and, much later, the brief insert of a man crawling painfully across a parking space that not only connects with the earlier shot but alludes to Charles Whitman, a student at the University of Texas at Austin, who shot ten people from the University's administration building on 1 August 1966, an event remembered with local pride by Old Anarchist (Louis

Mackey) in *Slacker*. Although *Elephant* (Gus Van Sant, 2003) would employ a similar aesthetic in its recreation of the Columbine High School massacre, Linklater's own brief embodiment of the assassin figure suggests a disturbing potential for violence within the spirit of rebellion associated with slacking.

For all the film's impassive objectification of Linklater's own athletic figure, the on-camera filmmaker remains a cipher for the manifesto of experience. This is not an autobiographical work in which Linklater considers, moulds, fixes and presents himself as knowable, but an auto-ethnographical work instead, somewhat in the manner of Chantal Ackerman and the Modernist Structural Realist cinema of the 1970s, in which the self is presented as a performance that is objectified and acknowledged as such. The staging of subjectivity is not even attempted by Linklater, who, as protagonist and filmmaker, cannot be in two places at once, so leaves the actual filming to the appa-ratus. Thus Linklater confronts the voyeurism of his own self by making it merely the content of a film whose subject is determined by the financial and logistic limitations of the project: one person, one camera. The film therefore meditates upon the indigent materiality of its own production and opposes what is culturally deemed to be private and mundane in order to imitate with railway carriages the interior journey of a film-maker who never really leaves Texas. The fact that this is an internal journey as much as a geographical trip is underlined in the sequence where Linklater hikes to the top of a mountain in Montana and deliberately fails to shoot and show the view. Correlatively, the long takes do not promise or comply with the predestination of those of Bresson but allow for an unpredictable interior journey of a filmmaker whose experience of America does not tally with the one advertised in the brochure for Reaganomics. Its trajectory of simple redirections may be hardly more considered than that of a pinball interacting with a flipper, but the film does accrue and exude a poetic sense of realism in being of its own time and movement.

Despite shots of railway tracks converging on an infinite number of allusions to westerns, *It's Impossible to Learn to Plow by Reading Books* is more sympathetic to the hobos who hopped freight trains during America's Great Depression. Like them, Linklater's onscreen character is seemingly in exile from his own country, alienated from its social pressures and estranged from its political system. Instead, identity is found in optimistic nomadism by way of meetings with like-minded folks such as the girl he meets and leaves sleeping in the train station (a prototype of *Before Sunrise*'s Céline). His forebears are literary, for Jack Kerouac, Jack London, Eugene O'Neill and John Steinbeck are all Linklater's illustrious ancestors, and their influ-ence on his cinema is seen not only here but in the hobo played by David Martínez in *Waking Life*, who jumps from a train to explain how 'things have been tough lately for dreamers'. This voyage through the backyards and bars, parking lots, waiting rooms and railway sidings of America is one of anonymous places that correspond to Gilles Deleuze's consideration of the concept of *l'espace quelconque* (any space whatsoever) that he attributes without reference to Pascal Augé (Deleuze 2005a: 112). The 'any space whatsoever' is a mundane place of transit, where the depersonalisation and isolation of individuals occurs, but also one that is surrounded by an out-of-field indeterminacy that holds the potential for unique and singular experiences. Deleuze writes: 'It is a space of virtual conjunction, grasped as pure locus of the possible' (2005a: 113). Linklater (in line with Deleuze) thus situates himself in the cinematic cloze test of filmmakers such as Michelangelo Antonioni and Monte Hellman, who each used such settings to place the identities of their protagonists in flux and/or crisis in their existential road movies, *Zabriskie Point* (1970) and *Two-Lane Blacktop* (1971) respectively. Yet the virtue of any space whatsoever is that the traveller can potentially choose to go in any direction whichever. For Deleuze, this choice 'is identical to the power of the spirit, to the perpetually renewed spiritual decision' (2005a: 120). Thus, in the early cinema of Linklater we can begin to identify techniques associated with representations of alienation in post-war European cinema and their application to a regional concept of American cinema that is also informed by the existentialist and Marxist undercurrents of slacking. Because films such as *Woodshock, It's Impossible to Learn to Plow by Reading Books* and *Slacker* associate slacker culture with a wider alienation brought on by 'withdrawing in disgust' from political and national institutions, Linklater's filmed round trip effectively points to the reterritorialisation of a part of America called Austin.

Furthermore, in personally embodying this concept of reterritorialisation by reflective exploration in *It's Impossible to Learn to Plow by Reading Books*, Linklater also appears to be imitating the Situationist International ploy of the psycho-geographical *dérive* (drift) in his attempt to leave Austin and investigate what truth lies behind the pre-packaged concept of Reaganite America. His quest connects with the definition of psycho-geography made by French Marxist theorist, filmmaker and founder of the Situationist International Guy Debord, which combined subjective and objective knowledge of the self and one's surroundings. Although predominantly urban and potentially anarchist in its strategy, Debord's 'Theory of the *Dérive*' (first published in 1956) was a guide and incitement to losing oneself gainfully in spaces thought to be under the control of a system:

> In a *dérive* one or more persons during a certain period drop their usual motives for movement and action, their relations, their work and leisure activities, and let themselves be drawn by the attractions of the terrain and the encounters they find there. (2006: 50)

This strategy has clear parallels with *It's Impossible to Learn to Plow by Reading Books*, which embodies the paradox of losing oneself in order to gain knowledge of one's potential, for 'the *dérive* includes both this letting-go and its necessary contradiction: the domination of psycho-geographical variations by the knowledge and calculation of their possibilities' (Debord 2006: 50). The *dérive* is a training course, an initiation rite and an exercise in reconnaissance that prescribes wandering as an adjunct to revolutionary theory or, to put it another way, insists that it is impossible to learn to plow by merely reading books. Despite Debord's advice that 'the interventions of chance are poorer' (ibid.) on predestined train journeys and wandering in open country, *It's Impossible to Learn to Plow by Reading Books* still exudes a spontaneity that 'is the freedom to travel aimlessly, to simply exist in the world without daily responsibilities, [which is what] Linklater's characters treasure most [and] *Plow* is his most direct embrace of this freedom' (Schwartz 2004). The *dérive* proposes the inhabiting of spaces that are revealed as junctions of potential narratives and thus inevitable crossroads in a labyrinth of paths less travelled. This is the structural conceit that also underpins *Slacker*, *SubUrbia*, *Before Sunrise*, *Waking Life* (in which Debord actually appears as Mr Debord, played by Hymie Samuelson), *Live from Shiva's Dance Floor* and *Before Sunset* in which space and time are wrested from stagnant notions, irrelevant hierarchies and redundant systems and reclaimed for imaginative, restorative and romantic endeavour. The America that Linklater wanders resembles that of *Paris, Texas* (Wim Wenders, 1984) and *Stranger than Paradise* (Jim Jarmusch, 1984), but the onscreen Linklater is already Jesse Wallace (Ethan Hawke) before meeting Céline (Julie Delpy) in *Before Sunrise*, staying still with his head against the window while watching the landscape move as if his train is a static, long, thin cinema with widescreen windows akin to the fairground ride in Max Ophüls' Vienna-set *Letter from an Unknown Woman* (1948). Ultimately, however, this is a return journey to Austin, where Linklater was reunited with the ten hours of exposed Super-8 film that he had mailed home in stages.

The playful-constructive *dérive* complete, Linklater proceeded to reassemble the objective terrain of his film in accordance with both the logical sequence of its occurrence and his understanding of the social awareness that he had at least pretended to experience. Following Emile Durkheim:

> [This] does not consist in a simple science of observation which describes these things without accounting for them. It can and must be explanatory. It must investigate the conditions which cause variations in the political territory of different peoples, the nature and aspect of their borders, and the unequal density of the population. (2003: 78)

Seeking to reconstruct this experience, Linklater transferred the film to video and edited at Austin's ACTV studios two nights a week for a year. Knowledge gained and explained was certainly limited by the solitude of the whole venture, however, and it is apt to see *It's Impossible to Learn to Plow by Reading Books* as a prequel to *Slacker*, whose preparation would now occupy Linklater. As Debord had indicated:

> One can *dérive* alone, but all indications are that the most fruitful numerical arrangement consists of several small groups of two or three people who have reached the same level of awareness, since cross-checking these different groups' impressions makes it possible to arrive at more objective conclusions. (2006: 50)

This notion of a cinematic game of tag between the various participants of various *dérives* was ideal for representing the drifting nature of fellow Austinite slackers. Even Debord's warning that 'it is impossible for there to be more than ten or twelve people without the *dérive* fragmenting into several simultaneous *dérives*' (ibid.) became a template for the cinematic drift in the more appropriately urban space of Austin, which thereby represented an alternative state of mind to that of the government and electoral majority of the country that enclosed it. As Debord warned: 'The practice of such subdivision is in fact of great interest, but the difficulties it entails have so far prevented it from being organized on a sufficient scale' (ibid.). This was the challenge met by *Slacker*.

Linklater filmed *Slacker* as 'sort of a group art project' (in Lowenstein 2009: 26) in the sweltering heat of July and August 1989, when the greatest obstruction to its production was the subscription to its ethos of its participants, many of whom could not be bothered to show up for Anne Walker McBay's casting session. Linklater's ambition was for a non-judgemental film made of all the unheralded individual activities, neighbourhood anecdotes, spontaneous street theatre and community art projects that made up the tolerant community of Austinites of which he was part. However, his vision was actually quite narrow, empirical and contained within a few blocks around Guadalupe Street. As he admits: '*Slacker*'s unique, because it's not just Austin, it's West Campus, so it's kind of the university. So it made it a little less diverse-looking than Austin really is.' He also claims to have imagined the film as a single shot: if *It's Impossible to Learn to Plow by Reading Books* was about disconnection, this was quite the opposite. Practicalities of filmmaking spoiled the single shot idea, but the ambition remained:

> The biggest visual idea was probably that I wanted very little editing, long takes, and the same lens. With the people changing constantly, I wanted it to seem real, like an unending flow. [...] I had this kind of flowing, real thing going on in my head. (in Lowenstein 2009: 27)

Through local interest in *It's Impossible to Learn to Plow by Reading Books*, the dissemination of a rough outline of sequences known as The Roadmap and a letter of support from Monte Hellman, who had liked *It's Impossible to Learn to Plow by Reading Books*,[13] Linklater scored a grant of $2,000 from the Southwest Alternate Media Project, a Houston-based organisation that fostered independent productions. This he added to all that had been saved and would be borrowed, including the same amount of money from his mother as she had spent on his sister's wedding, gained on the promise that he would never get married (Pierson 1996: 191). The total notional budget of $77,340 was slashed by borrowing equipment worth $11,700 and deferring wages totalling $40,550 for cast and crew so that everyone worked for free. With $10,820 for post-production (including three release prints for $2,500), the final cost would be around $23,000, which still allowed for the use of a crane and a Steadicam as well as a sound mix that added non-diegetic effects such as the typewriter 'splashing' into a dry river-bed and an 'offscreen' car crash. As Linklater recalls:

> I was going for a certain naturalism. It wasn't planned. I really wanted to be like Robert Bresson with a really highly structural, highly mannered style. That's how I thought about cinema. But when I started doing it it was something else entirely. I wanted it to have that eloquent documentary feel, but if you really

look at it, there's cranes, Steadicam, a lot of dolly shots; it's very technically ambitious for a no-budget film.

Nevertheless, money-saving short-cuts that opposed bought-in solutions with creative, personal ingenuity were plenty, including the recreation by two obliging friends of a sex scene from *Ai no korîda* that is glimpsed on the monitor of Video Backpacker (Kalman Spelletich). But some limitations were frustrating, with neither the Super-8 nor the 16mm lens wide enough to shoot any group conversation, thereby dooming Linklater to alternate set-ups and the obligation to cut into scenes. Uncertain how to end a film that should by nature be interminable, Linklater thought of concluding ironically with Peggy Lee's 'Is That All There Is?' but its expense prompted the substitution of 'Strangers Die Everyday' by the Butthole Surfers, whose drummer Teresa Taylor plays Madonna Pap Smear Pusher, a prescient conflation of pornography with celebrity culture.

In addition to the ideological factors that inspired the gambit of filmmaking, the possibility of actually making a film on such a small budget was due to the technological advances of the 1980s that enabled filmmakers to focus on the details of the everyday. In addition, this attention paid to the everyday meant that ideas of what was local and regional (to Austin, for example) were important at a time when America's foreign policy and globalisation were both driven by the alienating forces of capitalism. The regional cinema of Pennell, Linklater and others may also be understood in terms of what Hamid Naficy calls 'the interstitial mode of production' (2001: 40) of accented filmmakers for whom the idea of local, regional and home is especially important. *Slacker*'s collage of video, 16mm, Super-8 and Pixel vision (shot on a Fisher Price toy camera bought for $99 from Toys R Us) made collaborative multi-tasking the film's form, content and meaning with Linklater leading the way as the first character on screen. Should Have Stayed at Bus Station (Linklater) arrives in Austin, catches a cab and regales the driver with a stream-of-consciousness monologue that turns the tables on most cab rides. *Slacker* thus begins like a direct and immediate sequel to *It's Impossible to Learn to Plow by Reading Books* that offers the fresh contrast of community in a single place with the lack of same previously experienced around the country. Struck by an evolving notion of parallel and alternate realities inspired by *The Wizard of Oz* (Victor Fleming, 1939) and inspired by the possibilities revealed in daydreams, Linklater elucidates upon a variety of other yellow brick roads his life could have taken or may be taking – 'This one time I had lunch with Tolstoy, another time I was a roadie for Frank Zappa' – before regretting his own lack of faith in oneiric potential by not having stayed at the bus station. Although the film's specific and limited time-frame conforms to Linklater's view that 'time is a valuable, unreplenishable commodity steadily slipping away,' (Linklater 2004), *Slacker* insists that 'daydreaming is the place where all the new situations, narratives and acts originate' (ibid.). Dropped off to meander in Austin, it appears that Linklater might repeat the adventure of *It's Impossible to Learn to Plow by Reading Books*, but the camera, which is now subjective, loses interest in him when it comes across a hit-and-run victim and the imminent arrest of the victim's son. And when the cops have gone the camera picks on a bystander and

Walking and talking in *Slacker*

follows him to another passerby until encountering another re-acquaintance, and so on, thereby illustrating the parallel realities lived by characters in Austin whose common link is idleness followed by various degrees of happiness, sadness and madness.

The protagonist of this *dérive* is not Linklater or any other character but the camera itself, which drifts from one person to the next, lending its subjectivity to the spectator who is thereby empowered to daydream around Austin. As a satire of digressive pilgrimage, *Slacker* may be appreciated as Linklater's palimpsest of Luis Buñuel's *La Voie lactée* (*The Milky Way*, 1969), although Linklater's most direct reference to the Surrealist agitator is in the oft-quoted refrain of Hitchhiker Awaiting 'True Call' (Charles Gunning) – 'I may live badly, but at least I don't have to work to do it! – that originates with Don Lope (Fernando Rey) in Buñuel's *Tristana* (1970):

> I say to hell with the work you have to do to earn a living! That kind of work does us no honour; all it does is fill up the bellies of the pigs who exploit us. But the work you do because you like to do it, because you've heard the call, you've got a vocation – that's ennobling! We should all be able to work like that. Look at me, Saturno – I don't work. And I don't care if they hang me, I won't work! Yet I'm alive! I may live badly, but at least I don't have to work to do it!

The effect of this idle pilgrimage or *dérive* can change with successive viewings, with tedium, envy, beguilement, depression and exhilaration all possible cognitive affective responses to *Slacker* by new and repeating spectators. This apparent affective incoherence is explained by Old Man Recording Thoughts (Joseph Jones), who appears late in the film to proclaim 'the more the pain grows, the more this instinct for life somehow asserts itself. The necessary beauty in life is in giving yourself to it completely. Only later will it clarify itself and become coherent.' Thus diagnosed, this movement from person to person through the day and night in Austin is revealed as an urban *dérive* that Linklater has himself defined as 'a nomad education of movement that features a changing curriculum of [one's] own making, based on the passion and pursuit of the moment' (Linklater 2004). This *dérive* is the reterritorialisation of a time and place that effectively occupies the capital city of Texas, home-state of the recently elected President George Bush senior while he is away working in Washington. It therefore positions *Slacker* as a guerrilla film of sly tactics and great political resonance. *Slacker* is the film of a region whose inhabitants are in a kind of hibernation throughout three successive Republican presidencies. Moreover, its sense of lucid dreaming is conveyed in long takes that correspond to Deleuze's concept of time-images, whose form, content, subversive meaning and political resonance was a determining factor in the cinema that emerged in Europe after World War II (Deleuze 2005a; 2005b). The time-image, which evades objective criteria, is usually a long take that stalls the narrative, dislocating the protagonists and the audience in time, whose passing is made perceptible. Consequently, existential angst and a longing for metaphysical transcendence become the locus of an image whose meaning is heightened by, and inseparable from, its prolongation. A time-image makes time visible in the way protagonists and audience are subject to the sense of its duration; but it also embodies time's dimension as indefinable, thereby compounding limitations of language and making verbal description impossible. Instead, it forces the audience to scrabble for meaning by 'thinking' in terms of the image. Linklater relocates the time-image's technique and aesthetic of dislocation and alienation from post-war Europe to Austin in the early 1990s and uses it to explore the mindset of an isolated, regional community whose liberal, left-wing, existentialist philosophy and lifestyle is at odds with the electorate and its thrice-elected Republican government. The inhabitants/protagonists of *Slacker* have gotten along by rejecting society and its social hierarchy before it rejected them. They now inhabit and maintain a communal identity that is celebrated in a passed-along polyphony resembling Bakhtin's carnival of street-level interaction, in which all characters are unfinalised and truth is found in a multitude of carrying voices. For Bakhtin, then, 'in the whole of the world and of the people there is no room for fear. For fear can only enter a part that has been separated from the whole' (1984a: 256). Just as the voices and gestures of this slacker folk culture express an alternative to what Linklater calls 'democratic ineptitude' (Linklater 2004), so their freedom to think is gained, explored, observed and shared in the time-images that make up the carnival of their everyday *dérive*.

The most famous literary *dérive* (even before it was identified as such) is that of Leopold Bloom in James Joyce's *Ulysses*, first published in its entirety in 1922, which chronicles his drift through Dublin on the most ordinary day possible, 16 June 1904. The novel is divided into eighteen overlapping episodes that play with form and resemble Linklater's parallel and alternate realities. Description, monologue, lists, punctuation-free stream of consciousness, Q&A and a play take their turn like the passers-by in *Slacker*, making of *Ulysses* an experimental prose full of such rich characterisations, absurdist allusions and details of Dublin that it is one of the most highly regarded of all Modernist novels. Joyce signals that Bloom's *dérive* is based upon a similar subscription to the creativity of daydreaming: 'His eyelids sank quietly often as he walked in happy warmth' (1993: 55). Bloom, like Linklater's camera, is guided by an unpredictable instinct: 'Grafton Street gay with housed awnings lured his senses' (1993: 160). For Joyce, as for Linklater, this wandering in the streets entails an immersion in an otherwise unknowable culture: 'He walked along the curbstone. Stream of life' (1993: 148). Like *Slacker*, *Ulysses* may appear chaotic but a sense of burgeoning revolution is expressed in such intense and prolonged descriptions (literary long takes) of the commonplace and the working class from all angles that the Cubist element of Modernism is also evoked in 'the cracked looking glass of a servant being the symbol of Irish art' (1993: 16). In Cubist style, Joyce's text is 'an epic "body" with episodes comprising somatically interrelated and interconnected arts, organs and hours' (Johnson 1993: xxxii). Like *Ulysses*, *Slacker* begins with a matricide that is soon shrugged off for fear that its melodramatic qualities will swamp the *dérive* with plot. Joyce's novel is also referenced explicitly in *Slacker* when Jilted Boyfriend (Kevin Whitley) is advised to rid himself of an ex-girlfriend's belongings in order to get over obsessing about her as a perfect, pure and unrepeatable romance. Guy Who Tosses Typewriter (Steven Anderson) recites a passage from *Ulysses* that comments on the wrongheaded idealism of infatuated lovers while also making explicit the affined structural conceit of *Slacker*'s catalogue of Austinites:

> To reflect that each one who enters imagines himself to be the first to enter whereas he is always the last term of a preceding series even if the first term of

'It all makes sense if you'd just read from this passage here.' Filming Guy Who Tosses Typewriter (Steven Anderson) as he reads from James Joyce's *Ulysses* in *Slacker*

a succeeding one, each imagining himself to be the first, last, only and alone whereas, he is neither first nor last nor only nor alone in a series originating in and repeated to infinity. (Joyce 1993: 683)

Furthermore, this union of the *dérive* and *Ulysses* will also be felt in *Before Sunrise*, whose time-frame for wandering Vienna is pointedly Bloomsday (16 June) and in *Before Sunset*, where the *dérive* begins in the Shakespeare and Company bookstore in Paris which first published Joyce's novel in 1922.

Like slacking, the *dérive* is a means of empowerment, a therapeutic technique and a strategy of urban occupation. The drifter/slacker does not evade duties and responsibilities out of laziness but out of dedication to more spiritual aims. As Coupland states in *Generation X*: 'We live small lives on the periphery; we are marginalized and there's a great deal in which we choose not to participate' (1996: 14). Yet, as Robert Louis Stevenson asserts in his 1876 essay *An Apology for Idlers*: 'Idleness so called, which does not consist in doing nothing, but in doing a great deal not recognized in the dogmatic formularies of the ruling class, has as good a right to state its position as industry itself' (2009: 1). Even so, self-indulgence, sloth and arrogance is exhibited by several of the characters in *Slacker* (as well as by Joyce's Leopold Bloom), which also reflects Coupland's warning that 'we're not built for free time as a species. We think we are but we aren't' (1996: 29). Nevertheless, *Slacker* is ultimately an optimistic film in which street-level interaction between humans is still mostly enjoyed in a world before mobile phones and social networking websites transformed interpersonal communication. The fact that *Slacker* ends with a montage that recalls *A Hard Day's Night* (Richard Lester, 1964) constitutes a naive return to the optimism of the 1960s or at least a nostalgic recreation of same. It also signals a key theme in Linklater's films, namely that when allowed the time to express themselves freely, most people find a spiritual quality within themselves that suggests a potential for transcendence.

Much like the way grungy garage bands liberated rock music from branding and power ballads, *Slacker* demonstrated that the means of production that had once inspired the French New Wave were once more at hand for filmmakers like Linklater and Kevin Smith, who was so enticed by *Slacker*'s iconic poster image of Madonna Pap Smear Pusher that he travelled the fifty miles from New Jersey to the Angelika multiplex in Manhattan on his twenty-first birthday in August 1991 to have his imagination 'kick-started [by] a glimpse into the free-associative world of ideas instead of plot, people instead of characters, and Nowheresville, Texas instead of the usual California or New York settings most movies elected to feature' (2008). This solipsistic Nowheresville was an instant metaphor of creative freedom for Smith, who would make *Clerks* in 1994, although as he admits, 'the fact that "Nowheresville" was really Austin speaks volumes on how culturally bereft I was at that time' (ibid.). *Slacker*'s *dérive* thus revealed an alternative and parallel present for America as it was lived in Austin with its collaborative community, tolerant mood and creative behaviour. Although Philip Kemp asserts, 'there's little sense of serious deprivation, nor any suggestion that these marginal characters are the victims of callous economic policy' (2006: 130), the inhabitants of *Slacker* claimed a history based upon distrust of their political leaders

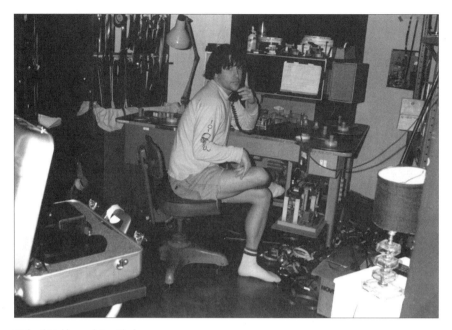

Richard Linklater editing *Slacker*

and the system that empowered them. And even if that history was almost exclusively white and straight in a city with a massive Hispanic population, black districts and a proud and highly visible gay community too, the culture of this collective was no less entitled to its cinematic expression in the new regional cinema of the so-called independents than that of San Francisco's Chinese in *Chan is Missing* (Wayne Wang, 1982), the Manhattan socialites of *Metropolitan* (Whit Stillman, 1990) or the lesbian community of *Go Fish*. Despite the colonising of America by firstly what Joyce called 'the sweepings of every country' (1993: 230) and later by big-name franchises and the uniforming of its citizens in logos, *Slacker*/Austin was a complementary example of an extant pioneer spirit. At a time when '75 per cent of young males 18 to 24 years old [were] still living at home, the largest proportion since the Great Depression' (Gross and Scott 1990), *Slacker* was a metaphor for independence and a clear indication to would-be filmmakers like Smith that regional American cinema could even settle in places like New Jersey. Like Coupland's novel *Generation X* and Nirvana's album *Nevermind*, Linklater's film indicated that expressions of independent thought could coalesce to form 'a sad, evocative perfume built of many stray smells' (Coupland 1996: 154). Most pointedly, although *Slacker*, like *Nevermind* and *Generation X*, described a period maligned by what Coupland defined as 'Historical Underdosing: To live in a period of time when nothing seems to happen' (1996: 9), it demonstrated that even this was not a hindrance once the vibrant inner life of imagination and reflection was liberated from 'low pay, low prestige, low benefits, low future' (Coupland 1996: 5).

Linklater screened a 16mm print of *Slacker* at Austin's Dobie theatre to the hundred or so participants, their friends and family, whose word of mouth and repeat viewings meant it went on to play a record eleven weeks. He also sent a VHS copy to independent producer John Pierson, who showed it to Michael Barker of Orion Classics, 'the undisputed leader in the art-film market' (Tzioumakis 2006: 261), and a group of enthusiastic students. 'Call back, something is happening!' was the message Pierson left on Linklater's answer-phone (Pierson 1996: 188). *Time* magazine had noticed something too and awarded its 16 July 1990 cover to a new demographic they called 'Twenty-something: Laid back, blooming or just lost?' (Gross and Scott 1990). Armed with this cover story, Pierson attempted to draw the attention of distributors to the relevance of *Slacker*, arguing that the article's description of a disaffected '48 million young Americans ages 18 through 29' (ibid.) promised a huge potential audience for the film, while the notion that they possessed 'only a hazy sense of their own identity' (ibid.) made them possibly ripe for synergetic branding as slackers/Generation X-ers. Supporting Pierson's claim was the article's assertion that these potential audience members 'reject 70-hour work weeks as yuppie lunacy, just as they shirk from starting another social revolution. Today's young adults want to stay in their own backyard and do their work in modest ways' (ibid.). Orion offered a $100,000 advance for distribution rights and an extra $50,000 on completion of the 35mm transfer and sound mix for the modest, backyard project that was *Slacker* (Pierson 1996: 188). But festival screenings were elusive. On Pierson's recommendation, Linklater hired lawyer John Sloss, who also represented John Sayles and Whit Stillman, and got *Slacker* into Sundance on his second attempt, where, as Pierson recalls, 'one third loved it, one third walked out, and one third fell asleep' (1996: 190). However, although its first public screening at the USA Film Festival in Dallas garnered unimpressed reviews, its showing in Seattle in June 1990 struck a chord with an audience that was just gearing up for grunge: 'It was like the spiritual wedding of the film and the audience,' recalls Linklater (in Lowenstein 2009: 35). The film also played well at Manhattan's Angelika and was then rolled out to campus cinemas nationwide. Unfortunately, by the end of 1991 Orion Classics had declared bankruptcy before the film could recoup much more than half the $100,000 advance and it was badly treated by a flustered home video division of the ailing firm. Nevertheless, a tie-in book published by St Martin's Press sold 20,000 copies and its title entered common media parlance, albeit somewhat incorrectly, as a synonym for layabout.

In capturing the drifting *zeitgeist*, however, *Slacker* may have effectively deprived it of the freedom that was essential to its survival. Like *Ulysses*, *Slacker* exhausted the conventions of realism by making the subject aware of itself, thereby rendering this single day in Austin's summer of 1989 (like Bloomsday 1904) instantly nostalgic and forever unrepeatable except in pastiche or performance. The film's emblematic status would thus endure not as a manifesto but as a touchstone for a generation that *Time* had stated 'pines for a romanticized past' (Gross and Scott 1990). In its marketing and cultish survival, *Slacker* was consequently inscribed in the process akin to that which Coupland called, 'Legislated Nostalgia: To force a body of people to have memories they do not actually possess' (1996: 47). Coupland later described the resentment it prompted in his novel *Microserfs*: 'Michael was on a rant, quite justified, I thought, about all of this media-hype generation nonsense going on at the moment. Apparently we're all "*slackers*". "Daniel, *who* thinks up these things?"' (2004: 242). However, the process is still relevant to *Ulysses*, which Dublin's Tourist Office has commoditised as a nostalgic treat for those who have probably never read it, just as *Slacker*'s working title – *No Longer/Not Yet* – indicated the illusory nature of a time and place whose film record could only ever be a tease: a cinematic construct. Nevertheless, the film's enduring relevance is partly due to the fact that its nostalgic quality naturally increases as its reputation grows as a metaphor for community-based, youthful rebellion of a non-violent sort.

Linklater, who was the oldest amongst his crew, was already in his thirties when he became spokesperson for those in their twenties and Austin was growing up too. Captain Quackenbush's Intergalactic Café on Guadalupe Street was closed. Esther's Pool on Sixth Street became The Flamingo Cantina. The Varsity Theatre was evicted by Tower Records and Café Les Amis, where several scenes in *Slacker* were filmed, became a Starbucks. Genuine slackers who were there in the early 1990s are now vastly outnumbered by all the non-contributing lurkers and relocated drop-outs who thought the film an invitation. The Austin of *Slacker*, like the Madrid of *La Movida* was a time rather than a place and the films that emerged were postcards from Coupland's 'periphery' rather than manifestos of revolutionary intent. Beneath the film's pose of loose-living there are also those who express and suffer intimidation, paranoia and depression, inspiring Jon Rosenbaum's observation that *Slacker* was 'at heart a very Russian film' (2001). A closer look at those who drift through *Slacker* reveals instances of mental illness, debilitating peer pressure, obsessive-compulsive routines, directionless anger and lost souls whose enervation is the darker side of idleness, such as the character who cuts out photographs of fellow students from his high school yearbook and burns them, the guy selling the T-shirt (made by Linklater) advertising gruesome methods of murder ('Thumb gouge to brain via eyes') and the woman who pesters diners not to traumatise women sexually. Much like Almodóvar was to struggle with bitterness and compassion for the events and characters of *La Movida* in later films such as *Tacones lejanos* (*High Heels*, 1991) and *Todo sobre mi madre* (*All About My Mother*, 1999), so Linklater would question the ultimate purpose of slacking and indicate that some of its criticisms were justified with *SubUrbia*.

Based on the 1994 play by Eric Bogosian, *SubUrbia* is a catch-up on where slackers are headed that finds nowhere fast has become a masochistic, even suicidal ambition. Five years on from *Slacker* and over a single night on a street corner, *SubUrbia* offers an ugly contrast to the gaiety of *Dazed and Confused* and a slovenly, resentful impersonation of the ingenuous purity of *Slacker*. Its twenty-something characters have attached themselves to causes that they barely understand: feminism, vegetarianism and civil rights are now branded campaigns that they subscribe to but cannot explicate or make relevant to their inaction: 'At least I admit that I don't know. I know that things are fucked up, beyond belief, and I have nothing original to say about it…' admits Jeff (Giovanni Ribisi). Instead, racism, addiction and impotence are beginning to define them. In self-defence, they catch each other posturing and call each others' bluffs, ultimately losing the struggle to identify anything in their group that is authentic and worthwhile. All attempts to drift away from the corner are frustrated: the *dérive* has stalled. Even Pony (Jayce Bartok), the old school friend turned nascent rock star, who steps out of his chauffeur-driven limousine to reconnect with some nostalgic notion of innocence and abiding friendship, is dragged down by the jealousy and frustration of the corner. Just as *Slacker* may be understood as a palimpsest of Luis Buñuel's *La Voie lactée*, so *SubUrbia* (which is analysed further in Chapter Two) might be one of *El ángel exterminador* (*The Exterminating Angel*, 1962), in which party guests find themselves unable to leave their dining room and descend to cruel, carnal and cannibalistic impulses. Once more, this is a defiantly regional cinema in which Bogosian's imaginary Burnfield provides a metaphor of Austin, where it was filmed almost entirely on the corner of Stassney and South First Street. Thus, Burnfield and Austin act as a two-way mirror that provides a clear illustration of what happened to Austin and its slackers in the mid-1990s.

Yet by then the real Austin had also become a viable base for film production and a stage for the performance of its independence. Says Linklater:

It's a real libertarian, leave me alone kinda place. Do do your own thing. But it's always tolerant. For instance, this is telling, especially in the South, the bigger cities would have a gay district, but Austin never had that. There was never a ghetto if you were gay. So it attracts people who are different, welcomes them with open arms. If you have any artistic ambitions or just want to be around culture, you'd choose to live here.

As a trendsetter of Austinite endeavour who, in addition to *Slacker, Dazed and Confused* and *SubUrbia* would also make *Waking Life* and *A Scanner Darkly* in Austin, as well as sections of *The Newton Boys* and *Bernie*, the Home Box Office (HBO) television pilot *$5.15/Hr*, the documentary *Inning by Inning: A Portrait of a Coach* and, little by little, the untitled twelve-year project known as *Boyhood*, Linklater has seen the city and his Austin Film Society flourish. By the mid-1990s the AFS was not only screening films but supporting their production with internships and apprenticeships, some of which would be administered through Linklater's own company Detour Filmproduction, named after Edgar G. Ulmer's 1945 B-noir (but also a viable synonym of *dérive*). The AFS, on whose governing board Linklater still sits as artistic director, also began managing the Texas Filmmakers' Production Fund and the Texas Film Travel Grant and was itself supported by the National Endowment for the Arts, the Texas Commission on the Arts, and the City of Austin under the auspices of the Austin Arts Council. On 24 November 1999 at the New York Hilton, Linklater and AFS executive Rebecca Campbell accepted the Directors Guild of America's first Honours Award from John Sayles in recognition of its contribution to regional film production and culture.

Ambitions were truly surpassed in 2000, moreover, when the AFS created Austin Studios by negotiating a ten-year lease of disused hangars at the Robert Mueller Municipal Airport from the Austin City Council for the token sum of $100 per annum. This was achieved by Linklater, Campbell and Robert Rodríguez convincing Austin City Council and the Mueller Neighborhood Coalition that there would be an immediate and enduring diffusion of dollars into the local small-business community as well as a real chance of maintaining a profitable regional film industry. True to this potential, Austin Studios now boasts five sound stages covering 100,000 square feet of production space, a state-of-the-art digital green screen and a roster of film and television productions bringing funds, film types and a growing industrial status to Austin. The non-profit AFS also supports short film production, the Austin Student Digital Film Festival and is associated with the South by South-West Music Festival (SXSW) and its film sidebar. Since 1995, the AFS has had its own paid staff and a website displaying copious links to screenings, archives and support services, including advice and referrals, workshops and a bi-monthly newsletter for subscribers. Alongside details of the fiscal sponsorship of projects on this website is found the proud history of the Texas Filmmakers' Production Fund, which has awarded $750,000 to over 200 film and video projects since 1996, including an After School Film Program and Summer Moviemaking Camps. In addition, the AFS still flaunts its mission to screen films that are otherwise unavailable and offer 'a model for presenting artistic works of cinema on a regional level' (Anon. 2009a). Thus the ethos of its early years remains intact, with recent seasons of Black Image in American Cinema, San Francisco Super-8 Film Happening and Women's Film Shorts, as well as retrospectives of Satyajit Ray, Raúl Ruiz, Douglas Sirk, Preston Sturges, Andrei Tarkovsky and old favourites like Bresson, Buñuel, Fassbinder and Dreyer alongside the work of regional filmmakers and a returning, annual ten-day festival at the Alamo Drafthouse cinema on Sixth Street that is curated by Quentin Tarantino.

This is a proud and proudly regional cinema despite or because of all the aforementioned ideological complexity that this entails, which includes Kinder's warning that 'there is always a close connection between regionalism and nationalism' (1993: 388) and that this may provoke conflict with centralised government and other regions. On 9 March 2007 the AFS inducted Linklater into its own Hall of Fame and on 2 July 2001, the ten-year anniversary of *Slacker*, it hosted a reunion screening in the Paramount Theater on Congress Avenue (the cinema visited in *Waking Life*) that also served as fundraiser for the Denise Montgomery Award in honour of the late actress-activist who had set up Austin Media Arts and played Having a Breakthrough Day in *Slacker*.[14] Yet the most pertinent recognition of Linklater's contribution to Austin remains its enduring boast of a tangible, viable, regional American cinema. The AFS's conflation of foreign, art-house, experimental, auteurist and regional cinema in its programming demands a respondent status for regional American cinema on the global circuit of art cinemas and film festivals. It also points to the fact that once they reach distribution on DVD all films are regional, being ascribed one of the marketable regions of the format. Moreover, because Internet distribution disregards all price-fixing, screen quotas, restrictive demographics and schedules it creates a truly world-wide film community that Linklater has always welcomed and explicitly encouraged by the copyright-free release of *Slacker* on the Internet in 2009.[15] Such actions as these make a tempting plinth for the beatification of Linklater as a patron saint of slackers, as already evidenced by a 2004 Channel Four documentary entitled *Linklater: St. Richard of Austin* in which he appears decidedly uncomfortable with the term.[16]

Austin is clearly more than the convenient hometown location of Linklater's films. It allowed a community of slackers to interact and nurture the chance to build an industry on other terms, to collectivise a creative urge and harness it to a notion of regional cinema that may have been sparked by the *zeitgeist* of *Slacker* but was maintained by the collaborative ambitions of other Austinites. In its first year, Austin Studios created 700 local jobs and brought in $41.5 million to the city, rising to 1,600 jobs and $110 million by the following year (García 2009). It ploughs back into maintenance and improvements the rents it receives from productions such as *Miss Congeniality* (Donald Petrie, 2000), *Friday Night Lights* (Peter Berg & Josh Pate, 2004), *Idiocracy* (Mike Judge, 2006), *Infamous* (Douglas McGrath, 2006), Rodríguez's *Spy Kids 3-D: Game Over* (2003), *Grindhouse* (2007) and *Machete* (2010) and Linklater's *Fast Food Nation*. As always, crucial to its success and Linklater's career is not a cliquey or solipsistic isolationism but a willingness to negotiate between the independent and studio sectors and with those who might facilitate the means to expression and advancement. In an interview in *The Velvet Light Trap* in 2008, Linklater reflected upon negotiations with the city government in 2000 and remarked that 'a lot of smart urban planning and thought [...] went into it. I think there was some good leadership at some crucial moments that kept us from going completely off the rails' (in Bozelka 2008: 55). In 2005, however, Austin dropped the ball when the Texas Legislature approved the Texas Film Incentive Program but failed to budget for its funding (Ward M. 2007). Incentives for filmmakers were thus limited to between 5 and 15 per cent based on the level of spending in Texas, which is why regional filming had relocated to the closest regional competitor Louisiana, where tax credits equal to 25 per cent of all in-state spending went to filmmakers and 35 per cent of the payroll went to Louisiana residents. Or New Mexico, which offered refunds equal to 25 per cent of in-state spending, including payroll. Or Michigan, where a 40 per cent film incentive drew the Austin-set *Whip It!* (Drew Barrymore, 2009) starring Ellen Page to its recreation of the Texas capital. In sum, Texas lost approximately 7,000 crew positions and $500 million in production spending to other regions and a closer look at the slate of films due to be shot in and around Austin revealed them all to be frugal, low-to-no-budget projects that might have been keeping the *Slacker* spirit alive, but in a grossly malnourished body (Anon. 2009b). It was only a public demonstration and lobbying of the State Capitol in March 2009 that prevented the collapse of filmmaking in Austin, when, true to form, Linklater was a central figure in this minor but significant revolution.

The plan was that the Texas Moving Image Industry Incentive Program (House Bill 873 and Senate Bill 605) would demand an increase in funding from $20 million to $62 million and give the Texas Film Commission Office greater flexibility in negotiating the incentive rate on a project by project basis. On 4 March 2009 approximately 600 red-shirted supporters responded to the call of the Texas Motion Picture Alliance (TXMPA) on the steps of Austin's State Capitol, where they were greeted by Governor Rick Perry (author of House Bill 873), Film Commissioner Bob Hudgins, TXMPA President Don Stokes, Senator Bob Deuell (author of Senate Bill 605), *Prison Break* producer Garry Brown and Linklater. 181 legislators were visited and duly lobbied in the Capitol building, resulting in additional sponsors, the recognition of TXMPA by the House and an address to the House Committee on Culture, Recreation, and Tourism by Linklater, who told his audience he was ready to go with a $17 million film set in Texas, but might have to shoot in Shreveport, Los Angeles instead if the improved film incentive package was not passed (Anon. 2009c). Thus, on 23 April 2009 Governor Rick Perry duly signed the bill that expanded the state's incentive program for film, television and video game production in Texas (O'Connell 2009). This allowed Robert Rodríguez to reinvigorate his slew of projects that included *Machete* (2010) and a reboot of the *Predator* franchise. In quiet contrast however, following the commercial disappointments of *Fast Food Nation* (barely $1 million USA box office), *A Scanner Darkly* ($5.5 million USA box office on an estimated $8.5 million budget) and a prolonged delay in the distribution of *Me and Orson Welles*, Linklater retreated to the refuge of an earlier Austin with his attempt (ultimately frustrated) to make 'a spiritual sequel' to *Dazed and Confused* that was entitled *That's What I'm Talking About* and set in 1980 (Graham 2009).

South-west of Austin in San Antonio is the site of another battle for independence called the Alamo, the fortress where 188 Texans led by Davy 'King of the Wild Frontier' Crockett stood against the Mexican General Santa Anna's force of several thousand in 1836. Back then regionalism did not signify parochialism but a demarcation of political and cultural boundaries worth dying for. This notion of America as a single nation is relatively recent and about as satisfactory as pretending that the term European could ever unite and pacify all the countries and cultures that make up the most war-ravaged continent of the twentieth century. Far better perhaps to recognise the variety and value of regional cinema in America, which also avoids any arrogance, cynicism, convenience or opportunism in labelling filmmakers and their films 'independent'. Nostalgia may intrude on history in identifying *Slacker* as one of the great 'indies' of modern American cinema, but the 'legend' of Linklater in a raccoon hat fighting off the forces of Hollywood, like any celebration of auteurist endeavour, is best countered by heeding Texan folklorist J. Frank Dobie's assertion that 'the history of any public character involves not only the facts about him but what the public has taken to be the facts' (Gellert 2002: 39). Nevertheless, what cannot be denied is that Linklater's cinema derives from an umbilical connection with Austin and that his own drift and drive persistently relocates him in a city that has always been the source of what Robert Louis Stevenson called 'a faculty for idleness [that] implies a catholic appetite and a strong sense of personal identity' (2009: 7).

Notes

1   *Easy Rider* was produced by Raybert (later BBS) and distributed by Columbia; *Slumdog Millionaire* was produced by Celador and Film4 Productions and sold to Warner Independent Pictures to distribute.
2   Representative films and filmmakers from the Mumblecore movement, which was featured in a ten-film series at New York's IFC in 2007 under the title 'Generation DIY: The New Talkies', include *Funny Ha Ha* (Andrew Bujalski, 2002), *Quiet City*

(Aaron Katz, 2007), and *In Search of a Midnight Kiss* (Alex Holdridge, 2007), all of which replay the 'boy meets girl, they walk and talk' premise of *Before Sunrise*.

3   *Hud* was adapted from McMurtry's *Horseman, Pass By* (1961). McMurtry also wrote the novels *The Last Picture Show* (1966), *Terms of Endearment* (1975), Pulitzer Prize winning *Lonesome Dove* (1986) and the screenplay (with Diana Ossana) of *Brokeback Mountain* (2005), based on the short story by E. Annie Proulx.

4   Cormac McCarthy was born in Providence, Rhode Island but moved to El Paso, Texas in 1976. His novels include *Blood Meridian* (1985), *All The Pretty Horses* (1992), *The Crossing* (1994), *Cities of the Plains* (1998), *No Country for Old Men* (2005) and Pulitzer-winning *The Road* (2006).

5   Another precedent was the German channel ZDF's backing for the work of Jim Jarmusch.

6   Gramercy was a joint venture between Universal and PolyGram Filmed Entertainment that would merge with October Films to become USA Films in 1999, and which would change its name to Focus Features in 2002.

7   Films produced by Castle Rock prior to 1994 (including New Line co-productions involving Sony) became the property of MGM. Post-1994 films are the property of Warner Brothers.

8   Examples include *The Last King of Scotland* (Kevin MacDonald, 2006), *Once* (John Carney, 2006), *The Savages* (Tamara Jenkins, 2007), and *Funny Games US* (Michael Haneke, 2007).

9   Warner Brothers basically got the *Ocean's 11* to *13* franchise in return for partly financing and guaranteeing some level of marketing and distribution for Soderbergh's *Full Frontal* (2002), *Bubble* (2005), *The Good German* (2006) and *Ché: Part One* (2008) as well as Clooney's *Confessions of a Dangerous Mind* (2002) and *Good Night, and Good Luck* (2005), all of which, to a greater or lesser extent, were commercial flops.

10   All quotations from Richard Linklater, unless otherwise attributed, are from interviews with the author in Austin, Texas, 30 July–1 August 2009.

11   These flyers are included as an extra feature on the region 1 Criterion Collection DVD of *Slacker*.

12   This Oblique Strategy, as verified by Lee Daniel in the Channel Four documentary *St. Richard of Austin* does not actually appear in Peter Schmidt and Brian Eno's deck of cards containing aphorisms designed to inspire creative thinking but is inspired by the writing of Albert Camus on *The Myth of Sisyphus*: 'Living the absurd … means a total lack of hope (which is not the same as despair), a permanent reflection (which is not the same as renunciation), and a conscious dissatisfaction (which is not the same as juvenile anxiety)'. Albert Camus (1991) *The Myth of Sisyphus and Other Essays*. New York: First Vintage International, p.23.

13   Linklater sent Monte Hellman a copy of *It's Impossible to Learn to Plow by Reading Books*. Hellman's influence is referenced in *Slacker* in the name of Lee Daniel's character GTO being that of Warren Oates in the existential drop-out film, *Two-*

Lane Blacktop. Hellman's thoughts on *Slacker* and Linklater are included in the booklet with the Criterion Collection DVD of *Slacker*, while Linklater's thoughts on *Two-Lane Blacktop* are included as an extra feature on the Criterion Collection edition of Hellman's film.

14   A record of the reunion is provided as an extra feature on the Criterion Collection DVD of *Slacker*.

15   http://www.hulu.com/watch/38316/slacker.

16   *Linklater: St. Richard of Austin*, The Art Show, World of Wonder, www.worldof-wonder.net. Thanks to Andrew Richards for providing a DVD of the programme, details for which may be found here: http://www.channel 4.com/culture/ microsites/A/art_show/linklater (accessed 3 July 2009).

CHAPTER TWO

Crafting Contradictions

Revellers in Linklater's *Dazed and Confused* kidnap bronze figures playing pipe and drum from a memorial to the American War of Independence and paint their faces black and white to resemble members of KISS, an American rock band of the 1970s whose image was based on this carnivalesque trademark. Strapped to the back of a truck and adorned with fireworks, they are a monument to irreverence in the midst of the Moon Tower keg party that commemorates the last day of school in May 1976.[1] However, by 1983 KISS had abandoned their face paint to seek credibility. It was not until 1996 that nostalgia prompted their reunion with reinstated make-up and a worldwide concert tour. But which of these incarnations might be taken as most representative of the cinema of Richard Linklater? Is it the original monument to American independence or the witty but vandalistic imitation? Is it a cinema that wears a youthful disguise or one that doffs it in order to gain credibility for maturing expression? Or is it all of the above? Answers may be found by an exploration of the contradictions in his cinema. Is Linklater an independent auteur or a collaborator in search of industry? Is he a director favouring original screenplays and improvisation or one dependent upon adaptable works and rehearsal? Do his films reflect an American sense or a European sensibility? Are they political or indifferent? Is he a Modernist or a Postmodernist filmmaker? Or, again, is he all of the above, making dazed and confused the most appropriate response to his cinema?

   Contradictions arise when attempting to assess the cinema of Linklater largely because his emphasis on collaboration undercuts any semblance of the kind of performative auteurism that posits the director as 'primary creator' during production. The possibility and pretence of a film director being somehow gifted to fashion films as ideological constructs that revel and reveal themselves in their own quirks, codes, conventions and signifiers is a common obstacle to complete appraisals of the invention, construction and reception of films. Yet it is the structuring process of filmmaking rather than the construction of any monument to its meaning that most consumes Linklater. Developing projects, negotiating funding, corralling collaborators, encouraging actors, promoting talent and hawking for distribution before moving on to the next project is what typifies his career, with the composite role of producer increasingly commanding most of his energy. Neither exclusively independent nor wholly dependent upon studios and distributors, Linklater's career must be plotted with an entire arsenal of sliding scales that includes the one that major studios use to calibrate film budgets ranging from those that are appropriate to the absolute autonomy of filmmakers whose talents suit a narrow marketing strategy to those that factor in the servitude of those whose skills can be applied to industrial franchises. Such calculations are exacting since few high-stakes gambles have been placed on contemporary American filmmakers by a major studio since the profligacy of the 1970's movie brats unless their boast of a marketable vision can be backed up by past grosses, the loyalty of box-office stars and a record of profitably pushing but never bankruptingly breaking generic formulas. Perhaps only the careers of David Fincher, Michael Mann and Christopher Nolan have begun to meet these criteria sufficiently, whereas other filmmakers who have emerged from the independent sector have seen their talents siphoned away from small, personal projects to add flavour to the industrial formula for superheroes.[2] Linklater seems unlikely to helm an episode in any supersized franchise any time soon, however, for he has mostly tried to skew the scale towards the privilege of autonomy that comes with low-budget filmmaking. Even with studio projects such as *Dazed and Confused* and *The School of Rock* there is a degree of independence to be found and/or fought for over their small-to-average studio budgets. On the other hand, any deal demands some respect for the investment and a consequent responsibility to the investor, which means that creative independence is arguably incompatible with an industry where a director is part of a manufacturing process. Contradictions thus arise because this also suggests that the kind of collaboration that Linklater most often seeks might actually be best found on a studio production. From the viewpoint of the filmmaker as well as the studio, the negotiation of financing and facilities for production and distribution makes independence something measurable in the kind of fractions that Linklater has agreed to with varying degrees of success and subversion.

In his working methods and practices Linklater actually opposes the notion of auteurism that Andrew Sarris introduced to America in his essay 'Notes on the Auteur Theory in 1962' (1962) as a structuring principle of enunciation that supported the concept of the authentically creative filmmaker at work within the studio system. This 'auteur theory' was also 'a surreptitiously nationalist instrument for asserting the superiority of American cinema' (Stam 2000: 89); for it was by adopting auteurism as a structural conceit and marketing tool respectively that critics and Hollywood somewhat displaced European cinema as the normative reference for the study and appreciation of film. At the same time, the structuralist basis of film criticism in the 1960s and 1970s empowered dissections of the work of directors such as Alfred Hitchcock and Howard Hawks and extended this courtesy to many lesser-known and contemporary directors. Critics sought the traits and building blocks of any director's supposedly singular vision and thereby elevated the likes of Michael Cimino, Martin Scorsese and Francis Ford Coppola to positions of indulged despotism within the major studios. Celebrating these filmmakers as auteurs was a critical construct that fed an academic need for structure, a critical need for recognition, studios' marketing strategies, directors' egos and the increasing public interest in celebrity. Despite correctives from critics such as Pauline Kael and numerous academics, however, auteurism survived to resemble a populist championing of the voice of the director as the sole point of enduring stability amongst so much rupture, fragmentation and change in a multimedia world. Thus an emblematic film such as *Pulp Fiction* (Quentin Tarantino, 1994) erected a matrix that 'suggests that every text forms an intersection of textual surfaces' (Stam 2000: 201). *Pulp Fiction* by which Tarantino duly dazzles with a glut of references that correspond to the multi-dimensional space that Roland Barthes described when a 'variety of writings, none of them original, blend and clash' (1982: 146). In *Revolution in Poetic Language* (1984), however, Julia Kristeva analysed intertextuality as 'the passage from one sign system to another' (1984: 59) and invoked the destruction of the old system and the flourishing of the new, while nonetheless maintaining an awareness of overlapping meanings in which the new system might use the same signifiers as the old one. It is in these terms, for example, that *Slacker* may be understood as a palimpsest, as a renewal and subversive application of Bakhtin's notion of carnival, which he posits as a social institution in which distinct individual voices interact. The film's respectful embodiment of carnival means that it avoids the traps of both pastiche and allegory and its polyphony remains true to the members of a community that made this film about itself instead.

Linklater is just one member of this community, of course, and as such must be recognised as an example of what Bakhtin posited as an unfinalisable self; that is, a person who cannot ever be completely known, understood or labelled. This overlaps with the theories of Henri Bergson (1992b), who wrote of an eternal becoming because it sees in people the eternal potential for change. However, in his writing on *Problems of Dostoevsky's Poetics* (1984b [1929]), Bakhtin also notes the influence of everyone on everyone else and therefore denies the possibility of isolation while simultaneously recognising creative works as representations of this polyphony, that is, of the many voices that go into creating a work or a person. This concept underpins the open auditions held for *Slacker* and *Dazed and Confused*, for instance, as well as the casting of people and their empathetic animators for *Waking Life* in which Timothy 'Speed' Levitch as Himself informs Main Character that their lives are 'adaptations of Dostoevsky novels starring clowns'. It also points to the incorporation of actors' own personalities in characters such as Jesse and Céline, Dewey Finn and the kids who play-acted in *The School of Rock* and *Bad News Bears*. Just as each distinct character in *Slacker* may speak for an individual self (including Linklater as Should Have Stayed at Bus Station), so the resultant film is an unfinished monument to the evolving community of voices, each of which carries its own truth, with which all-comers interact. Within this polyphony may 'also figure, but in far from first place, the philosophical views of the author himself' (Bakhtin 1984b: 5), which suggests that Linklater's relation to a work such as *Slacker* corresponds to how Bakhtin perceives of Dostoevsky:

> *A plurality of independent and unmerged voices and consciousnesses, a genuine polyphony of fully valid voices is in fact the chief characteristic of Dostoevsky's novels.* What unfolds in his works is not a multitude of characters and fates in a single objective world, illuminated by a single authorial consciousness; rather a *plurality of consciousnesses, with equal rights and each with its own world,* combine but are not merged in the unity of the event. (1984b: 6; emphasis in original)

For example, a character such as Dostoyevsky Wannabe (Brecht Andersch) in *Slacker* is worked up in writing and rehearsal and embellished in performance with the result that it 'possesses extraordinary independence in the structure of the work; it sounds, as it were, *alongside* the author's word and in a special way combines both with it and with the full and equally valid voices of other characters' (Bakhtin 1984b: 7; emphasis in original). The study of film as an academic discipline may have benefitted from a belief in a director's creative artistry because it empowered critics, academics and filmmakers to raise the status of cinema to that of other arts, but in the cinema of Linklater, as for the novels of Dostoevsky, 'the direct and fully weighted signifying power of the characters' words destroys the monologic plane' (Bakhtin 1984b: 5). Nevertheless, in addition to considerations of the economic viability of Linklater's career, his working practice in relation to studios and collaborators (including co-writers), his association (whether real or assumed) with contemporary filmmakers, the marketing of the films he has directed and, following Timothy Corrigan (1991), the commercial performance of auteurism (particularly in the context of it being so enthusiastically performed by several of his contemporaries), the cinema of Linklater must also be contextualised within World cinema and in relation to key influences such as Bresson and Godard. By these means may be plotted a schema of aesthetic development and its relation to political and philosophical thought and meaning.

Should have, could have, would have stayed at the bus station; but *Slacker* was made with $23,000 of Linklater's own money, grants and deferrals and was picked up for distribution by Orion Classics, while *Dazed and Confused* was a studio production that came in at $6 million for Universal. On it Linklater learnt that if a filmmaker seeks some degree of independence the film's price must be low, which he subsequently forgot on *The Newton Boys*, which was made for $27 million from the Twentieth Century Fox Corporation. Balancing the scale between independence and studio interference, *Before Sunrise*, *SubUrbia* and *Before Sunset* had Castle Rock Entertainment as intermediary between them and distributor Columbia Pictures; but *The School of Rock* was made for $35 million for Paramount, while *Bad News Bears* cost $30 million to produce and was locked into a distribution deal with Paramount and UIP. The variety of production deals and packages points to a volatile but versatile industry, although the piecemeal accumulation of independent funding as was the case with *Fast Food Nation* can prove as much of a challenge as distribution. The risk is such that the montage of funding required to attach a green light to any project is fraught with a collage of clauses. For all its period detail, *Me and Orson Welles* cost in the low $20 million range, for instance, but much of this came from The Isle of Man Development Fund on condition that the production was completion bonded, 'at least 50 per cent of all principal photography [took] place on the island [and] at least the equivalent of 20 per cent of the below the line budget [was spent] with local service providers' (Anon. 2009e). *Me and Orson Welles* was duly filmed in large part at the Gaiety Theatre in the island's capital, Douglas, but only after Linklater had submitted an application for funding that contained (as per conditions and criteria) a fully developed shooting script, a detailed synopsis, a biography and filmography of all key elements, including principal cast, producers, writer and director, and a 'proposed finance structure including principal conditions attached to all third party investment and projected budget [and proof of] some initial finance already in place' (ibid.). And upon completion it faced perhaps the greatest risk run by independently produced features, that of failing to secure distribution beyond festivals.

After a career spanning thirty years, as of May 2009 Linklater's career gross in America stood at $155,714,563 which was massively skewed by $81,261,177 from *The School of Rock* (Anon. 2009f). The remaining $75 million gave an average $5.7 million gross in the USA for the remaining features, putting only a few into domestic profit. Starting out, *Slacker* made $1.2 million and *Dazed and Confused* struggled just past break-even to $7.9 million. *The Newton Boys* made back only $10 million of its $27 million, *Waking Life* made $3 million, *Bad News Bears* barely covered its budget and *Fast Food Nation* scraped just $1 million. Nothing on Linklater's spreadsheet besides *The School of Rock* could ever excite a major studio such as Paramount, which duly showed interest in signing Linklater, writer Mike White and star Jack Black to make a sequel called *The School of Rock 2: America Rocks* that, says Linklater, 'Mike White was writing [...] a long time ago, but it's become dormant' (in Buchanan 2009). Yet this same CV does attest to Linklater's longevity at the low-cost level of American filmmaking, as well as the possible viability of regional filmmaking. It also indicates how important 'independent' American cinema's reception abroad is, for the afore-mentioned figures do not include international box office, where, for example, the $17.2 million gross of *Before Sunrise* is three times the domestic box office of $5.4m. In addition, the total gross for this film indicates a $20 million profit or an 800 per cent ratio of return on its $2.5 million budget. For comparison's sake, to achieve the same return on each dollar a blockbuster like *Star Trek* (J. J. Abrams, 2009) would have to earn $1.2 billion on its budget of $150 million. Moreover, the cult followings that make the likes of Criterion Collection DVD editions of *Slacker* and *Dazed and Confused* worthwhile also point to enduring critical, academic and popular interest in Linklater as well as the importance of the home viewing audience, ancillary markets and other evolving ways of disseminating films to the kind of fan base whose enthusiasm makes *Before Sunrise* the lowest-grossing film to ever spawn a sequel.

Survival is its own form of success, however, and Linklater has always claimed extra lives by pinballing from project to project with a collaborative ethos, breaking even and the chance to make another film seemingly ambition enough. The negotiation of the degree of autonomy necessary for the collaborative creative process to prosper is a cornerstone of his career, although the notion that this is primarily an auteurist objective is unrealistic. His reputation as an independent filmmaker endures because of the resonance of the emblematic *Slacker* and the kindred spirit of a succession of protagonists in his ensuing films rather than any refusal to work with the studios. Says Linklater:

> I love the studio system. I would like to have been Vincente Minnelli or Howard Hawks making a film or two a year in the studio system. But you know, that had its downside. I think you had to sublimate your own ego on the surface. Secretly you're making your film, but at least on the surface you had to show that you're being a company man. At least talk the talk. And it's a lot of hard work. When I do a studio film I'm not slumming. I work just as hard on that to make it be as good as it possibly can and push everyone around me to work well.[3]

In Paramount's *The School of Rock*, for example, the slacker-rocker Dewey Finn embodies this curious paradox by exhorting his inhibited pupils to 'Stick it to "The Man"!' within a potential film franchise for a multimedia corporation. These crafted contradictions are even highlighted with some irony in Finn's rallying cry to his class: 'You gotta get mad at the man! And right now, I'm the man. That's right, I'm the man, and who's got the guts to tell me off? Huh? Who's gonna tell me off?' Nevertheless, although Jack Black's performance of Finn imitating 'The Man' suggests a parodic impersonation of the major studio that funds the film/platform that he speaks from, Linklater subverts the whole project by constructing an audience-pleasing moral victory out of getting the pre-teen children of Republican parents to ditch their private elementary school studies and discover their truly creative vocations in rebelliousness and rock. Notwithstanding, Lesley Speed rightly defends the film against any accusation of complicity in the kind of anti-intellectualism that Jean-Pierre Geuens identified in the counter-cultural demand of the 1960s, namely that 'art [should] be directly apprehended by the senses, without any training, any research, or any effort by the mind' (Speed 2007: 100). Instead, she recognises an 'inclusive scheme' in the cinema of Linklater, 'in which reflective and sensory experience coexist and complement one another' (2007: 101). In other words, not only is it impossible to learn to plow by reading books, but rocking out and goofing off are vital to a fully-rounded education too.

Clues to the subversive nature of this finely-tuned family film begin with the very first shot of the leather-jacketed back of a figure entering a club that is a direct homage to Kenneth Anger's *Scorpio Rising* (1964), an underground cult film about sado-masochistic, gay, neo-Nazi bikers. Finn will later curse the noxious effect of MTV on rock music and blame 'The Man' for its invention in gleeful defiance of the fact that MTV is owned by Paramount, which produced *The School of Rock*. 'We tapped into rebellion [and] were having our own fun. [...] Even on the day [of filming that scene] we expected the phone to ring,' admits Linklater on the region 2 DVD commentary. Many treated *The School of Rock* as Linklater's sell-out, but, as noted earlier, it is argu-

'Sex Pistols never got an A!' Dewey Finn (Jack Black) in *The School of Rock*

ably the most subversive film to have come from a major American studio in recent years because it inspires kids to ditch their studies, disobey their Republican parents, band together and rock. As Linklater contends:

> It was the first time I was ever cast as a director as I would cast an actor. And that was a very different script when I first got it. Very cheesy: they win the competition, donate the money to the school. We'd already got the commercial notes, the kids, etc., but now we thought, 'Okay, let's make it cool!' And you could be really subversive!

Thus, any auteurist critique would define *The School of Rock* as Linklater's most qualifying venture because his creative input corresponds to the myth of a filmmaker within the system being able to place his or her artistic signature on alien material. Linklater does make the film personally relevant to the extent that it corresponds to a subversive exposition of the slacker ethos within a feelgood family film by a major studio. Here again therefore, it may be argued, the influence of Luis Buñuel, whose films played at the Austin Film Society under the title The Subversive in the Studio is evoked, for *The School of Rock* might be best understood as a joyfully Buñuelian perversion of the 'inspirational tutor' genre typified by films such as *Mr Holland's Opus* (Stephen Herek, 1995) and *Music of the Heart* (1999) directed by Wes Craven, a longer way from Texas than Linklater.

In addition, one of the main themes of *The School of Rock* is creative control, which suggests something of the contradictory role of its director. Linklater came to the project at the urging of writer Mike White after Stephen Frears turned it down. Although always intended as a vehicle for Jack Black (who had inspired White to write it for him by running naked, music blaring, through the corridors of the apartment block they shared), Paramount's removal of the script's darker elements (including Finn having run over the teacher whose supply job he takes, references to the drug use of rock stars, and Freddy the pre-teen-post-punk drummer justifying his extant nickname 'Spazzy' with a case of Attention Deficit Disorder) was meant to turn *The School of Rock* into a wholesome, family comedy. Under studio control but within his own working practice, however, Linklater still claimed a degree of autonomy for the creative process that is replicated in the way that the children are inspired to shape themselves into a rock band in montage sequences that Linklater claims on the DVD commentary are 'great for representing collaborative efforts'. Finn is on a mission: 'Dude, I service society by rocking, OK? I'm out there on the front lines liberating people with my music!' *The School of Rock* is not really about 'goofing off' as one child says, but a viable alternative to systematised education that amounts to a pre-teen revolution in search of freedom, and as such it carries philosophical weight and a subversive charge.

The catalyst of music in *The School of Rock* as in *Dazed and Confused* 'did what rock and roll was supposed to do – it unleashed a power and had a liberating and unifying effect,' (Linklater 1993: 5). However, naiveté is ultimately avoided by having the kids premonitorily emulate the Bad News Bears of Michael Ritchie's 1976 film (and Linklater's subsequent remake) by losing the climactic Battle of the Bands. Moreover, they lose to a manufactured boy-band, which adds corrective realism to the fantasy of competing against a 'Man-sized' corporation. What *The School of Rock* provides is a metaphorical illustration of the collaborative work ethic that originates with Linklater's experience of team sports: 'I was always the team-sport kind of guy: baseball, football, basketball. I think because of the team efforts I had been involved in I realized that I like being a part of a team' (in Smith G. 2006). This enthusiasm also corresponds to the political and social strategy represented in the production of most of his films including this, a studio project. In effect, although Linklater pragmatically assumed the responsibilities (no wastage, return a profit – check) and guise (apron, name-tag – cheque) of a director-for-hire, he still managed enough collaborative rebelliousness from Black, White and his child actors to twist the film into an assault upon the Republican values that govern institutions such as private elementary schools and major film studios. Far from a sell-out, *The School of Rock* is equal to the allegorical indictment of British public schooling and the class system that maintains it in Lindsay Anderson's *If...* (1968), although it arms its pupils with musical instruments instead of machine guns. Thus *The School of Rock* demonstrates there is clearly much to be derived from the resources of a major studio like Paramount, not least the expansive budget for music rights that has long evaded Linklater, who got to compile a soundtrack for *The School of Rock* that harks back to the pre-punk and disco era of *Dazed and Confused* with The Clash, KISS, The Doors, AC/DC, The Who, The Ramones, Metallica, David Bowie, T-Rex and The Velvet Underground. Most importantly, Linklater was able to back up his request to Led Zeppelin to use their 'Immigrant Song' with a filmed plea by Jack Black in front of several hundred screaming fans and, of course, ready payment from Paramount several years after failing to get their song 'Dazed and Confused' from the album *Led Zeppelin 1* (1969) for his film of the same name.

Dazed and Confused was one of several films that Linklater had been shaping since before *Slacker*. His usual working practice involves these 'superlong gestation periods'

(Anon. 1994) in which he makes and saves notes on cards: 'I have a lot of movies I'm always doing this for: scenes, exact memories, ideas, and it slowly comes together in my mind' (ibid.). His original idea for *Dazed and Confused* was for all the action and characters on the last day of school in 1976 to be seen from inside a car (Spong 2006: 35). However, when critic Gary Arnold put in a good word with Jim Jacks, producer of *Raising Arizona* (Ethan & Joel Coen, 1987), Linklater was invited to pitch the film to Universal. Asked to turn his awkward pitch into a script, Linklater structured his notes by adding a framework of songs from circa 1976 and then wrote the dialogue in a matter of days by using the music as an *aide memoire* 'to tap back into a period of my life I had long ago intentionally repressed [because] it was too painful' (Linklater 1993: 5). He claims this script is his 'most autobiographical moment to moment' (Corn 1996), which suggests that Mitch is his alter ego by dint of age, although it was the part of Randall 'Pink' Floyd (Jason London) that he most often read opposite auditioning actors. Meanwhile, Jacks talked up the project's similarities to *American Graffiti* (George Lucas, 1973) to Universal chairman Tom Pollock, while 'keep[ing] him away from *Slacker* for as long as possible' (Pierson 1996: 196). Thereafter, a decent budget (at least by *Slacker* standards) enabled Linklater to create his collage of characters, events and sounds within the time-frame of eighteen hours from noon on the last day of school on 28 May 1976, which was recreated in Austin during the summer of 1992. He entrusted the casting to Don Philips, who had excelled at the same task on *Fast Times at Ridgemont High* (Amy Heckerling, 1982), and selected his actors according to their correspondence with the available roles. Auditions yielded a roster of fresh talent, including Parker Posey, whose character of Tess Shelby in daytime soap *As The World Turns* (1991–92) was conveniently in a coma, Cole Hauser, Ben Affleck, Rory Cochrane, Adam Goldberg, Marisa Ribisi, Michelle Burke, Joey Lauren Adams and Austinites Wiley Wiggins, Cristina Hinojosa and Matthew McConaughey, whose casting and enlargement of the role of Wooderson was particularly catalytic for the production.[4] Linklater made individualised mix-tapes of their characters' kinds of albums for each actor and sent them all a 'Dear Cast' letter dated 16 June 1992 that promised: 'If the final movie is 100 per cent word-for-word what's in the script, it will be a massive underachievement' (Linklater 2006a: 52). His aim of prompting the cast into living their roles led to them being billeted together in an Austin hotel, but the

Slater (Rory Cochrane), Pink (Jason London) and Dawson (Sasha Jenson) in *Dazed and Confused*

mix of East and West Coast actors produced a hormone-led, highly unruly commune. Nevertheless, Linklater was protective of his cast and put himself between them and the studio in order to protect rehearsals and rewrites that incorporated the creativity of his actors within a stifling schedule. The success of this process, he claims, pointing at the script, is that 'all the best lines in *Dazed* are in the margins' (in Corn 2006). Indeed, great embellishment during rehearsal is evident in the workprint of the film, which features an extensive sub-plot about the pursuit of the KISS-ed bronze statues by the cops and several stand-alone scenes featuring aimless but entertaining banter amongst the actors.

Dazed and Confused firmly established Linklater's favoured, cost-effective working practice of prolonged preparation for both writing and filming with rehearsals leading to rewrites but little actual improvisation during filming. The myth of favouring improvisation during filming that pursues Linklater is not just wrong but illogical because any filmmaker who has graduated from very low-budget filmmaking and, indeed, chooses to remain there, simply cannot afford to allow improvisation during a shoot because the inevitably ruined or inappropriate takes will use up the precious daylight, film, budget and patience of a low-to-no-salaried crew. Thus, on all films except *The School of Rock*, where the studio budget did allow Black to riff in search of comic rhythm with the child actors, Linklater aims to exhaust the scope for improvisation in rehearsal so that the actual filming is not wasteful:

> I never have understood how people don't rehearse much in movies. They come in, rehearse it, block it, shoot it. I insist on a lot of rehearsal. People say: 'Three weeks of rehearsal! I'd rather be shooting!' But no. Every day of rehearsal saves you a week of filming. You're that much more prepared, that much more ready.

Linklater's ambition to transfer the working ethos of *Slacker* to the studio production of *Dazed and Confused* was also signalled by his letter to the crew, which resembles extracts from Robert Bresson's collection of working memos entitled *Notes on the Cinematographer* (1975). Bresson certainly influenced Linklater in the way he crafted spiritual themes by stripping back the aesthetics and the performances of his films in long takes that captured a delicate sense of time and expressed a potential for transfiguration. Bresson's aim was a distinction between the cinema that he derided as filmed theatre and cinematography that entailed not reproduction but creation, wherein cinematography, which he believed had the special meaning of creative filmmaking, 'thoroughly exploits the nature of film as such [and] should not be confused with the work of a cameraman' (1997: 16). This, for example, is echoed by Linklater when he writes: 'To avoid: the smell of the stage or theater. [...] We are not recopying life – we are creating a new, cinematic life' (2006b: 53). As would Linklater, Bresson aimed to 'apply myself to insignificant (nonsignificant) images, [to] tie new relationships between persons and things which are, and *as they are*' (1997: 19; emphasis in original) and to 'catch instants. Spontaneity, freshness' (1997: 34). In turn, Linklater writes:

Art is not in the mind but in the eye, the ear, the memory of the senses. [...] Our images must exclude the idea of image. Not beautiful photography, not beautiful images, but necessary photography, necessary images. [...] The real is not dramatic. Drama will be born after a combination of non-dramatic elements. (2006b: 53)

Such rhetoric also suggests Linklater's desire to prove himself capable, authoritative and resistant to the studio's expectations of a raucously sentimental teen movie. Although *Dazed and Confused* was a tightly controlled and slimly financed production by Universal, Linklater wrote that the mission of his cast and crew was: 'Turning liabilities into assets: making (monetary) limitations our (creative) freedom' (ibid.). He also snubbed the studio by prohibiting the use of fashionable Steadicam so that the film 'looked seventies' (ibid.) and clashed frequently with producer Jacks over scheduling, coverage and the amount of swearing allowed to actors such as Affleck, who tended towards a foul mouth when in full flow.

Linklater has said of *Dazed and Confused* that he 'sold out from the very beginning [but] want[s] credit for suffering Universal' (2006c). In pre-production he claims he 'quickly had to learn to drop all references to [Luis Buñuel's] *Los Olvidados* (*The Forgotten Ones*, aka. *The Young and the Damned*, 1950] and focus on the *Animal House/ American Graffiti/ Fast Times at Ridgemont High* holy trinity' instead (Pierson 1996: 196). Yet, rather than trace the template of that triptych, *Dazed and Confused* maintains some fidelity to Buñuel's nightmarish evocation of the slum-dwelling delinquents of Mexico City for it is a horror film about high school that takes nostalgia for its first victim. As regards the comparison with *American Graffiti*, which also takes place over one summer night (albeit in 1962), *Dazed and Confused* rejects what Robert Stam describes as that film's 'wistful sense of loss for what is imagined as a simpler and grander time' (2000: 304) and instead subscribes to Coupland's view that 'we can no longer create the feeling of an era ... of time being particular to one spot in time' (2004: 75). Thus, says Linklater, *Dazed and Confused* sees high school as 'a light prison sentence to be served. Once paroled you don't look back' (1993: 5). Instead of conjuring nostalgia, it presents the 'shitty time' (in Corn 2006) of high school with hazing rituals as horrific as the prom in *Carrie* (Brian De Palma, 1976), which was released the year *Dazed and Confused* was set. As with many of those in *Slacker*, the guise of being dazed and confused is one of self-protection for the film's teenagers, whose recent past is alien (Vietnam, Watergate) and whose present is stagnating in the kind of fearful inertia voiced by Cynthia (Marisa Ribisi): 'I'd like to quit thinking of the present, like right now, as some minor, insignificant preamble to something else.'

Ironically, Universal contradicted itself by planning for a marketing campaign based on nostalgia while declaring its intention to replace the original music with synergetic MTV-friendly cover versions by popular bands of 1993. In order to ensure the authenticity of the soundtrack, Linklater spent 15 per cent of the film's entire budget on acquiring the rights to what he calls 'the greatest hits of my freshman year' (in Corn 2006) but was obliged to give up all his rights to royalties from the soundtrack album that would go double platinum in order to do so. This strategy included spending

Wooderson (Matthew McConaughey), Slater (Rory Cochrane), Shavonne (Deena Martin) and Simone (Joey Lauren Adams) in *Dazed and Confused*

$100,000 on using Aerosmith's 'Sweet Emotion' over the opening credits because Led Zeppelin had disallowed the use of their version of the song 'Dazed and Confused', which meant that *Dazed and Confused* eclipsed the budget for *Slacker* in its first three minutes. Says Linklater: 'I got out alive with the film I wanted [and] the finished film was about 80 per cent of everything I needed' (in Corn 2006). Marketing was hideous, however, with Universal so focused on the massive profit-to-budget return of $115 million USA gross on a $777,000 budget earned by *American Graffiti*, with its nostalgia-trip to America before the assassination of JFK and Vietnam, that it ignored *Dazed and Confused*'s contrary time and attitude to nostalgia. Because 'Where were you in '62?' was the tagline for *American Graffiti*, it was decided that the poster for *Dazed and Confused* would provide a crass, intertextual riff on that sentiment: 'It was the last day of school in 1976, a time they'd never forget … if only they could remember.'

Dazed and Confused actually gets its title from being set just one year after the fall of Saigon (dazed) and during America's Bicentennial celebrations (confused) and is therefore resentful of the propaganda that underscores nostalgia. 'It's impossible to have much nostalgia for that time period,' insists Linklater (1993: 5). None of the teenagers in *Dazed and Confused* relish the time they are living in. Instead they adhere to Cynthia's complaint that 'the seventies obviously suck' and collude with Pink's summation: 'All I'm saying is that if I ever start referring to these as the best years of my life, remind me to kill myself.' As Linklater claims, the film explores 'the plight of the teenager: trapped and oppressed, but with the budding consciousness of being trapped and oppressed, but still trapped and oppressed nonetheless' (1993: 5). Where the film might have connected with the youth demographic on its release in 1993 was in its illustration of unease at the extent of policing in the year that saw the FBI raid the Branch Davidian compound in Waco, Texas and the beating of Rodney King by Los Angeles police. Resonance may be detected in the bullying team coach and his imposition of an anti-drugs pledge that is one of the film's few concessions to narrative, but *Dazed and Confused* ultimately illustrates this unease as a political divide that suggests an emerging social schism. On the one hand there is the hyper-aggressive selfishness of older males like sadistic bully Bannion (Affleck) and on the other there is the liberal teacher Ginny Stroud (Kim Krizan, co-writer of *Before Sunrise*), who warns her pupils that 'with all this American bicentennial Fourth of July brouhaha, don't forget what you're celebrating, and that's the fact that a bunch of slave-owning, aristocratic, white males didn't want to pay their taxes'. In between is the impulsive but harmless hedonism of those stranded in the 1970s between the hippie culture of the 1960s and the slacker culture of the 1980s. Only the kind of self-awareness expressed by Mike (Adam Goldberg), Cynthia and Pink recognises that even the most minor tactic of self-determination can become a viable crusade. Thus, Pink refuses to sign the pledge, Cynthia escapes her own bookish stereotype by hooking up with Wooderson and Mike answers the question of what he is going to do with his life if he does not go to law school with the line: 'I wanna dance!' Like Mike, perhaps, Linklater considers it 'part of the healing process to turn attention away from the society that has let everyone down and to focus on where the party is' (1993: 6). Unfortunately, after botching its marketing, Universal delegated the film's distribution to a short-lived company called Gramercy Pictures that was formed as a joint venture with PolyGram and fumbled a 'half-assed release' (Pierson 1996: 196). *Dazed and Confused* thus became what Linklater calls 'the worst of both worlds: a studio production with independent release' (in Corn 2006). Nevertheless, a cult was born on enthusiastic reviews from Roger Ebert, who called it 'art crossed with anthropology' (1993), Peter Travers of *Rolling Stone*, who also wrote of Linklater's 'anthropologist's eye' and described the film as 'a shit-faced *American Graffiti* … loud, crude, socially irresponsible and totally irresistible' (2000), and Owen Gleiberman in *Entertainment Weekly*, who argued astutely that Linklater was no mere pop anthropologist but the creator of an 'Altmanesque' film that represented 'the first era in which teenagers communicated by wearing their media-addled brains on the outside' (1994).

As Linklater was himself one of these teenagers it is tempting to draw parallels between his own graduation from the innocence of *Slacker* to the experience of *Dazed and Confused* and the hazing rituals inflicted on Mitch Kramer in the latter. Wooderson delivers the slacker philosophy late in *Dazed and Confused* but this only vaguely prefigures the spirit of the Austin that features in *Slacker*: 'The older you get, the more rules they are going to try and get you to follow. You just gotta keep on livin', man. L-I-V-I-N.' The moral certainly resonates with Linklater's dropping out of university to study literature and film on his own terms and his subsequent reluctance to deal with major studios on a scale that removes too much autonomy from his own productions. However, this determination to maintain his independence has also been contradicted by his never again writing an original script after *Dazed and Confused* without credited collaborators and, moreover, mostly thereafter seeking to adapt pre-existing material. Besides *Before Sunrise*, which originated with Linklater meeting a woman in a Philadelphia toy shop and spending the night walking and talking, no other film of his besides *Boyhood* foregrounds any autobiographical element. Instead, Linklater's relative autonomy has mostly obscured or operated as a shield for the collaborators who have vitalised and supported his own filmmaking ambitions. Thus, only *Slacker* and *Dazed and Confused* are self-penned originals and the interrelated *Before Sunrise* and *Before Sunset* were the only two jointly-authored original scripts prior to *Bernie* (2011), which was co-written with Skip Hollandsworth. Otherwise, there is but one self-penned adaptation of a novel (*A Scanner Darkly*) and two adaptations of works of non-fiction in collaboration with their authors: Claude Stanush's *The Newton Boys* and Eric Schlosser's

Fast Food Nation. The first of these involved Linklater and Stanush embarking upon a substantial research project; the second saw Linklater and Schlosser writing independently and together over a period of several years (Feinstein 2006).

More than writing, Linklater has indulged his enthusiasm for actors and acting by filming two adaptations of plays by their authors (Eric Bogosian's *SubUrbia* and Stephen Belber's *Tape* [1999]), as well as one adaptation of a novel with a theatrical background (Robert Kaplow's *Me and Orson Welles* [2008]) from a screenplay by Holly Gent Palmo, a former production coordinator on *Dazed and Confused*, whose first writing credit this was. *Bad News Bears* was based on a script by John Requa and Glen Ficarra that hewed so closely to Michael Ritchie's 1976 film of the same name that its writer Bill Lancaster, who also wrote its two sequels and died in 1997, received a posthumous credit on the rather redundant remake. And, finally, it might be noted that in Linklater's present filmography there are several sequels to films that Linklater has himself directed. Perhaps, for a filmmaker who takes time as his most enduring theme, whether it be depicted in time-frames, alternate realities or parallel lives, a sequel offers a particularly apt and significant vehicle for its exploration. Thus, there is *Before Sunset*, *Before Midnight* (and *its* possible sequel), the postponed 'spiritual sequel' to *Dazed and Confused* and *The School of Rock 2: America Rocks* written by Mike White. Another is *Last Flag Flying*, a sequel to *The Last Detail* (Hal Ashby, 1973), which further underlines Linklater's empathy with the generation of American filmmakers sometimes referred to as the 'Hollywood Renaissance' that included both Ashby and Ritchie alongside Altman.

Although debate may continue as to whether Linklater is a filmmaker dependent upon adaptable texts and rehearsal or one favouring originality and improvisation, there is no doubt about the importance to his cinema of collaborators. *Slacker* was a wholly collective effort on which Linklater found himself 'suddenly the head coach' (in Lowenstein 2009: 23). He even recalls 'at the end of the day, when the film came out, some were a bit surprised. Oh, so it's *your* film?' (in Lowenstein 2009: 26; emphasis in original). However, it would not be long before Linklater was invited to pose for a *Vanity Fair* article on new filmmakers illustrated by Annie Leibowitz's portraits of Robert Rodríguez, Alexander Rockwell, Allison Anders, Rob Weiss, Gregg Araki, Stacy Cochran, Todd Haynes and Carl Franklin that coincided with the release of *Dazed and Confused*. But such premature consecration apart, as for *Slacker* and every film of Linklater's thereafter, the script of *Dazed and Confused* remained unconditionally malleable throughout rehearsals. On *Waking Life* Linklater even estimates that only about one third of the finished material was scripted and another third was developed by the cast, while the final third was the product of ad-libs made possible by filming inexpensively on video. The original credit for the screenplay was to Linklater 'with additional dialogue by numerous cast members' but The Writer's Guild disallowed this. Yet, despite the Writers' Guild's failure to celebrate collaboration, Linklater clearly favours working closely with the writers and co-writers of stories, scripts and screenplays as well as with the cast. McConaughey's Wooderson in *Dazed and Confused* is a prime example of this, for his drawl and demeanour make an endearing icon out of what, as written, could so easily have resulted in a much sleazier hanger-on.

Some American actors like McConaughey, Affleck and Posey thrive on this freedom to embellish; others like Michelle Forbes, who gave a vibrant audition as Jodi, shrink away or become mannered during filming.[5] Nevertheless, Linklater deploys a similar methodology on all his films including *Tape*, for which he claims to have 'rehearsed the hell out of it before though. It was an old idea of mine to have something so well planned, then to shoot it very spontaneously' (in Anon. 2009d). As he says on the DVD commentary of *The School of Rock*, 'the ultimate compliment' an audience can make of a film is that it appears to have been improvised, even when the appearance of spontaneity comes from a confidence created in rehearsal and the natural fluidity of long takes that, *Dazed and Confused* apart, are often filmed with understated Steadicam. It also comes from casting actors who perform well in his more Altmanesque, multi-character films, while Jack Black in *The School of Rock* and Billy Bob Thornton in *Bad News Bears* provided not just an anchor but a spur for the performances of the child actors, although in *Bad News Bears* they barely transcend stereotyping, perhaps because they all have to share a baseball bat instead of exploring and expressing their identities on different instruments. In sum, it is Linklater's stated opinion that '90 per cent of filmmaking is casting your collaborators' (ibid.).

Most notably, this enthusiasm for collaboration often seeks correctives to Linklater's own weaknesses. Following what he describes on the Criterion Collection DVD commentary as the 'fairly Charlie-Brownish' script of *Dazed and Confused* in which grown-ups hardly appear and only Parker Posey and Marisa Ribisi transcend the stereotype of pliant femininity as the gleefully sadistic Darla and the warmly intellectual Cynthia, Linklater employed Kim Krizan to provide an authentic, adult voice for Céline in the writing of *Before Sunrise*. Krizan had played Questions Happiness in *Slacker* and the high school teacher in *Dazed and Confused* and would expound upon the theories of Ferdinand de Saussure in *Waking Life*, and was ideal for Céline, says Linklater, because he 'loved the way her mind worked – a constant stream of confident and intelligent ideas' (1995: 5). *Before Sunrise* was 'conceived to take place in San Antonio' (Pierson 1996: 197), just 60 miles south-west of Austin and, like *Dazed and Confused*, was a project that Linklater had been developing for several years; but it was only by working with Krizan that the basis for the film's dialogue was established in the working process. Krizan recalls: 'We'd pieced together a plot (or non-plot as some would have it, but I'd call it "internal drama") and then we'd duel with words via turns at the computer' (1995: 6). After many discussions 'the conversations that make up the movie' (Linklater 1995: 5) were written down and followed by a meeting with Hawke and Delpy in Austin that Krizan describes as an 'intimacy boot-camp' (1995: 6) that marked the beginning of a rehearsal process that 'didn't end until we shot the last scene in the movie' (Linklater 1995: 5). This working process made the production of *Before Sunrise*, 'an exploration analogous to the relationship in the movie' (ibid.) in which the writing and rehearsal merged naturally into the film's actual production, where Hawke and Delpy continued fleshing out their characters in Vienna.

One of the longest gestation periods in Linklater's career was reserved for *Before Sunset*, which in 2004 added nine actual years to the five or so that had preceded the prequel. Returning to characters that they had briefly revisited for a scene that had been rotoscoped for *Waking Life*, Hawke, Delpy and Linklater started writing the script together in 2002 and re-ignited the project properly over five months in 2003–4. In this collaboration that mirrored the fiction they were creating, their writing, rehearsal and re-writing produced 75 pages of dialogue that they would subsequently film in long, unbroken takes on a fortnight's shoot on the streets of Paris. Delpy claims the success of this collaborative process was self-evident: 'I wrote most of my dialogue, some of Ethan's dialogue, and Rick wrote some of my and Ethan's dialogue – and vice versa. We wrote the structure and story together. We came up with the concept together' (ibid.). Linklater also promoted Delpy's identification with the role by basing his contributions to Céline's dialogue on excerpts from a 'thirty-page essay that [Delpy] wrote after George Bush got elected, afraid that he's all about war' (Peary 2004). By the time of filming, as is typical of Linklater's budget-savvy avoidance of costly improvisation, the actors did not improvise much at all because everything was written, mapped out and rehearsed.

The myth of on-set improvisation that is erroneously attached to Linklater comes from his cast hewing so closely to their characters in rehearsals that the need for embellishment is exhausted with the result that their acting becomes seemingly more behavioural. In addition, the complementarily loose, naturalistic tone of his films comes from the long takes, fluid camerawork and evocative rhythms of the dialogue. The myth of spontaneity is the director's typically contrary objective, however, for it results from his dedication to prolonged writing and rehearsal and experimentation with filming methods. In sum, it takes a lot of time, practice and effort to look this casual, which is not to say that Linklater limits his eventual filming to single takes, but that the nuances of crafted dialogue come from an exploration of the words rather than from their dismissal. The centrifugal force of improvisation, which is based upon actors moving away from the core dialogue or direction, is avoided. Instead it is replaced by the centripetal emphasis on exploring the dialogue as written according to intimate direction until its delivery is wholly appropriate to the overall vision and in character. Linklater thus contradicts assumptions of his *cinéma vérité* style of filmmaking (which includes consideration of what lies beneath the animation of *Waking Life* and *A Scanner Darkly*) by being actor-centred and theatrically influenced in the manner that he challenges and dissects but ultimately wholly respects the text. And, therefore, at least one apparent contradiction that can be dismissed is the fact that he has directed faithful film adaptations of two plays for which he left the major task of their adaptation to the original playwrights.

Linklater's adaptation of Bogosian's play *SubUrbia* emphasises the darkness and potential for depression beneath the surface of several of his films while at the same time suggesting that Linklater may be unable or unwilling to reach those depths in his own writing. Nevertheless, an attempt to map a chronology of his cinema based on the evolution and ageing of the protagonists would begin with the initiation into adolescence of Wiley Wiggins in *Dazed and Confused* and move onto his metaphysical entry into adulthood with *Waking Life*, which ends with him drifting away and therefore becoming, perhaps, the 'drifter' of *It's Impossible to Learn to Plow by Reading Books*, who returns to Austin in the first scene of *Slacker*. There is the brief escape of *Before Sunrise*,

Richard Linklater (right) and Lee Daniel filming *SubUrbia*

which sees this American slacker connect with his European ancestry, heritage and soulmate, while the twenty-something slackers who hang out on the smalltown street corner in *SubUrbia* disprove the hope expressed by Cynthia in *Dazed and Confused* that 'maybe the 1980s will be like radical or something. I figure we'll be in our twenties and it can't get worse.' As stated, Linklater's universe is not very big, although at this point in the constructed chronology it does point to the buffoonish disciple of slacking that is Dewey Finn in *The School of Rock* and his possible destiny as the washed-up Morris Buttermaker in *Bad News Bears*. The fluke reunion of *Before Sunset* is a blissful option that is as yet undreamt of by the characters in *Waking Life* and an impossible ambition for those in Bogosian's play *SubUrbia*, which had its debut in the Lincoln Center Theater's 1994 Festival of New American Plays in New York and was described in *The New York Times* as 'Chekhov high on speed and twinkies' (Richards 1994).

Bogosian is an amalgam of playwright, actor, novelist and monologist, who developed *SubUrbia* as a character-based workshop with student actors and set it in the fictional town of Burnfield, which represents his home-town of Woburn, Massachussets. Linklater recognised Burnfield as a metaphor for Austin too and its characters as the subjects of a post-mortem of the city's slacker culture. Hanging out all night like slacker vampires, they throw their beer cans, cigarette butts and pizza boxes on the ground in front of the convenience store and themselves into or against the dumpster beside it. An attempted suicide, a suggested rape, and murder are just some of the night's events. Mostly listless and lacking focus, each of these characters will explode with anger over trivial matters, while the American dream is chased regardless by the Choudhurys, the immigrant Pakistani couple that runs the store. Links to the original

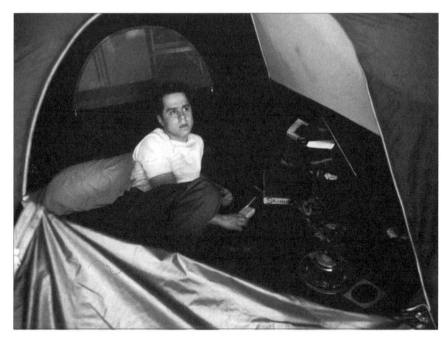

Jeff (Giovanni Ribisi) lives in a tent in his parents' garage in *SubUrbia*

play include Steve Zahn and Samia Shoaib repeating their roles as Buff and Pakeesa Choudhury, while Linklater hewed closely to the text and filmed with an emphasis on two-shots that best served the speed of Bogosian's dialogue.

The experience was similar for Stephen Belber when adapting *Tape*, which he wrote in 1999 as a vehicle for actor friends. *Tape* is a one act play/film depicting the abrasive, vengeful reunion of three people who have their distant high school friendship in common but also conflicting memories of a possible date rape inflicted by Jon (Robert Sean Leonard) on Amy (Uma Thurman), the ex-girlfriend of Vince (Ethan Hawke, Thurman's spouse at the time). Hawke sent Linklater the text of *Tape* after reading it at an acting workshop and it fitted the director's remit of a small-scale, inexpensive feature shot on digital video in one week for the InDigEnt collective of which Linklater and Hawke were part. After extensive rehearsal, *Tape* was shot very quickly on hand-held cameras by Linklater and Maryse Alberti on the single, cost-effective soundstage set of a motel room. Belber meanwhile found adaptation a natural progression from the play that he subsequently rewrote after finishing the screenplay and he has since collaborated with Linklater and Hawke on developing a screenplay for a biopic of Chet Baker (Smith G. 2006). He recalls the production of *Tape* as precise and faithful to the dialogue with improvisation limited to Hawke's 'P for Party' routine: 'Otherwise it was pretty word-for-word, and when there was a change, it was discussed by the group' (ibid.).

This privilege afforded fellow Austinite Ethan Hawke prompts recognition of the actor as the most visible of all recurring collaborators in the cinema of Linklater. Hawke has acted in *Before Sunrise*, *The Newton Boys*, *Tape*, *Waking Life*, *Before Sunset*,

Fast Food Nation and the ongoing project known as *Boyhood*. Consequently, he might get fitted for the role of Linklater's alter-ego in an auteurist approach to his cinema if it were not contradictory to seek an onscreen alter ego for a filmmaker who is so intensely collaborative. Only overriding directorial control can fashion a *doppelgänger*, otherwise the nature of true collaboration prevents it. Hawke's four incarnations of Jesse in *Before Sunrise*, *Waking Life*, *Before Sunset*, and *Before Midnight*, his charming drunk Jess in *The Newton Boys*, his wolfish Vince in *Tape* and his radical Uncle Pete in *Fast Food Nation* have little in common besides Hawke. There is therefore no recurring representation of Linklater in his cinema and little chance of a reading that might, following Barthes, be 'tyrannically centred on the author, his person, his life, his tastes, his passions' (1982: 143). The explicit emphasis on collaboration in form and content, the plethora of adaptations and the generic basis to much of Linklater's work means that there is simply no 'more or less transparent allegory of the fiction, the voice of a single person, the *author* "confiding" in us' (ibid.). Nevertheless, the grouping of disparate films around the figure of their director does allow for analysis of how a particular filmmaker influences the way films come to be funded, produced, distributed and received. Barthes contends that 'to give a text an Author is to impose a limit on that text, to furnish it with a final signified, to close the writing' (1982: 147); but the critical strategy of centring analysis on an individual whose role in the creative process is essentially collaborative in its ethos as well as in its practice does demarcate a field of study for discovering how that figure functions within specific contexts such as independent American filmmaking, Hollywood and contemporary art-house cinema. In addition to directing, Linklater is a writer, adapter and sometime cinematographer with special concern for actors and an interest in unusual technologies such as roto-scoping. To group together his films and the contradictions therein is not to 'find' or 'explain' the author but rather to enter into 'a multidimensional space [...] drawn from the innumerable centres of culture' (Barthes 1982: 146). The only myth to over-throw with Linklater is the one of 'independent' filmmaker and he characteristically collaborates on this with his audience by demolishing it himself. Pronounced and enduring collaborations, a reliance on the adaptation of other sources for the subject of his films, a career-long negotiation of production and distribution deals, occasional commissions for major studios, the comparative lack of a performative persona in the manner of, say, Quentin Tarantino, Kevin Smith or Spike Lee, his objective criticisms of slacking and his refusal to be the spokesperson or mascot of that 'movement' all add up to the dissolution of the qualities necessary to authorise the award of auteur to his work as a no less dedicated filmmaker.

Beyond reverential references to films such as Vincente Minnelli's *The Clock* in *Before Sunrise*, Hitchcock's *Rope* (1948) in *Tape*, and *Detour* (Edgar G. Ulmer, 1945) in the naming of his production company, Linklater's cinema is most similar in form, content, aesthetic and meaning to those American filmmakers whose European influences are evident in the practice and theory of their cinema. Cassavetes and Sayles are obvious touchstones for any filmmaker with aspirations to independence because of their individualistic response to major studios and distribution, but it is also their natu-ralism, collaborative working practice, dedication to the craft of acting and frequent emphasis on time rather than narrative as the structural determinant of their films that influences Linklater. Between Cassavetes, Sayles and Linklater, moreover, is Jim Jarmusch, whose sad and beautiful cinema turned a sense of pessimistic urban dislocation into optimistic nomadism. Anchorage in Jarmusch's cinema is provided not by family or tradition but by a universal pop culture sensibility that has proven contagious to much of the American 'indie' sector. Similarities with the cinema of Linklater are also revealing of a curiously philosophical approach to the way that Americana affects and informs human connections. *Permanent Vacation* (Jim Jarmusch, 1980) is a study of estranged youth with marked similarities to Linklater's *It's Impossible to Learn to Plow by Reading Books*, while *Stranger than Paradise* (Jim Jarmusch, 1984) evokes the terse approach to personal growth that is incorrectly interpreted as time-wasting in *Slacker*. Following this, Jarmusch's *Mystery Train* (1989) evokes the same waylaid romanticism of people passing through a city as *Before Sunrise*, while his *Night on Earth* (1991) is very much like *Waking Life* in the way that it evokes an ultimately unresolved search for a philosophical meaning to parallel lives and realities within a strict time-frame. Jarmusch's attempt at a western with *Dead Man* (1995) may have been far grimmer than Linklater's *The Newton Boys* but his *Coffee and Cigarettes* (2003) was a film in which successive, solipsistic scenes of dialogue between hangers-out in a bar referenced both Godard and Altman and brought to mind Linklater in its Cubist approximation of looking through a prism at a specific time and place. Jarmusch's low-budget intimacy is a clear influence on Linklater, as is the wayward pacing within a delineated time-frame of several of his films, the use of parallel, simultaneous storylines and an occasional dreamlike quality that are all in the service of films that seem meaningfully at odds with their contemporary American surroundings.

Jarmusch did not follow his contemporary filmmakers into working for the majors, although 'many of his films after *Stranger than Paradise* are increasingly responsive to commercial and genre filmmaking' (Suárez 2007: 47). The same is mostly true of Linklater, whose independence has not precluded his collaborations with the major studios nor his 'film attempts' at genres. Despite his reputation as a purveyor of structural, aesthetic and philosophical elements, as previously stated Linklater is remarkably adept with genres. To date he has directed a road movie, a western, a high school comedy, a romantic comedy and its sequels, a black comedy, a television situation comedy, a couple of claustrophobic dramas, a sports comedy, a sort-of musical family film, a science fiction film and animation combined, as well as two documentaries and the recently fashionable kind of multi-narrative, multi-character social drama that is *Fast Food Nation*; but none of these exercises in genre are particularly escapist. The road movies go nowhere, the western ends not in a shoot-out but on a chat show, the high school comedy finds nothing to laugh about in being a pupil, the first romantic comedy ends with separation and the second fades out before the kiss, the team in the sports comedy loses as does the rock band in the musical, the situation comedy finds little to laugh about in its particularly grim situation, the animated science fiction explains itself as madness and the social drama is ultimately about apathy more than activism. Adeptness notwithstanding, therefore, the appearance of genre filmmaking sits uneasily with Linklater because his films' idiosyncrasies undermine generic conventions, and whether this justifies an auteurist-by-default approach to his cinema is an argument plagued by unending contradictions.

After Jarmusch, the emerging American filmmaker with whom Linklater briefly had most in common in the early 1990s is Whit Stillman, whose *Metropolitan* (1990) utilised character-driven dialogue and camerawork that shifted between the individuals and alliances of a group of Manhattan debutantes to observe America from the other end of the social spectrum from *Slacker*. Stillman has directed only three films since (and an episode of *Homicide: Life on the Streets* for television) but he belongs with Todd Haynes, Hal Hartley and Linklater, who has stated:

> I think there are two kinds of filmmakers. Ones that had their little 8mm cameras and their trains and were setting fires and blowing them up and crashing them into each other, and then there were the ones who read a lot and were going to the theater and maybe reading philosophy. (In Price 2003)

Although Linklater belongs in the second group, like Pink in *Dazed and Confused* he has an ability to move between cliques that perhaps explains his comparative productivity and longevity. Theatre and philosophy apart, Linklater is also part of the home video generation that swiped cinephilia from the film school generation of Francis Ford Coppola, Martin Scorsese and Paul Schrader and used offbeat (if not always original) dialogue and characters to compensate for rudimentary production values (if not technique). Tarantino's performance of auteurism may be understood in terms of Timothy Corrigan's view of how the auteur operates at the level of post-production 'as a commercial strategy for organizing audience reception, as a critical concept bound to distribution and marketing aims that identify and address the potential cult status of an auteur' (1991: 103). However, that of Linklater operates more at the pre-production end of the process, as a name whose wavering bankability can sometimes attract investors and actors for low-budget, collaborative projects. In contrast, Tarantino exemplifies the manner in which 'today's auteurs are agents who, whether they wish it or not, are always on the verge of being consumed by their status as stars' (Corrigan 1991: 106). Whereas Tarantino is a star, Linklater is a character actor. Stars open pictures and get them green lit, whereas Linklater's recent films have either struggled at the box office (*Fast Food Nation*), failed to attract adequate distribution (*Me and Orson Welles*), not survived the endless negotiations of pre-production (*That's What I'm Talking About*) or fallen victim to economic crisis (*Liars (A-E)*), which was a casualty of the downsizing of Miramax in 2010. Thus, perhaps, the ultimate contradiction presents itself: might the popular and critical sense of Linklater's auteurism be based on exactly this kind of relative failure? As soon as he has success with *The School of Rock*, for example, his fan base with its auteurist dogma and reservist celebration of independence accuses him of selling out. On the other hand, Linklater blames the commercial failure of *Dazed and Confused*, *A Scanner Darkly* and *The Newton Boys* on their mis-marketing:

They ran from the period elements. I offered to make my own posters. *The Newton Boys* was a homage to the old cinema and they portrayed it as a shoot 'em up. They put it in a genre in which it couldn't compete. These guys weren't psychopaths, they didn't want to kill people, so it fails on that level.

However, following Corrigan, it is at least arguable how much of his own contradictory auteurist status is at fault. Does his fan base avoid these films because the marketing convinces them they are generic films for a general audience, or does the general audience avoid them because the marketing fails to convince them that, despite appearances to the contrary, they are probably introspective art-films with long pauses where the action should be?

This contradiction might at least suggest how audiences for both independent and mainstream cinema subscribe to an extant and media-inflated notion of auteurism. Nevertheless, in order to make sense of the cinema of Linklater as a unifying, structural concept it is useful to associate it more with aspects of filmmaking in Europe than with those of several of his American peers. The working practice that affected, informed and defined the most significant filmmakers from the UK, Italy, Germany and France in the 1950s and 1960s was developed in a post-war industrial vacuum that resulted from widespread destruction, not only of property but of confidence in the arts. It was the availability of lightweight cameras, portable sound equipment and faster film stock that enabled those filmmakers whose work would come to be classified as Italian Neo-realism, New Spanish Cinema, British Social Realism, New German Cinema and the French New Wave. However, although the post-war regrouping of battered nationalisms indicated by these labels reflects the particular origins and contexts of each group, it also limits appreciation of how they relate to each other. Post-war European cinema was often a transnational movement in mood at least in which the angry young men of British social realism had their counterparts in the German loners, resentful Spaniards, French rebels and Italian chancers (and, subsequently, Linklater's slackers). Their films illustrated in content, form and practice the necessary new freedoms afforded filmmakers. This was not even limited to Europe, for the same opportunity was grasped by Cassavetes, whose small-time gangsters and night owls suit the same social grouping so well. What key films by Fassbinder and Wenders, Godard and François Truffaut, Vittorio De Sica, Roberto Rossellini, Carlos Saura, Cassavetes and Jarmusch had in common was the guerrilla-style production that complemented the pursuit of meaning. Rough-edged and rebellious, the films and their protagonists were merged in street level tussles with the kind of obstacles that previously only documentary-makers had encountered. These in turn inspired experimentation and, arguably, an ingrained methodology and mythology of film production that became an inextricable knot of aesthetic and philosophical clichés. As Richard Brody writes of Godard:

The simplified technique of *Masculine Feminine* offered a method – one that specifically befit the director's independent film about young people, the modern cinematic Bildungsroman. It became a method that was used for more or less every first-person classic of beginning filmmakers, from *Clerks* and *Slacker* to *Go Fish* and *Judy Berlin*. (2008: 268)

Nevertheless, Brody is rather ungenerous in limiting the technique to films about youth, for it has also distinguished films that deal with adults, as well as pop culture. In recent years the ambit of American 'independent' cinema has been dominated by low-budget films that utilise the technique to support their marketing in search of breakout or crossover success. The glut of films that match naturalism to self-conscious quirkiness as evidence of an 'indie' sensibility (e.g. *Napoleon Dynamite* [Jared Hess, 2004], *Little Miss Sunshine* [Jonathan Dayton & Valerie Faris, 2006], *Juno* [Jason Reitman, 2007], *The Wackness* [Jonathan Levine, 2008], and so on) has overtaken the kind of 'indies' for adults made by Cassavetes and Sayles. What Linklater, Stillman, Lee, Smith, Hal Hartley, Rose Troche, Todd Haynes and Darren Aronofsky share is the same penchant for seeing the world through widescreen spectacles that afflicts the most movie-minded filmmakers such as Steven Spielberg, Scorsese and Tarantino. Yet, at least when starting out, in reflecting the media-saturated environment of their generation these exemplaries commented to varying degress upon that situation and condition rather than merely exacerbating it. Like *Slacker*, films such as *Metropolitan*, *She's Gotta Have It* (Spike Lee, 1986), *Trust* (Hal Hartley, 1990), *Poison* (Todd Haynes, 1991), *Clerks* (Kevin Smith, 1994), *Go Fish* (Rose Troche, 1994) and *Pi* (Darren Aronofsky, 1998) do not merely imitate but innovate. They make the techniques associated with the French New Wave and Godard in particular resonant and relevant to contemporary sectors or communities of American society. Arguing for the kind of political and philosophical depth that might close the space between Godard and Linklater may seem pretentious, but as Céline says in *Before Sunrise*, 'the answer must be in the attempt'.

Linklater's offices for Detour Filmproduction in Austin Film Studios are festooned with original Polish, French and American film posters and many of the largest advertise the films directed by Godard, whose influence on the cinema of Linklater is more than just working practice. Godard sought a form and style that would enhance meaning, and the rebellious youths he made the subject of his films were just as media-addled as Linklater's; but for them the only media was film. Michel (Jean-Paul Belmondo) in *À bout de souffle* (*Breathless*, 1960) may be a sociopathic thief hunted by the police but, spontaneous murder apart, he is also a slacker whose pursuit of leisure, Patricia (Jean Seberg) and the elusive cool of Bogart is an impulsive response to the fatalism that infects his left-ish view of burgeoning consumerism in post-war France: 'Shall we steal a Cadillac?' The techniques that Godard utilises to express the impulsiveness of this content in the film's form include hand-held camerawork, jump cuts, direct address (or at least sly asides) and a general disdain for such conventions as the 180 degree rule, which communicates the logic of action by the positioning of the camera but is here abandoned like the dog-end of a Gauloise. Here is life liberated from the limitations of filmmaking and, at the same time, teasing those same limitations of the frame, time, place, narrative and audience. Godard's decisive neglect of narrative conventions and continuity means that *À bout de souffle* combines Neo-realism with so many dislocating techniques that the effect is borderline Surrealism. Yet this does not preclude Godard's love of generic signifiers in the example of Michel's embrace of the tough-guy persona, which remains an ironic but affectionate pose right up until his death, when he accepts that his French imitation cannot but fail to embody the American myth precisely because the myth is a fallacy: 'C'est vraiment degueulasse' ('It is very disgusting'). Nevertheless, in Michel's imitation of Bogart that complements Godard's dedicating the film to Monogram Pictures, which made low-budget films between 1931 and 1953, there is an admission of addiction. As Michel says, 'informers inform, burglars burgle, murderers murder, lovers love', which explains the troubled relationship between the French New Wave and the hegemony of Hollywood, its resentment of Hollywood's control of distribution and the colonising iconography of its fictions, while, at the same time, acknowledging its surrender to the seductive beauty of Hollywood product. Although increasingly political in his film form and content, Godard does not pursue specificity but explores instead the complexity of any matter. A parallel with some 'independent' American filmmakers of the 1980s and 1990s thereby occurs, whereby the purposeful disdain for the specificity of conventional narrative in *Slacker*, for example, represents a refusal to conform to a single narrative or shape a quest for resolution that is rebellious in its form, style and content. Here, the long takes, fluid camerawork and resistance to remaining with any one of a hundred possible narratives is the form/style that expresses the content of these same slackers, following their intuition and refusing to conform to any conventional careers or lifestyles. It also embodies a rejection of Hollywood that is expressed not by the pretence of force but by one of ironised nonchalance. Like Jeff in *SubUrbia*, who protests about the 'mosh-pit of consumerism' that is a fast food joint but cannot afford to eat anywhere else, Michel in *À bout de souffle* rejects Hollywood while feeding his ego with its product.

Furthermore, what Godard has in common with several of his American contemporaries and followers is a concern with the causes and effects of the war in Vietnam. The French perspective on the conflict, with all its post-colonial baggage, is far more ambiguous than that of the superpowered USA's failed fight against Communism. When distance from defeat and its domestic shockwaves allowed, American cinema finally responded by imposing linear narratives onto a war that was as inconceivable and inexpressible within conventional arts as Godard and Deleuze claimed of the Holocaust. Instead, generic linear narratives such as *Platoon* (Oliver Stone, 1986) offered a *Bildungsroman* that allowed America to put the war down to experience. In contrast, Godard tackled the conflict in 1965 with *Pierrot le Fou*, which explores the collusion of film in the subject's complexity in its inclusion of a nonsensical playlet for American tourists put on by Ferdinand (Jean-Paul Belmondo) and Marianne (Anna Karina) in which the absurd stereotypes of her Vietnamese peasant woman and his Yankee sailor unite by scrawling 'Vive Mao!' ('Long live Mao!') in chalk. However, for Godard, politics was not so much present in rhetoric as in the Marxist underpinning of film form itself: in the allusions, edits, length of takes, framing and camera movement of the filmmaking process. Before becoming explicitly Maoist in the late 1960s and 1970s, Godard's cinema was at least anti-consumerist by default in the use and innovation of low-budget filmmaking techniques and equipment that rendered alienation as the common link between so many of its protagonists. This alienation of characters was nuanced and typically complex, evoked not just in their dislocation from each other but from their product (i.e. the film itself). Where this connects with Linklater is in his appropriation of low-budget techniques for an appropriate and unavoidably Marxist evocation of the slacker collective in *Slacker* by means of a film made by and about that very community in a form that reflected its own working practice and ethos. Not for Linklater the thrilling generic spin of *El Mariachi* (Robert Rodríguez, 1992) or *Reservoir Dogs* (Quentin Tarantino, 1992), rather the complex and nuanced filming of characters that interact in their immediate surroundings in order to assuage their alienation from the rest of America. The sympathy extended to marginal and underprivileged protagonists, the exploration of the politically conscious collaborative working practice and the extension of favoured, representational techniques wherever possible is what typifies the cinema of Linklater.

Further evidence of the impact of Godard on Linklater is found in addition to the indebtedness to Robert Bresson in Linklater's aforementioned letter 'To the film-makers' of *Dazed and Confused*. For example, 'cinema is the most truthful and poetic of art forms' (2006: 53) is Linklater echoing Godard's aphoristic 'the cinema is truth twenty-four times per second' from the screenplay of *Le Petit Soldat* (*The Little Soldier*, 1960) and Pier Paolo Pasolini's writing on the cinema of poetry (Ward D. 1995: 19–25). There are also direct homages in his films that include Richard (Zac Efron) and Gretta (Zoe Kazan) running through the museum in *Me and Orson Welles* like the lawless trio in *Band à parte* (*Band of Outsiders*, 1964) and the cuts in *Before Sunrise* and *Before Sunset* to shots from behind Jesse and Céline walking and talking *à la* Michel and Patricia on the Champs Elysees in *À bout de souffle*. Intertextuality rather than imitation or homage is the true test of influence, however, and it is therefore of interest to compare the early films of Godard with the most formally and evidentially European of Linklater's films. Besides the empathetic *Slacker* and *Waking Life,* whose mix of naturalism and metaphysics overlaps with Surrealism in the extrapolation of the mundane, it is to *Before Sunrise* and *Before Sunset* that *À bout de souffle* and other films by Godard such as *Une femme est une femme* (*A Woman is a Woman*, 1961), *Masculin féminin: 15 faits précis* (*Masculine Feminine: In 15 Acts*, 1966) and even *Pierrot le Fou* bequeath an appreciation for walking and talking while narrative stands still and speechless. Several of the dialogues in *À bout de souffle* suit Michel and Patricia striking poses that combine the heartfelt and the pretentious – 'It's sad to fall asleep. It sepa-rates people. Even when you're sleeping together, you're all alone' – and could quite easily come from *Before Sunrise*. Delpy, of course, made her acting debut for Godard as Wise Young Girl in his *Détective* (1985),[6] which is something that Linklater was aware of, while the reunion of the couple in Paris in the sequel suggests something of a pilgrimage to the streets of the French New Wave. However, the questioning, regret and even recriminations of *Before Sunset* reveal a sadness that comes from a loss of naiveté and recalls that of Michel in *À bout de souffle*: 'When we talked, I talked about me, you talked about you, when we should have talked about each other.' Jesse and Céline never get as far as the bored, resentful and ultimately vicious recriminations of Ferdinand and Marianne in *Pierrot Le Fou*, but it is easy to imagine another sequel in which Jesse might utter Ferdinand's line – 'Why do you look so sad?' – and Céline, copying Marianne, replies: 'Because you speak to me in words and I look at you with feelings.' In the rudimentary working practice, the rebellious anti-heroic characters and the emphasis on dialogue as an expression of character that undermines any pose with inherent feeling, Linklater and his cast clearly subscribe to Godard's oft-quoted dictum, 'all you need to make a movie is a girl and a gun'. Except they even do without a gun.

The cinema of Linklater relocated to regional American cinema the associated techniques and aesthetics that several European filmmakers had used to communicate dislocation and alienation from the post-war societies of Europe that had taken America as the model and patron of their reconstruction. Hand-held camera, naturalistic dialogue and an improvised feel to the performances, as well as authentic urban locations, limited time-frames and the exploration of time and space in long takes (some of which may be identified as time-images by reference to the theories of Deleuze) all feature in the cinema of Linklater, where they reveal an inheritance of a cinematic sensibility that opposes the power-broking of corporate America. What is often missed in appreciation of Linklater's cinema is the fact that its apparent indifference to narrative, generic conventions, industrial demands and audience expectations is not a result of apathy but a deeper political commitment. Asking whether the cinema of Linklater is political or indifferent should be the next Socratic gambit but this misses the point entirely; for it is inextricably both at the same time. This is not a contradiction, although it is crafted to appear as one. What occurs, in truth, is that indifference to conventions is the form taken by the protest. Just as not voting might not signify the lack of an opinion but the angriest protest, so slacking in its truest form and in its equivalent cinematic technique and working practice signifies both a rejection of the dominant system and an alternative methodology enacted by those who care to share. *It's Impossible to Learn to Plow by Reading Books*, *Slacker*, *SubUrbia* and *The School of Rock* are all politically charged in their opposition to the demands of a social, industrial and political system nicknamed 'The Man'. They each may smack of hippiedom but they still connect with the core beliefs of alternative priorities to consumerism and competition, such as the collectivisation of creativity and imagination.

Despite shirking from the role of slacker spokesperson (and what else would a true slacker do?) Linklater has occasionally spoken of his political beliefs. For example, he claims the films he directs are partly a corrective to his observation that 'everyone is required to see their lives, the world through the eyes of the rich' (in Walsh 1998). This is because the aforementioned techniques of time-frames, naturalism, hand-held camera, long takes, improvisational tone and time-images combine to suggest a refusal to obey, conform or provide conventional, linear, narrative-bound entertainment. Instead, they offer an alternative perspective on the lives of the characters, and so the audience; that of those whose marginal status is best expressed in the techniques available to low-budget filmmaking. The techniques associated with the kind of low-budget films that Linklater directs are not always random but designed to express the condition of their content in their form. That is to say, both the form and content of this oppositional cinema were determined when American society under Reagan was realigned towards free enterprise by the policies of low taxes and private sector growth. This caused increased deficits and a mild recession that President George Bush Senior responded to by cutting government spending and raising taxes. Consequently, by September 1992 the United States Census Bureau reported that 14.2 per cent of all Americans lived in poverty (Anon. 2009g), which generated the feelings of conspiracy, paranoia and depression that are so prevalent in *Slacker*, *SubUrbia* and several dialogues of *Before Sunrise* and *Before Sunset*, as well as in *Fast Food Nation* and *A Scanner Darkly*. Moreover, as successive Republican governments reduced spending on the arts, this had the effect of pushing creativity to the margins and prompting a degree of contrary support for independent and regional cinema that was associated with the slacker culture of Austin in the mid-1980s, when Linklater met and collaborated with many who agreed with his concern that he 'had always sensed instinctively from the earliest age that I was being lied to' (in Walsh 1998). Even during the tenure of Democrat President Bill Clinton (1993–2001), Linklater sided with those who took the official enquiry into the president's perjurious philandering with Monica Lewinsky to be damning evidence of the remoteness of national politics: 'Whatever politician takes office, our lives don't change. They're all doing the will of the Fortune 500, so what does it matter? Voting is a symbolic act. It doesn't mean anything because there are no choices anyway' (ibid.). Besides prescience about the banking and investment implosion of the late 2000s – 'I think this bloated thing is going to come crashing down' (ibid.) – Linklater also described the regime that the slacker culture of Austin and his films opposed as 'sort of a police state. No one is asking what happened to all the homeless. No one cares, because it's easier to get on the subway and not be accosted. Where are they? In Texas they throw the homeless in jail' (ibid.). In opposition, Linklater did become active in his stand for regional filmmaking in Texas and regime change through cinema in 2004, when he worked with MoveOn.org 'getting directors to do [anti-Bush] spots. I'm not your run-of-the-mill Democrat. I'm for regime change' (in Peary 2004).[7] Unsurprisingly, Linklater was no fan of his fellow Texan, President George W. Bush:

> I met him in a social situation. I'd be surprised if he's seen any of my films. He's affable, but I don't want that frat lunkhead running my country. […] I want to have a big rally here to let the world know not everyone in Texas is goose-stepping in line to his drumbeat. (In Peary 2004)

In attempting to identify and assess any political undercurrent in the cinema of Linklater, it may be noted that *The Newton Boys* is as subversive as *The School of Rock* (but with negligible impact due to its commercial failure) and as a western was always intended to have special meaning for Texans. *The Newton Boys* was a Twentieth Century Fox production based on the true story of four poor brothers with a strict moral code who take to robbing banks and, ambitiously, one train in the 1920s. Apart from Hawke's performance, the brothers are as underplayed as the potential drama and the film dispenses with most of the bank robberies in a ragtime montage. Yet the rambling narrative does typically check generic conventions (hats, rifles, breaking

Jess (Ethan Hawke), Dock (Vincent D'Onofrio), Joe (Skeet Ulrich) and Willis (Matthew McConaughey) in *The Newton Boys*

horses, gunfights, saloons and a train robbery) while undercutting them with sly, subversive humour. The hats for these 'bad' guys are not black but white so that they can see each other at night, their rifles are loaded with pellets so that nobody gets hurt, the wild horses to be broken are just placid ruses for their entrapment, the gunfight that succeeds the bank robbery and has the potential to resemble that in *Heat* (Michael Mann, 1995) is played as a screwball farce, the lead brother Willis (Matthew McConaughey) does not drink and the train robbery is mostly an amiable, chatty affair until one of the brothers loses his hat and gets shot accidentally by a nervous colleague. When the banality of their leisurely crime spree is interrupted by the greater banalities of narrative, it is to an innate reflexivity that the film recurs; for, if *The Newton Boys* has themes in common with Linklater's other films, they are the importance of collaboration for any project, even a bank robbery, and an empathy with the outlaws that refuses to judge or sanction the disguise of nostalgia. The bank robberies are justified by the brothers (and to an extent by the judge who finally sentences them to trivial prison sentences) on account of their crimes being 'just one thief a-stealing from another,' while the lack of any hermetic narrative arc has the effect of making the subtext relevant to those who were disempowered by Reaganomics. The contemporary relevance is emphasised by the inclusion of chat show footage accompanying the final credits of Willis Newton being interviewed by Johnny Carson in the late 1970s, shortly before Reagan's election in 1980. As Linklater has stated:

American mid-to-late 1970s' society was probably a lot like the post-World War One 1920s: after witnessing the horrors of war and realizing that humanity was capable of such large-scale corruption, destruction and loss one might as well, as Jim Morrison said: 'Get your kicks before the whole shithouse goes up in flames.' (1993: 5)

The Newton Boys thus demonstrates how the 1920s and the 1970s shared similar problems and their causes, just as *Me and Orson Welles* would later hold the cautious optimism of the 1930s as a mirror to the early years of Barack Obama's presidency. The research-based authenticity of the period details in both films are not for nostalgia's sake but, quite appositely, to make the period as real as that inhabited by the film's audience. Unfortunately, the audience did not materialise for either and the critical response to *The Newton Boys* was typified by the complaint that when 'saddled with plot necessities and genre expectations with which he is manifestly uncomfortable, Linklater doesn't possess the force and decisiveness to turn these burdens to his own ends' (Tracy 2008). On the contrary, however, Linklater proves with the screwball robbery sequence bursting with energy, wit and invention that he can direct generically thrilling scenes like this if so inclined. Yet, crucially, *The Newton Boys* seems to forcefully resist the combined pressures of studio and audience expectations and deliver a slacker western instead, one which takes on the sacred cows of Texas and the only verifiably American film genre to boot. Linklater's determination to fashion an outsider's view that was informed by prolonged research marks *The Newton Boys* as not only revisionist in the line of *Bonnie and Clyde* (Arthur Penn, 1967), *McCabe and Mrs Miller* (Robert Altman, 1971) and, more recently, *The Assassination of Jesse James by the Coward Robert Ford* (Andrew Dominik, 2007), but also more vital than any 'simple object of the author's consciousness' (Bakhtin 1984b: 7) and in this sense not given to representing 'the usual objectified image of a hero' (ibid.). In addition, this wary view of history (fact) and genre (fiction) being subject to perception (myth and its reduction to generic formula) is also very much in the line of narrative dissolution in search of trace elements by Godard. In *Alphaville: une étrange aventure de Lemmy Caution* (*Alphaville: A Strange Case of Lemmy Caution*, 1965), for example, Godard includes everything one might expect in a film noir, but in the wrong order, while *Une femme est une femme* has everything one could wish for in a musical, except conventional song and dance numbers. In an equal spirit of subversion, *The Newton Boys* is an introspective western without a frontier spirit in the same way that the more overtly political *Fast Food Nation* presents helplessness, apathy and conformity as a more common response to awareness than activism. In so doing, the cinema of Linklater does not merely illustrate the reach of the slacker ethos but also documents its failings, which suggests it remains a Modernist cinema by always questioning its own context and limitations.

Finally, then, might we consider whether the cinema of Linklater is Modernist or Postmodernist? As with previous puzzles, the basis of comparison might be a series of distinct alternatives or contradictions, but such a clear division is problematic and at times paradoxical. Colin MacCabe states that, 'Modernism can be understood as the reaction by artists to the new forms of capitalist culture kinked to mass audiences' (2003: xiv) and he notes that in relation to Modernism 'the work of Godard is particularly interesting because, unusually, it takes place within those very forms [and] poses the paradoxes of Modernism at their most acute' (ibid.). Unusual, certainly, but not unique; for although the cinema of Linklater does not by any means reject the stereotypical and the generic, it does require a level of active engagement by an audience that is willing to negotiate what little space there is between Modernism and Postmodernism. Modernism elevates rational thought, universal human rights and individualism, but its support for order, consensus and structural functionalism may be denounced as repressive by Postmodernism, which nevertheless concurs with Modernism in favouring new ways of understanding time and space, subjectivity, discourse, social structure and change (Johnson 2000: 232). The cinema of Linklater appears to lobby for change and new understandings in the rhetoric of characters as distant and similar as Bush Basher (Ron Marks) in *Slacker*, Mike in *Dazed and Confused*, Jeff in *Suburbia*, Timothy 'Speed' Levitch in *Live from Shiva's Dance Floor*, Céline, Dewey Finn, and Amber in *Fast Food Nation*. However, the emotional if not narrative progress of each of these characters is essentially based on a metaphysical struggle towards enlightenment beyond existing hegemonies. As such, they sometimes draw in similarly unfocused proto-activists such as the characters that surround and support Bush Basher's harangue, Mike's fight, Jeff's impromptu strip ('It doesn't matter what I do as long as I don't care about the results. And that's why now, I'm getting naked'), Céline's activism, Levitch's imaginative reconciliation with New York's Ground Zero, Dewey Finn's band ('Rock isn't about getting an A! Sex Pistols never won anything!'), Morris Buttermaker's sozzled pep-talk ('Come on guys, remember what I told you, there's no "I" in team') and burger-flipper Amber's need to do something, anything, whatever. Thus, consensus and structure is sought in relationships that enable activism and vice versa. The cinema of Linklater is not nihilist or even deconstructivist; it is innately defensive and distressed. Contradictory as ever, it mostly just wants to be left alone with other like-minded loners.

Nevertheless, the cinema of Linklater *is* quietly optimistic in the way it finds space for hope in times and places as unlikely as a trans-European passenger train in *Before Sunrise* and Ground Zero in *Live from Shiva's Dance Floor*. Meaning is found in connections between people, places, music and philosophies, but never in products, personas, packaging or policies. Theorists of Postmodernism may deny there is a centre to anything, thereby countering privilege, fixed subjects and verifiable origins (see Luis G. Pedraja 1999), but the cinema of Linklater rejects cynicism, institutionalised politics and religious dogma as anything more than shields and refuges for fragile emotions and seeks stability instead, not in success or status but in those very same connections. If there is a unifying theme to the cinema of Linklater, it is found in Céline's admission:

> I believe if there's any kind of God it wouldn't be in any of us, not you or me but just this little space in between. If there's any kind of magic in this world it must be in the attempt of understanding someone, sharing something.

Thus, the Postmodernist search for flux, chaos, disorder, fragmentation, open-endedness, destruction and deconstruction is contradicted. Postmodernism problematises representation by affirming aforehand that reality is a construct and that all attempts at representation are based on an ideology that seeks to narrativise the chaos of this world. As Lennard Davis states of novels, films 'do not depict life, they depict life as it is represented by ideology' (1987: 24). And if reality is a construct, then fiction is free to create rather than merely copy, re-create, reflect or represent, which in turn suggests that any attempt to define Postmodernism as somehow distant from reality is erroneous because reality is already elsewhere. Thus, instead of contrasting with reality, intertextuality becomes the matrix of meaning between an infinite number of unrealities of equal status. Postmodernists 'posit that there are no clearly superior, that is, "privileged criteria"' (Fishman 1999: 5) for recognising or attaining pure objectivity and argue about the impossibility of politics as a criteria for categorising all aspects of human thought, science and art. However, where Postmodernism tends to oppose Céline (and thus the cinema of Linklater) is in the way it derives pleasure from disconnection rather than connection, from what Bryan D. Palmer describes as a 'hedonistic descent into a plurality of discourses that decenter the world in a chaotic denial of any acknowledgement of tangible structures of power and comprehension of meaning' (in Southgate 2003: 168). Postmodernists might see chaos as a substitute for unknowable history, but Céline in *Before Sunset* aligns herself with Slavoj Žižek, who claims 'through fantasy, we learn to desire' (1992: 6). Thus she responds emotionally to Jesse's expression of a belief in the kind of human evolution that is possible in a person's lifetime or even a film's time-frame:

> Maybe what I'm saying is, is the world might be evolving the way a person evolves. Right? Like, I mean, me for example. Am I getting worse? Am I improving? I don't know. When I was younger, I was healthier, but I was, uh, whacked with insecurity, you know? Now I'm older and my problems are deeper, but I'm more equipped to handle them.

Like Jesse, the Modernist cinema of Linklater is purposeful in its objective search for meaning rather than any subjective reckoning and thus even posits a return to the kind of structuring narrativity that is increasingly evident in his more recent films. It simply believes that meaningful connections *are* possible, even when seemingly contradictory:

> Céline: Baby, you are gonna miss that plane.
> Jesse: I know.

It may be argued that Postmodernism breaks boundaries while Modernism explores the limitations of collective identity; or, to put it another way, Modernists are at their best in an orchestra whereas Postmodernists spiral away on interminable solos. The collaborative ethos that Linklater conducts is clearly more orchestral. Modernism speaks for a group in the language of that group, whereas Postmodernism, following Michel Foucault, 'is explicitly designed to liberate suppressed voices and struggles in history from the dominant narratives that reduce them to silence' (Best and Kellner 1977: 274). *Slacker* arguably manages both, but in general, the generic basis of Linklater's cinema with its reliance on adaptable texts and collaboration emphasises fusion over dissolution. However it is also experimental in the measure in which it explores from within the limits of genre, adaptations and studio commissions, as well as those of form (e.g. the subversion of low-budget limitations in the rehearsal of long takes and an improvisational feel to the acting that comes from prolonged rehearsal), content (e.g. limited time-frames and claustrophobic sets) and meaning (e.g. the amount of activism that is likely to emerge in the characters *and* the audience of a film like *Fast Food Nation*). Crucially, Modernists see time as a three-dimensional space (like the motel in *Tape* or Paris in *Before Sunset*). Postmodernists, on the other hand, believe in multi-dimensionality and non-linearity and although this belief is sometimes taken as characteristic of the cinema of Linklater, it is typically contradictory that the concept of parallel realities is actually contained entirely within talk such as the self-parody of Linklater's own opening monologue as Should Have Stayed at Bus Station in *Slacker*. It may be discussed by other characters in *Slacker* and by Jesse and Céline in *Before Sunrise*, but it is only in *Waking Life*, when the rotoscoped Jesse and Céline appear post-coital, that this parallel reality actually appears in the cinema of Linklater. Even then it is only a dream that is explicitly rendered as such by the animation and it will be duly unmentioned in the lovers' actual reunion in *Before Sunset*. In *Slacker*, Linklater is a metaphysician, but despite delighting in discussing options and possibilities he also accepts that, ultimately, consciousness entails unique awareness of the single chosen path that must be made the most of. In other words, Should Have Stayed at Bus Station didn't; but that's all right, because if he had done so his character would probably have been called Should Have Caught Taxi into Town.

Postmodernists may celebrate chance and the opportunities brought on by uncertainty and chaos but the cinema of Linklater actively avoids the dangers of this in improvisation and does not seek to destroy or dismantle conventions. *Slacker*, for example, does not really suffer from a lack of narratives or surfeit of it. Neither is *Slacker* haphazard. The lives depicted therein do not appear in a split-screen patchwork of all their doings and musings, but in the linear fashion of a relay race between walkers that subverts the underlying anxiety of Linklater's initial monologue. Far from chaos, the structure and grounding of *Slacker* in the slacker community of Austin thus accords with what Dragan Milovanovic (1995) identifies with Modernism in being transparent, reflective and territorialised. Whereas *Slacker* is a cheap, guerrilla shoot and *The School of Rock* is a studio-bound-and-enabled production, they share a sense of utopia because, as with most of Linklater's cinema, their collaborative production process illustrates their meaning, which is the potential of a slacker mindset in a community, a rock band and society in general. Yet it may seem that this recurring community of collaborators does not countenance the empowering of feminist, queer or racial differences because of fear or distrust of fragmentation. Perhaps as a reflection of a collaborative working practice that may even inhibit individualism, the feminist performance art entitled Burger Manifesto Part One of Sooze (Amie Carey) in *SubUrbia* is ridiculed, while the lone black-ness of Melvin (Jason O. Smith) in *Dazed and Confused* is treated with a liberal camaraderie that smacks of forced idealism. Besides the effeminate and prepubescent Billy (Brian Falduto) in *The School of Rock*, no gay characters come to mind at all. Thus, for all its emphasis on a collaborative working practice being centred and organised instead of chaotic and dispersed, the cinema of Linklater reflects white, straight, liberal, European and Western thought that encounters true multi-culturalism only when the effect of Mexican immigration on Texas is glimpsed in *$5.15/Hr* and *Bad News Bears*. In the latter, two non-English speaking players are included in the team because their father is another's parents' gardener, and in *Fast Food Nation*, the plight of the immigrant workers is arguably more symbolic than the problems of conscience affecting Don (Greg Kinnear) and Amber, whose ephemeral guilt is quickly subsumed into the kind of passivity that too often passes, and is mistaken for the confrontational inaction of true slacking. Consequently, despite an emphasis on collaboration that promotes integration and permanence by seeking communication, unity and objective truths, the cinema of Linklater might also reveal the contradiction of ultimately replacing one hegemony with another.

Several of the films directed by Linklater might also be said to appear consistently Modernist in form and content by operating at the very limits of Modernism but not post-it. It is, after all, rather conventional in the manner in which his films often base their resolutions on the formation or elevation of a community and/or the heterosexual couple as much as any Hollywood musical. Even when at its most metaphysical, a film such as *Waking Life* explores not freedom but the limitations of the consciousness of its own desiring because, in essence, the film's exploration of lucid dreaming is a pilgrimage to the Self protagonised by another of these recurring characters in a small and localised world. Having graduated from *Dazed and Confused*, Mitch becomes Main Character in *Waking Life*, but is buffeted, seduced and dismissed by such a plethora of philosophical suggestions for understanding his existence that the experience resembles a bout of intellectual hazing every bit as brutal as Bannion's batting in *Dazed and Confused*. Yet Wiggins' Modernist aim remains the same: endurance, reflection and growth. Postmodernists, on the other hand, prefer to think of themselves as permanently decentred and perpetually in the process of becoming their own eternally elusive subject of desire. Thus, perhaps, they inspire Linklater's scorn, which he delivers in *Waking Life* in the role of Pinball Playing Man when Main Character pretends to search for meaning beyond the moment: 'I mean, I'm not saying that *you* don't know what you're talking about, but *I* don't know what you're talking about.'

In conclusion, perhaps it would be wisest to posit the cinema of Linklater as the cinematic bridge between European Modernism and American Postmodernism, as 'this little space in between' Godard and Tarantino. Yet the collaborative, cooperative working practice that renders communities and couples onscreen is rather particular to Linklater, whose way of exploring limited time-frames by limited means results in films in which 'somehow it all feels true and accurate in a composite sort of way' (Linklater 1993: 5). Because Linklater's awareness of his financial and creative limitations prompts him to make them part of his craft and even add to them in thrifty long takes, claustrophobically tiny sets and constricted time-frames, so his cinema often reflects the experience of a specific time from all sides, although none of them are nostalgic. Instead they are all fleeting, immanent, transient and ephemeral. Any leaning towards nostalgia is curtailed by meaninglessness in *Waking Life* and by madness in *A Scanner Darkly*. Even in *Before Sunset*, nine actual years after *Before Sunrise*, neither Jesse nor Céline waste valuable time on what might have been. Neither of them, in other words, would ever countenance the epithet Should Have Stayed at (Vienna) Train Station. Consequently, this look back over his cinema suggests that Linklater is not a spokesperson for slacking or a leader of any movement, nor an auteur film-maker or a weary studio drudge, although a Cubist portrait rendered as collage would rightly include scraps of them all. As one of many but in his own equally particular way, however, he is a quiet revolutionary; as quiet as the character identified as Quiet Woman at the Restaurant (Mona Lee) in *Waking Life*:

When it was over, all I could think about was how this entire notion of oneself, what we are, is just this logical structure, a place to momentarily house all the abstractions. It was a time to become conscious, to give form and coherence to the mystery, and I had been a part of that. It was a gift. Life was raging all around me and every moment was magical. I loved all the people, dealing with all the contradictory impulses – that's what I loved the most, connecting with the people. Looking back, that's all that really mattered.

Notes

1   The statue was originally to have been one of Ronald McDonald, the clown that represents the fast food franchise, but the corporation objected.

2   For example, Bryan Singer directed *X-men* (2000), *X-men 2* (2003) and *Superman Returns* (2006), Jon Favreau directed *Iron Man* (2008) and *Iron Man 2* (2010) and Sam Raimi directed the first three *Spider-Man* films (2002, 2004, 2007).

3   All quotes from Richard Linklater, unless otherwise attributed, are from interviews with the author in Austin, Texas, 30 July–1 August 2009.

4   Brendan Fraser was cast but declined. Renee Zellwegger was hired as an extra and has no dialogue but her character is named Nesi White in the tie-in book and she may be glimpsed at the Moon Tower party and striding past the guys outside the pool bar. Ashley Judd and Claire Danes both auditioned but were not cast.

5   Several auditions including that of Michelle Forbes are included on the region 1 Criterion Collection *Dazed and Confused* DVD.

6   Godard dedicated *Détective* to John Cassavetes and Edgar G. Ulmer, the director of *Detour*, which gave its name to Linklater's production company.

7   In the ten weeks leading up to the 2004 presidential campaign, MoveOn released new advertisements each week featuring the work of American film directors and actors including Linklater, Matt Damon, Rob Reiner, Scarlett Johanssen, Kevin Bacon, Al Franken, Rebecca Romjin, Martin Sheen, Margaret Cho, Doug Liman, Darren Aronofsky, Donal Logue, Ed Asner, Charlie Fisher, John Sayles, Allison Anders, Illeana Douglas, Ione Skye, and many others. See http://pol.moveon.org/archive/.

CHAPTER THREE

The Form and Content of Slack

Modernist novels that explore the multiform potential and limitations of the written word such as James Joyce's *Ulysses* (1922), Douglas Coupland's *Generation X* (1991) and Julio Cortázar's *Rayuela* (*Hopscotch*, 1963), which effects a stream of consciousness that includes changing languages and has chapters that can be read in any order whatsoever, are often pronounced unfilmable. While the attempt at fusing form and content to create film meaning is a creative pursuit, attempts at true Modernism may collapse into the kind of complex, self-referential relationship between form and content that results in the pastiche of Postmodernism. However, the Danish Dogme movement did manage it with its purposefully disabled filmmaking process matching form to the content of films about mentally and physically disabled characters. Removing tracking, tripod and artificial lighting, for example, takes mobility, emotional stability and clarity of vision away from films such as *Festen* (*The Celebration*, Thomas Vinterberg, 1998), in which abused children strike back as traumatised adults, and *Idioterne* (*The Idiots*, Lars von Trier, 1998), where infirmity is present in both the collective pretence of a commune of 'spazzers' and the impaired morality of those they provoke with their 'spazzing'. More explicit still is the expression of the various psychological and physical ailments of characters in *Julien Donkey-Boy* (Harmony Korine, 1999) by means of constantly abrasive, blurry, underlit imagery, which is climactically 'owned' by the schizophrenic title character (Ewen Bremner) and Chrissy (Chrissy Kobylak), a near-blind girl, who explains that until someone told her she was almost blind she had thought her sight to be just as good as that of everyone else. Watching this film thus gives a literal insight into how it must be to sense the world when schizophrenic and almost blind. How then should a film about slacking look and feel or, to put it another way, what might be the form and content of slack?

A theoretical approach to what might be called the Modernist cinema of Linklater should begin by traversing the frequent motif of the street. In *It's Impossible to Learn to*

Plow by Reading Books, *Slacker*, *Dazed and Confused*, *SubUrbia*, *Before Sunrise*, *Waking Life*, *Live from Shiva's Dance Floor*, *Before Sunset*, and *Fast Food Nation* the street is a place and time of visual, auditory, sensual, romantic, spiritual and philosophical encounters. The locating of these encounters in the urban areas of Austin, Vienna, Paris, New York and *SubUrbia*'s metaphorical Burnfield suggests modernity and its flow of life, but also the fluid nature of the films themselves, for the movement of these films is the movement of the characters therein. Whether this follows the chain of passers-by in *Slacker*, tags along with Jesse and Céline in *Before Sunrise*, tries to keep up with them in *Before Sunset*, stumbles along with the proto-activists of *Fast Food Nation*, drifts with those of *Waking Life*, hangs out on the corner with the inhabitants of *SubUrbia* or takes the metaphysical guided tour of post-9/11 New York in *Live from Shiva's Dance Floor*, this movement is always temporalised; that is, defined by time. This time-wary movement also doubles as the cost-efficient process of the film being made, whether it is the ad-hoc guerrilla style of *Slacker* and *Before Sunrise* or the shifts from rehearsal to filming to rotoscoping of *Waking Life*. And, finally, this temporalised movement also negotiates the potential of cinematic subjectivity and the sharing of empathy and emotional effect, whether it be on the road to nowhere of *SubUrbia* and *Fast Food Nation* or the stairway to heaven of *Waking Life* and *Before Sunset*. Thus the cinematic apparatus, the working practice employed in their making and the active spectatorship required in their reception is conjoined. The cinema of Linklater is one of time-frames and the movement therein: life, fluidity and open-endedness of thought and action. Although the budgets of these films are always far too limited to afford fashionable 3-D trickery, they are nonetheless multi-dimensional in their basis in creating and dissolving spatial and temporal collages that include characters, events and ideas such as Cubism, the *dérive* (drift), the time-image and carnival.

As slacker characters in the cinema of Linklater explore, change, reflect upon and adapt to their time and place in the street, so the films they inhabit extend by means of the collaborative working practice of the actual filmmaking to accommodate their movements in a synchronous manner. Consequently, the real time and space of their action or inaction is continuously reterritorialised as a cinematic construct, as is the time that it takes to explore, pass through or reflect upon the space that becomes cinematic. Thus, when a character in *Slacker*, such as Should Have Stayed at Bus Station, (Linklater) expounds upon the wide variety of possible alternative realities besides the one that he and this camera (and so this audience) happen to be following, a particular sense of layered time and space is suggested. On one level, for example, any potential for narrative momentum is purposefully slackened in the filming (by a long take) and the editing (by not cutting into it) to allow his monologue to play itself out. On another, it should be clear that the actor/writer/director playing the role is a collaborative part of the filmmaking collective drawn from the slacker community of Austin who is making a film called *Slacker*, which is about this very community. Meaning, in the cinema of Linklater, is a composite of all these layers.

Although any attempt to identify an intellectual pattern in films associated with a specific filmmaker may be dismissed as an intellectual construct, so too is any film. In rejecting the option of meaninglessness, moreover, analysis of the cinema of Linklater is surely entitled to search for structure, meaning and significance in the spirit of Main Character in *Waking Life*. In that film, for example, when Main Character pauses to reflect upon his path already taken and the options that lie ahead, his dilemma is expressed by means of a long, hand-held take with a 360 degree pan from the subject's point of view that, in turn, reveals how the film itself prompts reflection and appears to share options with its audience. Inevitably, however, the key to understanding how meaning is constructed in the cinema of Linklater is found by going slacker-like with the flow. Because the low-budget, collaborative working practice that he favours demands fluid, imaginative, unwasteful filmmaking, so the flow of life onscreen tends to indicate a corresponding concern with efficient and necessary collaboration. Thus, the movement of slacker characters in *Slacker*, *Waking Life*, *Before Sunrise* and other films tends to mirror the flow of life behind the camera and vice versa, because slacking is not about laziness but imagination, reflection and collaboration as a rebuttal to convention, consumerism and competition. As Jean-Louis Comolli states, characters 'are constituted by gesture and word by word, as the film proceeds; they construct themselves, the shooting acting on them like a revelation, each advancement of the film allowing them a new development in their behavior, their own duration very precisely coinciding with that of the film' (in Deleuze 2005b: 186). The reality of Linklater's cinema with its emphasis on drifting characters, collectivised creativity, spendthriftness and exploratory dialogue means that *Slacker* is a film made by slackers about slackers in a very slacker kind of way. In the same way that Dogme '95 disables the filmmaking process to make films about disability and Ken Loach insists on working with a union-ised crew to make films about the lack of unionisation such as *Bread and Roses* (2000), *The Navigators* (2001) and *It's a Free World* (2007), so the cinema of Linklater makes its production appropriate to its content. Moreover, it is on these grounds that its political, philosophical and even spiritual sense is founded.

To appreciate this is not simple, however, for the equation connects various theo-ries relating to film form, content and meaning. These include Guy Debord's notion of the *dérive* as a model for narrative form and content, Jean-Luc Godard's playful and disruptive aesthetics of collage, and Gilles Deleuze's theory of the time-image that reveals the eruption of real time onscreen as both process and purveyor of meaning. In addition, attention must be paid to Henri Lefebvre's ideas on space as well as to Mikhail M. Bakhtin's notion of the street level carnival as a forum for dissent that finds expression in oppositional language. All this converges, moreover, in the struc-tural conceit of Cubism, which incorporates the influence of what might be called the 'tapestry' genre of multi-narrative, multi-character works in American literature, film and television, such as Sherwood Anderson's novel *Winesburg, Ohio* (1919) and the film *Nashville* (Robert Altman, 1975). Beneath all this must first be laid, however, an awareness of the nature of time that was put forward by Henri Bergson and was the instigator of much Modernist thought.

Bergson's theories were celebrated in his lifetime and following the revitalisation of his work in the 1960s by another French philosopher, Gilles Deleuze. In addition to ideas of multiplicity, perception, memory and creative evolution, Bergson prom-ulgated a distinction between intellect and intuition that is exemplified by apposite understandings of time. Bergson claimed the intellect is something that seeks comprehension in order to ensure its survival and attains it by reducing reality to moments or fractions in order to rationalise its purpose scientifically: 'Fixity is therefore what our intelligence seeks; it asks itself where the mobile is to be found, where it will be, where it will *pass*. [...] But it is always with immobilities, real or possible that it seeks to deal' (1992b: 15; emphasis in original). If the intellect alone were to analyse film it would first stop the projector in order to see each frame or press pause on the remote control. This is because the rational intellect believes time, like a butterfly, can best be seen by sticking a pin in it, thereby removing the distraction of its bothersome mobility and, moreover, its unpredictable life. Here, fragmenting, stopping or killing something in order to study its existence is not deemed a paradox but a scientific strategy. However, instead of bowing to the stubbornness of the intellect Bergson celebrated intuition instead, claiming that, by contrast with intellect, intuition was an ability to find reality in the flow of life: 'To think intuitively is to think in duration. Intuition starts from movement, posits it, or rather perceives it as reality itself, and sees in immobility only an abstract moment, a snapshot taken by our mind, of a mobility' (1992c: 34). Thus, Bergson not only favoured study of the living butterfly but reflection upon what it had been and what it was becoming. He rejected fixity and claimed: 'It is not the "states," simple snapshots we have taken once again along the course of change, that are real; on the contrary, it is flux, the continuity of transition, it is change itself that is real' (1992b: 16). Thus, a life cycle should not merely be reduced to the intellectual demarcation of caterpillar and butterfly as separate stages that can be pinned to a board in sequence. Instead, intuition concerns itself, like Céline says in *Before Sunrise*, with 'the space in between'. Following Bergson, a butterfly needs to be understood as existing in the permanent flux of becoming something else: 'Let us unfasten the cocoon, awaken the chrysalis; let us restore to movement its mobility, to change its fluidity, to time its duration' (1992b: 17). Bergson's theorising thus allows the intellect to play its role in offering a series of scientific or philosophical frameworks on which to pin stages, fragments and experiences, but, because the intellect ignores the flow of life, insists it is intuition that enables its perception.

Transposed to considerations of time, Bergson's theories were entirely revolutionary. For Bergson, 'time is what is happening, and more than that, it is what causes everything to happen' (1992b: 12). In contrast to the intellect, which does not so much countenance time as fluid but seeks to pin measurable moments of history to boards as seconds, minutes, years and centuries, Bergson presents the paradox of time as something that is always departing and always arriving: 'Its essence being to flow, not one of its parts is still there when another part comes along' (ibid.). He calls this flow of time *durée* (duration or 'what something lasts') and celebrates its 'uninterrupted up-surge of novelty' (1992b: 18). He writes that it should be considered as 'a creative evolution [with] perpetual creation of possibility' (1992b: 21), and he insists that it cannot be fractured into measurable parts or fractions. Instead it is unique, variable and delirious with its own capacity for change. The relevance of this idea to film is that time and film share the movement that constitutes the flow of life and is inseparable from their meaning. Unless one stops the projector or hits the remote control there is no single 'now' in film or in time. This informs *Slacker*, for example, when Working on Same Painting (Susannah Simone) apologises for turning up late to Having a Breakthrough Day, who replies: 'That's okay, time doesn't exist.' In a similar way, the image of a film is never frozen or still, not even in an intrinsic freeze frame because this still passes inexorably through a projector or the scanner of a DVD. A film never stalls in the present except in the intellect's pedantic insistence on the single frame that scientific manuals state stops for 1/24th of a second before the projector's bulb. This may be a rational explanation of film but the mind is as incapable of seeing a single frame before the bulb as it is of observing a similar period of time in reality. Furthermore, in digital film the problem is perhaps even more pronounced, with no single image ever discernible from amongst the myriad transforming pixels except by hitting the pause button, which negates the whole nature of film just as sticking a pin in a butterfly negates its existence.

Confusingly, however, writing so close to the birth of the cinema meant that Bergson was actually more concerned with the novelty of the cinematic apparatus (the camera and the projector) as a machine for recreating reality than he was with the potential of film as an artistic medium and a vehicle for political and philosophical thought. Thus, in his own time and from his own experience of the cinema, he saw film as an illustration of the working practice of the intellect rather than intuition. Perhaps, at least then, it was. He drew his simile from the fact that a filmstrip was a succession of immobile photographs that illustrated exactly how the intellect (not intuition) saw time and reality (i.e. as a series of still images or frozen moments). Bergson thus posited that reality for the intellect was not found in the illusion of movement onscreen, but in the images on the filmstrip itself. The perception of move-ment created by the projector's motor passing the filmstrip through the gate in front of a bulb was, he concluded, contrived, regulated and therefore repeatable. Unlike reality and unlike time, what was onscreen was not unique: 'Such is the contrivance of the cinematograph and such is also that of our knowledge' (Bergson 1998: 306). The dissolution of the critical standing of this simile after his death was perhaps partly due to the fact that the evolution of the filmmaking craft and art so quickly outstripped the initial remit of the cinematic apparatus to merely record reality. However, his theories of time endured and their resurrection in relation to cinema by Gilles Deleuze in the 1960s had important consequences for the development of contemporary film theory and underpins this analysis of the cinema of Linklater.

For instance, the relationship between intellect and intuition is the basis of *Waking Life* in which Main Character represents the wandering of intuition in the spaces in between myriad intellectual concepts. Main Character is at times a physical presence and at others a disembodied consciousness that still claims the film's subjectivity. He is part of the flow of life that he gradually comes to think of as a particularly lucid dream. Throughout the film/dream, his intuition negotiates a series of encounters with theory-spouting intellectuals that are rendered impressionistically by being rotoscoped; that is, by having stylised animation overlaid on the live-action footage. By discus-sion and observation, Main Character is a more active collaborator in the elaboration and dissection of philosophical thought than Sophie Amundsen in Jostein Gaarder's novel *Sofies Verden* (*Sophie's World*, 1991), which provides a basic and objective guide to philosophy. Each of the dialogists met by Main Character puts forward a theory that sticks a pin through an aspect of life but, as his name suggests, Main Character is not a cipher but always resolutely the main character, whose predicament starts out dreamlike and ends up nightmarish. Some of these dialogists are real academics, such as Lisa Moore (English professor at the University of Texas [UT]), David Sosa (Philosophy, UT), Robert C. Solomon (Philosophy, UT), who lectures on the value of an exuberant response to existentialism, and Eamonn Healy (Chemistry, UT), who is credited as Shape-Shifting Man and expounds upon evolution by interaction. In a literally animated fashion that employs both meanings of the word, Healy explains how time has sped up along with the evolution of communities and the individual to the extent that change should now be visible within one's own lifetime, and concludes 'that would be nice'.

Other dialogists given time and space to expound upon their intuitive ideas include Austinite individualists such as Burning Man played by J. C. Shakespeare, a writer for *The Austin Chronicle*, who argues that society and humankind are drawn to chaos despite the 'occasional purely symbolic participatory act of voting – you want the puppet on the right or the puppet on the left?' Then he turns himself into a media image by dousing himself in petrol and setting himself alight in the manner of the photograph taken by Malcolm Browne of the burning monk from Saigon 1963, whose self-immolation was the first televised image of violence and the first, therefore, to turn tragedy into mediated spectacle. Like other characters in *Waking Life*, Burning Man appears to illustrate a theory, making of his brief, animated existence an enactment of his thought. Here, for example, Burning Man extols and illustrates the theories of Jean Baudrillard, whose criticism of contemporary society and culture signalled an irreparable break with Modernism in the wake of his providing an explanation for the experience of 9/11 and its aftermath in *The Spirit of Terrorism* (2003).

In addition to the theories of Bergson and Baudrillard, still more are put forward by real and fictional characters from other films by Linklater, including the director himself, who appears twice in *Waking Life*. Firstly, he reprises his role as passenger from the first scene of *Slacker* but this time he passes the burden and illusory opportunity of chance onto Main Character when he improvises directions for Boat Car Guy (Bill Wise), who advises his passengers to 'go with the flow'. Another recurring character is that played by Wiley Wiggins, for Main Character may be read as the somewhat older but still struggling character of Mitch Kramer that Wiggins played in *Dazed and Confused*. In addition, Louis Mackey, the real-life professor of Philosophy at UT who played Old Anarchist in *Slacker*, turns up as Himself to talk about the divide between great thinkers and ordinary humans who reside at what he claims is 'at best, super-chimpanzee level'. Meanwhile, Kim Krizan, who was Questions Happiness in *Slacker*, the schoolteacher in *Dazed and Confused* and the co-writer of *Before Sunrise*, appears as Herself to discuss the theories of Ferdinand de Saussure, while Timothy 'Speed' Levitch, who will appear in *Live from Shiva's Dance Floor* and has a cameo as a waiter in *The School of Rock*, turns up in his role as New York tourist guide to quote Federico García Lorca and advise Main Character that 'life is a matter of a miracle that is collected over time by moments flabbergasted to be in each other's presence'. Jesse and Céline appear too, of course, in a post-coital discussion of the Taoist philosophy of Chuang Tzu and its relation to multiple consciousness that recalls Céline's concerns about her grandmother in *Before Sunrise*: 'It's like I'm looking back on my life, like my waking life is her memories.' Yet another intertextual reference is the appearance of the poet David Jewell, whose poem 'Delusion Angel' is used in *Before Sunrise*. Beleaguered by so many intellectual theories and frameworks of discussion, Main Character gradually becomes aware by intuition (not by intellect) that the only 'consistent perspective' in and on this flow of life is his own. Thus he intuitively comprehends that he is involved in lucid dreaming, which, as he describes it, 'is mostly just me dealing with a lot of people who are exposing me to a lot of information and ideas that seem vaguely familiar but at the same time it's all very alien to me'. Nevertheless, he escapes all the attempts of the dialogists to pin him down and finally floats away.

It used to be (and often still is) that a single and absolute belief in a god, a monarch or a dictator could subdue intuition with dogmatism. However, in *Waking Life* Main Character has to contend with the multitude of theories that emerged to fill the vacuum caused in large part by the wars of the twentieth century and no single theory dominates or concludes his search for meaning as long as his intuition and its instinctive searching elsewhere can resist. Made just before the 2001 destruction of New York's World Trade Center, *Waking Life* points to a world that will soon be perceived in a highly fragmented fashion. What emerges from *Waking Life* is the notion that the human consciousness is itself a moment of structure: the universe is chaos and only the time of being human is coherent. What is more, the structuring principle of this time is emphatically the Bergsonian concept of intuition. Thus the existence of Main Character is not merely spatial, but also temporal. He is a moving, vital essence in constant evolution from what he was to what he is becoming. Thus he too embodies the paradox of time as something that is always departing and always arriving. This is what Bergson meant by *durée*: 'pure, unadulterated inner continuity' (1992b: 14). It is the idea of time as something mobile and incomplete that cannot be fractured into measurable parts. Instead, *durée* is unique, variable, organic and delirious with its own potential for change. As such, it could only ever be grasped by the intuitive force of the imagination. Or, as Linklater himself puts it in *Waking Life*: 'There's only one instant, and it's right now. And it's eternity.'

Waking Life illustrates the movement of Main Character's intuition from theory to theory without ever getting pinned down, which in turn inspires Linklater and the animators to create the responsive form of the film with restless hand-held, intuitive camerawork and an overlay of stylised animation. Because of its odd angles, whip pans and floating aerial shots of Austin that Linklater filmed from a hot air balloon, the temporalised movement of the camera is fused with the film's content in the editing to create a meaning that becomes the temporalised movement of the film itself. This multiplicitous mental puzzle is akin to the process required to understand the meaning of *durée*, which requires the employment of intuition in order to experience it. For Bergson, intuition is 'the *sympathy* by which one is transported into the interior of an object in order to coincide with what there is unique and consequently inexpressible in it' (1992f: 161; emphasis in original). Thus, it is no wonder that *Waking Life* has such a sterling reputation as a 'trip' movie, for in addition to its visual fireworks and philosophical debate the film requires its audience to sympathise with its flow in order to empathise with its meaning. Although the dialogue was worked up by the cast and rehearsed beforehand, Linklater admits on his Region 1 DVD commentary that the structure of *Waking Life* was mostly discovered in the editing. Following this, the edited footage was rotoscoped using the Rotoshop computer program of art director Bob Sabiston that allows for animation to be overlaid on the footage, thereby adding a further, metaphysical level to the film that chimes with the oneiric status of the events onscreen. In terms of heightening the collaborative nature of the project, moreover, not only do most of those onscreen play themselves or characters based upon themselves, but the large roster of animators were also 'cast' or assigned to characters based on the appropriateness of their style of animation. In sum, therefore, it is the working practice of the film's making as well as its form and content that makes *Waking Life* a film about the communication and negotiation of ideas. In the context of Linklater's cinema, moreover, *Waking Life* also sports significant intertextuality, whether explicitly (in the reappearance of characters from other films, such as Céline and Jesse), implicitly (with the reappearance of actors such as Wiggins, Charles Gunning, Nicky Katt, Adam Goldberg, Kim Krizan and Linklater himself) or by direct reference to the work of key influences such as Guy Debord and Philip K. Dick, the author of *A Scanner Darkly*, who Pinball Playing Man (Linklater) quotes at length and clearly reveres.

Waking Life is also something of a palimpsest of *Slacker* in that it personifies anew the kind of Austin-based, low-budget guerrilla filmmaking that involves extended rehearsals and a collaborative script. Apart from the rotoscoping, the only difference is that a looser, more improvisational shooting style was enabled for *Waking Life* by its six weeks of filming on Mini-DV digital cameras. Thereafter, Sabiston and his team of animators coloured, layered and embellished the footage in styles ranging from realist to borderline abstract, from pointillism to pop. Sometimes it seems as if the animation is transparent and the actors can be seen beneath; at other times the characters are vibrantly cartoonish. Yet this interchangeability of appearance and reality only adds to the film's meaning by raising the question of how we can be certain of what we are seeing when the distinctions between reality and unreality are blurred, which is a dominant theme in the cinema of Linklater. In response, *Waking Life* features a variety of respondent theories that includes Céline's citing of biologist and author Rupert Sheldrake's concept of a vital, evolving universe with its own inherent memory: 'Maybe I only exist in your mind' (2009). In addition, more immediately relevant to Bergson and the cinema of Linklater is *Waking Life*'s rebuttal of the Postmodernist claim that people are merely social constructions. The torrent of dialogue that constitutes Main Character's search for meaning is not concerned with excuses for behaviour but with a concrete responsibility to communicate. For all its cerebral wanderlust, *Waking Life* is clearly not estranged from contemporary political activism either, for, as is noted: 'It's always our decision who we are.' In addition, the film is graciously not above self-criticism. As One of Four Men (Adam Goldberg) observes of the quixotic and stranded Man on the Lamppost (R. C. Whittaker): 'He's all action and no theory. We're all theory and no action.'

Nevertheless, of all the theories expounded upon in *Waking Life* the one that gets closest to an understanding of the slacker ethos is that of the aforementioned Guy Debord, who is actually present as Mr Debord (Hymie Samuelson) and makes the following declaration: 'Free the passions. Never work. Live without Dead Time.' It was Debord who contributed the notion of the *dérive* to the group of international revolutionaries of the 1960s known as The Situationist International (SI), which was formed in 1957 and dissolved in 1972 following the failure of workers, students, revolutionaries and the SI itself to capitalise on the achievements of the 1968 riots in Paris that the SI had done a great deal to instigate. This movement and its theories emerged from European Modernist tendencies that exalted a more instinctive response to life and drew upon Bergson's concept of intuition in order to promote a radical subjectivity. Consequently, this *dérive* became a favourite technique of the SI by which an environment that was appropriate to being explored by intuition would reveal itself in the *durée* of this exploration. The terms that were developed to classify a series of experimental fields of study for the construction of such situations included unitary urbanism and psycho-geography; but essentially, thought and action were fused in the *dérive*, which is a recurring motif in the cinema of Linklater, wherein walking and talking often features as content, inspires and determines the form of films, and contributes to their meaning. Thus, as Lesley Speed perceives, 'the relationship between Linklater's films and the SI is an instance of postmodern revivalism' (2007: 103). Speed concludes that 'Linklater's films posit worlds in which freedoms of thought and self-expression are presented in spatial terms' (2007: 104) and she correctly identifies *Slacker* and *Waking Life* as films that 'posit space as a locus of orientation in relation to fractured linear time' (ibid.). In part, the *dérive* was a kind of art project with a political objective, that of reterritorialising urban spaces by means of an intuitive revision of their potential. The SI utilised the *dérive* to express their scorn for materialism, authority and determinism, each of which had negated free will. Most at home (and at the same time deliberately homeless) in Paris (as is apparent in *Before Sunset*), the *dérive* was associated with the concept of the *flâneur* and the *flânerie* proposed by the poet Charles Baudelaire in the nineteenth century to describe the pedestrian's exploration of Parisian streets by those whose wanderings enabled their understanding of the evolving metropolis. The daylight wanderings of the *flânerie* (as for the participants of a *dérive*) rejected geometrical town-planning and the quantitative measurements of functional space and sought instead to realise new meanings and functions for the streets. In this they were much like their nocturnal associates of the 1920s, the Surrealists led by André Breton, who had sought dreamlike encounters in the streets at night. Like the Surrealists, the SI were against all repressive regimes and therefore made of the *dérive* something like a symbolic trespassing on official spaces, a pointed trampling of any prohibitive demarcations and a freeform remapping of the city for revolutionary pursuits. Their wanderings were intended to destroy old values and invent new truths, just as Austin was reterritorialised as an oasis of dissent against corporate America in *Slacker*.

This act of walking and talking that the cinema of Linklater shares with the *dérive* is not about defining the asphalt in any concrete manner but reterritorialising the streets by the flow of life. In effect, these streets become a psychological terrain that visually represents the exploration of an inner life by the protagonists. Following Bergson, this entails an intuitive exploration of visual, aural and sensual encounters in an urban area with the objective of transforming the meaning and dimensions of the space itself in order to illustrate the reflective process of the explorers. It is by these means that *Waking Life* redeems the entrenched limitations of Austin a decade after *Slacker* and how Vienna and Paris are reterritorialised as spaces fit for romantic and metaphysical transcendence in *Before Sunrise* and *Before Sunset*. These spaces, like these films, are mapped by fluid camera movements that are temporalised by following, entering into, and being subject to the flow of life. For example, any uninterrupted tracking shot following Jesse and Céline down a Parisian street must last at least as long as it takes them to drift down it. This temporalised movement seeks communication, and is therefore constantly creating and dissolving spatial and temporal collages such as those conjured in Jesse and Céline's encounters with objects and passers-by. There is even a clue to this Bergsonian temporalisation in *Before Sunrise*, when Céline comments on a poster in Vienna for an exhibition of the paintings of Georges-Pierre Seurat that, like her, is briefly estranged from Paris: 'His human figures are always so transitory, like they are disappearing into the background.' Moreover, as Siegfried Kracauer asserts in his essay on the redemption of physical reality:

> The street in the extended sense of the word is not only the arena of fleeting impressions and chance encounters but a place where the flow of life is bound to assert itself. Again one will have to think mainly of the city street with its ever-moving crowds. The kaleidoscopic sights mingle with unidentified shapes and fragmentary visual complexes and cancel each other out, thereby preventing the onlooker from following up any of the innumerable suggestions they offer. What appeals to him are not so much sharp-contoured individuals engaged in this or that definable pursuit as loose throngs of sketchy, completely indeterminate figures. Each has a story, yet the story is not given. Instead, an incessant flow casts its spell over the *flâneur* or even creates him. The *flâneur* is intoxicated with life in the street – life eternally dissolving the patterns which it is about to form. (1960: 72)

Clearly Kracauer defers to the Bergsonian notion of time as something that is a durational state of mind in which the elements of its coherent whole are not located spatially but dispersed throughout the passage of time. The notion of *flânerie* thus resonates in the cinema of Linklater, wherein and whereby it communicates subjectivity about life in the street to its audience.

The *dérive* used creative intuition to liberate spaces from their definition by rigid intellect, whereby a designated parking space for a government official might be danced across, for example, or a crossing might inspire a pause regardless of the Parisian traffic. The relevance to Cubism of such child's play with adult intent is that, as Gliezes and Metzinger stated in *Du Cubisme* (1912), it is by such means that 'sensory space is subsumed within a temporal concept of human consciousness' (in Antliff and Leighten 2001: 83). Any linear perspective invoked or represented by the lines of the crossing or the rectangle of the parking space is the product of a mathematical system of representation and the dictation of rules and regulations by officialdom and hierarchy. Consequently, it must be ignored, defied, debased, overthrown and recycled as a temporal space suitable for intuitive creation, for, as Douglas Coupland remonstrates in his post-apocalyptic slacker novel *Girlfriend in a Coma*, we must 'dismantle and smash everything that stops questioning' (1998: 263). Following the theories of the Marxist sociologist and philosopher Henri Lefebvre, moreover, the temporalised space in the cinema of Linklater may be understood in terms of its social function, as something that can be classified as either a basic natural space, which simply exists, or as a social space that both affects and is affected by its inhabitants. A social space, argued Lefebvre, is a product that is defined by perception and therefore liable to be valued: 'The space thus produced also serves as a tool of thought and of action' (1991: 26). Yet, because 'new social relations demand a new space, and vice-versa' (Lefebvre 1991: 59), it is also possible that space can be repeatedly reclaimed and reterritorialised as an arena of such thought and action. Thus it may be argued that the drunken Korean immigrant in *Sans soleil* who 'takes his revenge on society by directing traffic at the crossroads', the Chinese students standing up to tanks in Tiananmen Square in 1989 and the slacker community hanging out in Austin in 1991 are all engaged in a form of revolution by reterritorialisation.

The actions of a *dérive*, when perceived by intuition as occurring somewhere in the Bergsonian notion of time as a thing that is eternally dissolving and becoming, are truly immeasurable and unrepeatable. Time 'is a totally human idea – without people time vanishes. Infinity and zero become the same thing' (Coupland 1998: 263). Cubism illustrates this concept because it disperses the temporal condition of an object and challenges the spectator to synthesise it. Cubism may be included in the group of art movements known collectively as Modernism, which includes Post-Impressionism, Dadaism, Fauvism and Surrealism, but contrary to common assumption, it was not a complete break with Classicism (see Cooper 1999).[1] Surrealism subscribed to intuition in the production of art as well as its reception, but Cubism employed the intellect in its initial pictorial deconstruction of an object prior to its synthesis by intuition. This Cubist strategy is seen, for example, in Pablo Picasso's *Les Demoiselles d'Avignon* (1907), in which the artist first subjected the five human figures 'to a programme of conscious planning that resembled the great academic projects of Leonardo or Géricault, before finally painting his 8ft square canvas' (Jones 2007). The result was a painting that was a 'perpetual motion machine that never loses its vitality [.] Actually looking at the picture means moving constantly from one facet to another; it never lets you settle on one resolved perception' (ibid.). Thus, whereas the intellect measures and fragments objects, intuition is freed to consider an infinite number of ways in which to piece them back together. What Cubism and the cinema of Linklater have in common is that they both explore not just the spatial extent and location of an object or event but its multiplicity, its evolving place in fluid time: its *durée*.

Antliff and Leighten state that Cubism is 'the seminal art movement of the twentieth century' (2001: 7) but analysis of its effect and meaning has so far hardly extended beyond painting, sculpture and design. Nevertheless, its 'radical approach to imagemaking, employing some of the most important features of modernism in Europe and America: visual abstraction and obfuscation, spatial and temporal disorientation, avant-gardist rejection of past values, and breakdown of class hierarchies in the embrace of popular culture' (ibid.) is hugely relevant to cinema and the films of Godard, Altman and Linklater, amongst others. Cubism breaks up objects so that they are seen simultaneously from many different viewpoints. Braque's *Violin and Palette* (1909), for example, breaks apart, dissolves and suspends the still life identified in its title. Instead of painting the object according to the rules of perspective that govern spatial representation, Braque rendered the object in time: he painted its *durée.* Moving around the violin and palette, he depicted them so as not to privilege any perspective behind the objects or any point of view before them. Thus he depicted broken planes, floating transitions, discontinuous edges, contradictory shade and seemingly arbitrary light. Although disorientation is one result, the true potential for a contextual appreciation of the objects is multiplied. The disruption of depth of field and perspective creates a flat ambiguous space that is juxtaposed with the temporal multi-dimensionality of the 'exploding' objects within the painting. The violin and palette thus exist in various planes at the same time and are thereby depicted as evolving objects. At the same time, they can be reconstructed in endless ways by intuition taking any one of numerous elements in the picture as the starting point for their incomplete recreation. In addition, 'Bergson strongly affected French writers associated with the development of Cubism' (Antliff and Leighten 2001: 80) because of their shared notion that human consciousness also exists in an infinite moment of exuberant existentialism in which it is gifted an endless capacity for redirection. As Antliff and Leighten maintain: 'The Cubists welcomed Bergson's "intuitive" approach to science and studied his thought to justify their adaptation of [Jules Henri] Poincaré's alternative geometries to their mode of pictorial abstraction' (ibid.). Subscription to Bergson's theory of intuition as the key to experiencing time and the temporality of creation also enabled revolutionaries, artists and ordinary people to reject the dominant concept of measurable, deterministic time. Following Bergson, Cubists favoured 'a specifically subjective temporality in contrast to the mechanical time of the clock' (Antliff and Leighten 2001: 65). They thus aimed to develop an empathetic consciousness made of intuition that might grasp and reveal the inner nature of reality, fused as it was with the flow of time.

Because what is sought is creative insight, understandings of time have also underscored the films of several European filmmakers with an interest in religious, metaphysical and/or existentialist discourses, such as Dreyer, Bresson, Bergman, Tarkovsky, Kieslowski and Medem, who all share a concern with the form, content and meaning of the kind of long takes that Deleuze would call time-images. The Cubist aspect, which is based upon seeing these takes as overlapping, discontinuous perspectives on an object or issue, was first evident in the cinema of Alain Resnais and Godard, who was identified as a Modernist in 1965 by the poet and novelist Louis Aragon in *Les Lettres Françaises.*[2] Colin MacCabe writes that Godard 'travelled from a position of pure classicism (using established genres and an accepted language to address an established audience) to one of pure Modernism (deconstructing established genres and grammars to address an ideal audience)' (2002: 207). Godard, like Linklater, was involved in a cinematic *dérive* that disrespected the restrictive rules of cinematic conventions such as linear narrative and transition shots because he felt no confidence in them, although (for a time) he remained sufficiently affectionate towards those conventions to rework genres into unsettling but freeform 'movies'. Setting a template for low-budget, independent filmmaking that would be used for *Slacker*, Godard made *À bout de souffle* in just four weeks 'for a third of the normal cost because he was working with an extremely reduced crew' (MacCabe 2002: 115). Aiming to capture 'reality on the run' (MacCabe 2002: 116), he and his cast and crew worked so fast that 'passersby on the Champs Elysees didn't know they were there' (ibid.).

Moreover, the form of Godard's films of the mid-1960s, like many of those directed by Linklater, also leaned towards the aesthetics of collage rather than montage, offering what might be recognised as a Cubist fragmentation and dislocation of a subject such as contemporary France in *2 ou 3 choses que je sais d'elle* (*Two Or Three Things I Know About Her*, 1967) that made for an intuitive, associative filmmaking practice and aesthetic. In an affined close reading of *À bout de souffle* that accords with the notion of Cubism, Noël Burch writes of 'fragments of the subject appearing and then disappearing in accordance with a rhythm that is quite essential to the discontinuous structure of the film' (1992: 149). Because of this, Susan Sontag calls Godard 'the deliberate "destroyer" of cinema, hardly the first cinema has known, but certainly the most persistent and prolific and timely' (1969: 150). In addition to narrative disjunction, the appearance of improvisation in Godard's films signified a split from classical cinema and a new Modernism that would later blur into Postmodernism, which also correlates with the ideas of Bergson, for, as Jean-François Lyotard contends, Postmodernism, 'is not Modernism at its end but in the nascent state, and this state is constant' (1999: 79). The cinema of Godard illustrated Lyotard's view that, 'modernity, in whatever age it appears, cannot exist without a shattering of belief and without discovery of the "lack of reality" of reality, together with the invention of other realities' (1999: 77). Like Picasso and James Joyce, who 'attacked new formal problems in each of [their] works' (Hoffman and Murphy 1992: 8), Godard's experimentation with film form included its fragmentation, by which the space and time of each image was explored in an, at times, arguably Cubist manner. This was a reaction against traditional realism, one that substituted discontinuity and ambiguity for exact measurements, which is the same reaction expressed by the cinema of Linklater, which may also be diagnosed as perhaps having suffered from the kind of generational unease that re-emerges every decade or so with a vague sense of inheritance rather than any explicit taking up of the cause.

The notion of collage that informs how Godard compiles films such as *Une femme est une femme, Made in USA* (1966) and *2 ou 3 choses que je sais d'elle* is akin to the Cubist technique employed by Braque and Picasso around 1912, which also included adding fragments of reality: here, documentary footage and improvisation to fiction films, there postage stamps and strips of newspaper to paintings. Instead of a single, overarching perspective that governed a single, linear narrative, Godard explored the temporalised representation of objects and issues in films with the consequence of leaving them open and incomplete. For example, the twelve tableaux of *Vivre sa vie: Film en douze tableaux* (*My Life to Live*, 1962) reveal the temporalised representation of Nana (Anna Karina) as she becomes a prostitute in the manner of a Cubist portrait; that is, by discontinuous and incomplete sequences based on observation from over-lapping viewpoints that include a Marxist critique, a melodrama and a dance around a pool table. To truly grasp the potentially Cubist nature of this film, moreover, it helps to consider the twelve tableaux as being projected simultaneously onto a single screen. Technology permitting, it would have resulted in a near-opaque portrait of Nana as an object that is eternally dissolving between her twelve tableaux or 'flows of life'. And the film would have ended after six minutes, which is altogether more satisfactory than what Godard offers when actually obliged to end the film at a reasonable eighty minutes; that is, a cynical parody of the convention of a film ending in which Nana is gunned down in an overwrought shoot-out.

To classify Linklater as a Cubist filmmaker is probably overstepping the remit, but at least the suggestion may serve to reveal his cinema's connections with its own limitations and its indebtedness to Modernist filmmakers such as Luis Buñuel and Godard amongst others. Cubism is essentially about how an object exists in time more than it does in space and it is in this respect that its relevance to the cinema of Linklater is most profound, for his films variously offer multi-layered Cubist repre-sentations of specific time-frames, communities, collaborative working practices and issues that are reflected in the way the films are made. *Slacker*, for example, may be appreciated as a Cubist portrait of Austin's slacker community and its particularly collaborative creative practice, while *Dazed and Confused* is a Cubist picture of what it feels, looks and sounds like to have been born in 1960 and be sixteen years old on the last day of school in 1976. Similarly, *Before Sunrise* may be appreciated as a Cubist rendition of what it feels like to fall in love during a few hours walking and talking around Vienna, while the real-time drift of *Before Sunset* offers nothing less than the *durée* of a *dérive*. *Waking Life* too is the *durée* of a *dérive*, but one that is philosophically-minded rather than romantically-inclined. The emphasis on the streets in these and other films directed by Linklater is expressive of Bergson's dictum that 'though all the photographs of a city taken from all possible points of view indefinitely complement one another, they will never equal in value that dimen-sional object, the city along whose streets one walks' (1992f: 160–1). Consequently, the Cubist approach to filming/walking the streets in the cinema of Linklater corre-sponds to one of Bergson's key illustrations of thought.

This Cubist approach to the temporalised condition of an object also feeds off Roland Barthes' theorising that a text is 'a multi-dimensional space in which a variety of writings, none of them original, blend and clash. The text is a tissue of quotations drawn from the innumerable centres of culture' (1982: 146). Yet it does not court or risk the potential meaninglessness of Postmodernism because its fragmentation is never absolute. Instead the fragments always orbit a core issue or hypostasis (such as prostitution in *Vivre sa vie* or the horror of high school in *Dazed and Confused*) much like the lines, angles, light and shade of a Cubist painting always refer back to the object from which they came. Fragmentation may make the object indeterminate as a whole, but it is still the unifying element of the many pieces. Nana in *Vivre sa vie* may end up a cipher for female suffering in a Marxist equation, but what she illustrates is always vibrant, challenging and uncontained within the duration of any single, six-minute tableaux, just as slacking is not defined by any single character in *Slacker*, the meaning of life is not limited to any one theory in *Waking Life* and the issue of fast food does not reside solely in the matter of either animal welfare, immigrancy or consumer health in *Fast Food Nation*. Nevertheless, as the example of *Vivre sa vie* shows, because the literal application of Cubism to cinema was disallowed by the impossibility of showing all the tableaux or frames of a film all at once, Godard subscribed to an equivalent idea of film as tapestry instead: 'I don't really like telling a story. I prefer to use a kind of tapestry, a background on which I can embroider my own ideas' (in Roud 1980: 436). Thus, just as 'regional' cinema was replaced by the term 'independent' so the notion of 'Cubist' cinema was superseded by the peculiarly tactile (and textile) notion of 'tapestry' that is perhaps clearest in American cinema, where the term is used to denote the form and content of works of literature and film with multiple overlapping narratives involving multiple interrelated characters.

In American literature, for example, the 'tradition' or 'genre' of tapestry form and content is exemplified by Sherwood Anderson's 1919 novel *Winesburg, Ohio*. From this group of tales of Ohio smalltown life at the end of the nineteenth century there emerges a gallery of grotesques whose troubled lives are gradually revealed to be inextricable from each other. The accumulative sense makes of the work, like one of its main characters Adolph Myers, 'one of those [...] in whom the force that creates life is diffused, not centralized' (Anderson 2008: 15). The aesthetics of incompletion that signal the Cubist element of the work are also evident in Doctor Reefy, who 'had begun the practice of filling his pockets with [...] scraps of paper [on which] were written thoughts, ends of thoughts, beginnings of thoughts' (Anderson 2008: 19), as well as in the tales told by Doctor Parcival to young George Willard that, Anderson writes, 'began nowhere and ended nowhere. Sometimes the boy thought they must all be inventions, a pack of lies. And then again he was convinced that they contained the very essence of truth' (2008: 32). *Winesburg, Ohio* was a major influence on Linklater and Eric Schlosser during their writing of *Fast Food Nation*. As Schlosser recalls:

I love the novel *Winesburg, Ohio*, written in the 1920s [sic.], which is the portrait of one town, but in looking at this one town, it is looking at America. Rick [Linklater] likes the novel as well. Suddenly it seems like not an obvious way to approach the [adaptation of *Fast Food Nation* into a screenplay]. (In Badt 2006)

Linklater concurs, offering a useful definition of his cinematic Cubism besides:

It's a narrative strategy that has a lot of precedents in literature. It's a way to tell a story from multiple viewpoints and to try to get around subject matter that is pretty vast. It seemed logical to set it in one area and deal with the inhabitants of that area who get there from different angles. I have a history of ensemble film work, and I like that as a storytelling method. (In Feinstein 2006)

Fast Food Nation: What the All-American Meal is Doing to the World (aka. *Fast Food Nation: The Dark Side of the All-American Meal*) emerged from a series of articles for *Rolling Stone* magazine that were written by investigative journalist Schlosser, who published the complete text as a monograph in 2001.[3] Thus the work was always fragmentary in its creation and form. In it, Schlosser investigates the development of the fast food industry and the changes to America and Americans that have caused (and been caused by) this growth. He calls this spread of concrete and waistlines 'the malling and sprawling of the West' (2001: 9) and pointedly blames the centralised purchasing power and marketing campaigns of the fast food giants such as McDonalds for 'wiping out small businesses [and] obliterating regional differences' (2001: 4). Schlosser states:

> [I am] interested in [fast food] both as a commodity and as a metaphor [because] a nation's diet can be more revealing than its art or literature. On any given day in the United States about one-quarter of the adult population visits a fast food restaurant. During a relatively brief period of time, the fast food industry has helped to transform not only the American diet, but also our landscape, economy, workforce, and popular culture. (2001: 3)

It is easy to see why Linklater, who has been vegetarian since 1983, should have found *Fast Food Nation* suitable for a Cubist film treatment. There was always the cinematic model of Altman's *Nashville*, which might be considered the prototypical Cubist film in American cinema for the way it took American music and politics as the subject of its mobile and incomplete collage in the cause of satire. Like *Fast Food Nation*, *Nashville* is suggestive of a portrait of a specific object (a country music concert) but this object is just a detonator around which explodes a plethora of characters, scenes and comments that depict contemporary America and its politics in a Cubist manner. Following *Nashville*, *Fast Food Nation* also spins off vague, incomplete considerations of its object from many different perspectives. Like Braque's *Violin and Palette* and Godard's *Vivre sa vie*, therefore, each film presents numerous perspectives on a hypo-stasis to the observer, whose intuition is challenged to reconstruct a violin, palette, prostitution, France or America from different points of view. Consequently, *Fast Food Nation* may be appreciated as a Cubist film in which the elements of contemporary America explored in its many fragments include not just the dominion of convenience food but also immigration, migration, environmental abuse, the idealism of youth, health and its relation to issues of class, the plight of farmers, minimum wage, drug use, gender in the workplace, globalisation, corporate responsibility, unemployment, activism, exploitation, surveillance, paranoia, obesity, animal rights, slaughterhouse conditions, marketing, and many more besides. What *Fast Food Nation* is about depends upon the interest, knowledge, activity and subjectivity of each spectator, which informs the

Richard Linklater directing on the kill floor in *Fast Food Nation*

perspective or point at which the spectator chooses to anchor his or her understanding of the film. If it helps, in the manner of the hypothetical overlaying of the twelve tableaux of Godard's *Vivre sa vie*, the multi-narrative form and multi-character content of *Fast Food Nation* might be imagined as overlaid and projected simultaneously to provide a Cubist portrait of contemporary America with all the opinions, perspectives, angles and elements that supposes. Bergson had already conceptualised this possibility but surmised that 'in the case of time, the idea of superposition would imply absurdity, for any effect of duration which will be superposed upon itself and consequently meas-urable, will have as its essence non-duration' (1992b: 12). Nevertheless, the fact that outside of a gallery installation by the likes of Chris Marker and the experimental films of Kenneth Anger and Maya Deren film is limited to being rendered in a succession of images rather than as endless, bottomless superimpositions only makes the Modernist awareness of its limitations more relevant to the sense of helplessness that pervades *Fast Food Nation*.

Fast Food Nation begins with a cheesy commercial for The Big One, a burger that Don Anderson is steering to success for a fast food franchise called Mickey's. When the campaign is threatened by independent reports of 'shit in the meat', Don is sent to Cody, Colorado ('An All-American Town') to investigate the Uni-Globe meatpacking complex. Although set in Colorado, the film was also shot in Austin, albeit under the pseudonym *Coyote* so as not to enrage local industry (Gross 2005) and, as Linklater explains on the region 2 DVD, in a Mexican meatpacking plant, whose owners were swayed by the film's focus on the plight of Mexican immigrants. Uni-Globe by its name alone stands for globalisation and the nickel-squeezing policy that Don comes to suspect 'may be running the production line too fast', thereby occasioning accidents, animal abuse and shit in the meat. His movement towards the truth of the matter is hindered by corporate glad-handing and veiled threats, however, and is juxtaposed with the movement to Cody of illegal immigrants from Mexico, including Sylvia (Catalina Sandino Moreno). Furthermore, an ironic third juxtaposition is made with Amber (Ashley Johnson), a high school-age employee at Mickey's, whose contrasting movement away from Cody is stymied by the ennui that her developing awareness encounters in all but her radical Uncle Pete (Ethan Hawke), whose own philosophy of life is limited to the fact that, as he says, 'I'm really alright with what I'm not doing.' That Uncle Pete encourages Amber's vague ambition of becoming an astronaut does not indicate what might be Capraesque fulfilment of a smalltown wish but an ironic comment on the pointlessness of any ambition for a girl who cannot even get out of Cody.[4] At key moments these three perspectives on America overlap without giving a complete picture. At a stop sign, Anderson's car passes Leroy's Plumbing Supplies van carrying the Mexican immigrants and he banters amiably with Amber in the restaurant, even commenting on the friendly manner in which she gives him the 'right' answer to his asking what she likes on the menu: 'Oh, I like everything!' Yet Anderson's later exchange with a hotel receptionist, who is trained to smile and ask questions but does not listen to his answers, spoils the bonhomie he supposes with Amber by stressing the lack of communication between those who struggle to live by the rules of corporate America. Ultimately, the film explores a void of empathy and fills it with justifiable, even sensible paranoia: 'There's a reason why it only costs 99 cents!'

There is certainly no resolution; at the end of the film the cycle begins again as fresh illegal immigrants are met with a Mickey's Itty-Bitty meal. Ultimately, however, *Fast Food Nation* is past the point of possible activism and redemption. It exists bleakly and helplessly at the same evolutionary tipping point as Coupland's *Girlfriend in a Coma*:

> One hundred years ago – or even fifty years ago – the world would have healed itself just fine in the absence of people. But not now. We crossed the line. The only thing that can keep the planet turning smoothly now is human free will forged into effort. Nothing else. That's why the world has seemed so large in the past few years, and time so screwy. It's because Earth is now totally ours. (1998: 265–66)

Around Don, Ashley and Sylvia, who are well cast with intelligent actors capable of expressing ordinariness, are fragments of myriad characters whose lives are defined by the industry in this world 'so large' and time 'so screwy'. These include an immigrant-smuggler (Luis Guzmán), a burger-flipper who adds spit to the shit (Paul Dano) and a suitably mythic Kris Kristofferson as an embittered farmer: 'My granddaddy went up against the meatpackers in 1919.' It also features an unbilled Bruce Willis, who delivers a rational defence of the industry and its meat with bloody ketchup smears across his face: 'Just cook it!' *Fast Food Nation* is thus fair, at least, because it illustrates, in Coupland's words, that 'human beings and the world are now the same thing' (1998: 266). All the human beings in *Fast Food Nation* offer valid perspectives on contemporary America as emblematised by the fast food industry, and their incomplete, contradictory and discontinuous appearances add texture but no definable shape

Don Anderson (Greg Kinnear) wising up and hating it in *Fast Food Nation*

to the Cubist object. As Kristofferson's farmer says of the object of Don's investigation in words that also describe the film's intent: 'This isn't about good people versus bad people; it's about the machine taking over this country.'

Revolution is withheld, however. Don simply walks out of the film halfway through, Sylvia submits to sex with her foreman in order to take up her injured husband's job on the kill floor, and Amber tries to free the company's several hundred thousand cows by cutting their fence but is left simpering at the immobile, indifferent cattle: 'Don't you want to be free?' A semblance of underlying structure is provided by match shots of cows crammed in pens with immigrants in a cramped motel room, and of the camera movement from Sylvia being fucked by the foreman to Ashley sawing through the fence, but the ultimate point of the film is the ironic disconnection between its many parts and characters. Awareness raised, everyone just gets on with their duties in their tiny part of the machine. Don returns to corporate comfort, Amber retreats to meaningless debate and Sylvia will soon get used to the carnage and stop crying on the kill floor. As Geoff King contends:

> To impose the usually affirmative Hollywood arc onto such material – to portray characters lifting themselves out of their difficulties, triumphing through adversity, and so on – is to impose a typically American-capitalist ideological framework, rooted in the notion that America is a society in which even those from the lowest reaches can achieve the dream of prosperity. (2005: 67)

This is why *Fast Food Nation* purposefully deflates, becomes flat and discards all narrative drive, to the extent that the climactic scenes inside the slaughterhouse may seem curiously undisturbing. Instead, the white walls, steaming hoses, plastic-robed workers and conveyor belt on which cattle are stunned, killed and rendered, reek of an efficiency that makes the tragedy of the situation its coldbloodedness. Says Linklater:

> This efficiency model that my film demonstrates runs our world of mass production. [...] That is the product of the last hundred years of our so-called progress, but it is the world we live in, with no care about the people or the environment [...] and that's not just American, it's everywhere. (In Badt 2006)

As befits a Cubist approach, there is no overriding perspective or limiting point of view to *Fast Food Nation*. The bullshit is not just in the meat but everywhere. And we're all in it together.

In effect, *Fast Food Nation* embodies the idea that whereas Renaissance and classical artists focused their creative energy on a single vanishing point in space that governed their perspective, Cubists refused this in favour of a notion of simultaneity that referenced the theory of relativity, whereby many different moments could be depicted as occurring in time from different perspectives. Correlatively, *Fast Food Nation* rejects recognisable terms such as heroic characters and an uplifting conclusion and favours numerous instances of reflection instead. This simultaneity allows for many elements of contemporary America to be spun off centrifugally from the central object of fast food and thus sets the film apart from other issue-driven but centripetal ensemble films such as *Traffic* or *Crash* (Paul Haggis, 2004), which explore the topics of drugs and racism respectively. If the centrifugal force of *Fast Food Nation* also means, as *Time* surmised, that Linklater 'can't breathe life into any of the characters [and is] content to create stick figures' (Corliss and Corliss 2006), then this may be because, as Michael Koresky concludes in his review for *Indiewire*, that it is 'a film about huge subjects writ tiny' (2006). This Cubist approach removes life as the intellect knows it from an object, meaning that it is no longer fully formed, defined by perspective as three-dimensional, situated in space and probably functional with little potential for intuitive exploration. Instead, the Cubist approach renders it more temporal than spatial, more expressive of its occurrence in time rather than of the space it occupies. Instead of depicting the scientific rationality of an object, it may be stated that:

> The Cubist style emphasized the flat, two-dimensional surface of the picture plane, rejecting the traditional techniques of perspective, foreshortening, modeling, and chiaroscuro, and refuting time-honoured theories that art should imitate nature. Cubist painters were not bound to copying form, texture, colour, and space; instead, they presented a new reality [...] that depicted radically fragmented objects. (Anon. 2010a)

This 'new reality', albeit a metaphysical one, is a common theme in the cinema of Linklater, wherein it is defined by its occurrence in time. This is why so many of the films he has directed employ a time-frame within which time is rendered in the Bergsonian sense as a Cubist object. *Slacker* is one whole day from dawn to dawn, *Dazed and Confused* runs from noon to daybreak and *SubUrbia* is one evening and night, as are *Before Sunrise* and *Waking Life*. *Tape* and *Before Sunset* are as long as the events onscreen, their real-time occurrence being one with the developing consciousness of their protagonists. Given Linklater's academic interest in classical theatre and his experience of writing and directing plays in the second year of his university education, it is probable that the deployment and exploration of time-frames in the films he has written, co-written and directed stems in part from his knowledge of the classical precept of time and space that inspired the correspondent dramatic unity of the time-frame and single setting as upheld by Aristotle. However, an appreciation of this concern with time as object is also usefully informed by the theories of multiplicity that Bergson put forward in *Time and Free Will: An Essay on the Immediate Data of Consciousness*, (1888). In this essay Bergson defined consciousness, which is expressed in something like a moral response, as temporal and in a constant state of becoming, as free, undefined and incomplete. It was this theory that inspired Gilles Deleuze to write (and thereby revitalise) *Bergsonism* (1966), as well as *Cinema 1: The Movement Image* (2005a [1983]) and *Cinema 2: The Time-Image* (2005b [1985]). Bergson is vital to Deleuze's argument that film does not represent an external reality but a means of arranging and expressing time and movement. Deleuze claims that cinema does not describe figures in movement (as would a photograph), but rather cinema's own movement reveals the figures (2005a: 5). Because of this, he argued, cinema was 'capable of thinking the production of the new' (2005a: 8). The arguments put forward by Deleuze in these two volumes are vast and complex and as much about a philosophy of life and its perception as they are about cinema. However, boiling them down to a level of immediate relevance to the cinema of Linklater leaves us with a useful, expressive and revealing indication of the previously mentioned distinction between what Deleuze calls the movement-image and what he identifies as the time-image. The movement-image is the basis of narrative cinema and most films are just a linear succession of them. Each one serves the plot and brings the resolution closer. For Deleuze, the movement-image is not separable from the object which moves: the movement-image, like the film, is always moving towards its resolution. Movement-images are thus associated with editing rather than camera movement or the duration of the shot. And because 'image in movement constantly sinks to the state of cliché' (Deleuze 2005b: 20), these movement-images tend to serve generic conventions and deliver the expected, thereby satisfying audiences of the 'movement-image-universe' or 'the world of the film'. Essentially, this theorising proposes that within a narrative based on generic conventions (and therefore movement-images that are calibrated by the intellect) no true representation of time as it is perceived by intuition can be established without halting the flow of movement because this would betray audience expectations and withhold the required resolution. In dominant, everyday, mainstream narrative cinema this movement is more important than time. Time is merely subject to the events that take place within it such as a car chase or a kiss, which usually last just as long as the narrative needs them to.

However, Deleuze contends that the trauma of World War II meant that 'the sensory motor schema was shattered from the inside' (2005b: 39). This, he claims, provoked a crisis of the movement-image in post-World War II cinema that was necessary in order that a new 'thinking image [...] beyond movement' (2005a: 219) could reflect upon the unrepresentable: recent warfare, wholescale destruction and a crisis of faith exacerbated to inexpressible extremes by the atomic bomb and the Holocaust. In this Deleuze also responds to the theories put forward by André Bazin in *What is Cinema?* (1958–1962), wherein he advocated objective reality by means of deep focus and true continuity based upon resistance to montage. However, Bazin's sense of realism was swayed by his belief that every shot is a representation of God manifesting creation (a notion that inspires the discussion of 'Holy Moments' between the filmmaker Caveh Zahedi and the poet David Jewell in *Waking Life* that was filmed in Austin's Paramount Theater). In response, nonetheless, Deleuze observed that in certain post-war films 'the subordination of time to movement was reversed, time ceases to be the measure of normal movement, it increasingly appears for itself and creates paradoxical movements' (2005b: xi). He called these instances of time appearing for itself time-images and he identified them in films in which the 'sensory-motor schema is loosened and a little time in the pure state [...] rises up to the surface of the screen' (2005b: xii). The time-image was one of stasis, *durée,* reflection, alienation and resistance. Could the time-image be a slacker?

Despite what at first might be assumed, the ideas of Deleuze do correlate with those of Bergson. The classical, linear narrative cinema of the movement-image is akin to the intellect's notion of time, being linear, sequential, continuous and complete, whereas the loose, reflective, possibly non-linear cinema of the time-image is akin to intuition's notion of time being seemingly incomplete, discontinuous and happening all at once. Perhaps the finest metaphor for this (and a key indicator of how the cinema of Linklater is informed, constructed and received) is found in James Joyce's *Ulysses* and quoted verbatim in *Slacker.* As Guy Who Tosses Typewriter tries to jolly a jilted pal by reciting from what appears to be an antique edition of the novel, the self-deluding rationalisations of each of the many lovers of Molly Bloom stand for the ignorance of the intellect in relation to time, in contrast with the truth that comes from intuition:

> It all makes sense if you'd just read from this passage here. It's when Leopold discovers that he's just been fucked over by his wife. He says: 'If he had smiled, why would he have smiled? To reflect that each one who enters imagines himself to be the first to enter whereas he is always the last term of a preceding series even if the first term of a succeeding one, each imagining himself to be first, last, only and alone whereas, he is neither first nor last nor only nor alone in a series originating in and repeated to infinity'.

Contrary to what the lovers tell themselves, there is 'a continuity of flow' around Molly's bed that corresponds to 'a succession of states each one of which announces what follows and contains what precedes [.] In reality, none of them do begin or end; they all dove-tail into one another' (Bergson 1992f: 163). Such is the subject and structure of *Slacker* as well as the encounters of *Dazed and Confused, Before Sunrise* and *Waking Life,* and the multiple characters in *Fast Food Nation.*

Bergson was not wrong when he wrote of the cinematic apparatus as a symbol of how the intellect sought immobilisation and fragmentation, but in later years Deleuze added that the cinema was not limited to this single mode of perception. Rather, Deleuze surmised that the nature of film was to unfold in time. He therefore posited that like time it also existed in a state of becoming, always departing and always arriving. Thus, although Bergson and Deleuze might have differed as regards the function of cinema, they reunite, as Robert Stam explains, because 'Deleuze is drawn to Bergson as a philosopher of becoming, for whom being and matter are never stable' (2000: 258). In expounding upon this, Deleuze destabilised traditional understandings of representation and caused a significant shift in contemporary film studies by treating film 'as event rather than representation' (ibid.). Instead of bowing to mathematics or science, Deleuze emphasised the temporal nature of creation and thought on film. His theories therefore maintain that fixed representation is no longer rational or possible in the cinema. Instead, fluidity and temporality direct our intuition to the provocative experience of what Deleuze termed 'a direct time-image' (2005b: 41). This he claimed could inspire transcendence, fusing memory, perception, time, thought and movement. Ultimately, of course, the debate between Bergson and Deleuze is philosophical. Writing at the beginning of the twentieth century, Bergson had little inkling of what the cinema would become beyond its meagre advance on the photograph, and saw the novelty of the illusion of movement as a contrivance. On the other hand, Deleuze, writing towards the end of the century, saw a simplistic division between popular cinema and the European art house and, quite simply, did not see enough films besides the elitist, Modernist traditions of Godard, Pasolini, Alain Resnais and others to make his writing on the cinema complete. Nevertheless, this incompletion is itself a provocation that has inspired much philosophical, academic and critical debate, as well as work by filmmakers such as Linklater who aspire to capturing, creating and releasing images and ideas of time in their work.

In building his argument, Deleuze sought and identified time-images in the films of several filmmakers including Godard, who, without using the term, by the mid-1960s had already claimed the collage of time-images as the true art of the cinema. By definition, a time-image cannot be measured or identified by reference to criteria, only sensed by intuition. Thus the 'pointing out' of time-images rarely convinces as this same signalling triggers an intellectual response to the image rather than an intuitive one. Nevertheless, examples worth considering include the tracking shot along a traffic jam in Godard's *Week End* (*Weekend*, 1967) and Nana (Anna Karina) watching *La passion de Jeanne d'Arc* (*The Passion of Joan of Arc*, Carl Theodor Dreyer, 1928) in *Vivre sa vie*. There is even the witty spoof of the measurement of time by the intellect in the one minute's silence ordained by Odile (Anna Karina) in *Band à parte*, which prompts Godard to show how time is subject to intuitive interpretation by cutting the entire soundtrack for what is mischievously much less than a minute. Time-images like these are those in which we see and experience the passing of time itself, without measurement or the mediating influence of the protagonist or plot. These are most often experienced as long takes in the films of Godard, Truffaut, Antonioni, Bresson, Tarkovsky, Víctor Erice, Terrence Malick, Carlos Reygadas and Linklater, wherein certain images are released from their subordination to movement and become subject to time instead. Even so, the long takes of these filmmakers may harbour different intent. Those of Antonioni were often in the cause of estrangement and alienation, while those of Bresson spoke of fatefulness. In *Days of Heaven* (1978) and *The Thin Red Line* (1988) Malick used long takes to convey the timelessness of nature as a corrective to the often violent urgency of man, while Tarkovsky sought meditation in images whose duration was at times a kind of penance. The political resonance of the time-image in the cinema of Linklater comes from the fact that, by their very nature, time-images cannot be integrated within narrative and generic conventions. Thus, confrontational thought appears in shots that withhold functional spectacle and closure. The time-image is revolutionary, but by its refusal to act, rather than by its action. The time-image *is* a slacker!

As a bona fide slacker, the time-image allows for imagination, reflection and collaboration to occur as a rebuttal to the conventions of a hurrying mainstream narrative cinema. The time-image, like the slacker, deliberately ignores all pressures to conform, compete or consume. Instead the slacker, like the time-image, uses time to reflect, consider and explore. As both can be seen as creative layabouts, their conjunction in the cinema of Linklater is significant, while their predecessor, as Richard Brody suggests, is Godard, whose innovative long takes in *Vivre sa vie* occurred because he simply could not afford or be bothered to set up and shoot different angles of a scene, which is as good a way as any to produce an entirely new film language (2008: 129–41). The key to all this is that 'not being bothered' requires great effort, because only the authentic 'wasting of time' engenders alternative priorities to conformity, tradition, consumerism and nationalism. As Dostoyevsky Wannabe in *Slacker* comments: 'Who's ever written a great work about the immense effort required in order not to create?'

In *À bout de souffle*, *Une femme est une femme*, *Band à parte* and *Alphaville* it is apparent that although the imagination of the French New Wave had been colonised by Hollywood genres, Godard had in his idleness reflected upon this enough that he was beginning to sense betrayal. By 1965 in *Pierrot Le Fou*, it is partly this union of the time-image and the slacker ethos that points to the politicisation of Godard, when Ferdinand tires of being in a genre film that has him 'driving towards a cliff at 100 kilometres per hour'. 'I wonder what's keeping the cops. We should be in jail by now,' he muses before writing a great work about the immense effort required in order not to create by painting his face blue and blowing himself up. Correlatively, the union of the slacker ethos with time-images in the cinema of Linklater often signals the political aspect of his cinema too. Examples of this might include many scenes from *It's Impossible to Learn to Plow by Reading Books*, wherein Linklater films himself in a position of pending travel in 'any-spaces-whatsoever' (Deleuze 2005a: 112), numerous sequences in *Slacker* in which the discourse, reflection or direction of characters inhabits the *durée* of the image, and several indeterminate and unequal moments of reflection and re-direction in *Waking Life*. More specifically, personal subjectivity might argue for the term in describing (amongst others) the scene in *Before Sunrise* when Céline and Jesse react to the potential *longeur* of being left on the bridge by the two guys from the play about a cow. Glen Norton writes of this moment as *temps mort* (dead time), which he links to the *nouveau roman* movement in its Modernist use of 'microrealism' and may be correlated with that of the theory of the time-image (2000: 64). As deployed by Antonioni, *temps mort* results from a lingering camera and defines a scene retroactively because 'the power of the *temps mort* lies precisely in our attempt to define it; within the immediacy of viewing, it is nothing more than a flash of insight and emotion' (ibid.). Other approximations of the time-image in the cinema of Linklater include the shot of Jesse and Céline crammed together in the listening booth in *Before Sunrise*, that which Linklater holds on the sliding doors through which Don has departed in *Fast Food Nation* (but he doesn't come back), several pained close-ups in *Tape* in which furious thought is experienced as a response to the pressure of time, and a number of the long-takes that make up the similarly time-framed *Before Sunset*, including moments in the drift along the Seine, climbing the spiral staircase, and the embrace in which Jesse dissolves into molecules. In sum, these are all sequences that arguably accord with Deleuze's assertion that the emergence of a little time in the pure state destabilises the narrative mastery of space and diverts characters and audience from narrative. As Deleuze describes, characters like Jesse and Céline 'saw rather than acted, they were seers' (2005b: xi). Given too much time and space in which to look and think, they reveal themselves by a process of painful reflexive awareness, 'where the character does not act without seeing himself acting' (2005b: 6). Forced to fill the time-image with something other than cliché, the slackers, lucid dreamers, Don, Jesse and Céline confront the abyss of their existence beyond the narrative, while their dislocation is endemic to a similarly adrift audience.

The political element emerges because in *Pierrot Le Fou* and so in *Slacker* the 'time out' of the time-image opposes the notion of national narratives, or narratives of nationhood. Benedict Anderson argued that the nation was 'an imagined political community' (1983: 6) and that the time of the nation was linear and progressive, 'moving steadily down (or up) history' (1983: 26). More recently, however, Georg Sørenson has observed the dissolution of nation states in Europe and identified a new 'community of sentiment' in their place (2003: 83). David Martin-Jones contends that Deleuze is pertinent to this evolution because of the way that national history and identity is explored through narrative. Moreover, he echoes Derrida in de-centring Europe as a normative culture of reference when he claims that 'it is no longer enough to simply posit the time-image as the European other of the American movement-image' (2006: 223). Following King, who identifies *Slacker* as 'a point of transition' (2005: 84) between 'decentred, downplayed or fragmented narrative' (2005: 63) and 'multi-strand narrative' (2005: 84), the cinema of Linklater may be appreciated as one more 'product of attempts made by marginalised or minority groups to create a new sense of identity' (Martin-Jones 2006: 6) that has often resulted in and from the deployment of the time-image. In the cinema of Linklater, the time-image is aimed at reterritorialising contemporary America in the style of films that employ 'unusual time schemes [to] negotiate transformations of national identity' (Martin-Jones 2006: 19). More specifically, it relates to the way in which 'American independent films [...] use their narratives to deterritorialise dominant myths of American national identity' (Martin-Jones 2006: 11). Mirroring the origins of the time-image in the 'any spaces whatsoever' of post-war Europe, the time-image in the cinema of Linklater emerges from the streets of Austin both during and following the triumphalism of the first and second Gulf Wars conducted by the Texas-based Bush dynasty, when America was so media-addled by propaganda that victory in the Gulf was paraded as a foregone conclusion. The oppositional tactic and result, as identified by Stam, is that 'lately we find a *slackening* of narrative time' (2000: 318; emphasis added).

The time-image in the cinema of Linklater fuses with the ethos and practice of slacking because it refuses to conform and tends to enshrine alienation instead. It (and by extension the cinema of Linklater) opposes corporate America by inaction as surely as refusing to stand when President Bush enters a room. Where a montage of movement-images constitutes and enables a linear timeline of nationhood, the displacement of the narrative by a collage of time-images may deterritorialise this nationhood and even constitute a revolution against the overbearing myths of its identity. The occurrence of a time-image also signifies modernity's confrontation with its own limitations, which may explain why and how films directed by Godard, Antonioni, Tarkovsky, Wenders, Erice and Linklater have acknowledged the difficulties of France, Italy, the Soviet Union, Germany, Spain and the USA respectively, because it is the conflict between movement-images and time-images in their films that signals several national identities in crisis. It is, for example, in the cinema of Linklater that time-images occur as rare pauses in contemporary American cinema, denying the hastening of narrative and inspiring instead reflection upon agency and stasis. In several of them 'a cinema of seeing replaces action' (Deleuze 2005b: 9) because it is in these films that 'the action-image disappears in favour of the purely visual image of what a character *is*' (Deleuze 2005b: 13; emphasis in original). Moreover, Deleuze suggests that viewers who observe these temporalised bodies (such as Having A Breakthrough Day in *Slacker*, Mitch Kramer in *Dazed and Confused*, Jesse and Céline, and Don in *Fast Food Nation*) experience the same sense of hollow, hanging time that cannot be reconciled with their exterior life. To watch the films that enclose these characters is to read the image, seeking movement and pondering its infinite potential, especially when the slacker ethos denies the direction of that potential towards conventional objectives. Derided as pointless by those whose priorities it deliberately disrespected, *Slacker* was actually a collage of dissent against the era in which it was made. It rejected classical form and content and the intellect's understanding of time in favour of a Bergsonian celebration of intuition and the time-image, which is an entirely deliberate strategy because, as Linklater claims on the region 1 DVD commentary on *It's Impossible to Learn to Plow by Reading Books*, 'the ultimate rejection of Hollywood structure is to see time passing'. It is subsequently of note that the time-image was adopted by several American filmmakers of the 1980s and 1990s, whose grungy wave of alternative, regional and independent films such as *Ruby in Paradise* (Víctor Nuñez, 1993) and *Clerks* (Kevin Smith, 1994) often illustrated the antithesis of Republicanism. And it is clearly no coincidence, moreover, that the second tenure of President George W. Bush and the second Gulf War prompted the revival of cinematic slacking in the recent Mumblecore movement that was composed of no-budget, non-professional digital films that were highly indebted to the cinema of Linklater (and especially the 'plot' of *Before Sunrise*) such as *Quiet City* (Aaron Katz, 2007) and *In Search of a Midnight Kiss*.

What *Slacker* did quite uniquely for its time was follow the movement of ideas, which relates to the techniques of associative thought favoured by the Surrealists, the *dérive* of the Situationist International and the experiments with film language of Godard. *Slacker* and many of the films that Linklater wrote, co-wrote and/or directed afterwards thus allowed for the expression of ideas that simply could not be voiced or visualised within the pre-existing structures of dominant modes of production. Because 'the frame for Deleuze is unstable, dissolvable into the flux of time' (Stam 2000: 259), so life in *Slacker* seeps beyond the frame as it does so often in the cinema of Linklater. Time-images create this incessant flow of life and dissolve the patterns of street-based impressions and encounters within the film. The reterritorialisation of American values thus occurs in *Slacker's* alternative history of the neverending moment. *Slacker* is a blog or tweet of what is actually happening at street level long before online social networking sites cleared the streets of slackers. And, unsurprisingly therefore, when the time-image appears in the cinema of Linklater it is in its representation of the street as a Bakhtinian carnival that occurs with full awareness of its unique meaning in *this* time and *this* space.

Writing during the 1920s, when the Russian people and their customs were being homogenised and restricted under Soviet rule, Bakhtin drew his theories of folk culture from a study of François Rabelais, in whose satirical and scatological vision he identified the prospering of a cultural life based upon the interaction of distinct individual voices that opposed the official language and its version of culture. In *Rabelais and His World* (1965), Bakhtin proposed that the popular revelry of the Renaissance period described by Rabelais signified a spirit of resistance. He called this 'carnival' and described it as an organic form of life with its own time and place. What may now be examined is how Linklater, being part of Austin's mid-1980s slacker community, supposed himself to be involved in Bakhtin's concept of oppositional, street level, un-funded folk culture and how this contributed to the creation of *Slacker*. As Linklater states of the streets of Austin: 'That's where I saw the real world. It wasn't on the six o'clock news, it wasn't anywhere on the media. There was the official world and there was the world of people's real feelings and problems' (in Walsh 1998).

What happens in the street is central to the theories of Bakhtin, whose ideas of the chronotope and carnival conclude this investigation into the form and content of slack. As stated, Bakhtin defines a chronotope (literally 'time space') as:

> The intrinsic connectedness of temporal and spatial relationships that are artistically expressed in literature [in which] time, as it were, thickens, takes on flesh, becomes artistically visible; likewise, space becomes charged and responsive to the movements of time. (2006c: 84)

The convergence of this theory with that of Deleuze thus allows for the locating of the time-image within a certain space to attain specific meaning. Just as Bakhtin contends that 'the real-life chronotope is constituted by the public square' (2006c: 131), so the connection with the urban area traversed in Debord's *dérive* points to an affinity with the streets that feature so meaningfully in the cinema of Linklater. For Bakhtin, as for so many characters in *Slacker*, *Dazed and Confused*, *Waking Life* and others, 'time is collective, that is, it is differentiated and measured only by the events of *collective* life; everything that exists in this time exists solely for the collective' (2006c: 206; emphasis in original). Correlatively, the Austin of *Slacker* becomes subject to the slacker's Bergsonian intuition of time that is expressed by Having a Breakthrough Day:

> I've had a total recalibration of my mind, you know. I mean, it's like, I've been banging my head against this 19th century type of, um, what? Thought mode? Construct? Human construct? Well, the wall doesn't exist. It's not there, you know. I mean, they tell you, look for the light at the end of the tunnel. Well, there is no tunnel. There's just no structure. The underlying order is chaos.

Finally, therefore, in relation to the Cubist approach to film it is summative to note that Bakhtin contends that 'the single great event that is life (both human and natural) emerges in its multiple sides and aspects, and they are all equally indispensable and significant within it' (2006c: 211). Moreover, in what could serve as a description of Cubism, Bakhtin states that 'all of these [sides] were merely different sides of one and the same unified event, and all sides shared an identity with one another' (ibid.). Thus, where Bakhtin enables a conclusion to this theorising is in relation to carnival, which with its emphasis on form as an active component of meaning in art is, like Cubism, ideal for application to the cinema of Linklater. Bakhtin's concern for the folk culture that was under threat from an increasing totalitarianism certainly has its echo in the preoccupations of the people in the streets of *It's Impossible to Learn to Plow by Reading Books*, *Slacker*, *Dazed and Confused*, *Before Sunrise*, *SubUrbia*, *Waking Life*, *Before Sunset*, *Live from Shiva's Dance Floor* and *Fast Food Nation*. Prior to World War II, the rejection of folk culture in Europe was part of the rise of Fascism that took ethnic cleansing to be compatible with European cultural centrism. Direct parallels with the anti-Communist crusade of Vietnam-era Republican America are the stuff of extremists but, even so, a sense of oppression was definitely a characteristic of the post-Vietnam slacker community in Austin and a reason for its enduring collective approach to acts of creative expression that included music, art and filmmaking. Where this activity connects so firmly with the theories that Bakhtin puts forward in 'Discourse in the Novel' (2006d [1934–35]) is in his emphasis on heteroglossia (meaning co-existence and conflict in language that holds Socratic dialogue as a discursive mechanism), and on carnival as the structuring principle of streetlife and its consequent shaping effect on language, where film should be recognised as a language too. Carnival opposes official culture in form and content and is associated with Socialism, instinct and the kind of spontaneous but doomed creativity of the people in that same inter-war period that James Joyce captures in *Finnegans Wake* (1939), wherein the everyman protagonist goes by the initials H. C. E., one interpretation of which is 'Here Comes Everybody'.[5] This celebration of collective intuition duly opposes the kind of official language and culture that breaks people down in both senses of the phrase. Writing on the analogous pre-Renaissance period in which François Rabelais wrote (and thereby wresting a critique of Stalinism that effectively drew a parallel between the oppressiveness of sixteenth-century Catholicism and twentieth-century Stalinism, but metaphorically so and therefore less life-endangering[6]), Bakhtin's observations indicate that 'the generations that lived through those years had to work out for themselves fresh categories by which the utterly new and bewildering universe into which they had been thrust would let itself be known' (Holquist 1984: xiv). Such, in its purest form, was the ideal of slacking too.

Instead of the closed, single, linear, conventional texts of the official culture that brokered no independent interpretations based on intuition, Bakhtin described the notion of an 'open text' by which an audience might enter and bring about change from below. Parallels with regional or 'independent' attempts at a viable American cinema such as Linklater's Detour Filmproduction, the Austin Film Society and their Austin Film Studios are thus apparent. This is particularly evident in the way that the efforts of communities such as these that seek expression through independent means may find themselves embroiled in a political conflict with the kind of corporate machine that engineers a synergy of global production, distribution and marketing. As globalising conglomerates, major film studios might be said to supply an 'official' product made from franchises, generic templates and studio packaging, and it is perhaps only in 'independent' American cinema that the hubbub and brouhaha of carnival allows 'independent' American people to exist and express their intuition in their own time and space. At another level, moreover, it begs comparison with liminal cinemas worldwide and therefore the status of independent American cinema in the world market.[7]

In conclusion, where Bakhtin matches Bergson, Deleuze, Debord, Godard and Linklater is by seeking new relations between form and content that might inspire, enable and give meaning to revolution. A stifled language, for example, might be out-manoeuvred by an expressive physicality, just as limited access to cranes, tracking rails and Steadicams inspires an oppositional hand-held aesthetic in 'independent' cinema. It is by these means that the development of independent filmmaking practices tally with the carnivalisation of speech and physical expression in communities that oppose hegemony in their expression. Just as Bakhtin carnivalises the present because it is a hope for the future, so the cinema of Linklater carnivalises the time of its characters in order to oppose the entrenchment of corporate puppeteering in American politics. In cementing the validity of this approach to 'independent' cinema, moreover, it should be noted that carnival is a common synonym for festival, whereby the ritualised spectacles of the marketplace that so inspired Bakhtin find their counterpart in the likes of Sundance, Telluride and Austin. Just as Bakhtin defines carnival by its confluence of 'ritual spectacles, carnival pageants [and] shows of the marketplace [that] does not acknowledge any distinction between actors and spectators' (1984a: 5–7), so a festival full of filmmakers includes screenings (ritual spectacles), prize-giving (carnival pageants) and interviews and debates (shows of the marketplace). The carnival/festival is thus the culmination of the production process (of foodstuffs, crafts or films) that enables 'the second life of the people, who for a time entered the utopian realm of community, freedom, equality and abundance' (1984a: 9). Like a carnival, a film festival such as the one that takes place in Austin every October enables this utopian realm of community with workshops and a multitude of informal get-togethers. Together they enable the exploration of alternative viewpoints and practices that oppose the official versions provided by Hollywood, Fox News and MTV, which only offer what Bakhtin calls 'the triumph of a truth already established' (ibid.).

Clearly, in following this analogy one should avoid any utopian vision of streetlife that ignores the grotesquerie that Rabelais celebrated and the business of film funding and distribution sometimes resembles. On the one hand, Bakhtin's railing against the restrictions imposed on Russian novelists, who were required to imitate the official exemplification of Maxim Gorky as a more ideologically submissive dramatist, may even correlate with the manner in which 'independent' American filmmakers including Linklater have sometimes conformed to Hollywood commissions for generic product, albeit with different grades of subversion. Nevertheless, even here one may see the vampiric relationship that Hollywood nurtures with independent filmmakers and their ideas as one which resembles the Russian government's relationship to folklore and the carnival, which 'had to be tolerated and even legalized outside the official sphere' (ibid.). In opposition to the 'official' Hollywood emphasis on franchises and generic product that provide 'all that was ready-made and complete' (Bakhtin 1984a: 11), what might be termed 'unofficial' independently-made American films suffer limited distribution. Films like *Slacker*, *Tape* and *Fast Food Nation* must therefore be budgeted with fore-knowledge of this limitation because many will be unseen beyond the festival circuit. They are fated to bear the stigma of an unmarketable 'grotesque realism' that corresponds to the kind of low-budget filmmaking that matches raw-boned form to rough-edged content, and thereby relates to Bakhtin's observation that 'during the classic period the grotesque did not die but was expelled from the sphere of official art to live and develop in certain "low" non-classic areas' (1984a: 301–31). Yet what is grotesque about these films may be posited ironically as a deliberate affront to the conformist propriety of a society modelled on the ruling government. That is to say, the 'grotesque' is the threat of liberalism and the unhindered communication between members of an unregimented collective that is expressed in its creativity, music, dress, films and dialogue. Because the intellect perceives only an absence of logic when confronted by an image that confounds its scientific worldview, slackers were denounced as lazy wasters by those whose attention to competition, conformity and conventions could not countenance a world in which *not* working, *not* competing and *not* conforming could ever be worthwhile or respected.[8] Moreover, because slacking upholds the value of philosophy and reflection, it could be denounced as an absence of corporate values in the context of the Republican hegemony that encouraged the post-*Slacker* reterritorialisation of Austin in the 1990s by more than 350 high-tech companies such as IBM, Motorola, Tandem, Texas Instruments and Dell. Instead of being respected and maintained as a valid, alternative lifestyle, slacking was turned into an insult by the media and redeployed accordingly by President Bill Clinton in 1994 when he told 'cheering college students at UCLA that they ha[d] been unfairly maligned as "slackers," but will be called on to prove themselves worthy of the nation's promise' (Farrell 1994). However, just by walking and talking, the cinema of Linklater celebrates non-conformity as the 'new' grotesque, for walking and talking, as recognised by the writer and psychogeographer Will Self is predicated upon movement and expression at 'a pre-industrialised pace that opposes economic imperatives' (2009). Consequently, for all its cultural activity, a place such as Austin may still find itself defined as a 'low, non-classic area', which tallies with the ethos of the slackers who maintain the carnival caught in *Slacker, Dazed and Confused, SubUrbia, Waking Life* and other films directed by Linklater, including those that find metaphors for what is both valued and increasingly missed about contemporary Austin in Vienna (*Before Sunrise*), Paris (*Before Sunset*) and the New York of the 1930s (*Me and Orson Welles*). Indeed, this will always be so because, as Bakhtin describes, the function of the carnival-grotesque, which is explored in the cinema of Linklater, is:

> To consecrate inventive freedom, to permit the combination of a variety of different elements and their rapprochement. To liberate from the prevailing point of view of the world, from conventions and established truths, from clichés, from all that is humdrum and universally accepted. The carnival spirit offers the chance to have a new outlook on the world, to realise the relative nature of all that exists, and to enter a completely new order of things. (1984a: 34)

Even if, as Anti-Artist explains in *Slacker*, opposition by inaction means that in this new order of things you 'don't do much really, just read, and work here, and, uh, sleep and eat, and, uh, watch movies.'

Notes

1   Many art historians have recently concerned themselves with the reconciliation of Cubism with Classicism. In literary studies, for example, the resolution has been pursued by such academics as Edna Rosenthal, who inserts Aristotle's Poetics into Modernist aesthetic in Rosenthal, Edna (2008) *Aristotle and Modernism: Aesthetic Affinities of T. S. Eliot, Wallace Stevens and Virginia Woolf.* Brighton: Sussex Academic Press. Another example is María Dolores Jiménez Blanco in her keynote address entitled 'The Perception of Spanish Art in America' at the conference on Hispanic Visual Cultures: Fractured Identities held at Cardiff University on 3 July 2009.

2   *Les Lettres Françaises* was the literary supplement of *L'Humanité* and Aragon was its director. The comment on Godard appeared in the issue dated 9 September 1965.

3   Along with Naomi Klein's *No Logo* (2000), Schlosser's *Fast Food Nation* fostered awareness and even inspired radical activism. An extensive interview with Schlosser can be found on the Region 2 DVD of Morgan Spurlock's documentary *Super Size Me* (2004).

4   For a relevant and revisionist appreciation of what it really means to be 'Capraesque', see Girgus, Sam B. (2007) 'The Modernism of Frank Capra and European Ethical

Thought', in Paul Cooke (ed.) *World Cinema's 'Dialogues' with Hollywood*. Hampshire and New York: Palgrave. 86–102.

5   The main character in *Finnegan's Wake* is Humphrey Chimpden Earwicker, whose initials H.C.E. serve as an acronym for numerous phrases (including 'Here Comes Everybody') throughout the book, which is written in a highly idiosyncratic language that includes puns and made-up words, literary allusions, free association and a stream of consciousness style that dismisses plot and evokes instead a highly oneiric sensation.

6   Bakhtin is responding to the official 1934 campaign to promote obligatory Social Realism in the Russian novel. Instead, he proposes linguistic and stylistic variety that might counter the 'official version' of Russia. Thus he advocates the inversion of categories and the development of satire, Surrealism, and independent thought.

7   This will be analysed in Chapter Four.

8   The term may have been common in the 1950s if we are to believe the spiteful refrain of Mr. Strickland (James Tolkan) in *Back to the Future* (Robert Zemeckis, 1985): 'You've got a real attitude problem, McFly. You're a slacker! You remind me of your father when he went here. He was a slacker too.'

CHAPTER FOUR

American Art House

Whether hanging out in the real Austin (*Slacker*, *Waking Life* and the project known as *Boyhood*), a metaphorical one (*Dazed and Confused*, *SubUrbia*, *A Scanner Darkly*) or the metaphysical ones of Vienna (*Before Sunrise*) and Paris (*Before Sunset*), walking and talking is what characters in the cinema of Richard Linklater do best. Out of several themes that are common to the most emblematic films, including the impossibility of distinguishing between what is real and what is not, dialogue is the most determinant factor in their form, content, meaning, making and marketing. Dialogue is also crucial to the way in which the films are engendered, rehearsed, shot and more often than not find their audience, by word of mouth that is maintained by the extended grapevine of online chat and buyer reviews. On one level, this emphasis on dialogue attests to Linklater's directorial interest in the theatre and evident enthusiasm for collaborating with actors, but it is also what distinguishes the films from much of American cinema and, within that context, Linklater from many of his contemporaries. The emphasis on perambulatory dialogue also indicates the dialogic nature of films that, as Lesley Speed contends, 'are radical in their affirmation that intellectual and reflective thought can be pleasurable, an idea that deviates strikingly from the association of American society with "dumbing down" in government, the media, education, science, and religion' (2007: 101). Thus, this dialogue is oppositional, partly because it resists any hege-monic dictum such as conservative political doctrine or the action-driven template of Hollywood and partly because it serves as a vehicle for the expression, integra-tion and cross-pollination of European intellectual traditions with those of popular American entertainment, albeit primarily in relation to the audiences for art-house cinema. Accordingly, this dialogue-heavy account of the production, distribution and marketing of the cinema of Linklater considers the extent to which *Tape*, *Me and Orson Welles*, *Before Sunrise* and *Before Sunset* inherit, warrant, express, embody and suffer the notion of art-house cinema.

The artistic potential of film was recognised and exploited in early twentieth-century Europe by movements such as Surrealism and Expressionism. Meanwhile, the presumption of art in relation to American cinema had its precedent in the prestige pictures and literary adaptations of filmmakers such as the 'independent' D.W. Griffith, whose *The Birth of a Nation* (1915) begins with 'a plea for the art of the motion picture'. Post-World War II, this conflation of independence with art inspired the emergence of Italian Neo-realism and the French New Wave, the associated rise of film studies as an academic discipline with interdisciplinary potential, the consequent rise of repertory cinemas and the anti-establishment enthusiasm of certain audiences for alternatives to Hollywood filmmaking. The first art-house cinemas in America were 'exhibition sites [that] featured art galleries in the lobbies, served coffee, and offered specialized and "intelligent" films to a discriminating audience that paid high admission prices for such distinctions' (Wilinsky 2001: 1–2). Post-war European and Asian cinema played well in New York, Los Angeles and college towns as did documentaries, the avant-garde and the emerging cult films of the midnight movie circuit. In the 1960s and 1970s the notion of art cinema moved away from movements to embrace the practice and product of auteurism, when 'rising up as a new, emergent culture in reaction to changes in social values, cultural hierarchies, and industrial systems, art cinema shaped itself as an alternative to dominant culture' (Wilinsky 2001: 3). Linklater recalls the impact of the French New Wave as 'important to everyone probably, who has made films since then,'[1] but he also credits the art-house cinemas in the university cities of Houston and Austin (as well as his own Austin Film Society) for enabling him to see what was going on in World cinema:

I don't just leave it to the French: a little bit later and there was what was going on in German cinema, what was going on in England and Japan and America too. Having caught the tail-end of the golden era of repertory cinema when I was first falling in love with cinema meant I could go to a theater and watch double features. All the great films I saw in theaters. Even if it was a 16mm print and there were four other people in the cinema at two in the afternoon, it was still great.

In addition, his awareness grew of what was possible in America:

We don't call it an American New Wave but I was really inspired by those films too. Shirley Clarke, Cassavetes, Lionel Rogosin: American indies that were just sort of there. Once there was a market there were distributors and theaters, but that was pretty non-existent back in the seventies when I was growing up. Back then there was mainstream Hollywood and there were exploitation films at drive-ins. And if it wasn't an exploitation film, if it couldn't be shown at a drive-in, what was it? They weren't showing *Woman Under the Influence* at a drive-in. So Cassavetes had to kind of self-distribute his films.

This mix of art-house films from around the world with independent American cinema would have a definitive influence on Linklater. Like many of his generation who were able to study film, he saw the work of amateur, regional, and independent filmmakers such as Cassavetes alongside retrospective screenings of films from the Hollywood studio system that had inspired the French New Wave to champion what they claimed were auteurist filmmakers such as Alfred Hitchcock and Howard Hawks. Linklater was a prime example of those attending art-house cinemas, who sought such 'distinction from their film-going experiences [that they] searched for films and theater environments different from those offered at mainstream film theaters' (Wilinsky 2001: 2). However, although the American art-house circuit may have marketed itself and its programming as an alternative to that of the major studios and distribution chains, in truth it has always remained 'in constant negotiation with the mainstream cinema, a process that has ultimately shaped both cultures' (Wilinsky 2001: 4). Instead of mostly generic entertainment, art-house cinemas often offered films built from narrative experimentation and ambitious play with form to the extent that, perhaps inevitably, their determined distinctiveness led to an accumulation of so many conventions that 'by the 1980s this [art] film practice had become almost a broad-based genre in itself' (Sklar 1993: 508). Non-linear narratives, long takes and enigmatic stares, moody interiors, threatening exteriors and open-ended dialogues about faith, sex and death were to the art house what gunfights, car chases and happy endings were to the mainstream. Art films tended to explore psychological problems without resolution. Their protagonists could thus be inconsistent, while the films embodied the fragmentation that empowered the art film to become 'episodic, akin to picaresque and processional forms, or [...] pattern coincidence to suggest the workings of an impersonal and unknown causality' (Bordwell 1985: 206). The art film became that of loose ends, unanswered questions and uncertain futures. Yet, as Speed states:

> Despite European film's influence on the generation of American filmmakers that emerged from film schools in the 1960s, the counterculture's influence on American cinema failed to prevent Hollywood's gravitation toward the blockbuster phenomenon, from which the high-concept film emerged. (1994: 80)

Nevertheless, the impact of European art-house cinema on independent American filmmakers remained a factor in the form, content, marketing and reception of their films to the extent that it is possible to speak of a dialogue that opened up in the 1960s between American and European filmmakers, one that led directly to the New Hollywood era that was heralded by *Bonnie and Clyde* (Arthur Penn, 1967).

As described by Mark Harris in *Scenes from a Revolution: The Birth of the New Hollywood*, *Bonnie and Clyde* was an attempt to 'bring a Nouvelle Vague aesthetic to as American a subject as Dust Bowl bank robbers' (2008: 15). The script by Robert Benton and David Newman combined the generic conventions of the American period gangster film with the aesthetic stylings and 'live fast, die young' existentialism of several key films of the French New Wave. Benton and Newman based their script on the 'studied disregard for the moral and narrative strictures of Hollywood filmmaking'

(Harris 2008: 7) that they identified in Truffaut's *Jules et Jim* (*Jules and Jim*, 1962) and were delighted when it attracted the directorial ambition of Truffaut to make a film in America, as well as the bonus but more ambiguous interest of Godard. Incidentally, as a precursor to Linklater's *Before Sunrise*, there were clear Texan, even Austinite origins to this film about boy meets girl, America meets Europe, and mainstream genre film-making meets art-house stylings, aesthetics and philosophies. Benton had gone to the University of Texas at Austin in the early 1950s and, as he explained, 'everybody in Texas grew up with Bonnie and Clyde' (Harris 2008: 12). With its abrupt shifts of tone, jump cuts, elements of pastiche, emphasis on ambiguous and explicit sexuality and hard-boiled dialogue, *Bonnie and Clyde* picked up the baton proffered by Godard's *À bout de souffle*, which had itself taken it from Monogram Pictures, and passed it on to America's youth. Eventually directed by Arthur Penn, *Bonnie and Clyde* revealed the viability and relevance of New Wave stylings to the American public and major studios and thus opened up a dialogue that continues through the cinema of Linklater.

Key points in this dialogue include a preference *for* dialogue, as well as the affined expression of time through time-images that effect a contrast with the subscription to action and movement-images in the kind of Hollywood product that Bordwell theorised and Paul Cooke describes as 'action-driven fictions, produced in the "continuity style" which elides the constructed nature of film as a medium' (2007: 2–3). *Slacker*, for example and by name alone, promises, nay proclaims an oppositional *lack* of action, while *Dazed and Confused*, *Waking Life* and *Before Sunrise* are all titles redolent of sleepy hiatus. In truth, however, the cinema of Linklater is rarely still or silent. On the contrary, its supposed 'idleness' actually illustrates Samuel Johnson's contention that 'if we were idle, there would be no growing weary; we should all entertain one another' (in Stevenson 2009: 1). However, as Stevenson observes in *An Apology for Idlers* (2009 [1877]), conflict arises because 'the presence of people who refuse to enter in the great handicap race for sixpenny pieces, is at once an insult and a disenchantment for those who do' (ibid.). In comparison with the protagonists of action-driven fictions, slackers resemble what Stevenson described as truants from 'formal and laborious science, [who] for the trouble of looking [...] acquire the warm and palpitating facts of life [and] speak with ease and opportunity to all varieties of men' (2009: 6). Yet, where the hagiography of an auteurist approach might dress up Linklater's reputation for independence in the guise of a purposeful truant from industry, the truth is that a dialogue occurs here too. That is to say, the cinema of Linklater is engaged in dialogue with regional, independent and studio-made American cinema as well as European philosophies and film aesthetics, new technologies and the vagaries of marketing and distribution opportunities. This is no tournament of binary face-offs that sets independent cinema against Hollywood or the American intellect against European intuition, but a dialogue that is best understood in relation to the concept of dialogism proposed by Bakhtin in *The Dialogic Imagination* (2006a [1975]).

Bakhtin argues that 'all literature is caught up in the process of "becoming"' (2006a: 5), which corresponds to Henri Bergson's aforementioned concept of time as something incomplete and eternally becoming. Bakhtin also maintains that literary works may be divided into those that are dialogic and those that are monologic. The dialogic work is that which seeks correspondence with other multiple works and a revisionist approach to what has gone before. Although centered upon literature, Bakhtin's term extends to language and thought, suggesting that whatever is said must exist not only in answer to what has been said before but also in anticipation of response. As Holquist explains, 'a word, discourse, language or culture undergoes "dialogization" when it becomes relativized, de-privileged, aware of competing definitions for the same things' (1981: 427). Dialogism thus dissolves or explodes any attempt at monologue that aims to be authoritative or absolute and so confronts the monotony of all that is monolithic. It is a dynamic process that both demands and enables an endless revisioning of the world; but it is not merely intertextuality, which too often suggests that everything has already been said and done. Rather, it expresses something of an optimistic response to existentialist challenges. In relation to the cinema of Linklater, the conceit of a film as a dialogic work that is itself constructed from a collaborative dialogue amongst its makers and which features dialogue between protagonists as its primary mode of expression denotes a particularly meaningful coincidence. In respect of its commercial prospects this points to what the filmmaker admits is a default and problematic marketing position for many of his films: 'If it's too smart it becomes an art film.'

Alongside *Waking Life*, perhaps the most experimental and self-consciously smart film amongst those directed by Linklater is *Tape*, an adaptation of screenwriter Stephen Belber's own single set, one act, three character play that was financed by the New York-based InDigEnt (Independent Digital Entertainment) company that provided small budgets on a profit-sharing basis to filmmakers willing to embrace the potential and limitations of shooting on digital video.[2] The impetus to filmmaking and film movements from new technologies like this is a recurring phenomenon, although Linklater's first experience of digital filmmaking was a cautionary one:

> You can now just point and capture things, and that's a great thing, obviously, for the world and communication, but it doesn't necessarily equal art. [...] There's a skill involved, and one of the first things people find out in filmmaking is that the skill isn't being able to push a red button on a camera. The real skill is in storytelling. (In Savlov 2009: 41–2)

Tape tells the tale of the reunion of drug dealer Vince (Ethan Hawke) with high school friend Jon (Robert Sean Leonard), a documentary filmmaker who may once have date-raped Vince's ex-girlfriend Amy (Uma Thurman), an assistant district attorney who turns up to question the veracity and interpretation of the remembered events. However, as Geoff King describes, 'the aim, for Linklater, was to create something akin to a collage effect [that was] thematically motivated' (2009: 120). Although granted autonomy by InDigEnt, the challenge for Linklater was to shepherd a collective endeavour to fruition without overstating his authorial responsibility. Thus, in addition to filming with digital cameras and adhering to a specific time-frame, *Tape* was also somewhat experimental in its negotiation of authorship. As with *Slacker*, *Dazed and Confused* and *SubUrbia*, there was a cacophony of voices both onscreen and off, with Belber, editor Sandra Adair and the cast all arguing the work into existence. In particular, *Tape* was made in accordance with the kind of dialogue and collaborative working practice that Linklater coordinated at the start of his career:

> Yeah, as soon as I started working with other people, which was *Slacker*, that's exactly how we did it. I had these notes or texts, I would hand them to people and say: 'Lets read it!' And then they would start talking, taking notes, just a very collaborative thing.

Like Hitchcock's *Rope* (1948), *Tape* involves the construction of 'the specifically filmic [...] "between four walls" chronotope' (Stam 2000: 205) and the claustrophobia of its theatrical origins is exacerbated by Stephen J. Beatrice's four-walled set of a seedy Michigan hotel room. Set entirely within the time-frame of the film's 86 minutes, *Tape* leans towards experimentation and the 'smartness' of art while holding on to the mainstream, for, as a melodrama styled around the recriminations of a small number of people who challenge each other's memories, it is not unlike a particularly claustrophobic drawing room whodunnit. Linklater had directed theatrical productions while at university and professes great admiration for the British playwright Tom Stoppard, whose witty dialogue often addresses philosophical concepts and conundrums. His *Rosencrantz & Guildenstern Are Dead* (1966), for example, deals with two minor characters from Shakespeare's *Hamlet* who idly ponder their fate beyond the original work but find themselves equally sidelined and rendered powerless by their reality. Rather than take action, the two slacker courtiers kill time with absurdist, existentialist dialogue that would fit well into *Slacker*, *SubUrbia*, *Waking Life*, *Tape* and even *Before Sunrise* and *Before Sunset*. Similarly to Stoppard, the chance to explore existentialism in the shaping of a basic text like *Tape* into situation, character and dialogue is what attracts and inspires Linklater:

> It's always been my instinct to loosen it up with the actors and let them reimagine their characters. I tell actors: 'We've got to take this apart, find the beats!' My nightmare of an actor is someone who doesn't want to think much about it or work it through and personalise it and make it better. Even if I've written every word of the script and it happened to me, even if it's very personal to me, I'm not attached to the character. It's not me. This is the great thing about art. This is the beginning of it, but the end of it will be you. I'm not that beholden to recreating my own life specifically. I like it as a jumping off place but I'm really more interested in what we can come up with, getting to some level that's not pre-ordained.

Despite the potential for diversion and digression in this creative process, *Tape* is fittingly a film with a one-track mind. Whip pans between the actors, stark lighting and the kind of over-emphatic editing allowed by the Final Cut Pro software all conspire to pin Vince and Jon to the grimy walls. As the confined space and combative dialogue make it impossible for the digital cameras to take in the whole scene and the fluctuations of expression as might occur in the theatre, the editing hurtles from face to face in an attempt to keep up with the characters' evolution. Leonard is ingratiating and insufferable as the character whose moral superiority turns to arrogance, while Hawke is magnetic and repulsive, alternately strutting and cowed. Their discussion turns into interrogation and the act of remembering becomes their punishment for forgetting. Amy turns up fifty minutes in to confront the men with the redundancy of any confession to her present situation and so the meaninglessness of any apology that relates only to an irrelevant past. For a film with such an emphasis on time in both its narrative dependency on a past event and the time-frame of the present encounter, *Tape* finds no curative quality to its passing. Instead, the lack of any resolution to its intrinsic dialogue corresponds to the conjoined notions of time and the dialogic work as things that are constantly becoming. Moreover, the multiple, contradictory perspectives of the characters and the shifting debate over which of the three can lay claim to ownership of the 'historical' past denotes the previously analysed Cubist notion of form and content in the film's expression of time and its remembrance.

Koresky calls *Tape* the 'polar opposite' of *Waking Life*, seeing 'debate without philosophy' (2004b) as its failing, which does hold true in comparison with the cinema of Eric Rohmer, for example, whose similarly intense, dialogue-driven films often feature a melange of neurotics, romantics and pragmatists in mostly playful, ironic, melancholic badinage that rarely fails to ferment philosophical debate. However, the true importance of *Tape* in the cinema of Linklater is that it comes between the more reverentially Rohmeresque *Before Sunrise* and *Before Sunset* in a much more meaningful manner than the brief animated interlude shared by Jesse and Céline in *Waking Life*. If *Before Sunrise* corresponds to the idealism and potential of youth and youthful sexuality, *Tape* interrogates regret for wasted time and inexact recollection. It is therefore the halfway point on a journey to *Before Sunset*, which investigates the possible revival of idealism and the recapturing of all that potential. The space between *Tape* and *Before Sunset* is what Koresky calls 'the uphill journey from emotional retardation to a spiritual solace, from digital-video grime to 35mm splendor' (ibid.). *Tape* might be the visit home made by a young American played by Ethan Hawke between his visits to Vienna and Paris, for it is not merely a pause or digression but an exploration of the angst that occurs when separated from the idealism of *Before Sunrise* and the reclaimed potential of *Before Sunset*. As such it connects with and perhaps in part explains this enthusiasm for experimentation with film form, practice and technology that Linklater expressed in 2001, firstly with the digitally-filmed then rotoscoped *Waking Life* and then with his assault on the pre-fabricated limitations of the time-frame, single tiny set and theatrical text by means of hand-held digital cameras and editing on an Apple computer of *Tape*. Together, as Roger Ebert surmised, these two films served as 'instruction manuals about how to use the tricky new tools' (2001). Consequently, they extend the dialogue with film history and future film, not only by exploring the new dynamics of digital filmmaking, rotoscoping and other new technologies but in the way the emphasis on dialogue, character, time and the *durée* of the *dérive* draw on 'the SI [Situationist International] and other European movements to posit an avant-garde ancestry for recent American independent film' (Speed 2007:

104). That is to say, on the one hand *Tape* is a test drive of digital gadgets, while on the other it is a coked-up Rohmer that suggests how 'Linklater's allegiance to the European avant-garde explores what American cinema might have been if market-driven, high-concept films had not achieved dominance' (ibid.).

Tape was picked up for distribution by the independent Lions Gate and won the Lanterna Magica Prize at the 2001 Venice Film Festival as well as a nomination for Thurman as Best Actress at the Independent Spirit awards. Founded in 1984 and originally called the Friends of Independents Awards, the 'Spirits' were renamed in 1986 partly out of the aforementioned impossibility of categorising any film as truly independent. Instead, the 'spirit' of independence was celebrated then and since in awards made to films that arguably still 'felt' independent despite their distribution by such parent companies as Paramount (e.g. *Brokeback Mountain* [Ang Lee, 2005]) and Fox (e.g. *Juno* [Jason Reitman, 2007]). The matter of independence was thus ironised, which nevertheless fuels Speed's observation that:

> The studios in recent decades have absorbed modes of filmmaking that were previously associated with independent production [to the extent that] the contrast in Linklater's career between market-driven entertainment and contemplative art cinema can be understood in relation to [this] blurring of the distinction between independent and mainstream American film since the 1980s. (2007: 99)

This blurring is also a dialogue between independent and mainstream cinema involving technologies, demographics and systems that are in constant flux. As Linklater contends:

> Distribution and marketing have changed incredibly. The bottom line is that marketing has become so expensive. The radical thing that freaked everybody out was releasing movies on DVD around the same time as the cinema release. This gap business of either going to the movies or waiting six months for the DVD, that seemed like such an affront, such a threat to the theater-going experience; but I didn't really look at it that way. Different markets. By the 1980s it was already a different game really.

However, in relation to the recent fostering of independent films by the distribution wings of the majors, Linklater is less bothered by the irony of the matter than by prevailing cynicism:

> The studios have now abdicated that role completely. They're not interested in art. They're in a business that precludes something that might resonate with adults or anybody with a certain sensibility. I've seen that gap just get wider and wider and wider but at least they're really honest now. It's like, 'We're not in that business', you know? A lot of those distributors have gone out of business already. Two of my movies in the 1990s were distributed by Warner

Independent. Well, 'big Warner' just said: 'Ah, let's just close that division. It doesn't make much money, if anything. It's kind of a break-even business. No one's going to complain if that just goes away and we just concentrate on *Harry Potter*.' So we lost another outlet. That world was under attack anyway, and then the bigger economic situation in the world has been a second tidal wave right through it. So right now there's just nothing left.

In forging ahead with low-budget films shot on digital video, the InDigEnt enterprise and *Tape* in particular challenged the assumption that the audience for art-house cinema was different from that for the mainstream. Generically speaking, *Tape* is an intense hybrid of melodrama and thriller that for all its formal and digital experimentation remains conversant with the conventions of the theatre. At the same time, however, its use of digital technology points to new modes of reception for art-house and independent films that extend from home-viewing on DVD, Blu-ray, Netflix and computer to inexpensive digital distribution and projection. Linklater sees this use of digital technology as essential to safeguarding, enabling and extending the territory of independence:

> I was talking to Steven Soderbergh about this and he said, 'I can't wait until there's digital projection because all distributors do is ship prints and collect money.' And then if shipping the prints wasn't the deal, if the theaters could just download your digital film, even if you shot on film, they could project it digitally, which looks great and then you really don't need to make your separate deal with your distributor. All distributors are is kind of a middleman between the film and the audience anyway. You could almost cut him out.

As Linklater explains, this kind of cheap, direct distribution changes the process of marketing and, moreover, removes any middleman from the dialogue sought by filmmakers with their audience:

> Anyone can come up with an ad, a poster and a trailer if you really want to go all the way. Why would some guy spend 35 million of his own money and then give the film to some small company that spends a million distributing it? It's just a matter of time before the guy who spends 35 million says, 'They didn't even care about it! I could have hired three people also!' So that's what's happening right now.

This potential boost to the viability of independent and art cinema may also extend a filmmaker's responsibility towards distribution and marketing. Linklater welcomes this development in particular:

> I haven't had too many good experiences with marketing. You have no control over marketing. It's frustrating. Filmmakers are control freaks and, collaborative as I am, I'm still really specific about what I'm going for. [A film] can have

a horrible film poster, and for me, who knows the history of film posters, to have a horrible film poster for your movie, I cannot explain to you how heart-breaking that is.

In approaching the grand chaos of this dialogue with marketers, producers, investors, distributors and the audience, Linklater and any film of his might be best understood in relation to Lyotard's ruling that 'a *self* [...] does not amount to much, but no self is an island; each exists in a fabric of relations that is now more complex and mobile than ever before' (1999: 15; emphasis in original). Linklater is thus a participant in a dialogue resembling this complex and mobile fabric of relations that involves a film and its maker with new and old forms of industry as well as with diachronic and synchronic film histories, the tradition and subversion of culture, and revised forms of production, distribution and reception. Nevertheless, his ambition is tempered by caution:

> Most people who come up to you and say they liked your movie watched it at home. You just have to accept that. Every filmmaker in the world has this ideal-istic notion of, 'Oh, how nice they were sitting in a huge theater watching it on a big beautiful screen!' But they weren't. It used to not bother me much at all if people were bootlegging a bad video back in the video days when things were being passed around. Once that was happening, I was like, 'Oh, that's good, it means people want to see it.' When it was hand to hand it was good news. But now with the viral thing you've got to be a lot more careful.

In ensuring that the dialogue keeps pace with new technologies and evolving defini-tions of independence, Linklater was especially keen to learn how to distribute his own films from the USA and UK release strategy of *Me and Orson Welles*, an adaptation of a 2008 Robert Kaplow novel about an ambitious young man's involvement with Welles' Mercury Theater Company during the 1937 New York production of *Julius Caesar*. The film had its premiere at the 2008 Toronto Film Festival but its release was delayed so that Linklater could explore new forms of distribution:

> After Toronto we could have taken offers, but that delay was really okay. That at least showed us, right, we've got be smart about this. For those of us who worked so hard on this film and cared so much about it, we really had bigger ambitions for it. When it comes out, I want it to have a bigger and better chance. There's new distribution that's coming about and I'm going to learn a lot about how this goes. I'm more involved this time than I ever have been with the release of any of my films since *Slacker*. I thought it was time to jump back in there and pay a little more attention because it seems like such a crucial time. And it has so much to do with social networking that I'm going to have to use that part of my brain that isn't the most fun, but it just seems like it's an essential time to be a part of the new 'whatever-it's-gonna-be'. Something's definitely over but it hasn't been completely mastered yet.

Richard Linklater directing Zac Efron (right) and Christian McKay in *Me and Orson Welles*

Although *Me and Orson Welles* was not self-distributed, it was handled by a new company called CinemaNX set up by the Isle of Man Media Development Fund that had financed its production. The film opened in November 2009 through Freestyle Releasing, backed by a campaign by former New Line marketing executive Russell Schwartz's Pandemic Marketing, with Hart/Lunsford Pictures funding the promotional costs. CinemaNX was cautious, selling the DVD rights to Warner Brothers in a deal brokered by Cinetic Media (and an exclusivity deal to the Tesco supermarket chain in the UK) but, as Linklater explains, 'holding back too. Instead of giving it to the distributor for a million bucks they want no commitment beyond a certain level. They believe in the film.' As a period film with a theatrical setting, *Me and Orson Welles* seems a particularly contrary example of independent filmmaking, which tends to favour contemporary realism. At the same time, however, with its teen-dream star (Zac Efron) and generic conventions it is an unlikely inhabitant of the art house. Linklater agrees:

> Yeah, its weird we're even in the rubric of independence. To me this feels like a studio type of film: PG13, fairly family friendly, not inaccessible. And yet the ground has sort of shifted enough that Hollywood is not making this sort of film anymore.

The dialogue thus falters, until new directions appear. As Linklater contends:

> There are two markets for *Me and Orson Welles*. There's an art film market and there's this 'because of Zac [Efron]' and the youthfulness of the audience and the movie. I'm taking that audience for granted, the ones who'll read reviews; but you really have to see to the teenage audience and for that you really have

to use social networking sites. The studio said that audience wasn't going to go, but I disagree. You want to be able to say, 'Fuck you, you're wrong!'

Thus the dialogue extends naturally to chat rooms, social networking sites, Twitter and whatever else comes along.[3]

Most pointedly, however, *Me and Orson Welles* may be appreciated as a dialogic work for the manner in which it relates to Welles, who Linklater describes as 'the progenitor and the martyr' of independent filmmaking:

> That's how the US looks at him and I think he took on that role to a large degree. There's a sadness that he didn't get a film made a year for twenty-five years, but what's great is that he made what he did. Americans tend to look at Welles like he was something tragic [but] I was refreshed being in the UK and I saw a European attitude to him, which was more about, 'Well gosh, he made however many masterpieces, arguably five or seven in so many different decades.' Name a playwright who had that kind of longevity! That's a successful career! Sure he struggled, but that's not so bad. That's not a tragic life on the surface. Anyone would sign up for that. And yet it's not enough. America in particular tends to chew up and spit out its artists.

The dialogue with Welles that *Me and Orson Welles* upholds is also one that resonates down through the history of independent filmmaking in America:

> Honestly, he's a guy out of time, you know. He would have done so much better if he'd been born however many years later. By the time the 1980s and 1990s came around he would have been like an Altman character who could have gotten funding worldwide for his little Shakespeare adaptations. That would have been great. But when he was living, his struggle just wasn't possible. So it's heartbreaking when you see a masterpiece like his *Othello*, which I think is the greatest Shakespeare adaptation ever made. If ever proof were needed that this guy was just an absolute pure filmmaking genius, just watch *Othello*. And *Chimes at Midnight*, which is really even more obscure. Those two are just brilliant. To know that they were so neglected, so forgotten. The way he financed them himself, the way he put them together, it must have been tough for him. Meanwhile Olivier is winning all the Oscars for *Hamlet*, you know, which really isn't all that cinematic. It must have been tough for Welles, who had been at the height of his acclaim, to know that he had done something so great and just see nobody give a fuck. It really must be humbling.

And what, if any is Welles's influence on the struggle of contemporary indie filmmakers?

> The struggle's the same. It's just so much easier now though. What Welles was going up against in the forties was still the full-blown studio system, which I love. But Welles was too enlarged of a talent to fit in. Welles barely got his RKO

premiere in the day, though he was totally willing to take the film himself and show it in tents. There's a parallel world where Welles took the film himself around the country and created a sensation everywhere he went with his new film and became the P. T. Barnum of movies. And then he became this renegade who profited from that and had his own alternate film universe that was Orson Welles.

The proximity of this alternate reality to the one that Linklater collaborated on creating with the independent production and distribution of *Me and Orson Welles* exemplifies how the dialogic work for the cinema is not only indicated by intertextuality but by influence and resonance in all aspects. For Linklater the experience of making this film was 'completely refreshing just to hang out with the early Welles', even though the experience 'goes against the biggest Welles theme of all, particularly in [*Citizen*] *Kane*, which is the unknowableness of the individual'. In terms of aesthetics and film style, Linklater claims he 'really, intentionally, never tried to get Wellesian. That would be ridiculous to shoot it like Welles would have because Welles wasn't a filmmaker at this point.' Nevertheless, the film does feature a curious indication of dialogism when an extra in the audience for *Julius Caesar* is made up to look like Gregg Toland, the cinematographer of *Citizen Kane* (1941), for, as Linklater claims, 'that marriage is born right there and it's a key moment in film history'. Most significantly, however, the dialogic nature of the film is the manner in which Linklater, like Welles, had to go to Europe to get film funding: 'Yes, *that's* very Wellesian. Maybe it's the Welles curse, you know. Maybe this film *is* ultimately Wellesian.'

Nevertheless, in Linklater's view the dialogic work and its connection with an audience is most often forestalled by marketing executives. The problem was that post-Toronto offers of distribution came tied to limited marketing strategies:

Ultimately you have multiple audiences and that's kind of anti-Hollywood right now. They want to hear that you have one very specific audience that's going to love it, even if that audience is 14–17-year-old girls or 17–21-year-old boys, because it's easy to market. The last thing they want to hear is that everyone might like the film, which is the case here.

According to Linklater, the cost of marketing is 'one of the big burdens of the modern cinema, not that movies cost so much but that they're so expensive to market, especially with indie films'. Thus, although declarations of independence and art can be shields as well as badges, the reduction of a film's interest and worth to either term in its marketing potentially limits a dialogue in which Lyotard exhorts 'the interlocutors [to] use any available ammunition, changing games from one utterance to the next' (1999: 17). The eternal 'becoming' of this dialogue thus includes the evolution of terms as noted by King:

The term 'mainstream' can easily become a rhetorical construct that obscures numerous forms of differentiation [...] as can other terms such as 'dominant', 'commercial', 'alternative', 'distinctive', and so on. [It] is also an *operative* construct, a discursive category in widespread use, explicitly or implicitly, in the articulation of a range of points of distinction [and] often taken as a reference point against which other forms are defined. (2009: 33–4; emphasis in original)

The same is true of 'independent' and 'art-house', which both suggest a certain elitism in the marking of actual territory, while King ultimately admits that a formulation such as his own 'Indiewood', which he defines as 'an area in which Hollywood and the independent sector merge or overlap' (2009: 1) is also one that 'exists as, or has become, a largely marketing driven niche' (2009: 274). As King concludes, all these terms 'become vague to the point of lacking much capacity for closer discrimination' (2009: 237). However, it is precisely this blurry vagueness that inspires rather than stalls the need for dialogue that Lyotard likens to a war that 'is not without rules, but the rules allow and encourage the greatest possible flexibility of utterance' (1999: 17).

As a dialogic work, the cinema of Linklater, like that of many filmmakers, carries on a continual dialogue with other films and filmmakers. For example, the centrifugal and centripetal energy of this dialogism is ably rendered in *Me and Orson Welles*. 'Wouldn't this make a great story? Two people meeting like this. Nothing more,' exclaims Gretta (Zoe Kazan) to Richard (Zac Efron) in an affectionate nod towards *Before Sunrise*, although the dialogue and its expression of the spirit that infuses the cinema of Linklater come intact from Kaplow's novel:

'And what happens?'
　　She looked confused. 'What do you mean "what happens"? Nothing happens. Why does something have to happen?'
　　'No, I meant…'
　　'The whole story is what I told you. […] You know, mostly *mood*. The girl goes to the museum feeling blue. She thinks about time and eternity, and then she feels a little better.'
　　'Oh…'
　　She got defensive. 'There's no *action* in it, if that's what you're looking for. God, can't you just be walking down the street, and suddenly you're happy? […] Well, stories can be like that too. Why does everything have to have a big *plot*? All that melodramatic garbage?'
　　'Hey, I'm on your side, Gretta,' I said. 'I agree with you.' (2008: 126; emphasis in original)

Not only does the intrinsic Richard agree with her but the extrinsic one (Linklater) does too, who further extends the allusion throughout his own work and in this specific adaptation to the influence of Godard by ending the scene with Gretta and Richard running from the museum chased by a guard in a reprise of the scene from *Band à parte* in which Odile (Anna Karina) leads Franz (Sami Frey) and Arthur (Claude Brasseur) on an attempt to break the world record for running through the

Louvre. For Linklater, 'art house cinema was always European film, whatever was the latest film from France or Germany or Russia, you know'. His film-going, his university education in French and Russian literature and his curating of the Austin Film Society all engendered the dialogue that shapes his work as writer, co-writer and director and is especially loud in relation to *Before Sunrise* and its sequels. *Before Sunrise* is particularly emblematic of the dialogic and dialogue-driven cinema of Linklater because its production was 'always about the process of its own making, a process that never stopped and was always open for new thoughts and inspirations' (Linklater 1995: v). However, the cinema of Linklater is not aimed at curtailing the globalising force of the raucous action blockbuster with a calming whisper. On the contrary, it is simply the kind of cinema that enables a more complex 'notion of a "dialogue" operating on a number of at times competing economic, aesthetic or philo-sophical levels' (Cooke 2007: 8). The competitive economic level is based on the ratio return of profit to cost by which, in simple terms, cheaper films can get by on lower returns that still ensure the employment of those involved in their making and even allow for such things as a sequel. The occasional crossover success of an 'indie' to the mainstream is always welcome but, on the whole, independent filmmakers survive by keeping their costs down. For Linklater this has meant investigating the possibilities of new digital filming, editing and distribution technologies as well as cutting corners, improvising and getting stars such as Bruce Willis in *Fast Food Nation* to work for a reduced wage. This traffic goes both ways, however, with Linklater willing to work for a salary or fee within what he calls 'the full-blown studio system, which I love'. In addition, this literal 'crossover' is also Linklater's embodiment of a dialogue, one that prompts Speed to argue that 'Linklater's crossing of boundaries among experimental, independent, and entertainment cinema is utopian in its eschewal of any absolute filmmaking approach' (2007: 105). As previously noted, Linklater concurs: 'I would like to have been Vincente Minnelli or Howard Hawks making a film or two a year in the studio system.' On one level, this admission suggests his subscription to theories of auteurism:

> We know who had the great careers in and around the system – Wilder, Huston, all the Europeans that came over like Lang – and I think you had to sublimate your own ego on the surface. Secretly you're making your film, but at least on the surface you had to show that you're being a company man.

However, such a traditional view of auteurism is illogical and self-defeating in the type of collaborative production process required of an independent film and those of Linklater in particular, where there is no rigid hierarchy to subvert. Linklater's part in the dialogue between studio and independent filmmaking leads Speed to conclude that 'his career's juxtapositioning of experimental and formulaic films suggests a utopian view of film production as accommodating diversity without negative tension' (2007: 104). More than this, however, Linklater is sometimes able to reconcile any contra-diction by blurring the juxtaposition in a single film. At least on his own terms, for example, *Before Sunrise* is a Minnelli-esque musical.

Richard Linklater, Ethan Hawke and Julie Delpy rehearsing *Before Sunrise*

Before Sunrise is not the first musical without singing or dancing. Godard claimed his *Une femme est une femme* was 'a neo-realist musical … a complete contradiction' (in Anshen 2007: 93) and that film's wilful, neurotic Frenchwoman Angela (Anna Karina) is a fitting forerunner of Céline (Julie Delpy). What *Before Sunrise* and *Une femme est une femme* share is an enthusiasm for all the conventions of a Hollywood musical, including the segues and cues, the romantic tension, the sublimation of sex into song and dance, the way the numbers unite a couple or a community and the way a film is structured according to the various types of song, without ever breaking into any artificial musical number. In this they are aligned with James Monaco's view that 'abstractly, film offers the same possibilities of rhythm, melody and harmony as music' (2000: 55). However, neither is *Before Sunrise* the only all non-singing, all non-dancing musical in the cinema of Linklater, for the accumulative effect of *Slacker*'s supposedly unique structure is also musical. *Slacker* may even be appreciated as an epic 'passed-along' song of a generation that shares what Jane Feuer terms the 'socio-economic alienation' (1993: 2) of the Hollywood musical that makes up for 'the breakdown of community [by] the creation of folk relations' (1993: 3). In common with naturalistic musicals, *Slacker* 'cancels choreography' (Feuer 1993: 9). Instead, its 'passed-along' form and narrative embody Bakhtinian principles of the carnival by 'employ[ing] film techniques such as the travelling shot and the montage sequence to illustrate the spread of music by the folk through the folk' (Feuer 1993; 16). The only difference is that the 'music' in this carnival is the dialogue. The same is true of *Before Sunrise*, which is structured around a series of dialogues that are numbers: duets, in fact, punctuating the narrative of a nocturnal *dérive* around Vienna of a young American abroad and the French girl he persuades to walk and talk with him until dawn.

The dialogic nature of *Before Sunrise* is well illustrated by this allusion to the Hollywood musical genre whose greatest exponents were MGM producer Arthur Freed and director Vincente Minnelli, who together created *The Clock*, which Linklater screened for Delpy and Hawke during the making of *Before Sunrise*, because both films adhere to the brisk boy meets girl dynamic of the musical genre even if their walking and talking never turns into song and dance. The films may have different attitudes to destiny: in *The Clock* Alice Mayberry (Judy Garland) and Corporal Joe Allen (Robert Walker) are fated soulmates, while Jesse and Céline are the authors of their own togetherness (see MacDowell 2008). However, both resonate with the emotions of classic melodrama that in *Before Sunrise* are also felt in relation to the Viennese setting and the long, eloquent takes with a mobile or static camera that recall *Letter from an Unknown Woman*. Ophüls' intricate long takes expressed the journey or pattern of life, whereas for Robert Bresson they tended to indicate its destiny. In addition, for Linklater, 'Truffaut is the master of the planned sequence. You'd plan it all out, move the camera. You'd realise you didn't want or have to cut it a lot. You could spend half a day on one three-minute scene.' Thus, such shots as the five-minute take of Jesse and Céline on the tram or avoiding eye contact in the listening booth evoke a diffidence towards narrative that is rendered by the snub of going with the flow and just drifting with the movement and dialogue of the actors, whose temporalised existence is expressed in the guise of the time-image. 'Yeah, I just love it!' says Linklater:

> You know, to me that's the purest cinema, the André Bazin idea of pure cinema. There's no cutting, there's nothing else. It forces you into the reality of the moment. You could if you wanted to cut away, but I like this way of making film. You see it in Preston Sturges too. Go back and watch *Sullivan's Travels* and you'll realise, 'Holy crap, the whole scene is like one take!' You wouldn't know it because the camera's moving around and within the frame it's got so much energy. It's like a musical.

Before Sunrise also references *The Third Man* (Carol Reed, 1949) with the ferris wheel in the Wiener Prater, while Jesse is but the latest in a long line of cocky but sensitive Americans abroad, including Holly Martins (Joseph Cotten) from *The Third Man* (and Welles too as Harry Lime, for that matter) as well as Jerry Mulligan (Gene Kelly) in Minnelli's *An American in Paris* (1951) and Joe Bradley (Gregory Peck) in *Roman Holiday* (William Wyler, 1953). The film's dynamic also recalls *Two for the Road* (1967) directed by Stanley Donen, who like Minnelli was a master of the musical and capable of transposing its particular structure of numbers alternating with narrative to that of the dialogues between Joanna (Audrey Hepburn) and Mark (Albert Finney) on their bittersweet journey through the south of France. These films alone refute Paul Schrader's view that 'American movies are based on the assumption that life presents you with problems, while European films are based on the conviction that life confronts you with dilemmas – and while problems are something you solve, dilemmas cannot be solved, they're merely probed' (in Elsaesser 2003: 44). As Elsaesser observes:

[Schrader's] assessment is not that far removed from the view of Gilles Deleuze, who in his Bergson-inspired study of the cinema proposes a more dynamic, and self-differentiating version of Jean-Luc Godard's old distinction between 'action' and 'reflection' [,] contrasting instead the movement-image of classical cinema with the time-image of modern cinema. (2003: 44)

However, Schrader's dialectic model is an elitist binary equation that fails to take into account the European mainstream and the American art house and is consequently rendered redundant by the dialogism of a film such as *Before Sunrise*, which responds to the generic conventions of the melodrama and the musical as much as it blurs them with its enthusiasm for European philosophy and dialogue.

Initially, the problem-solving obsession of Schrader's American 'movies' is illustrated when Jesse resorts to a rational, intellectual (American) argument incorporating persuasive theories of time travel to convince Céline to do things. He tells her that getting off the train in Vienna with him is a jump back in time from her future self. The gambit works, but it is also countered in the original script by Céline's intuitive, spontaneous (European) response and her subsequent probing of his dilemma: 'Is this why you tried to get me off the train? Competitiveness? To make sure the guy behind you didn't pick me up?'[4] Thereafter, the dialogue gradually blurs, even subverts any distinction between the problem-solving intellect of American 'movies' and the dilemma-probing intuition of European 'films' by showing repeatedly how Jesse's capacity and need for reflection ('I feel like this is some dream world we're walking through') is answered by Céline's penchant for intellectual cynicism: 'Then it's some male fantasy: meet a French girl on the train, fuck her and never see her again.'

The existential fears that unite Jesse and Céline, who claims to 'always feel like I'm observing my life instead of living it', are ultimately rebuffed by the potential of their romance, which emulates those films of the French New Wave that posited the individual as self-determining in matters of the heart. In getting off the train together in Vienna and in separating at the end, Jesse and Céline take full responsibility for their actions instead of succumbing to any preordained role or convention. Thus their shared experience responds to the slacker ethos in its justification of the journey as a kind of exile. In the published script there is an excised section of dialogue on the train in which Jesse explains: 'That's what I like about traveling. You can sit down, maybe talk to someone interesting, see something beautiful, read a good book, and that's enough to qualify as a good day. You do that at home and everyone thinks you're a bum' (Linklater and Krizan 2005: 13). His observation also tallies with how, as Céline observes of Seurat's human figures, characters in the cinema of Linklater 'always seem so transitory'. Their physical and spoken exploration of the slacker ethos makes tangible the many alternative realities made possible by their determinism: 'If I was asked right now to marry you or never see you again, I would marry you. I mean, maybe that's a lot of romantic crap. But people have gotten married for a lot less. I think we'd have as good a chance as anyone else.'

The immediate, enlightened intimacy of this couple 'on the run' from reality expresses an affinity with the protagonist couple of Godard's *À bout de souffle*, wherein

'You're in my dream and I'm in yours.' Jesse (Ethan Hawke) and Céline (Julie Delpy) in *Before Sunrise*

(although the gender roles are switched) Frenchman Michel affects American intellectual pretension but ultimately succumbs to a romantic view of his own gangsterdom, while the American Patricia tries imitating French style and intuition but is finally revealed as a pragmatist. When Godard reconnects with the fleeing lovers in *Pierrot le fou* he expresses a particularly bitter response to the intellectual arguments put forward by America for its globalising business and military avant-garde, blaming it for the division of intellect and intuition as expressed in the remnants of the relationship between Ferdinard and Marianne: 'I can never have a real conversation with you. You never have ideas, only feelings.' Jump cuts from *À bout de souffle* to *Pierrot le fou* to *Bonnie and Clyde* to *Before Sunrise* suggest an accumulative persona for Céline, not least because Delpy made her main acting debut aged fourteen for Godard as Wise Young Girl in *Détective*; but in truth the allusion was unplanned because she got the role by auditioning. 'I bet on the smartest girl I met,' says Linklater, who based *Before Sunrise* on 'one very fun evening in Philadelphia' with a woman he met in a toy store.[5] Furthermore, as Linklater explains, the concept went through various incarnations and nationalities before he settled on the eventual dynamic:

> I met Julie [Delpy] really early and at that point I didn't know if it was going to be an American man and an international female or an American female and an international man. You know, I knew it was going to be cross-cultural, but it could have been switched if I hadn't found the right international female. So I interviewed a lot, just trying to piece it together and see which way it would go.

Linklater met Hawke after seeing him in a play featuring Anthony Rapp (Tony in *Dazed and Confused*) and invited him to an audition/rehearsal in New York. Linklater says he was 'looking for intelligence, seeing who was creative, seeing who would collaborate with me, not just ask, "What are my lines?"'. Finally, because he believed 'the script needed to be completely re-imagined through the two people'. he chose Hawke and

Delpy because 'a lot of actors don't have that imagination, they're not on the creative, collaborative process with you'. This confirmed the central dynamic as that between an American man and a French woman, while the film's location was switched from San Antonio, sixty miles southwest of Austin, to Vienna, capital of the Republic of Austria, which Linklater had visited for its film festival in November 1993. At the time he noted its affinity with Austin: 'Vienna had a lot of people who were just hanging out. It kind of reminded me of Austin in a certain way. [They were] café people, really smart people. It felt like a big college town, very laid back' (in Hicks 1995).

The collaborative process that Linklater sought with co-screenwriter Kim Krizan and his actors prioritised dialogue between the filmmakers as the key to making a script from a series of dialogues that had been worked up in rehearsal. *Before Sunrise* was not simply the result of 'a certain creative evolutionary process [...] in which everyone involved contributed to the essence being portrayed on screen' (Linklater and Krizan 1995: iv) but, correlatively, was a film about 'people who verbalize their inner thoughts [...] and thus reveal themselves to each other' (ibid.). In other words, both the offscreen and onscreen discussions belonged to a single dialogue to the effect that, as Robin Wood contends, 'the usual distinction between "being" and "acting" is totally collapsed' (1998: 321). In addition, references to Georges Bataille, whose extravagantly pornographic *Story of the Eye* (1928) is Céline's reading matter on the train, Sandro Botticelli, James Joyce, Georges-Pierre Seurat, Thomas Mann, W. H. Auden, Purcell's *Dido and Aeneas* with its evocation of 'past attitudes to romantic love' (Wood 1998: 321), Yo-Yo Ma playing Bach and an unseen harpsichordist playing the Goldberg Variations (a particularly resonant example of a dialogic work in which harmony, melody, rhythm and orchestration is purposefully altered) all originated in workshopped rehearsals that carried on throughout the shooting of a film that is not so much *about* love and death as it is a dialogue *between* them. In this respect, the film's key line of dialogue is Céline's admission of personal faith:

> If there's any kind of God, he wouldn't be in any one of us, not you, not me, but just this space in between. If there's some magic in this world, it must be in the attempt of understanding someone else, sharing something, even if it's almost impossible to succeed. But who cares really, the answer must be in the attempt.

Her words are a dialogue not just with Jesse but also with Hermann Hesse, the German-Swiss novelist and poet whose work invokes an individual's search for authenticity, awareness and spirituality, who wrote: 'No matter how tight the ties that bind one human being to another, an abyss looms that love alone can bridge, but even then only narrowly and precariously' (Hesse 2009). It is this sort of dialogue that illustrates the Bakhtinian strategy that prompts Speed to surmise that 'intellect is positioned as a source of pleasure in *Before Sunrise*' (2007: 10). As Bakhtin argues: 'The central and basic motif in the narrative of individual life-sequences becomes *love*, that is, the *sublimated* form of the sexual act and fertility [for which] language serves as the most readily available medium [of its expression]' (2006a: 215; emphasis in original). According to Freud, sublimation is a psychological strategy that effects a defence mechanism, which suggests that Jesse and Céline's dialogue is the refined expression of love. As motif, moreover, love opposes death, which means the only way to keep death at bay is to keep talking. As for *Slacker* and *Waking Life*, therefore, all the walking and talking of *Before Sunrise* asserts the importance of the individual (and the couple) within a society debased by the commodification of love in the consumerist hard sell of 'aesthetic values made possible by Postmodernism' (Geuens 2000: 3). Dialogue, like the sex it sublimates, is an intuitive response to death and dying. As Henri Bergson wryly states, 'the ancient philosopher who demonstrated the possibility of movement by walking was right: his only mistake was to make the gesture without adding a commentary' (1992e: 144).

Walking and talking is not just proof of life but its defiant declaration. This is obvious in the way that death utterly dominates the dialogue between Jesse and Céline and in the way they keep walking and talking in an effort to deny death its dominion. Jesse recounts stories of when 'my mother first told me about death' and he saw an image of his dead great-grandmother in the spray from a hose, while Céline is 'afraid of death twenty-four hours a day' and leads him to the Friedhof der Namelossen (the Cemetery of the Nameless) where 'almost everyone buried here washed up on the bank where the Danube curves away'. Jesse has an elaborate theory about reincarnation that means 'at best, we're just these tiny fractions of people' and Céline professes to 'this strange feeling that I'm this very old woman, lying down about to die, you know that my life is just her memories or something'. When she was younger, Céline used to think 'that if none of your family or friends knew you were dead, then it's not like you were really dead', while Jesse wants 'to be a ghost, completely anonymous', and for his fortune to be 'when you die you will be forgotten'. For all its reputation as a romance, therefore, *Before Sunrise* is almost unremittingly morbid.[6] All its walking and talking is but a negotiation of respite – 'No delusions, no projections; we'll just make tonight great' – that is even more explicitly stated in the published script, when Jesse concludes their conversation on the boat with: 'So it's a deal? We die in the morning?' (Linklater and Krizan 2005: 93). Continuing this theme, Céline even confesses to murderous fantasies about an ex-boyfriend and to being 'obsessed that he's going to die from an accident, maybe a thousand kilometres away, and I will be accused', although Jesse, who Céline thinks 'must be scared to death' of her, actually believes that 'women don't mind killing men on some level'. Thoughts of death even permeate ideas of birth when Jesse recites the tale of a friend, who 'at the birth of his child, all that he could think about was that he was looking at something that was gonna die someday'. Crucially, where sex might be expected to repulse the encroachment of death, it is dialogue that truly thwarts the reaper. Jesse struggles to admit this – 'I don't want to just get laid. I want to … um … I mean, I mean, I think we should, I mean we die in the morning, right?' – and the consummation of the relationship is elided. The only thing that really opposes death is walking and talking: a drift and a dialogue that quietly rages against W. H. Auden's thoughts, as quoted by Jesse, on how 'vaguely life leaks away'.[7]

In comparison to the vitality of dialogue, moreover, love and sex is initially judged dormant as a defence mechanism because its complication by post-feminist attitudes is signalled as seemingly dead-ended. *Before Sunrise* begins with a row between a married

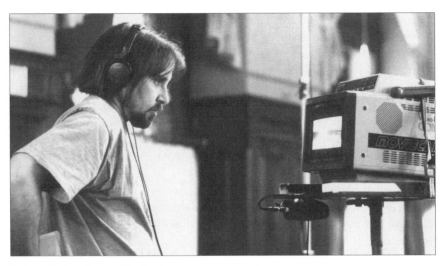

Richard Linklater filming *Before Sunrise*

couple on the train and Céline's opening line points to the curtailment of dialogue when she observes 'as couples get older, they lose their ability to hear each other [.] I guess they sort of nullify each other or something.' This premature disillusionment is echoed by Jesse, who admits that 'my parents are just two people who didn't like each other very much, who decided to get married and have a kid', while Céline is upset that her grandmother 'just confessed to me that she spent her life dreaming about another man'. Thus she believes that love is 'a complex issue, you know. Yes, I have told somebody that I love them before and I have meant it. Was it a beautiful thing? Not really. It's like … love.' And Jesse is hardly more optimistic, saying he knows 'happy couples, but it seems like they have to lie to each other'. However, such declarations are ironised because they actually emphasise how Jesse and Céline's ability to maintain a dialogue is what keeps the demise of relationships and death itself at bay. Their dialogue may begin with the unpromising clichés of gender-speak in the scene on the tram when Jesse asks Céline to 'describe your first sexual feelings towards a person', and she in return asks him if he has ever been in love, but this awkward exchange is arguably the only moment in the film when audience identification with retrograde gender politics and stereotyping is allowed and quickly, quite rightly dismissed. Away from other people, the two of them share what a line in the published script describes as 'a strange feeling. When we were talking on the train, it's like we were in public. There were people around us. Now that we're actually walking around Vienna, it's like we're all alone' (Linklater and Krizan 2005: 28). Alone except for the camera, that is, which, unlike in *Slacker*, refuses to break off from these people to follow others because, as soon becomes evident, the joy of dialogue rather than sex is what saves these two by elevating their *dérive* through night-time Vienna into a metaphysical experience: 'It's so weird, it's like our time together is just ours. It's our own creation. It must be like you're in my dream and I'm in yours.' Even though they recognise mortality again abruptly at dawn – 'Oh shit, we're back in real time' – they are also gifted with the souvenir of knowing the transcendental quality of dialogue. As Jesse says of Céline: 'She was literally this Botticelli angel, telling me that everything was going to be okay.'

All the singing and dancing of a musical usually culminates in a happy ending that sees the couple brought together and the community united around them. Here, however, the lovers part. Consequently, as Wood explains, 'everyone [...] raises the question of whether or not Jesse and Céline will keep their six-months-ahead date' (1998: 322). The discussion is complicated by emotion, however, for Wood clearly subscribes to Bazin's notion of appreciative criticism in admitting that *Before Sunrise* 'was a film for which I felt not only interest or admiration but love' (1998: 318). For Wood, *Before Sunrise* is 'characterized by a complete openness within a closed and perfect classical form [in which] the relationship shifts and fluctuates, every viewing revealing new aspects, further nuances, like turning a kaleidoscope, so the meaning shifts and fluctuates also' (1998: 324). Thus the dialogic work evolves through repeat viewings, special edition DVDs, intertextuality and influence, all the while trailing a cult following that extended the relevance of an emotional response to a dialogue about the fate of the characters that included Wood's prescient idea of a one-sided reunion for which only Jesse turns up and Linklater's possible response to this suggestion, for Wood suggests that his writing about this notion may have influenced Linklater, with whom he enjoyed a correspondence (1998: 324). More than this conjecture, however, just as the influence of *Slacker* is felt in such films as *Baka no hakobune* (*No One's Ark*, Yamashita Nobuhiro, 2003), *Die fetten Jahre sind vorbei* (*The Edukators*, Hans Weingartner, 2004), *3-Iron* (Ki-duk Kim, 2004), *Azuloscurocasinegro* (*Dark Blue Almost Black*, Daniel Sánchez Arévalo, 2006), and *Slackistan* (Hammad Khan, 2009), so the cost-effective simplicity of 'boy meets girl, they walk and talk' became a template and reference point for independent filmmakers who saw the intimacy and dialogue of their protagonists as a way of achieving the same with their audiences. *Once* (John Carney, 2006) actually *is* a neo-realist musical, while *Quiet City* (Aaron Katz, 2007) matched co-writer Erin Fisher as Atlantan Jamie to Brooklynite Charlie (Chris Lankenau) for twenty-four hours of coleslaw, galleries, after-party musing and a directionless race in the park between soulmate slackers who have no idea how fast they can run. *In Search of a Midnight Kiss* was another no-budget variation on the theme that paired gloomy Wilson (Scott McNairy) with pragmatic Vivian (Sara Simmonds) in Los Angeles and met with critical success that rarely failed to mention the influence of *Before Sunrise* or note that both films shared a producer (Anne Walker McBay) and that Holdridge thanks Linklater in the credits (Ebert 2008; French 2009). Yet another was *Monsters* (Gareth Edwards, 2010), commonly described as *Before Sunrise* meets Godzilla.

The generic lineage that connects classic melodrama with the more contemporary romantic comedy also exemplifies the dialogism that is explicitly retained in *2 Days in Paris* (2007), which was written and directed by Delpy. Here, Marion (Delpy) and Jack (Adam Goldberg, who played Mike in *Dazed and Confused*, One of Four Men in *Waking Life*, an uncredited man asleep on the train in *Before Sunrise* and was Delpy's real-life partner for several years) bond and bicker in comedic but barbed illustration of how, as Marion moans, 'there's a moment in life where you can't recover any more from another break-up'. In a similar vein, *Lost in Translation* (Sofia Coppola, 2003) finds palliative philosophy in the platonic May–September romance of Charlotte (Scarlett Johansson) and Bob (Bill Murray). More recently still, *Last Chance Harvey* (Joel Hopkins, 2008) employs the template for an October–September affair between Harvey (Dustin Hoffman) and Kate (Emma Thompson), while *(500) Days of Summer* (Marc Webb, 2009) finds extra mileage and a twist revealed in its tagline: 'Boy meets girl. Boy falls in love. Girl doesn't.' The dialogic work is clearly one that empowers the filmmaker (as it would an artist or writer) to ward off irrelevancy and stagnation. In contrast, solipsistic and centripetal works such as Julio Medem's *Caótica Ana* (*Chaotic Ana*, 2007) can temporarily scupper a career with their exclusive introspection, whereas the dialogic work is a centrifugal presence in art, culture and society that both sweeps up and throws off influences. In this respect the dialogism of *Before Sunrise* is most evident in relation to its sequel *Before Sunset*, which both revives the potential of Jesse and Céline's love by re-infusing it with dialogue and revitalises the cinema of Linklater by the same means.

Reuniting in Paris in 2004, the time that has passed for Jesse and Céline in *Before Sunset* is the same nine years for Linklater, his actors and the ideal audience that first saw *Before Sunrise* in 1995. The morbidity that pervaded *Before Sunrise* was a projection of fears around which was built philosophical conjecture, but the increased proximity of death in the sequel is more tangible and therefore conducive to a more practical and immediate response that is expressed in the urgency of the film's 90-minute time-frame. In addition, the dialogue between the films is rendered explicitly in the questions that each asks of the other in their taglines. *Before Sunrise* asks, 'Can the greatest romance of your life last only one night?' while *Before Sunset* wonders, 'What if you had a second chance with the one that got away?' The use of the pronouns 'your' and 'you' also indicates a dialogue with the film's ideal audience. In the first case, there

'I don't want to be one of those people that don't believe in any kind of magic'. Jesse and Céline take the barge on the Seine in *Before Sunset*

is a clear suggestion that *Before Sunrise* is about 'you' in the promise of identification with the protagonists, while the 'your' of *Before Sunset* insists upon an evolution of this dialogue between the audience and the films to the extent that it has been personalised in the way that André Bazin intended and to which Robin Wood admitted. Linklater recognises the 'omnipresent feeling of the audience, even when you're writing. I don't think you cannot consider that and work in this medium' (in Hewitt 2004) and even admits to finding this dialogue at times invasive:

> Ethan, Julie and I talked and said, 'No one wanted a sequel.' There were three people in the universe who wanted a sequel, who wanted to get back into this, nobody wanted to do it. And now that we did it, and now we get asked if there's going to be another, the idea that there's an expectation now almost makes us feel like we do not want to make it. What was so cool was that every day on *Before Sunset* we looked at each other and it was like 'How are we getting to do this?' And it was like this gift from the film gods that we even got to make this movie, because there were zero expectations and zero pressure. It was just for us. But you do two and: 'What's next?' People have expectations.

Long before talk of a second sequel, Linklater noted the growing fanbase for *Before Sunrise* and discussed the possibility of a first sequel with Delpy and Hawke in 2001 during the rehearsal for the brief oneiric reunion of Jesse and Céline in *Waking Life*. Yet it still took five more years for the project to evolve and the budget to be secured for a tiny fifteen day shoot. Firstly, Linklater and his actors agreed to co-write and met to work on a specific outline containing all the emotional beats. Then Hawke and Delpy invested in their characters by separating to work on their dialogue, which they emailed to Linklater, who collated contributions and re-wrote. Considerations of cost, schedule and filming restrictions made rehearsal and rigorous planning essential to the filming of *Before Sunset*. This time there would be no cutaways from the single conversation between Delpy and Hawke, whose greatest challenge (in addition to the rekindling of onscreen chemistry) was to appear spontaneous on top of so much rehearsal. 'In the first film we were just getting to know each other,' says Linklater:

> But then that's sort of why I cast both of them initially, because they seemed like the two most creative actors. Then, you know, cut to a couple of years later, they've both made a couple of features, they're both writers. These people are really fucking talented and they really know what they're doing and they're really smart, visual artists.

At the same time, Linklater faced the challenge of maintaining a sense of spontaneity during a production that was inhibited by the practicalities of filming in Paris:

> Paris was a tough city to film in. Vienna and other cities, they're glad you're there. Paris is the complete opposite. It doesn't mean anything to them that

Julie Delpy and Ethan Hawke filming *Before Sunset*

you're making a film in their city. In fact, if you need to come back tomorrow and finish a scene: 'Go to the bureaucrat's office and fill out the paperwork and maybe we can get you into that location next Thursday.'

Bureaucracy apart, Paris was also the home of the French New Wave. Linklater recalls 'staying in the Latin Quarter and I would just walk to the set from my little apartment I was staying in and some of my favourite filmmakers have shot on these streets'. Inevitably, the influence of Truffaut, Godard, Rohmer and Agnés Varda, whose *Cléo de 5 à 7* (*Cleo from 5 to 7*, 1962) has a similar time-frame, infused the tracking shots, sense of time, dialogue and urgency respectively, while all four informed the film's empathy and melancholy about youth, particularly in relation to Céline, who prompts specific consideration of the effect and resonance of the events of 1968. In *Before Sunrise* Céline described her parents as 'angry young May '68 people revolting against everything', who had conformed to 'this constant conversion of my fanciful ambitions into practical moneymaking schemes'. But in *Before Sunset*, the actual parents of Delpy, who was born in 1969, appear as jolly sybarites in the courtyard of her apartment block, thereby underlining this film's theme of rejuvenation.

Initially, however, the lost potential of youth, the inexorable passage of time and the increased proximity of death are all themes that dominate the dialogue of *Before Sunset* and are expressed in the long takes that approximate time-images and the 80-minute running time that suggests the *durée* of the *dérive*. 'It was such a huge challenge,' recalls Linklater:

It was like a play. There was no room to cut out anything, so for Julie and Ethan it was tough. For most movies, if something doesn't work, or doesn't work as well as you'd like, you can always cut it, you can still work on the internal pacing with the editing; but that movie was totally designed one hundred per cent and then executed as designed. We made our choices and then lived with them. You're painted into a corner, even geographically. We started here and ended here and the dialogue had to fit or we'd be timed out.

Consequently, dialogue is rendered as an even more urgent activity than it had been in *Before Sunrise*, because its existential nature is now expressed in the form and content of the 'real-time' conceit and its expression of 'the volatile lightness of the dangerous present' (Rosenbaum 2004). The guerrilla shoot may still have relied to some extent on improvisation, but, as Linklater explains, in a typically collaborative manner:

> That's the dynamic between Julie, Ethan and myself, we're all just brutally honest with ourselves and with each other. There's no bullshit. We have a great time collaborating on these movies and it's all pure honesty and it's the best kind of collaboration. If two of us feel strongly about something and something's working for us and the third party doesn't quite get it, it goes away. So everything in that movie was signed off by all of us. There's never a point where I have to look at Julie and say, 'I know you don't like it but trust me on this.' No, we're all equally invested in everything. And that's what just evolved in the second film particularly.

Nine years after the separation that concludes *Before Sunrise*, Jesse is a debut author on a book tour of Europe to promote a novel titled *This Time* in which he relates the events of the first film. On the Parisian leg of the jaunt, he meets journalists in the Shakespeare and Company bookstore in the Latin Quarter by the Seine and, while parrying personal questions from the press, sees Céline listening between the book-cases. They re-introduce themselves and, noting the brief amount of time before Jesse has to catch a plane, resolve to stroll a little way while catching-up. Thus the 'walking and talking' dynamic of the first film re-emerges. *Before Sunrise* was about killing time; now, however, the ticking clock adds tension. It also intrudes upon the dialogue, making the characters more target-oriented at first instead of just going with the flow. Gradually, Jesse's pending flight at Charles de Gaulle Airport becomes a symbol of all the high-tech urgency that the younger couple of *Before Sunrise* found so easy to ignore when they alighted from the train in Vienna. Then, in their full-blossomed youth, they were barely conscious of time when they resolved not to exchange contact details but to meet up six months later. Now the challenge will be to dismiss the ticking clock and return to that lost, Bergsonian, intuitive sense of time. *Before Sunset* is therefore a rescue mission for those trapped in the rigid timeline that connects the potential of youth with the resignation of middle age. In the nine years of their separation both Jesse and Céline have succumbed to thinking of life as finite and sequential, as something that demands compromise and submission. Jesse has turned quietly into his parents, being married with a son in a loveless, sexless marriage. Céline, meanwhile, is in a perfectly sterile relationship with a photojournalist who is always away, a man she can respect as an ideal without having to deal with in person, because she is clearly so addicted to missing a man (i.e. Jesse) that she recreates and therefore justifies the emotion in her current relationship. Unsurprisingly, they are now more guarded and defensive, either lying to each other (as Céline does when she refuses to countenance his memory that they had sex) or failing to mention things (as Jesse does in relation to his marriage). Instead, they reveal themselves slowly in a manner that accords with and enables the film's gradual dismissal of the constraints of the time-frame. Linklater is not, therefore, entirely appropriate for comparison with Wong Kar-Wai as a filmmaker whose main theme is 'the romance and poetry of moments ticking by' (Rosenbaum 2004), precisely because, in contrast, he finds poetry and romance in ignoring the clock.

The film's restrictive, antagonistic time-frame is posited in the initial bookstore scene by an urgent curtailing of dialogue by the manager (Vernon Dobtcheff): 'We have time for one last question.' However, it is the couple's gradual transgression of such time constraints that points to the revival of their potential. On leaving the bookshop, Céline leads Jesse down a series of streets and alleys on a purportedly short walk to a cafe ('there's one a little further that I like a lot') that immediately wrecks his bearings, endangers his punctuality and points to what Ryan Gilbey recognises in comparison with *Before Sunrise* as 'a transfer of power from Jesse to Céline' (2004: 44). Supposedly linear time is then dissolved when the couple offer conflicting memories of their initial meeting in Vienna and ambiguous explanations for their one-sided, failed reunion six months later. In addition, this dialogue revisits the theme of *Tape* as well as the debates over time and memory in Alain Resnais' *Hiroshima, mon amour* (1959) and *L'année dernière à Marienbad* (*Last Year in Marienbad*, 1961). *Before Sunset* then invites the audience to question the validity of these statements by drawing on their own memories of *Before Sunrise* as well as their own suppositions about the possible reunion, when to this collage of time and memory is added:

> Five intertwined threads of awareness: the fictional (Jesse and Céline confront their estrangement from their younger selves), the real (Hawke and Delpy do the same), the objective (the audience observes this critically), the subjective (the audience responds emotionally to the changes) and the metaphysical (the ideal audience experiences the changes in Jesse and Céline as a reflection of the changes in themselves). (Stone 2007: 231)

Thus the dissolution of time in a Cubist manner that is begun by the inserts from *Before Sunrise* that punctuate Jesse's chat with the press is expanded into a picture of the relative 'truth' of their first encounter in which the audience is fully integrated as subject as well as spectator. In addition, the way *Before Sunset* begins with images of the Parisian locations that will be traversed by the couple points to both the collage of those visited during *Before Sunrise* at its close, and the fact that this paradoxical, premonitory flashback dismantles any possible sense of linear time. That is to say, its collage of future locations shows in effect that their reunion has already happened, is already happening, and will happen again in a Bergsonian universe ruled by Linklater's dictum from *Waking Life*: 'There's only one instant, and it's right now. And it's eternity.' In other words, *Before Sunset* expresses the movement from the exactingly

'This is it. What do you see? What do you feel?' Jesse and Céline in *Before Sunset*

specific, linear and lost *This Time* of Jesse's novel at its start to the more relaxed, unfettered flow of *Just in Time*, the song sung by Nina Simone, who Céline imitates in the film's final scene.

Before Sunset thus effects a paradox: its set-up is a goal-oriented convention but its resolution requires its dismissal. The gradual return to an intuitive, Bergsonian understanding of time is referenced in the dialogue between allusions to Joyce's *Ulysses* that appear in both *Before Sunrise*, which takes place on Bloomsday 16 June, and *Before Sunset*, which begins in the Shakespeare and Company bookstore that took the name of the company run by Sylvia Beach that first published Joyce's novel. It is also reinforced by time-images that by their nature purposefully ignore the 'ticking clock' of the plot. The countdown is frustrated, for example, by the practical expedient of the film being shot during the so-called 'golden hour' (aka magic hour) that delivers the kind of ephemeral perfect twilight previously captured for Terrence Malick's *Days of Heaven* (1978) and *The New World* (2005). The golden hour has a warm, diffuse light with longer shadows and is thus ideal for expressing both the memory shared by Jesse and Céline, which is comforting but vague, and the very long shadow that it casts over everything else in their lives. It corroborates David Martin-Jones's theory that 'there is, then, always an aspect of the subject in both past and future, an actual I in the present and a virtual I in the past. [...] Time divides the subject in two, just as time itself is perpetually splitting into a passing present and a preserved past' (2006: 60). In addition, the golden hour evokes Linklater's view that 'film gives you these moments of bliss but the reality tries to crush you at the same time'. In sum, because the expression of time as an incomplete, centrifugal force is the biggest affront to mainstream cinema's determined linearity, so *Before Sunset* slips the binding of its generic conventions under cover of dusk and aligns itself with the reflective bias of the European art film.

Linklater contends:

> All films have a time-frame, it's just a question of how big a part that time plays
> in the story itself. You do a romance that takes place over a year, then it gets a
> typical time-frame: boy meets girl, the seasons change. It doesn't matter, you're
> just telling a story, whereas if you really condense it or elongate it to some really
> crazy extreme then it becomes part of the story. It becomes like another lead
> actor. It becomes the subject in a way.

Whereas the dialogue of *Before Sunrise* invoked death as a finite, linear concept, that
of *Before Sunset* rescues time from man-made fragmentation and revives it as a holistic,
infinite and incomplete Bergsonian concept that extends the thesis on time built up
throughout the rather youth-oriented cinema of Linklater towards a consideration of
ageing. While comparing how they have aged, both Jesse and Céline attempt physical
regression: Céline lets her hair down and Jesse tries to rub away his frown lines. Céline
thinks 'time gets faster and faster', while Jesse claims to 'like getting older. Life feels
more immediate. You can appreciate it more.' Both of them appear to have shrugged
off the sensation felt by Cynthia in *Dazed and Confused* of 'thinking of the present, like
right now, as some minor, insignificant preamble to something else'. Instead, Céline
rhapsodises about being 'truly in the moment' while Jesse lauds monks of his acquaintance who 'are trying to live and die in peace and be close with God or whatever part
of them they feel is eternal'. Thus attuned, they resume the dialogue that warded off
death in *Before Sunrise*, but in a more practical manner that seeks to validate the self-
sufficiency of shared moments.

Their revitalisation is not immediate, however. If the dialogue of *Before Sunrise*
revealed two twenty-somethings on a search for meaning who find and then lose each
other, that of *Before Sunset* first has to shed the resigned mimicry of the commodification of meaning that underpins their political and philosophical posturing. For all her
environmental activism, Céline's utterances, as Jesse remarks, have become the stuff
of bumper stickers. Faux-profound lines such as her 'memory is a wonderful thing if
you don't have to deal with the past', and his 'a memory's never finished if you think
about it', may be gratingly pretentious, but they are also overcompensation for the
hollowness they both suffer. Céline no longer believes in ghosts, spirits or reincarnation. 'What about God?' asks Jesse. 'No, no,' she replies, 'but at the same time I don't
want to be one of those people that don't believe in any kind of magic.' In terms of
Nietzschean philosophy, their defensive, Apollonian, intellectual and critical reasoning
gradually waivers in the face of each other's teasing sarcasm and creative-intuitive questions and answers. Faint traces of Dionysian instinct emerge in his irrational impulses
('Hey, let's get on that boat!') and her intuitive desires ('I want to paint, write more
songs, learn Chinese, play my guitar each day') and culminate in their cross-wired
confessions of misery in the chauffeur-driven cab. Seeking release, they search for
meaning in the moment: 'This is it. What do you see? What do you feel? What do you
think is funny?' Céline says she wants to be like her cat because 'every single morning
he looks at everything like it's the first time,' while Jesse 'wouldn't mind still talking

about magic in the universe. I'd just like to do it in a hotel room in between sessions of us, like, wildly fucking till we die.' 'Why waste time going to a hotel?' asks Céline. Thus, the way that dialogue sublimated sex in *Before Sunrise* (as does song and dance in the musical) is revived and made explicit, along with their potential: 'Do you like dirty talk during sex? Which words do you like to hear?' The dialogue is so successful, in fact, that they are empowered to ridicule the defeat of Dionysius by Apollo in the nine years in between their meetings. Céline: 'You think you would have finished your book if you were fucking someone every five minutes?' Jesse: 'I would have relished the challenge.' And finally *Before Sunset* does indeed turn into a musical when Delpy performs her self-written songs before miming playfully and dancing seductively to Nina Simone before the exquisite fade-out.

The time-frame that becomes irrelevant and is ultimately dismissed in *Before Sunset* (Céline: 'Baby, you are gonna miss that plane.' Jesse: 'I know.') is often mistaken as the subject of the cinema of Linklater, but it is the *picture* of time inside it that really matters. Linklater himself contends: 'I used to joke about that. A few films in and people would say, "Oh, all your films take place in a time-frame." But that really wasn't conscious. It was just the way those stories were being told.' In this, Linklater is allied with Tarkovsky, who calls film to the task of philosophy in his book *Sculpting in Time: Tarkovsky the Great Russian Filmmaker Discusses his Art* (1989 [1986]) in which he writes: 'The rhythm of the movement of time is there within the frame, as the sole organising force of the – quite complex – dramatic development' (1989: 114). Above all else, it is time as subject *within* the frame rather than the frame itself that typifies the cinema of Linklater, who, in what Céline might recognise as 'the space between' Hollywood conventions and commissions and European influences and philosophy, is responsible for a peculiar time-wary hybrid of action and dialogue, of walking and talking.

Finally or not, in positing the Bergsonian concept of time as a cure for the angst of growing older, *Before Sunset* also rescues the slacker generation from the indignity of ageing gracelessly. Jesse and Céline both evolve from treating each other as fearful memories towards self-consciousness about the present that posits the passing of every moment as a cause for immediate joy rather than a premature wake for its ending. This is existentialism as a reason for celebration rather than despair. And, ultimately, this may just be the perfect union of the Hollywood happy ending with the reflective pause of the European art film.

Nevertheless, following highly secret filming in Messinia in southern Greece in the late summer of 2012, Linklater, Hawke and Delpy announced that they had wrapped a third instalment in the lives of Jesse and Céline. It was titled *Before Midnight* and it was bought by Sony Picture Classics at the 2013 Sundance Film Festival. Previously, when asked if we should look forward to Jesse and Céline reuniting, however, Linklater had laughed:

I wonder what city, yeah? I get asked about that a lot. I've had filmmakers say like 'Here's what you do!' They have it all figured out. The next one will be dot-dot-dot, you know. Fill in the blank. I have a hunch we'll do it when the time is right. Like the second one. It happened to be nine years later that the planets aligned and we felt totally compelled to do it and it worked out well for all of us.

Any thoughts on what direction the next sequel will take?

Maybe we should go another way. Make it a little slice of life, talk about something that would take on the domestic beast a little bit. What happens when life is a little less… The first movie was like a dream, they were ships passing. The Paris thing, in the second film, that was her town and he's there for such a little time and there's this quick little moment in time. But we should look at some place that they both have attachments to, where they both have obligations.

So is this a lifetime thing?

It might be some lifetime thing, who knows. We make jokes about it. What's been the longest collaboration? The archetype seems to be Truffaut and Jean-Pierre Leaud: four little touchdowns in a twenty-year period. We can top that. We started early so if I'm lucky enough to live long enough… I wish Truffaut had lived longer; this is one of the great cinema tragedies. We take it for granted because he did make twenty wonderful movies but he died so young it was like, 'Oh my god, we've all been robbed of twenty more beautiful Truffaut films that would have dealt with ageing, getting older, the romance of older people!' He probably would have got Jean-Pierre Leaud and done a couple more.

But for that you'd have to turn into a European filmmaker?

Yeah. I've done it enough now. I can see myself just settling in and being a European filmmaker. I certainly have enjoyed my three times making films there. I'm kinda ticking off the great cities, you know. I need to do one in Rome. I like that Woody Allen is becoming a European filmmaker for the same economic reasons. But you adapt. It's more interesting. What the hell!

Notes

1   All quotations from Richard Linklater, unless otherwise attributed, are from interviews with the author in Austin, Texas, 30 July–1 August 2009.
2   *Tape* was brought to Linklater's attention by Ethan Hawke, who would also direct *Chelsea Walls* (2001) for InDigEnt.
3   See, for example, http://www.meandorsonwellesthemovie.com/; http://www.myspace.com/meandorsonwelles; http://www.facebook.com/home.php?ref=home#/meandorsonwelles?ref=nf; http://www.youtube.com/meandorsonwelles; http://www.twitter.com/meandorson; http://www.bebo.com/meandorsonwelles.

4   According to the published script, Jesse will later copy Alvy Singer (Woody Allen) in *Annie Hall* (Woody Allen, 1977) when using a similar argument to persuade Céline to kiss him on the ferris wheel: 'I propose we jump in time to that moment when we would naturally do that, probably a couple of hours from now after a certain amount of awkwardness and stuff.' But he is rumbled by Céline: 'How come every time you want me to do something, you start talking about time travel?' (Linklater and Krizan 2005: 46).

5   The casting of Julie Delpy in the role of a woman named Céline also suggests a dialogue with Rivette's New Wave classic *Céline et Julie vont en bateau* (*Céline and Julie Go Boating*, 1974).

6   Linklater reveals his indebtedness to what he calls the 'spirit-and-the-flesh titles' of European cinema in his list of 'top ten films' on the Criterion website. They include Bresson's *Pickpocket* (1959) and *Au hasard Balthazar* (1966), Dreyer's *Vredens dag* (*Day of Wrath*, 1943), Rossellini's *Francesco, giullare di dio* (*The Flowers of St. Francis*, 1950), Tarkovsky's *Andrey Rublyov* (*Andrei Rublev*, 1969), Bergman's *Fanny och Alexander* (*Fanny and Alexander*, 1982) and Powell and Pressburger's *I Know Where I'm Going!* (1945).

7   The line is from the poem 'As I Walked Out One Evening', which is included in *W. H. Auden; Collected Poems* (1976). New York: Random House.

CHAPTER FIVE

Dreamstate, USA: The Metaphysics of Animation

Rotoscoping? 'It was one of those magical marriages of technology and ideas,' asserts Linklater.[1] Which begs the question of exactly what ideas could best be betrothed by tracing over live action footage, colouring it in and animating it on a computer. Crudely psychedelic and at the same time languorously mundane, rotoscoped imagery evokes a dream whose lucidity insists upon its reality while simultaneously suggesting that its monsters are being barely kept at bay. Its history can be traced by a series of shortcuts through that of screen animation, but perhaps a more telling antecedent might be plate 43 of 80 comprising *Los Caprichos* produced by the Spanish painter and printmaker Francisco José de Goya y Lucientes (1746–1828), who is commonly considered the first modern artist 'because of his fascination with the irrational and his critical rage against church and class' (Hughes 1989).

Entitled *El sueño de la razón produce monstruos* (*The Sleep of Reason Produces Monsters*) and etched with aquatint in 1799, the print was intended as the frontispiece of the collection and depicts an artist (self-identified as Goya in an early sketch) asleep at his drawing table. From the darkness that surrounds him arises a huge nocturnal swarm of bats and owls and a tense and pensive big cat. The demonic beasts observe the artist intently with a mix of hunger and awe but these shadowy symbols of superstition, paranoia and threat do not penetrate the light of reason that bathes the dreamer. Thus the imagination is rendered as something macabre and irrational that consumes the artist, who must struggle to fend off fear in order to present the truth. Here is the eternal battle between reason and instinct, between intellect and intuition rendered as the dangerous but essential bipolarity of the creative mind, which must investigate what lies beyond reality in order to return with lessons learned about its truth, while running the risk of never returning. This branch of philosophical enquiry into the nature of reality and the notion of whether the world actually exists outside of the mind is commonly termed metaphysics, which amongst much else incorporates the study of abstraction, determinism, identity, change and mind over matter. And thereto the happy union with rotoscoping, which fuses technology and ideas in order to realise metaphysical enquiries on film in *Waking Life* and *A Scanner Darkly*. As Linklater explains:

> The literalness of film was too harsh for the idea of a lucid dream. It would cancel it out, whereas this kind of more ephemeral style that was real and yet was an artifice, that was an artist's rendering of real – that's what a dream is! That 'show' that your head processes! That was the marriage right there. The ideas found the right form.

Rotoscoping is rather appropriate to the slacker ethos as its ingenuity was fostered by idleness. The technique of tracing over live action frame by frame to create an animated film was first utilised by Jewish *émigré* Max Fleischer, founder and head of the Fleischer Studios, in the second decade of the twentieth century. Fleischer made Betty Boop, Popeye and Superman into animated film stars and his first experiments with the technique of rotoscoping were on animated shorts that he produced with his brother Dave, who worked as a clown at Coney Island Amusement Park and acted in the footage that would be turned into the animated misadventures of Koko the Clown.[2] Fleischer patented the Rotoscope in 1915 as a device that focused a film projector onto an easel covered by a frosted sheet of glass that offered a drawing surface, thereby allowing the animator to trace the image on successive sheets of paper while advancing the film frame by frame. He deployed the process in his innovative series *Out of the Inkwell* (later renamed *Inkwell Imps*) that ran from 1919 to 1929. Although an independent filmmaker, Fleischer produced this series under the patronage of Paramount before establishing his own-brand studio in 1923 and hiring Dick Heumer to be Director of Animation. Heumer subsequently weaned the Fleischer brothers off their dependence on merely tracing by forging the interaction of live action footage with rotoscoping and more traditional cel and modelling animation techniques.[3] However, because more creative animators were frustrated by having their talent and imagination limited to tracing, rotoscoping fell into relative disuse with only occasional revivals of its unique qualities for such film events as the inclusion of the jazz singer and bandleader Cab Calloway in three original Betty Boop cartoons – *Minnie the Moocher* (1932), *Snow White* (1933) and *The Old Man of the Mountain* (1933) – for which Calloway performed his inimitable dance steps for footage that was later rotoscoped by the animators.[4]

The advantage of rotoscoping was that it reproduced the realistic physical movement of one-offs like Calloways as well as the jobbing actors who modelled for the Superman cartoons (1941–42) and *Gulliver's Travels* (1939). Walt Disney employed the technique sparingly in *Snow White and the Seven Dwarfs* (1937) and *Cinderella* (1950) for the delicate movement of the heroines and the more naturalistic ones of the many animals that were featured, but the technique was mostly relegated to preparatory work intended to train and inform the animators in the most basic elements of human and animal physiology. However, the technique was adopted by animators in China and the Soviet Union who deployed it as a way of inserting a sense of social realism into folk tales by the inclusion of realistic human figures. In American cinema, meanwhile, rotoscoping was denigrated to the status of shortcut as evidenced by Ralph Bakshi's extensive use of the technique for the otherwise unaffordable fantasies of *Wizards* (1977) and *The Lord of the Rings* (1978), for which financial limitations demanded time-saving battle scenes rendered in chaotic silhouette. More interesting was Bakshi's use of rotoscoping in the more personal *American Pop* (1981), which told of four generations of musicians in an immigrant Russian-Jewish family in America and at least maintained, however inadvertently and infrequently, the peculiar twist on social realism provided by the contrast of rotoscoped humans in an animated world. This same disconcerting juxtaposition of fantasy and realism was apparent in the Canadian film *Heavy Metal* (1981) produced by Ivan Reitman, but was mostly thereafter consigned to the toolboxes of animators working on conveyor belt animated television series such as *Blackstar* (1981–82) and *He-Man and the Masters of the Universe* (1983–85) as well as the emerging video game industry, whose motion capture gadgetry has since largely bypassed the tracing stage altogether.[5] Thus, from this undignified history, it is perhaps surprising that a graduate researcher named Bob Sabiston should emerge from the Massachusetts Institute of Technology (MIT) Media Lab as the craftsman of a computerised form of rotoscoping and, moreover, that he should pass on his precision tools to Linklater.

Sabiston had worked as a software developer at MIT from 1986 but moved to Austin in 1993 where he set up Flat Black Films and developed a programme for simulating three-dimensional computer animation. For the four-minute *Beat Dedication* (1988) he synchronised an animated robot drummer to the input of a beat and duly admits to both the influence of Pixar's short film *Luxo Jr.* (1986) with its father and son dynamic between two anglepoise lamps and his delight at hearing of head of Pixar John Lasseter's approval. However, Sabiston subsequently turned down an offer from Pixar to work on *Toy Story* (1995) to remain in Austin: 'What a brave little trooper I was!' (Sabiston 2009a). Thereafter, his company survived on cash prizes for early film attempts such as the nightmarish, Tim Burtonesque two minutes of *God's Little Monkey* (1992) and *Grinning Evil Death* (1990), a six-minute gross and goofy tale of a boy superhero fighting extraterrestrial bugs that was inspired by Frank Miller's Batman redux *The Dark Knight Returns* (1986) and which featured prominently on the MTV channel's *Liquid Television* show. Sabiston's concern for reviving and redeveloping rotoscoping began properly with *Project Incognito* in 1997, a twenty-minute feature that responded to another MTV contest requiring ninety seconds of animation featuring characters talking about themselves to the camera. Inspired this time by Nick Park's claymation figures in the *Creature Comforts* (1989, 2003–) series that features a menagerie musing dolefully on mundane concerns, Sabiston sought to both capture the everyday attitudes and embellish the personalities of his vox-pop subjects. *Project Incognito* therefore has a distinct affinity with *Slacker*, not only in comparison with its sequential talking heads but in the working practice that engendered it. Sabiston placed an advertisement in *The Austin Chronicle* asking for volunteer interviewees, who were subsequently selected for the film by an informal audition process based on the interesting qualities of the person rather than any aptitude for performance. While tracing over the live footage of these interviewees, Sabiston realised that the workload would be significantly eased by the invention of a computer programme that he would have to write himself. Instead of copying a projected image, the animator would 'draw' with a pen-shaped mouse that could be 'dipped' in an electronic palette for any colour, texture, thickness or transparency. The drawing is then created on a computer screen which can be overlaid the original footage to check its veracity or simply embellished and adapted at will. Sabiston developed the programme further to allow for the interpolation of animation between one frame and one a dozen or so later. By these means an animator might trace an image of, say, a face on one frame, then one several frames later and the computer would fill in the movement in between, mostly correctly but sometimes oddly, which only added to the effect. Thus was invented what became known as interpolated roto-scoping, where what is left out by the animator and 'imagined' by the computer can often create a shimmering, floating quality and a plate shifting dissonance between the backgrounds and the figures. On *Project Incognito* the black-and-white imagery is sketchy, but this only aids the characterisation of these vague, impulsive individuals who could so easily have dropped out of *Slacker* (Sabiston 2009b). Sabiston won second place in the MTV contest with *Project Incognito* and moved to New York for nine months to develop the software and oversee its use as the medium for a series of brief filler segments or interstitials. However, he fell out with the corporate-ethos and obsession with product and universal branding of MTV and returned once again to Austin.

From the personal and informative website of Flat Black Films offering stills, clips and descriptions of every short and full-length project the company has undertaken, it is clear that Sabiston and his team always saw rotoscoping or Rotoshop (to give the program its name) as very much a developing technology and a dialogic work in progress that suited the team-building exercise of those involved. Like Linklater, Sabiston chose against the corporate-bound production culture on the east and west coasts of America and dedicated himself instead to the 'third coast' of southern Texas, where he collaborated with local artists in Austin on developing the software. According to this website:

> Despite some appearances to the contrary [rotoscoping] does not use filters, image-processing or any kind of motion capture technology. Rather, it is an advanced program for hand-tracing over frames of video. The program will interpolate between brushstrokes to save time and smooth motion, but the process is user-driven and can be extremely time consuming. (Sabiston 2009c)

The blurb also denies any intention to market the software and claims 'there isn't even a manual for it – training just happens on-the-job' (ibid.). As a collaborative work in progress and, indeed, a collaborative working *practice* in progress, it was perhaps inevitable that the similar ethos should have captured the interest of fellow Austinite filmmaker Linklater.

On the drive home to Austin from New York with Tommy Pallotta (who had appeared in *Slacker* as Looking for Missing Friend), Sabiston shot live action footage of interviews with travellers and bystanders that he had in mind to rotoscope for a film called *RoadHead* (1998) that would be 'the first "independent" use made of Rotoshop' (Sabiston 2009d). For its production, Sabiston did what Linklater had done on *Slacker* and posted flyers inviting volunteer animators from around Austin:

> I got about a dozen people to give four hours of their time at a stretch. It was a great way to meet new friends and try out the 'exquisite corpse' style of animated filmmaking. Each animator just got a little piece of the film to work on, with each interview subject in the film being drawn by three or four people. (Ibid.)

The result was a hectic collage of scribbled images of talking heads, drive-by sightseeing and road signs with ticker-tape dates and times to plot the route with an overlaid soundtrack of idle chatter and radio music, whose *cinéma vérité* element is foremost in the rotoscoping of interview subjects fiddling with microphones and querying the format of the piece: 'What is this? Can I just start over?' As they would for *Waking Life*, the animation styles vary greatly, mutating between minimalist broad strokes and Disneyesque outsize features. The subjects discuss God and astrology as well as astronomy, determinism, sociobiology ('It's about how we're hardwired for narrative [...] and how we are in a complicated dialogue with reality') until an animated 'Tape Out' warning flashes in the corner of the screen. Seen now, this drifting narrative and ragbag of philosophies makes *RoadHead* seem like a prescient early draft of *Waking Life*. It took four months to make and was forestalled when MTV demanded their computer back. As Sabiston recalls, 'I think the first place we showed it was at the Fringeware Film Festival down on Guadalupe Street next to Mojo's. They were projecting all kinds of stuff on a big sheet late at night' (ibid.).

Snack and Drink (1999) was next and marked the move into colour for this three-minute pursuit of Ryan Power, a six foot tall autistic resident of Austin on his way to a local 7–11 convenience store, where he demonstrates and expounds upon his characteristically solipsistic philosophy by mixing bursts and squirts of all the soda drinks into one Big Gulp container. Brash and hasty, the film gives the impression of the animators hurrying to catch up with the determined movement and thought processes of their subject and spinning off into increasingly abstract illustrations of his world view and empirical interactions instead (Sabiston 2009e). *Snack and Drink* tied for second place with Pixar's *A Bug's Life* (John Lasseter & Andrew Stanton, 1998) in the 1999 Prix Ars Electronica, was selected for inclusion in the video collection of New York's Museum of Modern Art (MoMA) and inspired The Independent Television Service (ITVS) to commission twelve short animated documentaries in the same style for a series named *Figures of Speech* (1999) that again featured subjects drawn from the streets of Austin. This was animated at the Detour Filmproduction studios of Linklater, where the project served to recruit the key team of animators that would work on *Waking Life*. At liberty to experiment with their rotoscoping of the live action footage, the animators produced work that Sabiston describes as 'the wildest and weirdest we've ever done' (2009f). Such was the infectious energy of the project that Linklater was drawn into considerations of the potential of the technique and its suitability for a long cherished project of his that had originated in a particularly lucid dream during which the sleeping Linklater had been convinced of both the passage of a substantial period of time and his entrapment, before waking to find that only a few moments had elapsed:

> The idea for that narrative came to me as a teenager, before I was a film person. I'd had that kind of lucid dream that the Wiley character seems to be having and I'd always felt that I would deal with that somehow, some way. So I always had this idea of how I can tell the story. *Slacker* came about in a similar way and what I described in the scene in *Slacker* where I'm talking about it, that dream, that becomes *Waking Life* some year later. You know, you make films in your mind for years before you really make them. And the *Waking Life* idea had just never worked as a film in my mind. I could never wrap my mind around it in my head. It seemed cheesy. It never worked as a film. But then these friends of mine, Tommy [Pallotta] and Bob [Sabiston], were developing this animation technique and the first time I saw it – it was black-and-white lines – they were doing some shorts and when I saw that it was – Wow! Something clicked in my mind – that this ephemeral idea might work in this form. Bob [Sabiston] was still working on the software so I thought about it for about another year I guess, started writing, putting it together, just at the moment where it came together, the colour and all that.

Thus, *Waking Life* would be a palimpsest of *Slacker* in which the repeated drift around Austin would be punctuated by all kinds of philosophical dialogues that would be subsequently transformed by rotoscoping into an oneiric, metaphysical exploration of consciousness.

The recurring motif in the cinema of Linklater of a young man or woman daydreaming or nightsleeping with his or her head against the window of a moving bus, car or train features in *It's Impossible to Learn to Plow by Reading Books*, *Slacker*, *Dazed and Confused*, *Before Sunrise*, *SubUrbia*, *Waking Life* and *A Scanner Darkly*. It is in the limbo between reality and dream that this common point of origin for the consciousness of characters in the cinema of Linklater appears paradoxical, because the traveller is at any moment on his or her journey both departing and arriving. This connects with Bergson and his intuitive sense of time while signalling a concern for the metaphysical musings of adolescents, torn as they often are between what William Blake posited as the freedom of innocence and the burden of experience. Suffering may be countered by heeding Boat Car Guy (Bill Wise) in *Waking Life*, who advises Main Character that 'the idea is to remain in a state of constant departure while always arriving'. This awareness of limbo constitutes a metaphysical act that is also a philosophical enquiry into the limits of reality and the unreal. As the aforementioned Goya knew well, the Spanish mystics of the sixteenth century, Saint John of the Cross and

Arriving while departing. Main Character (Wiley Wiggins) takes instruction from fellow passenger Richard Linklater and Boat Car Guy (Bill Wise) in *Waking Life*

Saint Teresa of Ávila, both suffered and craved visions that inspired and motivated them.[6] Their metaphysical experiences allowed them to leave reality behind and explore ecstasy in the pursuit of enlightenment before returning to the waking state in which these thoughts would be expressed in poetry and theological writing. Saint Teresa even essayed a structuring of the experience into four stages that began with concentrated prayer and moved onto meditation in which human will surrendered itself to what she identified as God. Thereafter, reason and imagination slipped their bindings with reality and allowed the subject to float into an ecstatic state in which reason is given up to God while memory and imagination are liberated. Finally, the state of devotion is a passive one of acceptance in which the self is wholly absorbed into the trance and during which Saint Teresa was said to have levitated before returning to the ground tearful and weak. Remove God from the equation and one is left with an analogous, oneiric experience that has similarities to the practice of lucid dreaming associated with non-secular meditation, recreational drug use and *Waking Life*.

Confusing the real and the unreal in this manner can also be a deliberate ploy aimed at questioning the nature of being and the world. Metaphysical enquiry is sometimes referred to as the first philosophy because the first major work to bear the term was a treatise by Aristotle (384–22 BC), although Aristotle himself did not name it thus. Within the field of metaphysical enquiry, however, the key question for characters in the cinema of Linklater appears to be whether the world exists outside the mind. This prompts conceptual musings on the interaction of the mind and the body that gives rise to the monologues and dialogues of *Slacker* as well as informing those in *Before Sunrise* and *Before Sunset*. It also inspires the banter and debate of the protagonists of *Waking Life* and the manic monologues of Barris (Robert Downey Jr.) in *A Scanner Darkly*. The ingredients of these dialogues include a belief in Dualism as propagated by the French philosopher René Descartes (1596–1650) in *Meditationes* (*Meditations*, 1641), which tends to locate intelligence in the brain while saving accumulated wisdom, intuition and self-awareness for a non-corporeal 'soul' or 'mind'. Other ingredients include the thoughts of later disciples of this philosophy, such as the Anglo-Irish George Berkeley (1685–1753), who maintained a belief that neither material objects nor ideas exist unless they are perceived by the mind, and Immanuel Kant (1724–1804), who went so far as to propose that time and space are merely mental constructs that humans utilise in order to structure and classify that which is perceived. Consequently, this once more connects with Bergson and his differentiation between the intellectual measurement of time and its intuitive perception.

The use of rotoscoping for a film such as *Waking Life* and its relay discussion of metaphysics is apt because the animation adds that extra level of transcendence sought by saints and philosophers alike to the reality of the live action footage. That is to say, the original, mostly hand-held digital footage shot by Linklater and Pallotta is a record of a reality that is rendered dreamlike by the animation process. In so doing, rotoscoping effectively facilitates the displacement of our attention from the real that was advocated by Bergson as essential to metaphysical enquiry: 'A question of *turning* this attention *aside* from the part of the universe which interests us from a practical viewpoint and *turning it back* toward what serves no practical purpose' (1992e: 138; emphasis in original). For Bergson, 'this conversion of the attention would be philosophy itself' (ibid.). The appropriateness of rotoscoping to the illustration of metaphysical enquiry is that it 'breaks away from the appearances here below and attaches itself to the realities above' (Bergson 1992e: 139):

> More precisely, for Plato and for all those who understand metaphysics in that way, breaking away from life and converting one's attention consisted in transporting oneself immediately into a world different from the one we inhabit, in developing other faculties of perception than the senses and consciousness. (Ibid.)

The irony remains, however, that this different world beyond the one we inhabit is merely rendered that way by rotoscoping, which challenges our perception of a familiar world by making it uncanny, at the same time both recognisable and strange. Yet this does not render *Waking Life* entirely Surrealist because it seeks meaningful relevance as well as incongruous absurdity and the struggle of Main Character, who is crucially gifted knowledge of his somnambulant state, is to learn to control his lucid dream through a somewhat paradoxical surrender to its logic. In a sense, rotoscoping might even invoke Immanuel Kant's view that 'if metaphysics is possible, it can be so only through an effort of intuition' (in Bergson 1992e: 140) because it enables a conflict of sorts between the intellectual force required to 'think through' its many dialogues and our more intuitive perception of its imagery. The mind is arguably thus torn between the logic and rationality of arguments as profound as a library full of theses and the bizarre, fantastic illustrations of those thoughts that are as ephemeral as a dope-fiend's enlightenment. In order to 'survive' this we should do as Bergson advises: 'What is required is that we should break with certain habits of thinking and perceiving that have become natural to us. We must return to the direct perception of change and mobility' (1992e: 142). This is the function and purpose of rotoscoping, the fluidity of which invites and reminds us to go with the flow, for it is only through our surrender to the imagery that we can intuitively understand what is being discussed.

The spontaneous, unrehearsed nature of several of the discussions filmed by Linklater and Pallotta made up about one third of the finished live action draft of *Waking Life*. Another third was scripted and the rest was worked up by the cast. After handing over the edited footage, Linklater did not participate in the rotoscoping: 'There were all these great artists. We hired these great illustrators, but that's not one of my skills.' Although he initially instructed the animators to be literal in their animation of the talking heads, they escaped his control and their potential boredom by extrapolating Expressionist digressions out of the speakers and their dialogues. It became a game in which in-jokes, gags, wild transformations and ghost images ganged up on Linklater and forced him to grant amnesty and inclusion to anything that suited the spirit of a scene. Nevertheless, he worked on the music and dialogue tracks, oversaw the casting of the various animators to specific characters and retained editorial control of the conglomeration of animation styles proffered by Sabiston's team. Recalls Linklater:

> I always describe that collaboration as working with a composer or even with an actor. It's like it's their skill but you're overseeing the bigger design. I end up in the position of approving the final design. They draw the character once and I'm like, 'Eww!' And they come back and, 'Okay, let's go with that!' You're kind of in this weird middle position. But that's kind of what a director does anyway, even with an actor. There's things you control completely – the shot, the camera – but on everything else you're collaborating completely with everyone.

To a certain extent in *Waking Life*, as in the positioning of Mitch Kramer in *Dazed and Confused*, Main Character played by Wiggins (who also worked as animator on the film) is initially positioned as the dominant subjectivity and thus the perceiver of the objects, events and ideas that surround him. Consequently, by learning to appreciate and even tentatively control his condition, Main Character finds himself transcending reality by adding floating to this uninhibited *dérive* around Austin, suddenly relocating his consciousness in disparate times and places (such as New York) and even approaching the extracorporeal sexual fulfillment that Guy Talking about Turning the Light on in Dreams (John Christensen) professes to achieve. The rotoscoped animation simply allows for the expression of an experience that is *beyond* the physical and thus the illustration of metaphysical ideas and philosophies. Because Main Character is aware that he is trapped in an increasingly bizarre succession of scenes, the simmering terror beneath his calm veneer resembles that of the guests in Luis Buñuel's *Le charme discret de la bourgeoisie* (*The Discreet Charm of the Bourgeoisie*, 1972), who respond with desperate decorum to the evermore bizarre interruptions of their attempts to dine in a film that can also be understood as a series of dreams within dreams. What rotoscoping adds to Main Character's plight is an immediate Surrealism that plays at the border between the real and unreal, just as, for example, Buñuel's guests react with strained amusement at discovering their dining room is actually a set on a theatre's stage. As

Linklater explained: 'What I needed was a way of depicting unreality in a realistic fashion' (in Arnold 2001).

However, Main Character is not merely a narrative cipher or pawn in *Waking Life*, for his dilemma increases as the film progresses and he is assailed by all manner of competing explanations for his experience of the kind of fairytale found at the other end of a rainbow or rabbit hole. He repeatedly tries to wake and is frustrated when the dream continues. Sleepwalking towards a cognitive state that allows him to explain his problem to others, Main Character is increasingly rebuked by their self-absorption and resignation towards their own dislocation from reality. The disconnection from those he encounters is exaggerated by *Waking Life*'s 'inclusion of a range of animation styles [that] reinforces its presentation of various philosophical perspectives similar to *Slacker*' (Speed 2007: 102). Yet, unlike in *Slacker* where a united sense of community extends beyond the frame, *Waking Life* accumulates nothing quite as dynamic, offering instead an evasive resignation to what is potentially an ultimately ineffectual and solipsistic existence. As Speed observes, 'the film's narrative trajectory through a series of separate, dreamlike episodes implies a perpetual evasion of an unspecified, absolute boundary' (2007: 105). The film, as One of Four Men (Adam Goldberg) admits, is potentially all talk and no action, which is also a criticism Goldberg's Mike levels against himself in *Dazed and Confused* and the proto-activists struggle to disprove in *Fast Food Nation*. As Old Man (Charles Murdock) in *Waking Life* contends: 'As the pattern gets more intricate and subtle, being swept along is no longer enough', which is why, as the dreamstate becomes paradoxically more real *and* more oneiric, Main Character strives to reclaim his human will. Unlike Linklater, who awoke, however, Main Character finally drifts away; heavenwards if one believes the saints.

In addition to the expression of a metaphysical transcendence of reality, rotoscoping is appropriate to the project because it renders the characters in *Waking Life* so grotesque that it connects with Bakhtin's views on the carnival:

> The fairytale world can be defined as strange and unusual, but it is not a world that has *become* alienated. In the grotesque, on the contrary, all that was for us familiar and friendly suddenly becomes hostile. It is our own world that undergoes change. (1984a: 48; emphasis in original)

Thus, the metaphysical realm of *Waking Life* may be understood as a distorting mirror's image of reality in which 'the grotesque liberates man from all the forms of inhuman necessity that direct the prevailing concept of the world' (Bakhtin 1984a: 49). What *Waking Life* makes explicit is the carnivalesque nature of *Slacker*, for it is a visual and thematic palimpsest of that film with an additional layer of rotoscoping that renders its protagonists grotesque. *Waking Life* is also America at the beginning of the new millennium, of course, but distorted as much as the England of Lewis Carroll's *Alice's Adventures in Wonderland* (1865) or the Spain of Goya's *Black Paintings* (1819–23) and *The Disasters of War* (1810–20). Remaining in Spain, there is also a great affinity between the manner in which rotoscoping renders its subjects and the work of Ramón María del Valle-Inclán (1836–1936), whose *esperpento* was a literary style of distorting reality in the service of irony and satire in which dreams and nightmares are invoked as analogous to the reality of the day. Furthermore, the conclusions drawn from the dreamstate of *Waking Life* have a marked affinity with the Golden Age play *La vida es sueño* (*Life is a Dream*, 1635) by Pedro Calderón de la Barca (1600–81). Like *Waking Life*, *La vida es sueño* is an allegorical illustration of philosophical enquiry into the meaning of life and the perception of reality. Its most celebrated passage is spoken by an imprisoned character called Segismundo, who questions whether he dreamt a brief period of liberty and extrapolates this to posit that all of life (and so all the lives he perceives therein) are also dreams: 'And in all the world, I see, / Man dreams whatever he be, / And his own dream no man knows' (1961: 65).[7] The conclusion of this soliloquy is even more convinced and convincing and warrants the status of Hamlet's soliloquy in Spanish literature as well as direct comparison with the resolution of *Waking Life*:

> What is life? A frenzy;
> What is life? An illusion,
> a shadow, a fiction;
> and the greatest good is small,
> for all of life is a dream,
> and dreams, dreams is all they are. (Ibid.) [8]

Here is 'the transience of life, the illusion of the material and the reality of the spiritual, the liberty of the individual and the frustration of the will' that Sloman writes of in his introduction to *La vida es sueño* (1961: xxii) and that, in a sense, rotoscoping revives and illustrates. It does so by locating all the dissenting and competing philosophies and belief systems of its contemporary characters in an alternative America to that of 2001. In other words, as did *Slacker* a decade earlier, the transformation of Austin, Texas into this 'Dreamstate, USA' effects both a refuge and a stronghold for ideas of non-conformity, spirituality and freedom that were perhaps subdued, even defeated, in the reality of the year 2001, in which the 46th Governor of Texas, George W. Bush, was elected the 43rd president of the USA. As Old Man exclaims: 'Man, this must be like parallel universe night!'

Although *Waking Life* received its premiere in the Sundance Film Festival in January 2001 it was not released until 19 October 2001 following screenings at the Austin Film Festival and the New York Film Festival, little more than a month after the destruction of New York's World Trade Center. In this context, Linklater was described as formulating a 'diplomatic response' (Arnold 2001) to questions about what was incorrectly perceived on its release (for the film had been completed long before 9/11) as *Waking Life*'s peculiarly evasive or palliative response to the recent tragedy and trauma:

> 'I feel weird thinking about it', he says. 'I don't want to find myself thinking, "Oh, God, the country has been forced by this great calamity into being in a friendly frame of mind for my new film"'. He does admit the film 'very consciously brings up fundamental questions about reality, unreality, existence,

free will – all the stuff that you realize will elude simple answers but you still need to ask, since the questions are always worth thinking about.' (Ibid.)

Interestingly, the fundamental questioning of reality that dominates *Waking Life* coincided with the academic and mediatic uptake of the French cultural theorist and philosopher Jean Baudrillard's denomination of the Gulf War as a non-event in *The Gulf War Did Not Take Place* (2001). His denial of the physical conflict as anything more than a media event that was 'a masquerade of information: branded faces delivered over to the prostitution of the image, the image of an unintelligible distress' (2001: 40) illustrated and invoked kindred doubts about reality itself. In addition, Baudrillard's 2001 essay *The Spirit of Terrorism* posited the destruction of the World Trade Center as 'the pure event which is the essence of all the events that never happened [which] through its unbearable power, engendered all that violence brewing around the world, and therefore this terrorist imagination which – unknowingly – inhabits us all' (2009). This 'terrorist imagination' was even oneiric, claimed Baudrillard, when he stated 'that we have dreamed of this event, that everybody without exception has dreamt of it, because everybody must dream of the destruction of any power hegemonic to that degree' (Ibid.).

The notion that 9/11 was in some way a metaphysical experience whose ocurrence in reality could only be assimilated by those who witnessed it live and on television by reference to the unreality of disaster movies and science fiction, aids more than a conspiracy theory, for it adds momentously to the debate about whether or not the world exists outside the mind. When confronted by this shock to the system, this slap to the side of the face that was the footage of the planes hitting the towers and the edifices crumbling into dust, the mind resorted to the refuge of unreality as practised by the artist in Goya's etching. That is to say, the monstrous event was removed from its frozen grip on the intellect and consigned to dreams or at least dreamlike imagery that was remembered from disaster films instead. Denial also played its part when the world expressed disbelief, thereby subscribing to George Berkeley's notion that the event could be erased from reality by the mind's inability to perceive of its magnitude. If it could not be received, contained or expressed within the mind, then it might be judged never to have happened. Thus, our consciousness needed to be raised or expanded in order for the event of 9/11 to have taken place. New structures and classifications for the scale of the event had to be mapped and, whereas news media took almost no time at all to reduce the event to a repetitive, emotionless cliché in its edited loop of the planes impacting the towers from various angles, our minds struggled to recall the impact *of* that impact and situate it within reconstructed parameters of time and space in which it *actually* happened and we *actually* experienced it as something real. Linklater would literally revisit Ground Zero in *Live from Shiva's Dance Floor*, whereas in *Waking Life* there is only a premonition of the imminent cataclysm. This is because rotoscoping, as practised by Sabiston and his team, had progressed far beyond its time-saving and realism-adding functions to allow for deviations and stylisation that made for an accumulation of layers or *sur*-realities whose malleability was ideal for representing and expressing metaphysical thought. If Linklater had completed *Waking*

Life after 9/11, for instance, it is possible that the destruction of the World Trade Center would have been fittingly rotoscoped into a metaphysical experience for Main Character, whereby its unreality would not have jarred with that of any other of his unreal experiences. This would conceivably have managed what news media and the personal endeavour of millions had failed to do: the assimilation of the event within the collective consciousness through the medium of a lucid dream or (which is the next best thing) the experience of watching *Waking Life*.

Nevertheless, merely communicating ideas such as these outside of literature, academic conferences, broadsheet newspapers, televised and streaming debate was, said Linklater, a major challenge for film culture, which he clamed 'had no room for ideas':

> There's no way to communicate it in a wide way. The pop culture tends to go to the lowest denominator, so cinema is a weird place, due to its mass nature. It's diluted down to very little: simple stories and simple politics. So this movie is really challenging in that way. I thought it was sort of a conduit to a lot of ideas and energies and I honestly spit it back out in an interesting way. One of the themes of the movie is that we're all connected on some psychic level: we come back to that a lot of times in the movie. And so, I think humans really feel that and they explain it in different ways. (In Kaufman 2001)

Waking Life thus raises a plethora of questions without answers in a manner that is playfully begun by Linklater's own daughter, Lorelei, appearing as Young Girl Playing Paper Game in the opening scene, in which 'Dream is Destinie' (sic.) can be seen scribbled on the inside of the origami paper contraption (a cootie-catcher), and concluded by Linklater himself playing the ultimate respondent to Main Character's questions. As Pinball Playing Man, Linklater recounts an anecdote of Philip K. Dick's that not only connects with *A Scanner Darkly* but also dismisses the now obsessive quest for meaning of Main Character: 'You know, just … wake up!'

If rotoscoping had worked commercially in the sense of connecting with a broad and youthful audience, Hollywood would doubtless have acquired Sabiston's programme (or developed a variation thereof) and deployed it for a summer blockbuster; but the minor cult status of *Waking Life* only supports Justin Wyatt's assertion that Hollywood's assimilation of avant-garde styles 'depends on the extent to which artists are interested in engaging with narrative in their creative projects' (1994: 199). Critical response to the film was divided between the nonplussed and the enchanted. *Senses of Cinema* christened Linklater 'the poet of American freedom' while also catching the contradiction by noting 'the scary question at the heart of *Waking Life*: in the end, how important is the distinction between our perception and the world we perceive?' (Jones K. 2002). Freedom, in other words, might just be an illusion, while the metaphysical return journey from reality to unreality is not necessarily one of guaranteed enlightenment but always liable to veer away from transcendence towards terror. Metaphysics cannot define 'being', only describe it. Metaphysical enquiry is thus not a destination but a journey through prayer, reflection, dialogue and debate that is always ripe and relevant in the cinema of Linklater, who might thus be placed alongside a small band of metaphysical filmmakers whose works are not limited to the avant-garde but possessed of political and philosophical resonance.

Andrei Tarkovsky, Krzysztof Kieslowski, Terrence Malick and Julio Medem, for example, are phenomenologically-minded filmmakers whose most metaphysical films make what appears local or personal into something more universally relevant. As for Linklater, each of these filmmakers has made places in Russia, Poland, America and Spain respectively into the setting for characters stumbling between chaos and order towards an eternally elusive explanation of time and its meaning. Each of them combines oneiric imagery with realism in a manner that questions the veracity of both, although it is Linklater who plays closest to the borders with mainstream, genre-based cinema and so his insistence on daydreaming appears all the more rebellious. He is, after all, a citizen of a country that withholds the 'American dream' in lieu of profit and results. As a counterplot philosophy to focus, drive, conformity and acceptance, Linklater's musing in *Slacker* that 'every thought you have creates its own reality. The thing you choose not to do fractions off and becomes its own reality', effects a potent rebuke to any demand to put all one's energy into one single reality defined by a government and ruling class that otherwise ignores you. Thus, there is daydreaming to be actively pursued as a survivalist technique or there is its flipside: death in life. This paradox is thrown into relief in *Waking Life* by the counter-paradox of what appear to be spontaneous moments of animation that make it seem as if the film itself is daydreaming. As characters talk seriously about great themes, the backgrounds morph and bud witty details that punctuate their dialogue: characters float, their ringlets curl and unfurl, creatures in an aquarium noticeably evolve and lightning bolts shoot from the hands of Caveh Zahedi as he attempts to explain Bazinian principles of realism by means of animation (another paradox). In sum, rotoscoping is not employed to represent unreality but to express the reality of the imagination.

The fact that dreaming features as a topic of conversation in so many of the films directed by Linklater points to their respondent fluidity and the dialogic nature of them all, wherein the walking and talking follows an endless stream of thoughts, ideas, tales and suppositions that creates an oneiric, sublime dialogue that approaches eroticism. Hand-held camera, long takes and time-images are thus well complemented by rotoscoping, which, with all its colours, movement and amoebic forms appears organic, growing atop characters that assume hallucinatory forms that evolve with an immediacy provided by the digital technology. Nevertheless, as with much of the cinema of Linklater, *Waking Life* posits loneliness as a theme, as the sad result of so much introspective disassociation from reality. Even the miracle of meeting one's soulmate (twice) as illustrated by *Before Sunrise* and *Before Sunset* is tainted by the loneliness that otherwise devours Jesse and Céline, although no protagonist is quite as isolated as the ironically named Main Character. From the lolloping individuals and tense couples of *Slacker* to the stilted activists, illegal immigrants and wilfully ignorant company men of *Fast Food Nation*, loneliness is the common consequence of thinking differently and thinking too much that plagues the protagonists of the cinema of Linklater. Walking and talking may temporarily alleviate the loneliness, as well as the symptoms of paranoia, depression and incipient madness, but there is always too the fear that *this* time, *this* youthfulness, *this* life will end. The fact that by committing to each other either Jesse or Céline will one day suffer the other's death is perhaps the only morbid thought missing from their dialogue.

Main Character also approaches intimations of his own mortality that the dream-state may actually have supplanted with a purposeless purgatory, identified as such by one of the 'oneironauts' who warns him 'the worst mistake you can make is to think you are alive when really you're asleep in life's waiting room'. By way of comparison, the same situation and emotion envelops the childlike Ray (Colin Farrell) in *In Bruges* (Martin McDonagh, 2008). A hitman in hiding after accidentally killing a child, Ray is sent to the Belgian town that he soon realises (following clues from Hieronymous Bosch's painting of *The Last Judgement* [c.1482]) is a kind of purgatory fashioned with Surrealist imagery that he is also incapable of escaping:

> Prison … death … didn't matter. Because at least in prison and at least in death, you know, I wouldn't be in fuckin' Bruges. But then, like a flash, it came to me. And I realised, fuck, man, maybe that's what hell is: the entire rest of eternity spent in fuckin' Bruges. And I really, really hoped I wouldn't die. I really, really hoped I wouldn't die.

Does Main Character die in *Waking Life* or does he just never wake up? And what, pray, is the difference? Because, as Sabiston states, 'the software has become a tool for blurring the lines between reality and the imagined' (Ward P. 2006: 42), the quivering, shape-shifting, flowing imagery of rotoscoping effects the expression of this fearfully conscious somnambulism. However, as Main Character passes through a second, third and fourth false awakening, he is dulled rather than revived by the experiences. Thus a final paradox emerges: for all the dreamlike *dérive* (drift) and unmeasured *durée* (duration) of *Waking Life,* it is arguably the most plot-driven, suspenseful and linear of all Linklater's films. Main Character struggles towards nirvana: the realisation that if reality (waking life) is a dream, then dreams must be reality. But he also drifts inexorably towards a death that, in opposition to all the walking and talking, is hastened by his increasing solipsism. Consequently, the cure offered to him by Linklater as Pinball Playing Man to 'you know, just … wake up!' is also extended to an audience that might as well be exhorted to 'you know, just … turn off the film!' In sum, if we take as given that reality is a dream and dreams are reality, and then correlate the dream-state with the experience of watching a film, we end up with a particularly cinematic philosophy that sees life, dream and film in a state of constantly becoming each other. Watching a film, in other words, can be a metaphysical act.

Such debate is irresolute but must end somewhere. Thus, after the exhaustion of its illustration, Sabiston sought 'a good break from the endless parade of human faces that was *Waking Life*' (2009g) and made a three-minute short called *Leaves* (2001) about Austin's summer chorus of cicadas followed by a series of documentary shorts for the PBS television show *Life 360* (2001). Then in 2002 his gadgetry was featured in *De Fem benspænd* (*The Five Obstructions*, Lars von Trier, 2003), an examination of film authorship in which von Trier challenges his old teacher Jørgen Leth to remake his short film *Det perfekte menneske* (*The Perfect Human*, 1967) five times with different sets of obstructions. As punishment for an infraction of one rule, von Trier threatens Leth with the commission to make an animated version, which prompts a comical exchange between the two as they take turns accentuating the stress on the phrase 'I *hate* cartoons'. The reason for their hatred and Leth's fear of the challenge is that animation supposedly removes every possibility of chance from the production process. Everything is premeditated, calibrated, revised and approved, which von Trier and Leth assume prohibits spontaneity and accident and so elides any semblance of realism and interest. However, Leth rises to the challenge by passing it on to Sabiston, who appears in the film presenting a catalogue of sketches and images for Leth's approval. In fact, as Sabiston recalls, the call came from Leth's son: 'They didn't pay us very much … but it was the ultimate in creative freedom. It was cool also to appear in the film and have our Austin office-house pop up all out-of-place in this erudite, multicultural piece of "*cinema*"' (2009h; emphasis in original). Leth and von Trier ultimately admire the rotoscoped short without much enthusiasm, but the platform for rotoscoping provided by *De Fem benspænd* was a remarkable boon to the recognition of its status as something other than a plaything or shortcut. In 2004 Sabiston reunited with Linklater to make *A Scanner Darkly* 'the best-looking animated movie ever made' (Sabiston 2009i).

While making *Waking Life*, Linklater recalls 'thinking about other films that would work in that style. You could do it with any movie technically – but why?' He first considered an adaptation of Philip K. Dick's *Ubik* (1969) about psychic warfare, time shifts, decomposition and the customary confusion of reality and unreality, but the rights were 'a mess, whereas *A Scanner Darkly* was available'. *A Scanner Darkly* is a semi-autobiographical novel written in 1977 in which Dick asserts, 'I am not a character in this novel; I am the novel. So, though was our entire nation at this time' (2006: 218–19), and it ends with a dedication to those of his acquaintance who were killed or brain damaged by drugs. It was optioned for Linklater to direct by Steven Soderbergh's Section Eight production company (with Soderbergh and George Clooney credited as executive producers). 'We had a meeting and they worked really fast,' remembers Linklater, although in order to convince the daughters of Philip K. Dick to grant the rights he had to swear he 'would not do the typical thing. Take the core idea, get rid of the rest and make a Hollywood narrative out of it'. Instead, he promised 'to just take those characters and go all the way with the story':

> His daughters responded to that. I had to get their rights and blessing and get them to take a discount. When I first met with Isa [Dick-Hackett], she said: 'Just so you know, the little dedication at the end, this is my dad and this is my mom, she's on the list too.' And I'm like: 'Oh, you're one of the little girls in the house that went away?' She goes: 'Yeah, we went away and those guys moved in.' So I was like: 'I really want to make this!'

Thereafter, Linklater approached Keanu Reeves about taking the main role and found him 'intrigued but unavailable, and then nobody wanted to do it for a couple of years'.

The project simmered, however, and was gradually reduced to a less risky budget that was covered by Warner Independent Pictures in association with Thousand Words (which had also produced *Waking Life*), Section Eight, Detour Filmproduction and 3 Arts Entertainment, which went on to have a hand in the science fiction epics *I Am Legend* (Francis Lawrence, 2007) and *The Day the Earth Stood Still* (Scott Derrickson, 2008). Linklater insisted that he 'wanted it to be faithful' and therefore claims the low cost 'actually helped, because it was low-budget, six million dollars, no one got paid anything and with that budget I thought I could make a faithful film, leave in all the digressive humour'. Unfortunately, as Sabiston recalls: 'The studio allotted only $2 million dollars and five months to animate an entire Hollywood feature film, and then treated us like criminals when we said it could not be done' (2009i). As for *Waking Life*, Sabiston had hired local aspirational animators with the promise of hands-on training in Rotoshop, but these five teams exhibited uneven commitment to the project and little in the way of completed footage with which to calm the increasingly frustrated Mark Gill of Warner Independent Pictures or Linklater, who was busy filming *Bad News Bears*. Seeing Sabiston's animation team and schedule faltering, producer Tommy Pallotta locked Sabiston out of the studio and replaced his amateur animators with a more Disneyfied production line of experienced artists (see La Franco 2006). Recalls Sabiston: 'In the end we left, and they finished it without us (spending another two, three, four million?). But the movie turned out okay, and if we'd had the resources allotted to say, two episodes of *Family Guy*, I think we could have done it' (2009i).

Linklater's quite faithful adaptation of *A Scanner Darkly* recounts the California drug culture of Philip K. Dick's day but films it in Austin and sets it in the 'neon ooze' (Dick 2006: 22) of a dystopian police state of 1994 in which paranoia is rife and, as Dick describes, time has become wholly subjective:

> The illumination for the room came from a pole lamp into which he had screwed nothing but spot lamps, which shone day and night, so as to abolish time for him and his friends. He liked that; he liked to get rid of time. By doing that he could concentrate on important things without interruption. (2006: 3)

Bob Arctor (Keanu Reeves) lives a double-life as a junkie and as a police agent named Fred who is not only obliged to report on his housemates, the befuddled Ernie Luckman (Woody Harrelson) and the paranoid, deceitful James Barris (Robert Downey Jr.), but to spy on himself as well in order not to arouse suspicion. Themes of duality are thus central to the plot and emphasised in an eminently Cubist manner by the scramble suit that agents like Fred must wear. Dick writes that this mutating shroud means that agents like Arctor 'cannot be identified by voice, or even by technological voiceprint, or by appearance' (2006: 15):

> He looks, does he not, like a vague blur and nothing more? Basically, his design consisted of a multifaceted quartz lens hooked up to a miniaturized computer whose memory banks held up to a million and a half physiognomic fraction-

representations of various people: men and women, children, with every variant encoded and then projected outward in all directions equally onto a superthin shroud-like membrane large enough to fit around an average human. As the computer looped through its banks, it projected every conceivable eye color, hair color, shape and type of nose, formation of teeth, configuration of facial bone structure – the entire shroudlike membrane took on whatever physical characteristics were projected at any nanosecond, and then switched to the next. […] In any case, the wearer of a scramble suit was Everyman and in every combination (up to combinations of a million and a half sub-bits) during the course of each hour. Hence, any description of him – or her – was meaningless. (2006: 15)

The scramble suit, which largely inspired the decision to deploy rotoscoping as the means of its representation, so clearly evokes the Cubist aesthetic and meaning that it is described by Dick as having been invented by a man who 'for about six hours, entranced […] had watched thousands of Picasso paintings replace one another at flash-cut speed' (2006: 16). As Anna Powell describes in relation to the theory of Bergson, the scramble suit is a 'dynamic and multi-faceted model [that] stresses change and multiplicity' (2008: 121). However, because Arctor is increasingly addicted to the psychoactive Substance D or 'Death' his ability to distinguish between reality and unreality is diminished. Thus, the scramble suit both illustrates and exacerbates his mental fragmentation, for, as Dick states, it is something like a canvas for a Cubist portrait of an Everyman that complies with Bergsonian notions of time in being constantly shifting and evolving. 'You will notice that you can barely see the man,' says the Brown Bear Lodge Host (Mitch Baker) somewhat paradoxically when introducing the suited Arctor as guest speaker to his audience: 'Let's hear it for the vague blur!' Because of the millions of fragments of human features and clothing that are replaced at a maddening

The mental and physical fragmentation of the scramble suit in *A Scanner Darkly*

rate, the scramble suit is both perpetually arriving and departing to the effect that 'Fred, Robert Arctor, whatever' (Dick 2006: 18) fragments into 'a composite of all sorts of guys at their desks' (Dick 2006: 21). This thus illustrates what Bergson called 'this indivisible continuity of change [that] is precisely what constitutes true duration' (1992e: 149). The perpetual Cubist fragmentation of Arctor's persona and appearance culminates in the dissolution of any single vantage point from which to ascertain the truth: 'What is identity? He asked himself. Where does the act end? Nobody knows' (Dick 2006: 21).

Like Main Character in *Waking Life*, the rotoscoped Arctor is forced into a questioning of time, reality and the mind's ability to construct a meta-reality that results in self-induced paranoia:

> To himself, Bob Arctor thought, *How many Bob Arctors are there?* A weird and fucked-up thought. Two that I can think of, he thought. The one called Fred, who will be watching the other one, called Bob. The same person. Or is it? Is Fred actually the same as Bob? Does anybody know? I would know, if anyone did, because I'm the only person in the world that knows that Fred is Bob Arctor. *But*, he thought, *who am I? Which of them is me?* (Dick 2006: 74–75; emphasis in original)

Arctor/Fred's dilemma may be partly explained by reference to Bergson, who defined this dual topography of the psyche in *Time and Free Will* (2003 [1889]) as an outer surface that functions in spatial and social contexts and an inner sense of self that experiences the *durée* or 'durational process of perpetual becoming' (Powell 2008: 121). As described by Dick, when Arctor is dressed in the suit (which briefly resembles Philip K. Dick in its very first appearance in the film), his exterior appearance allows him to pass unobserved through these 'spatial and social contexts' while his shrouded inner self experiences the suit's constant flux as an arduous state of 'perpetual becoming' because it will never, ever resemble the man inside. Bergson and Dick therefore seem to concur in their convictions that there are two selves to each Everyman: the one that is projected externally and which allows us to adapt and function in society (but which may not be wholly truthful), and the other which simmers within and whose relationship with the outer self is complicated by deep introspection. Each Everyman is thus both performer and audience, obliged to achieve and maintain this split personality in order to observe or 'spy on' himself and thus ensure his or her anonymity. Interestingly, this duality is actively advocated by some psychologists as a decentering of the self by which a subject may step outside restricted perceptions of behaviour and appearance by accessing those areas of the mind that are not prisoner of negative assumptions. The aim, which is illustrated so frequently in the cinema of Linklater, is to *think* about one's *thinking*. Termed metacognition by psychologists, the practice is essential to the enabling of perceptual shifts. For example, just as someone suffering from anorexia might undergo cognitive behavioural therapy in order to challenge and overcome the negativity that springs from an ingrained neural pattern connecting any intake of food with the exacerbation of feelings of being unloved, so Main Character in *Waking Life* must 'think about his thinking' in order to shift his perception of a traditional distinction between wakefulness and the dreamstate.

Thinking about one's thinking is, of course, also a common theme and subject in *Slacker*, *Before Sunrise*, *SubUrbia* and *Before Sunset*, where it feeds off both a European cult of Rohmeresque introspection and an American exuberance for Altmanesque self-expression. The caveat of *A Scanner Darkly*, however, is that Arctor's 'thinking about his thinking' results in the conflict between the two hemispheres of a divided mind. His perceptive and cognitive areas split and oppose each other, offering only exhausting 'cross-chatter' between the intellect and intuition, which are polarised to the point of stasis, resulting in Arctor's final conversion into the stupefied Bruce, who seems as somnolent as Main Character in *Waking Life* and as lobotomised as R. P. McMurphy (Jack Nicholson) in *One Flew Over the Cuckoo's Nest* (Milos Forman, 1975). The very similar endings of *A Scanner Darkly* and *One Flew Over the Cuckoo's Nest*, in which both Bruce and McMurphy are lobotomised, signals a congruent backlash against all the rebellious youths played by Nicholson and his peers in the films of the new American cinema of the late 1960s and 1970s, when, as Dick writes in the novel's final dedication/epigraph, 'some people [...] were punished entirely too much for what they did' (2006: 218). Normally, there is some dialogue between the intellect and intuition that allows for adaptation and evolution as new neural paths are mapped, but in cases of mental illness, drug use, paranoia, bipolarity or all of the above as experienced by Arctor, neural paths stagnate in obsession and psychosis, fragmentation occurs and multiple personality disorders may result. The scramble suit perfectly illustrates this movement from a single, stable personality to a shifting, unstable multiple personality disorder, while the finally unsuited 'Bruce' signifies the erasure of all personality that results. Because putting on and taking off the suit is also a metaphysical gambit of moving from the real to the unreal and back again (with all the risks that this involves), so it is apt that it should illustrate and express this in its Cubist representation of an Everyman who is constantly arriving and departing. It was the potential of rotoscoping to express this Cubist rendering of the suit that so enthused Linklater, who admits that the inspiration for the film was 'the scramble suit, but also the mindset of the whole movie':

> [Arctor]'s losing his mind and there's the ultimate Philip K. Dick question of how do you know what is real and what isn't – ultimately the picture puts you in the headspace. *Waking Life* puts you 100 per cent in the headspace too, but this movie has various headspaces: the perspective of the person being watched and the perspective of the government that's doing the watching and I'd always wanted to feel as if you're in Bob Arctor's mind. And I knew for that to work the same way that [rotoscoping] works on your brain will be the way to take in this particular story.

As a Cubist work, the scramble suit's constantly changing form expresses the limitless duration of its own event, making it possible to appreciate an analogous relationship between the suit and the form of Linklater's films. For example, the structure of *Slacker* is itself a kind of scramble suit in which the constant flux of protagonists creates a Cubist expression of the slacker community in Austin. Like the suit, *Slacker* is a collage of human expressions whose figures are constantly arriving and departing, to the extent that its detractors might describe this seemingly formless, aimless film as a vague blur. The multi-character collages of *Dazed and Confused*, *SubUrbia*, *Waking Life* and *Fast Food Nation* might also function in the light of Bakhtin's theories of carnival as costumes that are appropriately and ironically grotesque. As a costume, the scramble suit is both clown and demon. Its appearance is both foolish and terrifying. As Bakhtin writes of the Harlequin figure from the Italian *Commedia dell'arte*, who may have originated with one of the devils named Alichino in Dante's *Inferno* (1321) and who also wears a mask and multi-coloured suit, he 'represented a certain form of life, which was real and ideal at the same time. [He] stood on the borderline between life and art, in a peculiar midzone as it were' (1984a: 8). The suit, which both requires and inspires rotoscoping, rarely has two eyes the same colour. Its hair sprouts, recedes, curls, falls and recoils. Its clothing sags, bunches, clings and flows through an endless catalogue of styles and colours. This quivering being has features that exist in a constant blur of gender, race and age. However, the irony of the suit's grotesqueness is that it is only projecting elements of normal human physiognomy back at 'normal' humans. Finally, therefore, this ironic twist to its grotesqueness refers *A Scanner Darkly* back to the cinema of Linklater and the aforementioned affront to conformity offered by *Slacker*, whose 'scrambled' narrative and its protagonists so oppose the dominant, conformist, materialist society of Republican America that they are accused of being lazy, even degenerate, and thereby labelled grotesque. Thus, as suggested by Nick Bradshaw, *A Scanner Darkly* 'suggests the pitfalls awaiting the post-beatnik heroes of *Slacker* should they stray from the path of principled resistance to the bourgeois orthodoxy' (2006: 41).

For all the layered meanings of rotoscoping, the animation also gave the tale what Linklater describes as 'a certain pulpy feel' that was further required of the actors, who were encouraged to exaggerate their gestures and expressions for the eventual animators. It may even have helped that several of the main cast were associated with drug use: Downey Jr. had passed through several rehabilitation programmes, Harrelson is a keen activist for the legalisation of marijuana, Winona Ryder, whose godfather was drugs guru Timothy Leary, was accused of using non-prescription drugs during her 2002 trial for shoplifting for which she was ordered to attend drug counselling, and Rory Cochrane, of course, played the permanently stoned Slater in *Dazed and Confused*. Of the live action filming Linklater recalls 'the actors were intrigued: "So I'm a cartoon character?" "Yeah, everyone's a cartoon character." I always used to want to be a cartoon character when I was a kid.' Cochrane, Downey Jr. and Harrelson duly comply with cartoonish behaviour, whereas Reeves and Ryder, who both worked for the Screen Actors Guild scale rate, are more reserved in their playing of their multiple roles of Arctor/Fred/Bruce and Donna/Hank/Audrey respectively. Although unnecessary to both the animation process and the overdubbing of Fred and Hank's voices by other actors, they also performed these characters in the scenes when the characters were supposedly wearing scramble suits. Thus the film constantly points to a layering of reality and unreality that the audience is challenged to map, which begins in the opening sequence of Freck's (Cochrane) attack by phantom aphids, which are animated instead of just imagined by the character and thus indicative that the audience shares his hallucination due to that fact that, like taking Substance D, the audience has effectively chosen to watch a film whose rotoscoping replicates the psychedelic experience of a drug trip. Thought bubbles appear above characters' heads and at one point the film itself is fast-forwarded with resultant lines of interference as in Michael Haneke's *Caché* (*Hidden*, 2005), as if agent Fred is watching the surveillance footage. Otherwise, however, a contrasting context of reality is maintained by the familiar streets of Austin standing in for the low-tech representation of 'seven years from now' in Anaheim, California, which Linklater filmed separately and gave to the animators with instructions to create composite landscapes. After two weeks of rehearsal there was a six week shoot on digital video with little care for visible film equipment such as boom mikes which could all be erased during animation. Consequently, rotoscoping retains its reputation for enabling the kind of thrifty short cuts that allowed Linklater to spend/ save the film's tiny budget on basic local sets that could be embellished in the animation process.

Subsequently, when Linklater handed the footage over to the animators he convinced his departing cast that the rotoscoping process was 'just another interpretation of an actor: another layer. You bring in an actor, dress them, put make-up on them: this is just another layer.' For the team of thirty-five animators, however, this was a much less creative process than their forebears had enjoyed on *Waking Life*. They were equipped with Wacom graphics tablets connected to Power Mac G5 towers but instead of experimentation with animation styles they were restricted to a slim range of permissible tones of hair and skin colour, the precise shape of the actors' features from every possible angle and a limited palette of colours with which to render Austin as California. 'It was very different from *Waking Life* in the design,' recalls Linklater:

> It kind of put off a lot of the animators who had worked on both films. On *Waking Life* we thought that every character could have a different style, because the styles were by scenes, whereas with *A Scanner Darkly* I wanted it to be more like an illustrated novel, to have that constant look. The characters had to have the same look throughout. They couldn't just change styles. The animators were more restricted. There were style-sheets, old-style style-sheets: 'Here's how you draw Keanu!' 'Here's how you do his nose!' 'Here's how you do Winona!' A little less creative all round. Yet there was still so much to do; so much detail. It was really tough.

Again, the paradox of hard work as indication of a slacker ethos finds its expression in the cinema of Linklater, in which slacking is a unique, dignified and proto-metaphysical form of political activism. Moreover, *A Scanner Darkly* responds to a common question in the works of Dick, that of asking what counts as real, because it is a science fiction adventure that posits inactivity as a valid revolutionary act in a society in which invasive surveillance and the propagation of crippling paranoia force or inspire many citizens to retreat from the world. In other words, the best way to oppose a surveillance state is to do nothing. Like the time-image, these characters oppose by inaction. Instead of violent revolution, citizens concentrate on breaking down their own 'external' selves into the kind of atomised consciousness allowed by drug use or the kind of reflective, imaginative, creative activities of Austin's slacker community in the 1980s. To this extent, Barris, Luckman, Freck and Arctor are not just the science fiction descendants of the protagonists of *Slacker* but also of the verbose but inactive young proto-revolutionaries in Godard's *La Chinoise* (1967), whose legacy of inactivity remains a peculiar kind of protest.

Instead of shiny futurism, *A Scanner Darkly* presents 'seven years from now' as 'a second-generation of planned communities that mask their sprawling replication with simulated-organic winding roads and cul-de-sacs [.] Cloned homes for human propagation, flanked by identikit malls' (Bradshaw 2006: 42). This is the same landscape that sprawls behind the credits to *SubUrbia* as well as the one traversed in *Slacker*, *Dazed and Confused* and *Waking Life*, while, if Jesse and Céline had met in Anaheim they would surely have walked and talked around these streets too; for the future world of *A Scanner Darkly* is but a multi-level palimpsest of our own. Scratch away the rotoscoping and, like Arctor/Fred, we see ourselves as through a scanner darkly: 'What does a scanner see? Into the head? Down into the heart? I hope it sees better than me, because I see only darkly.' The title of the novel is a reference to St. Paul's first Letter to the Corinthians (c.56 A.D.) in which he writes 'For now we see through a glass, darkly' in a missive that is a call to unity and understanding found in 'things which eye has not seen and ear has not heard [...] combining spiritual thoughts with spiritual words' (1 Corinthians 13:12). That is to say, it is the metaphysical plane where understanding is found. However, in response to any religion's 'ownership' of such transcendental experiences or claims to own the wisdom found therein, *A Scanner Darkly* ultimately posits metaphysical experience ironically, as the reduction of discourse and experience to the kind of panacean banality that is particularly evident in the verbiage of Barris. As rendered by Downey Jr., these monologues express a wholly faithful embodiment of the rich vein of black humour in Dick's writing: 'That's the D talking!'

In her analysis of *A Scanner Darkly* in *Deleuze and the Schizoanalysis of Cinema*, Powell explores the element of transcendence offered by the flux of the scramble suit, which she reads as sympathetic to 'a new map of the body and psyche' (2008: 118). For Powell, 'fluid and shifting, this body in process draws on the pre-subjective mental and emotional forces of the "orphan unconscious"' (ibid.) that was delineated by Gilles Deleuze and Pierre-Félix Guattari. Focussing on the face as 'the site of socially projected identity' (2008: 127), she notes that 'identity is radically destabilized [because] the scramble suit has been cynically invented to produce false multiplicity in order to enforce conformity by pushing deviation' (ibid.). In relation to wider considerations of the cinema of Linklater therefore, the scramble suit is revealed to be emblematic of its most persistent themes. In sum, because the suit effects a Cubist expression of a human in a state of constant becoming it also represents Bergson's notion of real time as 'flux, the continuity of transition' (1992b: 16). For Bergson as for the scramble suit 'it is change itself that is real' (ibid.). The suit thus embodies Bergson's definition of time as a thing whose 'essence being to flow, not one of its parts is still there when another part comes along' (1992b: 12). The irony is that the suit actually mimics the efforts to fit in of 'unsuitable' humans who are constantly adapting in order to survive in society, even at the risk of anonymity. The struggle is such that schizophrenia may result, however, which Deleuze and Guattari nonetheless claim in *Anti-Oedipus: Capitalism and Schizophrenia* (1972) is capable of resisting the 'normalisation' of conformist Western society in which citizens are trained to desire their own repression. At least the schizophrenic may have half a mind to revolution. It may not be enough to take up arms, but sufficient introspection might still engender enough resistance to conformity to posit stubborn inactivism as a revolutionary act that might be objectively identified as slacking.

In contrast, the film does examine the perception of change in society and the individual, which, as exemplified by those who view the scramble suit, becomes a subject of philosophical contest. Bergson typically questions whether anything is ever stable:

> We say, for example, that an object changes colour, and that change here consists in a series of shades which would be the constitutive elements of change and which, themselves, would not change. But in the first place, if each shade has any objective existence at all, it is an infinitely rapid oscillation, it is change. (1992e: 146)

Perhaps the suit does not really have to scramble itself because the subjective, intuitive perception of its observers does all the work for it? However, as Bergson states:

> The perception we have of [change], to the extent that it is subjective, is only an isolated, abstract aspect of the general state of our person, and this state as a whole is constantly changing and causing this so-called invariable perception to participate in its change. (Ibid.)

That is to say, it is not just the suit (the form) that changes but the man (the content) inside it. Unfortunately, because Arctor must spy upon himself in order not to give away his true identity, his deliberate schizophrenia degenerates into oxymoronic duality. Writes Dick: 'He had a peculiar air about him: tense and bummed out both at once, a sort of dulled urgency' (2006: 151). When the condition deteriorates, Dick has Fred/Arctor visit the police psychology testing lab for a diagnosis:

> 'Competition,' the other psychologist said, 'between the left and right hemispheres in your brain. It's not so much a single signal, defective or contaminated; it's more like two signals that interfere with each other by carrying conflicting information. [F]or you neither hemisphere is dominant and they do not act in a compensatory fashion, each to the other. One tells you one thing, the other another.'
> [...]
> 'The two hemispheres of my brain are competing?' Fred said. (2006: 168)

The problem of 'cross-chatter' resulting from 'split-brain phenomena' (ibid.) is attributed to Fred/Arctor's illegal intake of Substance D while operating undercover. The red pills chugged by Arctor recall the one offered to Neo (Keanu Reeves) by Morpheus (Laurence Fishburne) in *The Matrix* (Andy Wachowski & Larry [now Lana] Wachowski, 1999): 'After this, there is no turning back. You take the blue pill – the story ends, you wake up in your bed and believe whatever you want to believe. You take the red pill – you stay in Wonderland and I show you how deep the rabbit-hole goes.' Here, however, there is no cure or even the possibility to go cold turkey. For Arctor/Fred there is only a final half-life as the somnolent Bruce, who Dick describes as receiving only '*partial* impressions – incoming sense data – for the rest of his life. Instead of two signals, he gets half a signal' (2006: 168; emphasis in original). Moreover, because the notion of live action footage beneath the rotoscoping is arguably gradually forgotten, so the film ends up as a 'cartoon' that poignantly underlines Arctor's complete disassociation from reality. As Dick writes: 'Time ceased as the eyes gazed and the universe jelled along with him, at least for him, froze over with him and his understanding, as its inertness became complete' (2006: 216). Arctor's last act as Bruce is to pick the blue flower from which is extracted Substance D and is a primary symbol of Romanticism, symbolising desire and the ultimately hopeless metaphysical struggle of reaching for the unreachable infinite.[9] By these means, the novel and the film conclude the theme of what is meant by freedom of choice and the loss of it due to addiction.

In his editor's note, Dick reflects that 'drug use is not a disease, it is a decision, like the decision to step out in front of a moving car' (2006: 218). He describes addiction as 'a speeding up, an intensifying, of the ordinary human existence [that inspires the refrain] "be happy now because tomorrow you are dying", but the dying begins almost at once' (ibid.). The vicious juxtaposition of choice and its lack is what befalls a person whose decision to use drugs obliterates from life all the other options he or she might ever have. As Barris says, Substance D boils all of life's options down to just one choice: 'You're either on it or you're not.' This fragile duality is evoked in *A Scanner Darkly* by references to other choices that must be made between good and evil, and between reality and unreality, but are mostly fumbled under the influence of drug-induced paranoia. In relation to the context of the novel's writing, moreover, it is important to note that Philip K. Dick believed himself to have been identified as an enemy of 'the establishment', which he was convinced had him under surveillance, although following the Freedom of Information Act, which allowed people access to their own FBI files, his was found to be almost empty. Nevertheless, the paranoia that infused the writing of *A Scanner Darkly* was not just fed by drugs but justified by the same post-Watergate period that inspired several of the conspiracy thrillers of the 1970s such as *The Parallax View* (Alan J. Pakula, 1974) and *Winter Kills* (William Richert, 1979). Correlatively, the production of *A Scanner Darkly* during the second tenure of President George W. Bush points to a resurgence of paranoia amongst those left disturbed and disenfranchised by government policy both at home and abroad during his presidency. Says Linklater: 'Post 9/11 I re-read [*A Scanner Darkly*] and saw it in a whole new way. The way power works and surveillance and government control. All those elements make it more relevant than ever. What was paranoid then is our reality' (in Russell 2006).

Like *Blade Runner* (Ridley Scott, 1982), which was very loosely adapted from Dick's *Do Androids Dream of Electric Sheep?* (1968), *A Scanner Darkly* may be understood in terms compiled by Bradshaw as 'the ultimate postmodern detective noir' (2006: 42). Like *Blade Runner* it is also possible that *A Scanner Darkly*'s dystopian view of the near future put off audiences and studios that would nevertheless continue to raid Dick's short stories for the ideas upon which more adventure-filled but less adventurous science fiction films such as *Minority Report* (Steven Spielberg, 2002) and *Paycheck* (John Woo, 2003) could be based. Rotoscoping may also be blamed for the film's poor box-office return because it confused any potential core and/or crossover audience. Nevertheless, what had always and uniquely inspired Linklater to attempt a faithful adaptation of *A Scanner Darkly* was his conviction that he could 'tell the story the way I thought [Dick] saw it, which was just about people hanging out' (in Russell 2006). The scenes of the disaffected characters lounging around, bullshitting about a repressive social order, goofing off and obsessing about the number of gears on a bicycle could, like any from *Waking Life*, have easily come from *Slacker*. In addition, such meandering scenes as that with the bicycle were only made possible because, the film's budget was so low that it allowed for a degree of creative freedom. Thus the main theme of *A Scanner Darkly* asserts itself in its familiar production process too, as does its affinity with *Slacker*, *Dazed and Confused*, *SubUrbia*, *Waking Life*, *The School of Rock* and the rest of the cinema of Linklater, which in turn, perhaps, finds its prophet in Philip K. Dick, whose 1972 essay on *The Android and the Human* contains this defence of 'unreliable' slackers:

> Either through laziness, short attention span, perversity, criminal tendencies – whatever label you wish to pin on the kid to explain his unreliability is fine. Each merely means We can tell him and tell him what to do, but when the time comes for him to perform, all the subliminal instruction, all the ideological briefing, all the tranquilizing drugs, all the psychotherapy are a waste. He just plain will not jump when the whip is cracked. (1995: 191)

The fusion of slacking with the filmmaking process meant that it was perhaps inevitable that the slow craftsmanship of rotoscoping should have frustrated the film's producers at Warners. 'Some people were just extremely upset with the realities of how long it takes' (Ward P. 2006: 42) remembers Sabiston, whose disillusionment was somewhat shared by Linklater:

> *A Scanner Darkly* made me not want to do another animated film. I didn't really have any more ideas. Even as I did it I thought I'm not an animator, I'm a storyteller and I'm using this technology to tell a particular story but it's not a particular passion or anything.

Furthermore, the lack of support experienced during production was compounded by the attitude of Warners to its distribution and its $5.48 million gross at the American box-office and £561,707 in the UK was a paltry return on an estimated $8.5 million budget. 'They dumped it,' says Linklater: 'Good news is Warners made it as a little film; bad news is that internationally: "Here's our slate: *Harry Potter* and *A Scanner Darkly*. Let's just go straight to video with this title"'. Thus, despite a Cannes screening for which *A Scanner Darkly* was awkwardly positioned as an auteurist, generic, star-driven curio, Linklater remembers:

> It didn't really get a theatrical release. Nevertheless, I figured it would find its audience though. You know, have its life. I knew this film was going to be seen on a screen at three in the morning. It's been downloaded by BitTorrent like a million times, so yeah, what the hell! I was never going to see any money on it. You're just glad people watch it. It just proves that there was an audience out there for it. A lot of films find their audience that way. You never know.

Ultimately, if there was an ideal audience for *A Scanner Darkly* it was the daughters of Philip K. Dick, who visited the set during production and, says Linklater, 'really liked it. I was sitting at a screening when they first saw the film and saw some tears'. In turn, Linklater claims that he 'was just proud to be able to do Dick authentically. He's a good enough writer to have his whole narrative recreated'.

Alas, rotoscoping may not have much future. Sabiston has since worked on sound-synchronised animation for the videos of the Austin-based psychedelic rock band The Black Angels, a short film entitled *The Even More Fun Trip* (2007) that reacquainted him with Ryan Power ('star' of *Snack and Drink*), thirty commercials (some in Hi-Definition) for Charles Schwab and eighteen episodes of a comic series called *Get Your War On* (2008) that was based on the recycling of five minutes of stock live action footage with the mouths reanimated for new dialogue on every episode. Despite their growing cult success, the perception of *Waking Life* and *A Scanner Darkly* as financial failures is inextricably linked to the animation process. Rotoscoping does look decidedly low-rent in comparison with the more sophisticated and infinitely more expensive filmmaking technologies developed by Robert Zemeckis, with his motion capture and IMAX 3-D 'experiences' *Beowulf* (2007) and *A Christmas Carol* (2009), and James Cameron, whose *Avatar* (2009) based its plot and marketing on the *Waking Life*-like promise of its hero Jake Sully (Sam Worthington) that 'everything is backwards now, like out there is the true world and in here is the dream'. Nevertheless, the ideas that rotoscoping expresses are uniquely appropriate to the inexpensive, independent, experimental, and collaborative cinema of Linklater because metaphysical concerns are the everyday obstacles encountered by slackers, who, like Bruce, 'looked forward inside [their] mind[s], where no one could see' (Dick 2006: 217). Thus, although it is likely to remain a minor footnote in animation history, rotoscoping adds a vital layer of extroversion to the often introverted cinema of Linklater.

Notes

1   All quotations from Richard Linklater, unless otherwise attributed, are from interviews with the author in Austin, Texas, 30 July–1 August 2009.

2   This may be viewed online at http://www.inkwellimagesink.com/pages/cartoons/
    MaxFleischer-OutOfTheInkwell3.shtml.

3   Several of these short films can be viewed online at http://www.inkwellimagesink.
    com/pages/cartoons/MaxFleischer-OutOfTheInkwell1.shtml.

4   The rotoscoped footage of Cab Calloway is also re-used in the compilation film
    Betty Boop's Rise to Fame (Dave Fleischer, 1934).

5   Rotoscoping was notably revived to popular effect in the video that illustrated the
    song 'Take on Me' (1985) by the Norwegian synth-pop group a-ha.

6   See St Teresa of Avila (2007) *El castillo interior / Interior Castle*. Mineola, NY:
    Dover Publications. Also St John of the Cross (2003) *La noche oscura / Dark Night
    of the Soul*. Mineola, NY: Dover Publications.

7   The original Spanish: 'y en el mundo, en conclusión, / todos sueñan lo que son, /
    aunque ninguno lo entiende.'

8   Author's translation. The original Spanish: '¿Qué es la vida? Un frenesí; / ¿Qué es
    la vida? Una ilusión, / una sombra, una ficción, / y el mayor bien es pequeño; /
    que toda la vida es sueño, / y los sueños, sueños son.'

9   Blue flowers are especially common in German literature. Its symbolism originates
    in Novalis's unfinished *Heinrich von Ofterdingen* (1876) and extends to Werner
    Helwig's *Die Blaue Blume des Wandervogels* (*The Blue Flower of the Wandervogel*,
    1998), a history of the German youth movement of the 1960s. Blue flowers are
    also the prime ingredient of a hallucinogenic drug in *Batman Begins* (Christopher
    Nolan, 2005).

CHAPTER SIX

The Spaces In Between

By definition no Cubist portrait can ever be complete because its subject exists in the time that it expresses and is therefore constantly changing, evolving, arriving and departing. So too is the cinema of Richard Linklater, whose movement between independent film and the studio system, between genres, European and American cinema, politics and philosophy is a product of versatility and variation. Linklater certainly disproves the assumption of idleness as a defining characteristic of the slacker ethos. Not counting all the work that he will go on to make, this portrait still lacks four vital fragments: a short documentary on the opportunity for creation and evolution provided by Ground Zero in post-9/11 New York that is *Live from Shiva's Dance Floor*, a buoyant pilot for a sunken HBO series about minimum wage earners entitled *$5.15/ Hr*, the extrapolation of a sports metaphor into philosophy that is the documentary *Inning by Inning: A Portrait of a Coach*, and the project being filmed a few scenes every year known as *Boyhood*. These fragments appear and disappear in the spaces between better-known projects, offering sketches, digressions and reaffirmations of themes and aesthetics. Although little known and in the case of *Boyhood* as yet unseen, they are all dialogic works that point to interwoven lines of political and philosophical enquiry and as such they illustrate and comment upon American society and its changing values.

For any American artist, writer, filmmaker or performer, the urge to commemorate the destruction of New York's World Trade Center on 11 September 2001 was complicated by the crashing of this imperative into a taboo of unseemly enthusiasm. Nowhere was this concern about premature recovery or reflection more explicitly revealed than in the debate over what would become of the area where the twin towers had once stood. Suggestions were mostly dismissed as inappropriate because they either came unseemingly soon, were too opportunistic or too crass. Meanwhile, the area became both a place of pilgrimage for those seeking closure and a tourist attraction for those wishing to gawk at the rubble. The assimilation of 9/11 in the psyche of Americans in general and New Yorkers in particular was a painful process aided only by time and forgetting and perhaps the involuntary contextualisation of the event within the remembered grammar of disaster movies. But when speechlessness was cured, the event was incorporated into the history of the city and the intrahistory of its inhabitants. Iron girders fused in the shape of a cross were salvaged from the wreckage and erected on the site as a monument to the need for immediate memorialisation rather than to the event itself. A glimpse of the twin towers was edited out of the credit sequence for the HBO series *The Sopranos* (1999–2007) and the trailer for *Spider-Man* (Sam Raimi, 2002) and the airport signs pointing to Manhattan were doctored to cover the towers. The Lower Manhattan Development Corporation (LMDC) held an international competition to create a memorial that would 'respect this place made sacred through tragic loss' (Anon. 2009h) and tour guides revised their itinerary and commentary to both incorporate the event and participate in the reimagining of the area.

One such guide was Timothy 'Speed' Levitch, who worked on the Gray Line tour buses but had been in San Francisco at the time of the attack. Levitch was born into a middle-class Jewish family of five in Riverdale, the Bronx, in 1970. He attended Horace Mann, a respected co-ed private school but endured a painful adolescence as 'a wallflower in the darkened corners of the cafeteria, acne-infested' (Bruni 1998). However, his consequent introspection allowed him to embellish and philosophise upon his existence with such zealous eloquence that it earned him the nickname Speed. He studied creative writing at New York University, graduating in 1992, whereupon he took the examination to be a tour guide and started work with Big Apple Tours in a role that combined performance, language and philosophy:

> I came to the tour route with the understanding that it is one of the great opportunities for self-expression and I do think that the people who really moved mountains in human history were all great tour guides. I do think that being a tour guide – understanding it to be a great opportunity for self-expression – enhanced my own use of language. It enhanced my understanding, if you will, that language is the instrument of life. It is the music of life and really a shamanic journey in its own right. (Levitch 2009)

He switched to Gray Line Tours in 1994 for a two dollar pay rise (making $9 an hour plus tips) and, as *The New York Times* recounts, 'around the same time, Bennett Miller, an aspiring filmmaker whose younger brother had gone to Horace Mann with Mr. Levitch, caught up with Mr. Levitch at a party' (Bruni 1998). Miller proposed a documentary to be filmed during 1996 and 1997 that would observe and preserve Levitch's Muppet-like performance of poetic improvisation, nasal eloquence and edgy, attitudinal quirks. Long before Linklater met Levitch, Miller's *The Cruise* (1998), which won the Don Quixote award at the 1999 Berlin International Film Festival, details Levitch's fanciful guided tours or 'loops' around New York – 'The sun, another great New York city landmark, above you on the left!' – in the company of bemused, delighted and annoyed tourists for whom Levitch claims 'each loop is a search for perfection'. This grainy black-and-white documentary takes in the sights from Levitch's peculiar viewpoint while engaging with his resentment at having to observe his employer's strict dress code and rigid timetable, and his vocational zeal at the possibility of 'rewriting the souls' of his passengers. Crucially for Levitch the world as it is represented in the microcosmic Manhattan exists exclusively in the present tense: 'We are two blocks from where D. H. Lawrence lives! Two blocks from where Arthur Miller contemplates suicide!' He justifies his state of eternal Bergsonian rapture by claiming that it is 'in that active verb "fleeting" that I reside in the moment'. And in seeking erotic fusion with the time, place and space of his anthropomorphised metropolis he literally embraces the Brooklyn Bridge, claiming the city as 'a scintillating, streamlined mermaid who sings to me at night'. For Levitch, New York City is 'a living organism [with which] my relationship is in constant fluctuation'. Consequently, he berates the business and busy-ness of the city dwellers, describing commuters arriving at the World Trade Center as 'running towards their destinations and from themselves' and claiming that only the joggers and cyclists found 'lounging or kissing in the park are historically accurate'. Most determinedly for Levitch, the 'vocational double-decker tour' itself is a motorised *dérive* or drift (aka cruise) through the urban jungle for which chance and improvisation is essential to the success of its application of psycho-geography. Thus he rails against the 'anti-cruise' of the grid plan of the metropolis and informs his tour group that their driver 'Martínez continues to audaciously improvise, not only with the tour route but with his own life'. A traffic jam, for example, is not a headache but an opportunity for all on board to 'sense the grandeur of [their] power' as their bus causes chaos and gridlock.

Levitch's conviction that time and all its subjects exist in a Bergsonian eternal present tense, his enthusiasm for the psycho-geographical experience of the *dérive* as propagated by Guy Debord, the Situationist International and the protagonists of *Slacker*, and his depiction of New York as 'a self-orchestrated purgatory' as well as his innate, extant romanticism ('We are wreckage with beating hearts!') is what impressed Linklater when he first saw *The Cruise* in which Levitch pointedly exclaims that 'one of the great tragedies of civilisation is that people have to work for a living'. Linklater met Levitch in 1998 after a screening of *The Cruise* and was impressed by his physical and verbal combination and expression of the infantile and the cerebral that is a common contradiction of so many of the protagonists of the films he has written, co-written and directed. In his unkempt adenoidal exuberance Levitch is a mix of jester and prophet, benign but boasting of self-aggrandising martyrdom:

Creativity I think of as the pursuit for the original exuberance that we all came into this world with – the exuberance that we all had until it was taken off to an abandoned dock somewhere and shot in a gangster assassination by the outside world. With that said, I've always thought of myself as a renaissance man and I'm pouncing with avarice on all opportunities and doing my best to experience complete self-expression and pursue the fullest applications of self. Yeah! (Levitch 2009)

'Where others see fragments, Speed sees connections', says Linklater (2003), who would re-team with Levitch in 2012 to create an episodic travelogue for subscription website Hulu titled *Up To Speed*. Levitch's undeniable erudition and the results of his reflection can be both intoxicating in their realignment of priorities and overpowering in their verbose extemporisation. For example, in *The Cruise* he gushes:

> I think, most notably, that our true state is the greatest party that has ever been thrown. On the cruise, we define life as an ongoing opportunity for celebration. I would say that it is an unintentional meditation and an elongated journey into our own forest. I think life is a gigantic adventure that leads back to ourselves. I think that meaning is just a subsequent invention, if you will, a rivulet off the original river that is our learning process. It seems to me at this point in my life that we are all involved in a process and that process is about learning. I think the earth in the long run is a giant classroom. Is that what you were asking? I could go on a long time.

The appropriateness of Levitch to *Waking Life* was such that Linklater obliged Main Character to take the astral plane out of Austin to Manhattan purely to meet Levitch as 'Himself' on the Brooklyn Bridge. With hair like a roman candle and eyes like Catherine wheels, the rotoscoped Levitch in *Waking Life* informs Main Character that 'on really romantic evenings of self, I go salsa dancing with my confusion'. He then prefigures the Bergsonian conclusion to the film offered by Linklater as Pinball Playing Man that 'there's only one instant, and it's right now, and it's eternity' with his declaration that 'the ongoing wow is happening right now'. Life itself, he proclaims, 'is a matter of a miracle that is collected over time by moments flabbergasted to be in each other's presence'. As both clown and commentator, Levitch comes at us live, direct from Bakhtin's carnival.

Live from Shiva's Dance Floor is a response to Levitch's premonition of 9/11 in Miller's *The Cruise*, when he had spun like a child between the twin tower monuments to crammed-in Capitalism in order to summon up the dizzy feeling when 'it looks like the buildings are falling on top of you' and concluded: 'This is ludicrousness and it cannot last.' However, the destruction of the World Trade Center on 11 September 2001 meant that New York City no longer existed in the present. Instead, so defined was the metropolis by the absence of the World Trade Center that the only valid frame of reference for the reality-shattering event was the contrast with its presence in the past. Commentators were plentiful but mostly cautious and the majority looked to historical causes and global consequences. In *9–11* (2001) Noam Chomsky argued, 'nothing can justify crimes such as those of September 11, but we can think of the United States as an "innocent victim" only if we adopt the convenient path of ignoring the record of its actions, which are, after all, hardly a secret' (2001: 35). Meanwhile, Susan Sontag weighed in with an article in *The New Yorker* that argued, 'a lot of thinking needs to be done [but] the public is not being asked to bear much of the burden of reality' (2001). Linking these two truths was a groundswell of feeling that all those affected by the event should accept some measure of personal responsibility for both its occurrence and its cure. Never mind that Jean

Baudrillard had declared this was 'the absolute event, the "mother" of events, the pure event which is the essence of all the events that never happened' (2009). Gradually a feeling grew amongst some New Yorkers that the overwhelming magnitude of what had happened was no excuse for evading personal obligation to comment, communicate and contribute to this opportunity to reform relationships, priorities and policies. The problem was that Ground Zero spoke only of what was gone, thereby locking New York forever into the past. Correlatively, the Levitch who appeared in *The Cruise* no longer celebrated the eternal present because Miller's imagery and Levitch's rhetoric was now impossibly frozen in a pre-9/11 past whose very completion signalled an end to Bergsonian time and the curtailment of the present tense. As Baudrillard stated, 'by collapsing (themselves), by suiciding, the towers had entered the game to complete the event' (ibid.). The problem thereafter was that the whole world would similarly regress; it would stop living in 'the ongoing wow' and reside forever after in the moments pending what Baudrillard called 'the brutal irruption of death in direct, in real time, but also the irruption of a more-than-real death: symbolic and sacrificial death – the absolute, no appeal event' (ibid.). For Levitch and Linklater this was never more explicitly problematised than in the competition administered by the LDMC to select a design for a memorial 'that would remember and honor all of those killed in the attacks of September 11 2001 and February 26 1993' (Anon. 2009h). From the 5,201 submissions it received, the LMDC selected 'Reflecting Absence' by architects Michael Arad and Peter Walker, which would 'consist of two massive pools set within the footprints of the Twin Towers with the largest manmade waterfalls in the country cascading down their sides' (ibid.). The structure would be engraved with the names of the dead in order to serve as 'a powerful reminder of the Twin Towers and of the unprecedented loss of life from an attack on our soil' (ibid.). But when Levitch and Linklater visited Ground Zero together in late 2001, they, along with many other artists, demurred.

As Linklater recalls, 'while respectful of the tragedy, [Levitch] was his usual optimistic, present-tense self' (2003). Instead of a redundant monument to the receding past they imagined a 'delightful, benevolent opportunity' (ibid.) to install a living thing that would speak of ongoing change. They rejected the notion of a monument to loss which would also serve as a mnemonic for revenge. Instead, they attempted to transcend the supposed sacrilege of simply appreciating the new skyline and its freshly unencumbered view. 'The World Trade Center towers did not die, they created more space,' says Levitch in *Live from Shiva's Dance Floor*. His idea was to rescue New York City from the past and return it to the eternal present. 'The gap between the twin towers represents non-communication,' he declares with a jarring but curative use of the present tense, whereas 'every citizen of every city I've ever met certainly deserves a hug'. Instead of attempting to embody meaning in a new construction based on the clichés of waterfalls, pools and the engraved names of the deceased, *Live from Shiva's Dance Floor* proposes: 'Sixteen acres of blazing green grass, a place for togetherness, healing out loud, and spontaneous culture. And in the middle of the park, the memorial should not be an inanimate slab of stone, but should have a heartbeat.' In fact, as Levitch expounds, this heartbeat could be both literal and multiple:

It's called 'The Buffalo Idea'. It's an idea that came about from a whole conversation of artists. And we'd like to use the land currently called Ground Zero and turn it into a Joy Park and grazing land for American Bison. The idea is that the central monument should not be an inanimate piece of stone but it should be something that's alive, that has a heartbeat and that propagates. I think that a lot of what was felt by the people who came up with the idea is that the American Bison represents an indigenous American community that has been experiencing September 11th for 400 years. (In Dashevsky 2003).

Although 'The Buffalo Idea' would never be realised, *Live from Shiva's Dance Floor* is its impassioned pitch. Shooting guerrilla-style on just one day (23 June 2002) emphasised the rescuing of the present tense, which was also underlined by the film's opposing the gritty monochrome of *The Cruise* with its vibrant colour. The hand-held camerawork and jump cuts also evoke a palliative immediacy while its subjectivity puts the spectator in the position of Main Character in *Waking Life*, whose fleeting pilgrimage to Levitch is enacted in the dreamstate that Levitch now prompts us to recover: 'I don't like New York City but it's my favourite place to get lost in. Now take out "New York City" and put "consciousness" in.' Once again, the recourse to metaphysics prescribed by Linklater and Levitch is anchored to a paradoxically profound sense of place: 'To be lost in New York City is to actually be quite precise about your place in the universe,' says Levitch, who Linklater presents by way of jump cuts that aid disorientation while also framing the experience exclusively on this prophet in order to emphasise just how personal is the tragedy of the city. This profound personalisation of the event is also what deflects any potential outcry at their radical alternativism. America, says Levitch to camera, is 'a land that is terrible at commemoration'; which is why Linklater reasoned that 'an entirely new way of looking at the issue was what was needed. What the hell – so many of the things we take for granted and enjoy as part of our lives were initially crackpot ideas the establishment scoffed at' (2003). No stock footage of the attack is included, diluted and perverted as it is by memories of disaster movies and looped newsreel. Instead, at a chatty 21 minutes, *Live from Shiva's Dance Floor* seeks to affectionately persuade its audience of its strategy for a 'joy park that is our strategy for survival'. Ground Zero, it is argued, is where destruction meets creation: behold the cosmic big bang coming to you LIVE! from Shiva's dance floor in which the libidinous Levitch aims to involve us. This is 'counter-intuitive. It has nothing to do with rationality,' admits Levitch, who claims the idea of relocating roaming buffalo offers 'a complete illustration of subconscious expectations for the future'. Consequently, even if it never actually happened, there was some triumph in just having people imagine it.

Live from Shiva's Dance Floor received its premiere in January 2003 at the Sundance Film Festival, one week after the public hearings on the new site proposals for the World Trade Center that were met by *The New York Times* with the headline 'New Trade Center Plans Draw Some Old Complaints':

Since the attack on the World Trade Center 16 months ago, the public has responded to calls for comment on rebuilding the World Trade Center with a host of new ideas, innovative thinking and considered debate. Last night, however, when officials tried to engage a citywide audience in a discussion about a new set of designs for the trade center, the public appetite for it seemed to hit a dead end. (Wyatt 2003).

Public apathy stemmed from disillusionment with bureaucracy, stated the *New York Times*, which reported calls from the audience for the LMDC to 'pay more attention to the needs of low income people on the Lower East Side' (ibid.). But the city's government was clearly regressing to ignorant, irrelevant, inconsequential ideas of monuments to capitalist excess. Aiming to break this interdependency with *Live from Shiva's Dance Floor*, Linklater allows Levitch to preach from on top of the eleven feet tall, 3,200 kilogram bronze sculpture called *Charging Bull* (1989) by Arturo Di Modica that stands in Bowling Green near Wall Street. This act not only shows Levitch taming Capitalism (a bull market is a strong stock market) but fulfils the title of the film, for a bull was the mount of Shiva, the Supreme God in the Shaiva tradition of Hinduism. Moreover, Shiva (like Levitch) is noted for his matted hair and most often represented either meditating or dancing the vigorous Tandava that sets in motion the cycle of death and rebirth that Levitch evokes explicitly in locating Ground Zero at 'the corner of creation and destruction'. Perched cross-legged atop the public statue, he appears to disprove the either/or of Monty Python's *Life of Brian* (Terry Jones, 1979) in being both messiah and a very naughty boy.

In the associations that make up Levitch's stream of consciousness, it is fitting that he should claim the symbolism of this bull for Shiva, thus elevating the film's concerns, as he states, 'beyond the duality of the bull and bear market'. He was certainly not alone in finding distasteful the erection of a monument that might be read as the rebuilding of Capitalism. And, although the debate he engenders cannot extricate itself from the mournful hush that dominates discussion over 'moving on' from 9/11,

Timothy 'Speed' Levitch atop Charging Bull in *Live from Shiva's Dance Floor*

Live from Shiva's Dance Floor does make a brave stab at reclaiming the public space of Ground Zero in an oppositional monologue that renders Levitch every bit as defiantly optimistic a performer as Gene Kelly 'laughing at clouds' in *Singin' in the Rain* (Stanley Donen and Gene Kelly, 1952). Indeed, there is great musicality in his speech, which Linklater allows to develop in long takes. Ground Zero is thus reclaimed for carnival with Levitch as Bakhtin's jester. Although some may find his ideas (and appearance) grotesque, *Live from Shiva's Dance Floor* presents him as a leader of the dance and Linklater is 'excited to be part of it – anything that might help put Speed's ideas further out into the public discussion could only be a positive thing' (2003). Their joint aim is to inspire the public to join in the *dérive* that leads to the dance and thereby recognise the potential for reterritorialisation and communication, although, as Koresky observes, 'Linklater's cinematic gesture is warm and undidactic, unable to provide answers to tragedy, he simply holds your hand' (2004a). Levitch and Linklater want people to reclaim the streets for human connection (as folk do in *Slacker*, *Dazed and Confused*, *Before Sunrise*, *SubUrbia* and *Waking Life*) and in this at least they were in tune with public opinion, for, as *The New York Times* reported:

> The Civic Alliance to Rebuild Downtown New York, a consortium of planning and civic groups, also played host to a multiday workshop last month to consider plans and ideas for downtown. A strong element that emerged from that effort was a desire for reinvigorated street life. (Wyatt 2003)

The task of identifying clear political affiliation in the cinema of Linklater is always problematised by the characteristic blending of any political sense into a philosophical sensibility. In *Slacker*, *Waking Life*, *Before Sunrise*, *Before Sunset* and *A Scanner Darkly* it might be argued that the protagonists use philosophy as a shield and, therefore, that in *Live from Shiva's Dance Floor* Linklater employs an actual philosopher like Levitch as a shield-bearer. However, it is also apparent that although Linklater speaks on camera himself in *Slacker* and *Waking Life*, his perspective as director is arguably expressed in the films' aesthetics. Here, in appropriating the Dogme-style criteria for realism (handheld camera, colour film, diegetic sound, and so on), he subscribes to immediacy as a revolutionary act that opposes media manipulation and the crawl towards consensus of committees that is so often overruled by the ultimate dogmatism of accountants. Recognising that the attack on the World Trade Center had expressed this very immediacy in the impact of what Baudrillard called its unrepeatable, real-time, pure event, Linklater responds by twinning the destruction of the towers with the instantaneous aesthetics and production process of this film. Levitch is an improvisational collaborator, but also a clown handed a pulpit by his director. However, this is not to say that their working relationship is imbalanced, for each relies on the talents of the other, with Linklater providing the ideal platform on which the hyper-kinetic Levitch happily performs. Nonetheless, if one demands a more explicit statement of political commitment in the cinema of Linklater than that which can be deciphered from its plentiful philosophical discussion, its valuing of metaphysical experience and expression, its protagonism by dedicated slackers, its affined aesthetics of immediacy and its *durée*, and the association of so much of its form and content with the purpose of the *dérive* and the meaning of carnival, then one may encounter frustration. Asked straight out whether he considers himself a political filmmaker, Linklater himself colludes in this theory:

> Not on the sleeve. But everything's politics. The politics of everyday life is in all my films. I wade into politics in art really carefully, but I admit there's a rebellious, subversive streak in everything I do. It's never from the overclass perspective or of the status quo. If I had to do that it would be like a Buñuel film.[1]

As has previously been noted, many of the films he has directed bear affiliation with those of Luis Buñuel, who summarised his own career in film when he wrote that:

> The thought that continues guiding me today is the same that guided me at the age of twenty-five. It is an idea of Engels. The artist describes authentic social relations with the object of destroying the conventional ideals of the bourgeois world and compelling the public to doubt the perennial existence of the established order. That is the meaning of all my films: to say time and time again, in case someone forgets or believes otherwise, that we do not live in the best of all possible worlds. I don't know what more I can do. (1985: 107)

As Linklater admits when pressed to consider his films from a Buñuelian perspective, 'many of these are perverse subjects, when you talk about social strata and expectations.' Thus, as previously indicated, *Slacker* is his *La Voie lactée*, *Dazed and Confused* is his *Los Olvidados*, *SubUrbia* is his *El ángel exterminador* and *Waking Life* is his *Le charme discret de la bourgeoisie*. Even *Before Sunrise* and *Before Sunset* have something of *Cet obscur objet du désir* (*That Obscure Object of Desire*, 1977) about them in their emphasis on love as an irresistible force and their discussions of that which Peter William Evans describes in relation to Buñuel's final films as 'a prevalent aura of anguish, the reflection in the microcosm of the wider *inquiétude* that governs the world' (2007: 47; emphasis in original). *Live from Shiva's Dance Floor* is therefore Linklater's *Simón del desierto* (*Simon of the Desert*, 1965), for Levitch is a prophet adrift in Manhattan, just like the fourth-century saint who sits alone on a pillar in the desert in Buñuel's short masterpiece, until the devil tempts him down with entry to a bohemian party in 1960s' New York.

Unlike Buñuel, however, Linklater subscribes to metaphysical creation rather than Surrealist destruction. In films such as *Viridiana* (1961) and *Tristana* (1970), Buñuel rendered beggars and cripples as a gallery of grotesques whose base instincts made a mockery of Christian charity (which was admittedly Buñuel's target, for these films were aimed at Spain's Church-backed dictatorship of Franco). But the protagonists of the cinema of Linklater are often on minimum wage by choice and their slacker lifestyle is redolent of a kind of low-key heroism for their oppositional retention of youthful idealism, non-conformist attitudes and cynicism. Where Buñuel aims 'to explode the social order' (1985: 107), these characters seek to transcend it. If there is a common theme in the cinema of Linklater it is the awakening consciousness of un-moneyed drifters on their *dérives*, starting with the director himself in *It's Impossible To Learn To Plow By Reading Books* and including all those in *Slacker* and *Waking Life*, on through *The Newton Boys* and Mitch in *Dazed and Confused*, Jeff in *SubUrbia*, Jesse and Céline, Dewey Finn in *The School of Rock*, Morris Buttermaker in *Bad News Bears*, Amber in *Fast Food Nation* and Levitch in *Live from Shiva's Dance Floor*. Even Richard in *Me and Orson Welles* works for nothing but the privilege of being in the company of Orson Welles in the 'rebuilt' New York of the film's authentically detailed 1937. Moreover, in relation to the rebuilding of New York and the awakening consciousness of its inhabitants, it is worth considering how it was that only 2,801 people died in the attack on the twin towers, when 'some 50,000 people worked in the World Trade Center [and] another 150,000 to 200,000 business and leisure visitors came to the center daily' (Anon. 2009i). This may partly be explained by the fact that the first plane hit at 8.46 in the morning, which meant that not too many business people had arrived for the beginning of the working day. But this also suggests that many of those killed would have been cleaners, technical staff, support staff and the like: low-wage workers finishing up the night shift or starting the early morning shift before the main workforce arrived. Thus, as *Live from Shiva's Dance Floor* argues, it is quite wrong that the concrete monument to world trade should be rebuilt because those who died were arguably victims of Capitalism too.

Levitch's buffalo never made it to Lower Manhattan, of course, while another failed attempt at pitching a monument to those on minimum wage was *$5.15/Hr*. This is Linklater's pilot episode for a series that was never picked up by the subscription cable television channel HBO, which had contributed greatly to a new golden age of writer-based quality drama on American television with shows like *Six Feet Under* (2001–5), *The Sopranos* and *The Wire* (2002–8). Set in Grammaw's (Texan for Grandmother's) diner in South Austin, the orphaned 25-minute pilot episode for *$5.15/Hr* is an affectionate but barbed portrayal of the workplace from the viewpoint of the powerless. Co-written by Linklater and Rodney Rothman, who had been head writer for *The Late Show with David Letterman* from 1996 to 2000 and supervising producer of Judd Apatow's series *Undeclared* (2001–3), its unforced characterisation, narrative drift, particular sense of time and tetchy empathy amongst the co-workers is very much in the mould favoured by the cinema of Linklater, who admits, '*$5.15/Hr* was something I'd been trying to do for a while. It's hard to do a pilot because you have to hint at what future episodes will be like. But that was something I really felt strongly about.'

Anyone who has ever had a job they hated will recognise the drudgery of dragging shifts offset by the in-jokes and hi-jinks that get one through the day of *$5.15/Hr*. As Linklater points out, 'there's a long tradition of workplace comedies, particularly in the UK' that American television has also maintained in shows like *Cheers* (1982–93) and *Scrubs* (2001–10), although the closest kin to *$5.15/Hr* is early *Roseanne* (1988–97) and the less zany moments of *My Name is Earl* (2005–9) to which it matches its realistic view of America's white working class and its affectionate look at their eccentricities.[2] That said, the tone of the pilot episode wobbles precariously between the observational, character-based humour in the diner and the absurdity of the scenes at the headquarters of the parent company Hoak Industries, where the tense banter between executives and the eccentric but dictatorial owner seems to have strayed in from a screwball farce. If it had been picked up by HBO, it is probable that the jarring 'bookend' scenes at Hoak would have been discarded much like the faux vox pops in the pilot episode of HBO's *Sex and the City* (1998–2004) or the blackly comic adverts in that of *Six Feet Under*, although without them the ramshackle narrative of *$5.15/ Hr* lacks any conventional hook to bring the audience back for the next episode. In sum, one either likes hanging out with these ordinary folk or one does not, much like the HBO executive who cancelled the commission after viewing the pilot. As Linklater recounts:

> They just thought it was depressing, this idea that people work so hard in a really shit job. They didn't get it. But the people at the studio wouldn't. They go from a rich upbringing to an Ivy League school and then into a position at a major corporation and work their way up from there. So a lot of people who are making these big decisions have no feel for working people. And I was like: 'Hey! That's my background!' I threw it out there.

For Linklater, 'throwing it out there' meant regurgitating all that is distasteful about a fast food franchise and the conditions of the minimum wage earners it both feeds without nourishment and pays without perks. *$5.15/Hr* begins with a montage moving from the CEO of Hoak Industries to scientists testing flavours in a laboratory, industrial-sized pastry mixers and a conveyor belt of new apple desserts called fandangos that are frozen, boxed and delivered to Grammaw's ('Eat Till It Ouches You!'), whereupon the short order cook dumps them onto the counter and proclaims, 'it looks like something that dropped out of someone's ass'. Following this, the already weary staff congregate for the daily pep talk called by Mitch the manager (Mitch Baker), whose corporate-speak marks him out as both the inadequate alpha male and fall guy for all the resentment of his 'human resources'. Bitter banter between short order cooks Vince (Clark Middleton) and sassy 'soul sister' Joy (Retta) adds an obscenity-laden corrective to Mitch's slogan-filled rhetoric (the graveyard shift is now 'the third shift' and customers are to be referred to as 'guests'), while Brianna (America Ferrara before stardom in the more up-market *Ugly Betty* [2006–10]) is a timid waitress whose habit of wishing customers God's blessings leads to Mitch's admonishment: 'Not all of our customers are Christians, so from now on the only G word is Grammaw's.' Completing this collective is waitress Wing (Missy Yager), two Hispanic wage slaves who speak no English, and Bobby (William Lee Scott), who is late for the pep talk because he has fallen asleep on top of a (HBO-obligingly naked) bar-room pick-up: 'Bobby, get up! You're still in me.' 'I'm still hard.' 'I think that what's called a piss-boner.'

$5.15/Hr is, like *Slacker*, *Dazed and Confused*, *SubUrbia* and *Fast Food Nation*, from the perspective of those who have realised they have few options but to work for minimum wage in convenience stores and fast food joints like Grammaw's. Unlike Kevin Smith's *Clerks*, which was directly inspired by *Slacker*, *$5.15/Hr*, which might be expected to share Smith's youthful dislike of customers and duties, expresses a mostly

Brianna (America Ferrera), Bobby (William Lee Scott) and Joy (Retta) dance the night away in *$5.15/Hr*

flat acceptance that life is happening elsewhere. Obliged to beg for extra shifts, the wage slaves take their revenge by collective slacking. These are the people that time, President George W. Bush and all those 'guests' who never left a tip forgot.[3] And, as the third (graveyard) shift drifts into the lull between late dinner and early breakfast, it is in the small hours that *$5.15/Hr* makes its case for the collective when Joy puts some funky soul on the stereo and the staff spontaneously dance with each other amongst the empty booths. The touching gaiety of this sequence makes one regret that the true musical is one of the few genres not attempted in the cinema of Linklater, for, apart from the sports movie, this genre offers the most opportunities for celebrating the community. To borrow Peter Gibbons' (Ron Livingston) classic line in the kindred Austinite slacker comedy *Office Space* (Mike Judge, 1999), it's not that these people are lazy, it's just that they don't care. However, as the graveyard shift proceeds like chronic jet lag, the waiting staff push fandangos on their diners, who can claim one free if they forget to do so and its cost comes out of their wages. Wing obeys but follows up her no-hearted sales push by telling customers: 'It's disgusting. It's about a thousand calories and it's probably been deep fried in a factory full of rat shit.' But when drunken frat boys order them anyway, at least she gets to win 'customer bingo' by crossing 'vomit' off the grid full of already spotted 'numbers' such as 'hand tattoo', 'leopard skin' and 'ugly guy with hot chick'. *$5.15/Hr* is about doing what it takes to get through one's shift without sacrificing one's integrity, imagination or humour.

Although too brief to even aspire to being episodic, this pilot still shows relationships deepening as the staff's nocturnal dislocation effects a contrast with sleeping America. Bobby and Wing share a kid daughter whose maintenance is a matter for negotiation, while the pathologically cheerful Brianna endures harassment from lascivious male diners and initiates 'positive action' by pulling African-American diners from the queue first when Mitch points out she once left a couple waiting over a minute for a table at Grammaw's, which is currently responding to a class action lawsuit on a racial matter. One significant advance on the smalltown Texan films in the cinema of Linklater is the acknowledgement of an explosion in their multi-culturalism since the period in which the almost all-white *Dazed and Confused* was set and *Slacker* was filmed. The 24/7 convenience stores are now all managed by Pakistanis, which was something new in *SubUrbia*, and all have booths offering Cambio de Cheques (cash for cheques) at exorbitant commissions to Hispanics without social security numbers. Where *$5.15/Hr* shows advancement is in its recognition of various strata of the Hispanic community in Austin and other towns that include the wage-earning but fearful Brianna, the bus-boy who gets fired for stealing tips and the anonymous illegals queuing to cash their cheques. This points to a new awareness of the complex social conditions of the Hispanic community in southern Texas. Consequently, *$5.15/Hr* had specific consequences for the cinema of Linklater:

> If HBO had followed through it would have been fun. Even if I hadn't directed all the episodes of the series it would have been fun to see something live and breathe. But I experimented with it and I learnt a lot from it. A lot of the technical stuff and a lot of my feelings about that stuff ended up going into *Fast Food Nation*.

It was the experience of making *$5.15/Hr* that convinced Linklater that a fictional extrapolation was the most appropriate way of adapting Schlosser's journalistic exposé *Fast Food Nation*, although persuading Hollywood to back such a project after the demise of *$5.15/Hr* was out of the question. Says Linklater: 'Hollywood doesn't want to finance stories about people at work, even if they're comedic' (Robey 2007: 24):

> When you examine the fast-food industry, it's a loser on every level: systematic cruelty to animals, environmental degradation, low-paid workers and a final product that's horrible for the end user. You couldn't design a more harmful, cruel situation. And yet it persists because everyone involved is answering to the bottom-line thinking that permeates our culture. (In Robey 2007: 26)

Nevertheless, Linklater persisted, finding funding for *Fast Food Nation* from the British Broadcasting Corporation's film wing (BBC Films) as well as HanWay Films, led by Jeremy Thomas, and Participant Productions, which had produced mindful documentaries such as *Murderball* (Henry Alex Rubin and Dana Adam Shapiro, 2005), *An Inconvenient Truth* (Davis Guggenheim, 2006) and issue-based fictions such as *North Country* (Niki Caro, 2005), *Good Night, and Good Luck* (George Clooney, 2005) and *Syriana* (Stephen Gaghan, 2005). The line between documentary and fiction is often unclear anyway; for, as Douglas Morrey points out in consideration of Jean-Luc Godard's dictum that all great fiction films tend towards documentary, just as all great documentaries tend towards fiction:

> Even in the most artificially contrived film narrative, the *real world* caught on film, will nevertheless make its presence felt; even the most rigorously factual

documentary, by virtue of being organised through montage, partakes of fictional construction. (2005: 4; emphasis in original)

For Linklater this lesson would be learnt during the filming of the slaughterhouse scenes for *Fast Food Nation* – 'I felt like a war correspondent who'd snatched a photograph of something horrific!' – and corroborated by his subsequent production of a documentary on the University of Texas baseball coach Augie Garrido, *Inning by Inning: A Portrait of a Coach*.

Augie Garrido coaches National Collegiate Athletic Association (NCAA) Division 1 college baseball and has more wins to his credit than any other coach in the league's history.[4] Since 1997 he has coached the Longhorns of the University of Texas at Austin, which raised his salary to $800,000 per annum in 2008. Having gotten to university on a baseball scholarship and remained a lifelong fan of the game, Linklater has been known to participate in batting practice under Garrido's tuition. The documentary that this friendship inspired is not really about baseball, however, but uses the sport as metaphor for a philosophy that Garrido expresses on the training ground. *Inning by Inning: A Portrait of a Coach* is thus, like *Live from Shiva's Dance Floor*, a highly subjective documentary given to 'fictional construction' in which Linklater positions a gifted but workaday philosopher as spokesperson for the fusion of cerebral and practical expressions of slacking. In effect this continues Linklater's characteristic presentation of the rhetoric of everyday philosophers such as Levitch, Garrido and Louis Mackey, who appears in the artificially contrived fictions of *Slacker* and *Waking Life*, just as the protagonists of the fictional films he has directed often express themselves through the philosophies and anecdotes of others. Jesse and Céline first get to know and then reconcile with each other by trading beliefs and values propagated or embodied by physical and literary acquaintances, for example, while Dewey Finn and most of the characters in *Dazed and Confused* rely on attitudinal music to shape their thinking. Thus the catalogue of thinkers, writers and musicians that fictional characters posit as their spokespeople ultimately resembles the scramble suit of *A Scanner Darkly* because it is constantly changing in its unending search for a connection with other people. However, in documentaries there is no fictional intermediary between the filmmaker and those who are quoted, there is only Linklater positing Levitch and Garrido as his spokesmen.

Inning by Inning: A Portrait of a Coach came about because Linklater 'had gotten to know Augie [Garrido] over the years a little bit. As a former player, I just kind of liked his style. He has a kind of philosophical Zen attitude towards baseball' (Moreno 2008). The affinity peaks with Garrido's belief that players should focus on the moment at hand rather than the overall match or overriding objective of winning, thereby demanding investment in the Bergsonian notion of what Levitch calls the ongoing wow. 'It's what's required in filmmaking for sure,' says Linklater: 'The end gratification is so deferred in a way. If you just want to make a good movie, if you don't enjoy every step and become a master of each little moment, then you shouldn't be doing it' (ibid.). *Inning by Inning: A Portrait of a Coach* took two years to complete, of which 18 months were spent editing the 600 hours of footage down to 106 minutes for its premiere at Austin's Paramount Theater on 3 June 2008 to an audience of past and present University of Texas baseball greats, family, fans, and Garrido. It was sold for broadcasting to the American television cable Entertainment and Sports Programming Network (ESPN) and released in 2009 on a DVD that contained both broadcast-censored and unexpurgated versions of Garrido's rousing, expletive-laden rhetoric. For the ESPN audience, the documentary fits snugly into the genre of hagiography as observational footage of Garrido pep-talking his players on the training ground alternates with televised footage of him shouting in the faces of umpires and rousing his team during games. All this is interspersed with talking head interviews with past and present players, childhood friends and family. Yet this is also a raw and simple portrait of a man who, like Levitch, lives his real life according to the philosophy that often guides fictional characters in the cinema of Linklater.

Garrido is the grandson of Spanish emigrants, whose father was a sharecropper in the Texas dust bowl and wanted his son to work on the shipyard. But at an early age Garrido saw a man performing with a yo-yo on the *The Ed Sullivan Show*, 'getting paid and having fun doing it', and was struck by the knowledge that his own skill with a yo-yo was much better. Thus he realised 'that if you're the best at what you do, you can make a living at it' and he resolved to build a career 'based on passion and the fact that I didn't want to work'. Channelling this ambition into playing baseball, he became a coach when he 'found out late that it wasn't the game I loved, it was the people involved in the game and the relationships and the experiences'. His career as 'the winningest coach in Division 1 NCAA history' makes him a prized employee of the University of Texas, whose on-campus stadium dwarfs all its faculty buildings. Yet Garrido is not about winning; instead he sees baseball as 'preparation for life, ethics, focus, ability, the courage to act on your thoughts'. In several scenes Linklater takes up a position with the camera in the huddle of capped and helmeted players to listen to Garrido's paternal tirades: 'Baseball is about coming to terms with failure without it becoming overwhelming. [...] Do your best, you're gonna fail. So you do your best again. [...] This isn't about some game, it's about our lives!'

Garrido could very easily have strolled into *Slacker* or accosted Main Character in *Waking Life*, so redolent is he of the limited universe of the cinema of Linklater. His philosophy is centred on the collective, for which he insists that playing for fun is infinitely more important than competing for the prize. At heart, he espouses a simple formula: 'Eliminate the fear – it's fun!' But he also makes sure his players understand their privilege in being able to reach for that ambition: 'Let me put it this way. How many guys your age in Iraq have died? Now ask yourself if you're doing your best.' When asked if Garrido's overriding philosophy of 'you can be as good as you can be' is also his own, Linklater replies: 'Yes it is. He's a friend of mine but in some ways it's a self-portrait of a process.' This process is one of self-fulfilment and creativity through the challenge of preparation at a sensible remove from injurious competition, for it is preparation, teamwork and positive thinking that give rise to the possibility of inspirational performance during a match. As such, Garrido's approach to baseball serves Linklater as a metaphor for a philosophy of filmmaking:

I saw a complete analogy with filmmaking, with the team just preparing for the game. Filming is not as important as pre-production but it's never totally worked out. It's like for an athlete. All that stuff is practice, but the shooting is the final game where you maybe discover something extra. You may wake up the morning of the game with the final good thought. That's why I always pace it so you're absolutely peaking when you're shooting that scene. Otherwise you're driving home at the end of the day having new thoughts that would have made the scene better. But it's too late then. I never do that. I've always thought it to death first and peaked in the game. You work out everything you possibly can, but you peak in the game. You save it for the film.

As Garrido maintains that pacing and preparation is crucial to life, so Linklater transposes this philosophy to the project known as *Boyhood*, filmed in short sequences over the space of twelve years in order to map out the stages in a boy's adolescence. In adding fragments to a Cubist portrait of the cinema of Linklater, *Boyhood* appears as a meta-portrait for its own fragmentation of a fictional life that reflects contemporary America too:

It's about a boy. It's contemporary, very contemporary. What I'm shooting is what's happening. It starts when he's about six or seven, just getting out of first grade. It's kinda like the public school here goes first to twelfth grade, so it's twelve years. This year he'll be in seventh grade. So it's in and around school but it's not always in school. And right now [2009] he's turning thirteen. I'm halfway through. I shot my sixth episode last fall. I'm gearing up to shoot another one.

The protagonist of the film is Mason (Ellar Salmon, who played Jay Anderson in *Fast Food Nation*), whose divorced parents are played by Ethan Hawke and Patricia Arquette. 'They're around about every other episode,' explains Linklater: 'Last year Ethan had a camping trip with his son and Patricia wasn't in it.' However, the subject of the film is time and cinema or as Linklater puts it: 'Pure cinema, where the lead character is really time.' To this end, every year Linklater stages both a 'family' reunion and one with a tiny but committed crew. Shooting in a documentary style, Linklater recognises the influence of Michael Apted's *Up* series of films charting the lives of fourteen children since 1964 with seven year ellipses that also resonates within the relationship of *Before Midnight* to its prequels and the series of films featuring Antoine (Jean-Pierre Leaud) directed by Truffaut. This is because the sense of pure cinema he purports to seek in recording the actual growth of a boy similarly blurs the distinction between character and actor that underpins the portrayals of Jesse and Céline; although here, for all the potential cruelty of adolescent growth spurts and hormonal highs, the changes to Mason/Ellar Salmon will be so gradual as to resemble what might be Linklater's holy grail of a *dérive* (drift) through life. And not only for Salmon, as Hawke and Arquette will also expose their ageing in a film that Linklater believes will show them as crumbling portraits in the fashion of Dorian Gray: 'The film is not in chapters, it's segued,' says Linklater: 'That's the interesting thing; it just follows. I'm shooting on 35 mm so I'm hoping it will all look the same. So you'll sit and watch one movie and everyone just ages.'

Perhaps the biggest obstacle to a project such as this is securing the long-term commitment of the cast, which explains the collaboration of the dependable Hawke, who, Linklater recalls, 'was on board easy because it sounded so crazy':

> Patricia I'd only met once. She was dating a friend of mine and I just called her up as I knew she had been a mother fairly young, about nineteen or twenty when she had a kid. And we talked for a couple of hours on the phone, and she just committed over the phone. You know, it was like: 'What are you doing twelve years from now? I'm going to be trying to make a film and you're going to be looking for a good part.' This is what we do. It's such a weird thing but this is what we do.

Other roles had to be filled with those who Linklater could rely on too: 'My daughter plays his older sister, just because I knew where she would be. Because it's hard to commit. You can't contract anyone to do anything for twelve years. It's against the law.' How then does one limit the risk of losing Ellar Salmon, his star? 'He could quit. He could move,' accepts Linklater:

> When you cast a little kid like that, you're really casting the parents. And his mother's a dancer. His dad's a musician. They have deep Texan roots and Austin ties. And I kinda looked at it and figured, 'Okay, I don't know if their marriage will survive.' And it didn't. They got divorced somewhere in the middle of it. But that's okay, that's fine. It works for the story. I meet with him pretty regularly. He's an interesting kid.

However, at a time when Linklater and most independent filmmakers are struggling to find funding and combine it with coherent distribution for even the smallest projects, perhaps what is most remarkable about *Boyhood* is that a production company has been willing to invest in a film that will show no possible dividend for at least fifteen years. That company is the Independent Film Channel (IFC), which co-produced *Tape* and *Waking Life* and has distributed the *Saw* horror film series (2004–) in the US. 'I somehow talked them into this,' says Linklater:

> They're so brave. They give me enough every year to shoot just that little, fifteen- or twenty-minute piece, which is long. I thought it would just be ten minutes every year, but I can't help it. There's just too much stuff. Last year was kind of short but this will be another big year. So at the end of the day it'll be around three hours hopefully.

Adding to the realism of the project is its dismissal of any narrative beyond the combined ageing/filming process and the ongoing, semi-improvisational shaping of the events onscreen. Linklater insists 'what they're doing is pretty banal, you know? He's in school and doing all the little petty things that you do growing up, but there's some drama in the family, the mother gets remarried and they move around a lot.' Moreover, Linklater professes to 'kinda have an eye on what I think is going on to some degree. Last fall they were campaigning for Obama door to door, for example. You know, putting signs in yards, whatever's going on.' The notion that the film will have value as a time capsule and as a time machine, is also recognised by the film-maker:

> Like one year, when the *Harry Potter* books come out, there was this launch. My daughter and I have been to these things. It's at midnight, people dress up in character and you go through the little railway station and there's people handing out books. And I said, 'next year we're going to film this', because it didn't happen when I was a kid and it might not happen ever again that people are that excited about a book. So I had my characters waiting and worked that into thinking retrospectively from eight years into the future, thinking, 'Yeah, that'll seem weird.'

Editing, on the other hand, is an accumulative process subject to regular revision: 'I edit every year and every two or three years I edit the whole thing again just to keep it all in mind. So I've got a pretty good cut of the first six years.' And so the production continues, with Linklater expressing commitment to Coach Garrido's dictum of thorough preparation for the game:

> We get about three days of production per year, we don't have much money, and we shoot about fifteen to twenty minutes. It's pretty concentrated, the days are tough, but you have to prepare. There's new casting, whatever. Most movies you prepare eight weeks and shoot ten weeks. This is like 'prepare three weeks to shoot three days', so at the end of the day you'll have a year of pre-production and forty days of production. So it's crazy. Every year it gets to be a lot more fun but it gets a lot more demanding too.

Proof, if any were needed, of the demanding nature of filmmaking is also evident in the many projects with which Linklater has been associated throughout his career without ever adding them to his CV. His independence and resolution to remain in Austin has often borne that downside of being adrift without backers or distribution for projects that a closer relationship with the major studios might have fostered, especially after proving his bankability with *The School of Rock*. Yet he continues to nurture long-term projects such as *Boyhood* and scripts that await technology or their right time: 'I have a couple of films now that I'm into my second decade on, that I can't even see doing in the next few years.' Amongst these waylaid also-rans are a sequel to *The Last Detail* (1973), which was directed by Hal Ashby and based on Robert Towne's adaptation of Darryl Ponicsan's 1971 novel about Seaman Larry Meadows (Randy Quaid) being reluctantly guided to prison by his military escort Billy Buddusky (Jack Nicholson).

Another casualty is *That's What I'm Talking About*, the 'spiritual sequel' to *Dazed and Confused* that ran aground on a lack of distribution in 2009:

> I spent seven or eight years outlining or plotting and then finally I get a strategy and a script and I go, 'Okay, now I'm ready!' It was a college comedy. I think it's the funniest thing I've ever written. I really thought I had it financed, but we couldn't really get a distributor. I couldn't believe I couldn't get distribution. It used to be if you had any money, if you had half your budget from equity or foreign sales… I got *A Scanner Darkly* made like that. And this was kinda shocking. So anyway, I'm in a holding pattern with that and a couple of other projects, scripts I've had for a while.

Working outside the major studios, Linklater admits that he has 'always struggled with that anyway: to get certain films made.' These include 'a script about an auto assembly line worker in Flint, Michigan' (Robey 2007: 24) and a black comedy called *Bernie* that finally went into production in 2010. *Bernie* recounts a true story from 1998 when the richest widow in the town of Carthage, Texas, Marjorie Nugent (Shirley MacLaine), was found in a large freezer in her home after being missing for nine months. Bernie Tiede (Jack Black), a popular and generous, assistant funeral director who had befriended Nugent when he supervised her husband's funeral, admitted to killing her for her money but was supported by the townsfolk, who had neither cared for nor missed the snooty widow. In August 2010, an open casting call for *Bernie* was posted on www.shortfilmtexas.com asking for 'Townspeople – Texans who are not necessarily professional actors … the real deal – funny and interesting folks. There are a lot of small parts in the movie, mostly for people over 40' (Weidner 2010) and attracted online responses from many who had known the real Bernie.

Also on the 'to do' list is *College Republicans* starring Paul Dano as future Deputy Chief of Staff and senior advisor to George W. Bush Sr. Karl Rove., who worked on Richard Nixon's 1972 presidential campaign and was nicknamed Bush's Brain. The film, which will be partly produced by Maya Browne of Bratt Entertainment, explores the formative relationship between Rove and fellow student Lee Atwater, who would become Chairman of the Republican National Committee. In addition, there is the still unlikely sequel to *The School of Rock* as well as a biopic of Chet Baker co-written with *Tape*'s Stephen Belber and due to star Ethan Hawke. And there is also *Liars (A–E)*, which was offered to Linklater by producer Scott Rudin but fell foul of Disney's downsizing of Miramax in late 2009 after Rebecca Hall and Kat Dennings had been cast as friends on a road trip to Obama's inauguration, collecting items left with ex-boyfriends on the way. At the time of this interview, nonetheless, Linklater was excited about the challenge:

> It's a change of gears for me: two women on a reflective road trip. I've got to do my *Alice Doesn't Live Here Anymore*. Everyone has to do their purely female movie and I've always been amazed that I haven't. You know, *Before Sunrise* and *Before Sunset* have a strong female character and sensibility, but I'd liked to

have been a Fassbinder or a Bergman or someone; someone who makes more female movies.

Linklater retains the ambition to create a drama as complex and powerful as Rainer Werner Fassbinder's television series *Berlin Alexanderplatz* (1980): 'The cinema isn't doing anything adult. I might have to get involved in television drama. Never say never. The right timing, the right subject matter…'

Periods of unemployment do not denote inactivity and are mostly subsumed within the fits and starts of any filmmaker's career. Gaps also provide opportunities for other endeavours, such as Linklater's involvement in lobbying for film incentives on behalf of the Austin Film Studios and working with MoveOn.org in 2004, which describes itself as 'a service – a way for busy but concerned citizens to find their political voice in a system dominated by big money and big media' (Anon. 2010b). Linklater made an advertisement for MoveOn prior to the 2004 presidential election aimed at encouraging voters to get involved in civic and political action. He also participated as judge alongside Susan Sarandon in the Fairview organisation's Upgrade Democracy video contest, which invited amateur filmmakers to upload short films to YouTube that answered the question: 'If you could change anything you wanted about elections, what would our democracy look like?' And he judged the 'Why We Don't Vote' essay-writing contest of the Center for Voting and Democracy and Midwest Democracy Center (Anon. 2010c). In addition to small parts and cameos in his own films that include him playing foosball in the music bar that Jesse and Céline enter in *Before Sunrise* and as the third member of the rock group in the photograph of Dewey and Ned (Mike White) in their younger days in *The School of Rock*, Linklater contributed the voice of a bus driver to *Beavis and Butthead Do America* (Mike Judge, 1996) and appeared as Ember Doorman in *Underneath* (Steven Soderbergh, 1995), Cool Spy in *Spy Kids* (Robert Rodríguez, 2001) and Principal Mallard in *RSO (Registered Sex Offender)* (Bob Byington, 2008). Finally, for insomniac completists only, there is *Heads I Win/Tails You Lose* (1991), a piece that Linklater compiled from the countdowns and tail ends of film reels that passed through his hands while curating the Austin Film Society between 1987 and 1990, thereby creating a cinematic monument to the excitement and frustration caused by films that are always arriving and forever departing. Thus, the climax of every film's launch procedure is elided with the result that the spectator exists in a constantly aroused yet frustrated state of expectation that expresses Bergson and Linklater's eternal moment as perpetual cinephiliac priapism.

And, having exhausted the CV, what is missing? In relation to what Corrigan calls the 'commercial performance of the business of being an auteur' (1991: 104), Linklater does not position himself as a celebrity or artist in comparison with various of his contemporaries but as a mostly non-Hollywood filmmaker who has been both liberated and limited by remaining in Austin all these years. To the extent that a commitment to recurring themes, a particular aesthetic and an insistent point of view is the basic criteria for an auteurist reading of any filmmaker's work, one might at least identify all three in the disparate projects that he has directed, although the finished films differ greatly in genre, tone and style. Nevertheless, while mainstream cinema often exaggerates all it can, that of Linklater appears to embody the attitude of Uncle Pete in *Fast Food Nation* of being quite all right with what it's not doing. Whereas narrative convention exudes a compulsion towards resolution tantamount to a capitalist imperative to speculate greedily on the future, the cinema of Linklater most often digresses through dialogue that prompts characters such as Jesse and Céline to perceive and reflect upon the contrary experience of an eternal, incomplete present. Consequently, it is not the movement of any narrative-bound protagonist that defines the cinema of Linklater but the time that encounters between them take to transpire in any space whatsoever. Linklater and his collaborators may play at the generic boundaries of the western, romantic comedy, science fiction, sports movie, musical, documentary and television situation comedy, but instead of making things happen with a stage kiss or a pulled punch they mostly allow time to foster far more intriguing and authentic connections. That said, the cinema of Linklater continues to pull in contrary directions while at the same time insisting that the best way to win a tug-of-war is to let go of the rope. This enthusiasm for genre filmmaking, for example, means that these character-based films stop short of the subtle, enigmatic observations of a filmmaker such as Claire Denis and may even seem hurried and cluttered besides the stripped-down films of the Mumblecore generation that references the cinema of Linklater on their way to that of Yasujiro Ozu; but that's okay.

Or is it? The cinema of Richard Linklater may observe an American underclass but it rarely contends with the explicitly political causes of their condition. His cinema remains white, straight and well-fed even though it proffers empathy with the underprivileged and marginalised that includes the 34.5 per cent of blacks, 28.6 per cent of Hispanics and 15 per cent of whites currently living in poverty in America (Anon. 2009j). Consequently, one might question the solipsism of slacking and wonder whether remaining in Austin has rendered Linklater a regional filmmaker of diminishing relevance. The fact that slacking is often celebrated as a lifestyle choice might even be considered irresponsible in a country where over 15.5 million people were living below the poverty line in 2007 (ibid.). In retrospect, his is not an outsider cinema such as that boasting queer or black credentials, although he once thanked Todd Haynes publicly during a panel discussion at Austin's SXSW festival on 17 March 2009 for saying that *Slacker* could be part of New Queer Cinema because of its alternative notions of time and narrative. The problems faced by the protagonists of the cinema of Linklater are mostly not those of survival but of classical Hollywood genres: how to rob a bank, how to get the girl, how to put on a show, how to rally a sports team, how to break into showbusiness, and so on. While the world was watching the progress to the White House of America's first black president, Barack Obama (who is a year younger than Linklater) in 2008, Linklater was back in the 1930s with Orson Welles and trying to make it on Broadway. Neither non-white, nor gay, nor poor; instead of a *Do The Right Thing* (Spike Lee, 1989), a *Go Fish* or a *Wendy and Lucy* (Kelly Reichardt, 2008), Linklater built a career over almost two decades before taking on the privileged moral issue of vegetarianism in *Fast Food Nation*. Thus, in considering the cinema of Linklater, one might well ask, where's the meat?

To be fair, the question of the extent to which any filmmaker is enabled, entitled or obliged to comment on society and its values is one that will often overbalance any appraisal. Linklater never sought the position of spokesperson of the so-called slacker generation and in his subsequent absence from the podium and pulpit it was hardly his fault that MTV and the iPod took his place. Instead of making his own statements, he is more likely to position and enable more verbose philosophers to carry the weight of the word in the films he has directed and sometimes even rotoscopes to add an extra protective layer. As Deleuze says of Godard, 'he provides himself with the reflexive types as so many interceders through whom I is always another' (2005b: 181). Perhaps, as Welles (Christian McKay) admits in *Me and Orson Welles*, 'if people can't find you, they can't dislike you'. Then again, as Linklater admits, 'on one level I have to acknowledge now that I've made fifteen films and a couple of little side things and, yeah, that's enough to have to account for it all I guess'. Thus, in formulating this account, it must be questioned whether true social realism, for example, is beyond his scope as a filmmaker; although an expectation of realism misses the point of his cinema entirely. Linklater is, after all, a metaphysician whose cinema often dismisses what passes for reality as a fallible and untrustworthy construct in order to seek truth and fulfilment elsewhere. Instead, by focussing on the *durée* (duration) of the *dérive* (drift), this cinema posits unreality as something that becomes tangible through imagination, reflection and emotional investment in those who might join one there, even to the extent that the shared experience replaces reality altogether. The metaphysical gambit of Jesse, for example, is to invite Céline to join him for a night in Vienna, while that of Céline is to lead him down twisting alleyways nine years later in Paris. In the same way, *Slacker* reterritorialises and so reinvents Austin, as do *Dazed and Confused*, *SubUrbia*, *Waking Life*, *A Scanner Darkly* and *$5.15/Hr*, while *The Newton Boys* revises the glamour of America's past, *Fast Food Nation* reveals the horror of its present and, nonetheless, *Live from Shiva's Dance Floor* and *The School of Rock* express hope for its future. Moreover, it is in long takes, fluid camerawork, an emphasis on dialogue and the movement and interaction of the protagonists that this alternative reality is communicated as a viable surrogate to the one experienced by the audience. In *Slacker*, for instance, contextual and textual analyses are not separate but interwoven so that the film's aesthetic carries political resonance. As *Slacker* opposes Hollywood narrative with its drifting, incomplete sequences, so the subaltern community in Austin also opposes Republicanism and its identical, analogous obsession with striving for resolution and speculation on the future. When *Slacker* is appreciated in the context of the end of Reaganomics and the beginning of the Bush dynasty, it should be recognised that textually and contextually it is a profoundly oppositional film in both form and content and, perhaps most influentially, in the way it simply illustrated an alternative reality to the one that was contemptuous of its carnival of grotesques.

Subsequently, the illustration of an alternative reality was achieved by more explicit metaphysical strategies that employed film itself as an analogy for the dreamstate. If *Dazed and Confused* conveys the feeling that every day has the potential to be the worst one of your life, it also ultimately resembles the adolescent fantasy of the best day in Mitch's life, when this geeky kid spends a night hanging out with the coolest guys in school, buying beer, smoking pot, cruising in cool cars, drinking at a keg party and making out with an older chick till dawn. Consequently, here is proof that the metaphysical strategy has worked, for the film itself aspires to the dreamstate that can be rendered more real than reality itself by the investment of genuine emotion in its potential. As Dawson (Sasha Jenson) says of him: 'Not bad for a little freshman.' Time and time again, therefore, the cinema of Linklater shows its audience a way out of conformity and surrender by acting upon imagination. These films are not escapist, but they do present an escape plan. In their possibly naive idealism, they nonetheless hold out the promise of self-determination in a manner that defies all pressures to conform to an unimaginative, unreflective, unemotional life. In addition, their insistence upon human interaction through walking and talking means that they aspire to the standards by which 'film is made accessible [when] it destroys the luminous cult value or presence of the putatively unique, remote, and inaccessible art project' (Stam 2000: 65). *Slacker, Dazed and Confused, SubUrbia, Before Sunrise, Tape, Waking Life, Before Sunset, Live from Shiva's Dance Floor, Inning by Inning: A Portrait of a Coach* and *Boyhood* are also determinedly collaborative projects in their production process, involving the same core crew repeatedly and the welcoming of their casts' own investment in their characters even when (or especially when) playing themselves. As an oppositional form of cinema at a time when the mainstream is piling on the bombast, that of Linklater illustrates independence and alternative priorities in its very making.

Such idealism as is celebrated in some of these films, however, is often spoiled by contact with reality in others. Just as the train timetable intrudes so wretchedly upon the otherwise timeless tryst of Jesse and Céline in *Before Sunrise*, so anxious considerations of one's place in history and the subservience of the present to the future is what does for the protagonists of *The Newton Boys* and *SubUrbia*, in which the fun of robbing banks and just hanging out are both based upon an initial lack of consideration for consequences. This is fine as long as one is able to invest imaginatively and wholeheartedly in one's immediate legend or ongoing rebellious reputation, but neither the Newton siblings nor the old kids on the block in *SubUrbia* are able to hold off considerations of ageing that make their behaviour and even existence increasingly anachronistic. From here is but a step inside to the burgeoning paranoia of *Tape*, moreover, in which two twenty-something males are trapped in the past of a grimy motel room, unable to break free from a cycle of recriminations that has become more important to their identities than the dimly remembered cause of a grievance whose resolution eludes them. However, the means of escape from entrapment in such a stagnant sense of time is illustrated by *Waking Life*, which evokes aspirations to transcendence through metaphysical gambits that are illustrated by the grotesque rotoscoping of its carnival of philosophers, one of whom, Timothy 'Speed' Levitch, is so animated as to make the rotoscoping that adorned him in *Waking Life* appear redundant when he preaches transcendence to post-9/11 New York in *Live from Shiva's Dance Floor*.

However, giving up on the lost cause of converting fearfully conformist adults, the cinema of Linklater turns its attention to the potential of a new generation in *The School of Rock* and *Bad News Bears*, in which playing for the fun of it rather than the prize is its own form of rebellion. As Augie Garrido demonstrates in *Inning by Inning:*

A Portrait of a Coach, it is collaboration rather than competition that is the key. It is by celebrating that redemptive, mutual commitment to the moment that Jesse and Céline are rescued from their stalled romance and reunited in real time in the Paris of *Before Sunset*. Nevertheless, it seems that such romanticism can only exist outside America, within which the second four-year tenure of President George W. Bush prevents much optimism from emerging in the meagre *$5.15/Hr*, the impotent *Fast Food Nation* and the ultimately forlorn and paranoid *A Scanner Darkly*.

Yet self-assertion through personal growth is revived as a literal ambition in the evolving *Boyhood*, while the potential for creative expression emerges anew in *Me and Orson Welles*, in which an analogous period of American optimism to that of Barack Obama's presidency is identified in the 1930s – a period that was similarly imbued with what Linklater identifies as 'the spirit of youthful ambition'. Aiming *Me and Orson Welles* at elusive cinema-goers in 2009, Linklater underlined the analogy when he declared: 'I want you to feel like you're a young person in 1937 and the future's all ahead of you!' Thus, *Me and Orson Welles* finds this robust dialogue in the communication of ideas and fosters a cautious commitment to integrity, collaboration and creativity at a time when Obama was campaigning with the promise, 'Yes We Can.' All the same, as Linklater admitted, the message of *Me and Orson Welles* was not immune from the lessons of experience: 'You can have pure integrity for yourself but you have to take the consequences.'

Way back in *Slacker*, Linklater appears onscreen in profile behind the film's opening title with his head against the window of the bus that drives past the golden arches of McDonalds and pulls into Austin at dawn. Identified in the credits as Should Have Stayed at Bus Station on account of the wry conclusion to his monologue on alternative realities and roads not taken, Linklater nevertheless ventures onward into downtown Austin. With its constant arrivals and departures, the bus station is an 'any space whatsoever' that signifies a Bergsonian state of mind. It is a place of interaction with countless individuals but little meaningful communication. It is also a place, like a train station in Vienna or an airport in Paris, whose purpose is to offer countless paths away from itself. It resembles, even symbolises, therefore, a billiard-break state of mind based upon an awareness of one's infinite potential to go in any direction in the eternal single moment. However, although it might seem to be a place of decision rather than chance, there is also scope for bucking the schedule and getting on any bus whatsoever, just to see where one ends up. Had Linklater stayed at the bus station, he may have taken any one of an infinite number of routes leading to different lives that might have included a career in Hollywood or a succession of 'McJobs'. But the fact that he remained in Austin makes the cinema of Richard Linklater a story of consequences. Asked why he chose to remain there, Linklater replies: 'It's home':

> I like Austin more now. I like its music. It's a very literary, academic environment. And I'm one of the non-nostalgic citizens. The 1980s were really slow here if you had any ambition. There was a depression in Texas and everyone was out of work, but *Slacker* really grew out of that Austin, you know: lazy, complacent, no economic activity.

Contemporary Austin is very different. Once the ban on construction any higher than the dome of the Texas State Capitol was challenged and overthrown, glassy banks shot up in the downtown area around Congress Avenue and turned the still vibrant streetlife into a bohemian Lilliput. But Sixth Street is still one of the rowdiest and most colourful venues for nightly carnival and South Austin still boasts the best Tex-Mex food in Chuy's and Gueros. The rents are higher but, as Linklater maintains, 'if you want to live in Nowheresville you can do it':

> I like to kid my friends in New York or LA: 'For that little two bedroom apartment you just bought in Tribeca, I have 37 acres and several houses. I built it myself; I got a pool I built myself.' On the other hand, the burden of being a local is that you're expected to participate in everything: aloofness versus asshole.

Has your life changed much here?

> It's not much different. It's more complex because I've got three kids, but Austin's always been a good niche for me. I love New York and all the great cities of Europe that I've spent time in. Los Angeles, however, is just too much industry and it's depressing because it's all film industry, just the industry of entertainment. It's so depressing to see it so commodified. All the trade magazines are obsessed with money.

Do you ever wonder how different your career might have been if you had headed for Los Angeles instead of Austin?

> Sure. But I always feel like a little bit of a failure there. I fit in. I have a toe in that world. But I couldn't see me being creative there.

So you can't imagine having set up the Los Angeles Film Society and building your own studios there?

> He laughs:

> The Austin Film Society was purely selfish. I was trying to see movies I hadn't seen and I thought I could sucker other people into helping me pay for that! But there's another reason why I have a film society: the absolute essential belief that those experiences are so much better as a communal experience, even with people you don't know. People need that.

Finally then, for all the walking and talking in the cinema of Linklater, one finds that its director has remained in the same place, one that is part refuge, part realm, and all about the people and the present. Beginning with the question 'is it the place or is it the time in which nothing is happening?', this attempt at exploring the films he has written, co-written and/or directed must ultimately surrender to what Henri Bergson

Richard Linklater, aka Pinball Playing Man

posited as the 'uninterrupted up-surge of novelty' (1992b: 18), Gilles Deleuze identified on film as 'a little time in the pure state [rising] up to the surface of the screen' (2005b: xii) and 'Speed' Levitch calls 'the ongoing wow'. What might be termed the 'newness of the nowness' is what is redeemed throughout the cinema of Linklater, from Having a Breakthrough Day (Denise Montgomery) in *Slacker* for whom everything is okay because 'time doesn't exist', to Cynthia in *Dazed and Confused* who 'would like to quit thinking of the present, like right now, as some minor, insignificant preamble to something else'. This is also true for Jesse, who wonders 'what good is saved time if nobody uses it?' in *Before Sunrise*, in which the lovers embark upon a futile search for permanence that is finally accepted as illusory when Jesse recites W. H. Auden's poetic counsel that 'time will have its fancy, tomorrow or today'. And so to Pinball Playing Man in *Waking Life* exclaiming 'there's only one instant, and it's right now, and it's eternity' in response to the Oblique Strategy offered by Linklater's entire cinema, that of 'walk, don't run'.

In conclusion, if this book ultimately resembles a Cubist portrait of the cinema of Richard Linklater with each film a fragment and all those fragments resulting in inevitable incompletion, at least that might evoke some sense of a filmmaker whose cinema walks and talks in the spaces between more profitable careers, more blockbusting films and more publicly celebrated figures, no matter how small those spaces have become. At least, as he recounts, there is evidence that its playful, collaborative, oneiric philosophy might have broken through when President Barack Obama declared himself a fan. 'He's not focused on the film industry,' admits Linklater:

He likes movies though. And Jack Black was at the inauguration. I got a text from him. It's like one in the morning and I get a text and I look at it and it says, 'Obama loves *The School of Rock!*'

A slacker in the White House? Like everything in the cinema of Richard Linklater, it was all just a matter of time.

Notes

1   All quotes attributed to Richard Linklater, unless otherwise attributed, are from interviews with the author in Austin, 30 July–1 August 2009.
2   As regards British television, Linklater is referring to *The Office* (2001–3) and *Fawlty Towers* (1975–79), but the tradition extends to *On The Buses* (1969–73), *Are You Being Served?* (1972–85), *Open All Hours* (1976–85), *Dinnerladies* (1998–2000) and many others.
3   President George W. Bush is actually glimpsed on a television jetting off to a conference in Germany and witheringly awarded the epithet, 'there he is, the man who saved Texas'.
4   Garrido's record is 1,629 wins, 755 losses, and 8 ties over 37 seasons of collegiate coaching.

FILMOGRAPHY

Woodshock (1985, short)
Distributor: The Criterion Collection
Director: Richard Linklater
Cinematography: Richard Linklater
Main Cast: Daniel Johnston

It's Impossible to Learn to Plow by Reading Books (1988)
Production Company: Detour Filmproduction
Producer: Richard Linklater
Director: Richard Linklater
Screenplay: Richard Linklater
Cinematography: Richard Linklater
Editor: Richard Linklater
Main Cast: Richard Linklater, James Goodwin, Daniel Kratochvil, Linda Finney, Tracy Crabtree, Linda Levine, Lisa Schiebold, Erin MCafée, Denise Montgomery, Scott Van Horn, Daniel Johnston, Tammy Gómez, Keith McCormack

Heads I Win / Tails You Lose (1991, video)
Producer: Richard Linklater
Director: Richard Linklater
Editor: Richard Linklater

Slacker (1991)
Production Company: Detour Filmproduction
Producer: Richard Linklater
Director: Richard Linklater
Screenplay: Richard Linklater
Cinematography: Lee Daniel
Editor: Scott Rhodes
Main Cast: Richard Linklater (Should Have Stayed at Bus Station), Rudy Básquez (Taxi Driver), Jean Caffeine (Roadkill), Jan Hockey (Jogger), Stephan Hockey (Running Late), Mark James (Hit-and-Run Son), Samuel Dietert (Grocery Grabber of Death's Bounty), Bob Boyd (Officer Bozzio), Terrence Kirk (Officer Love), Keith McCormack (Street Musician), Jennifer Schaudies (Walking to Coffee Shop), Dan Kratochvil (Espresso Czar/Masonic Malconten), Maris Strautmanis (Giant Cappuccino), Brecht Andersch (Dostoyevsky Wannabe), Tom Pallotta (Looking for Missing Friend), Jerry Deloney (Been on the Moon Since the 50s), Heather West (Tura Satana Look-Alike), John Spath (Co-op Guy), Ron Marks (Bush Basher), Daniel Dugan (Comb Game Player), Brian Crockett (Sadistic Comb Game Player), Scott Marcus (Ultimate Loser), Stella Weir (Stephanie from Dallas), Teresa Taylor (Pap Smear Pusher), Mark Harris (T-Shirt Terrorist), Greg Wilson (Anti-Traveller), Debbie Pastor (Wants

to Leave Country),Gina Lalli (Sidewalk Psychic), Sharon Roos (Devoted Follower), Frank Orrall (Happy-Go-Lucky Guy), Skip Fulton Jr. (Two for One Special), Abra Moore (Has Change), Lori Capp (Traumatized Yacht Owner), Gus Vayas (Cranky Cook), Louis Black (Paranoid Paper Reader), Don Stroud (Recluse in Bathrobe), Janelle Coolich (Shut-in Girlfriend), Aleister Barron (Peeping Kid), Albans Benchoff (Coke Machine Robber), Nigel Benchoff (Budding Capitalist Youth), Zara Barron (Coke Heist Accomplice), Kevin Whitley (Jilted Boyfriend), Steven Anderson (Guy Who Tosses Typewriter), Robert Pierson (Based on Authoritative Sources), Sarah Harmon (Has Faith in Groups), David Haymond (Street Dweller), John Slate ('Conspiracy A-Go-Go' Author), Scott Van Horn (Nova), Lee Daniel (GTO), Charles Gunning (Hitchhiker Awaiting 'True Call'), Tamsy Ringler (Video Interviewer), Luke Savisky (Video Cameraman), Meg Brennan (Sitting at Café), Phillip Hostak (Hit Up for Cigarettes), D. Angus MacDonald (Video Playing Store Security), Shelly Kristaponis (Shoplifter), Louis Mackey (Old Anarchist), Kathy McCarty (Anarchist's Daughter), Michael Laird (Burglar), Jack Meredith (Get-Away Accomplice), Clark Lee Walker (Cadillac Crook), Kalman Spellitich (Video Backpacker), Siqgouri Wilkovich (Slapping Boyfriend), John Hawkins (Choking Girlfriend), Scott Rhodes (Disgruntled Grad Student), Denise Montgomery (Having a Breakthrough Day), Mimi Vitetta (Teacup Sculpter), Susannah Simone (Working on Same Painting), Bruce Hughes (Card Playing Waiter), Keith Fletcher (Café Card Player #1), Eric Buehlman (Café Card Player #2), R. Malice (Scooby Doo Philosopher), Mark Quirk (Papa Smurf),

Kim Krizan (Questions Happiness), Annick Souhami (Has Conquered Fear of Rejection), Regina Garza (Smoking Writer), Stephen Jacobson (S-T-E-V-E with a Van), Eric Lord (Doorman at Club), Kelly Linn (Bike Rider with Nice Shoes), Rachael Reinhardt (Cousin from Greece), Stewart Bennet (Sitting on Ledge), Kevin Thomson (Handstamping Arm Licker), Nick Maffei (Pixl-Visionary), Nolan Morrison (To Be Buried by History), Kyle Rosenblad (Going to Catch a Show), Ed Hall (Band Playing at Club), Lucinda Scott (Dairy Queen Photographer), Wammo (Anti-Artist), Marianne Hyatt (Late Night Pick-Up), Gary Price (Watching Early Morning TV), Joseph Jones (Old Man Recording Thoughts), Kendal Smith (Post-Modern Paul Revere), Sean Coffey (Super 8 Cameraman), Jennifer Carroll (All-Night Partier), Charlotte Norris (Convertible Driver), Patrice Sullivan (Day Tripper), Greg Ward (Tosses Camera Off Cliff)

Dazed and Confused (1993)
Production Companies: Alphaville Films, Detour Filmproduction
Producers: Sean Daniel, James Jacks, Richard Linklater
Co-Producer: Anne Walker-McBay
Director: Richard Linklater
Story: Richard Linklater
Cinematography: Lee Daniel
Editor: Sandra Adair
Main Cast: Jason London (Randall 'Pink' Floyd), Rory Cochrane (Ron Slater), Wiley Wiggins (Mitch Kramer), Sasha Jenson (Don Dawson), Michelle Burke (Jodi Kramer), Adam Goldberg (Mike Newhouse), Anthony Rapp (Tony Olson), Matthew McConaughey (David Wooderson), Marissa Ribisi (Cynthia Dunn), Shawn Andrews (Kevin Pickford), Cole Hauser (Benny

O'Donnell), Milla Jovovich (Michelle Burroughs), Joey Lauren Adams (Simone Kerr), Christin Hinojosa (Sabrina Davis), Ben Affleck (Fred O'Bannion), Jason O. Smith (Melvin Spivey), Deena Martin (Shavonne Wright), Parker Posey (Darla Marks), Nicky Katt (Clint Bruno), Catherine Morris (Julie Simms), Christine Harnos (Kaye Faulkner), Esteban Powell (Carl Burnett), Mark Vandermeulen (Tommy Houston), Jeremy Fox (John Hirschfelder), Parker Brooks (Kyle Eschenbrenner), Terry Mross (Coach Conrad), Kim Krizan (Ms. Ginny Stroud, high school teacher), Julius Tennon (Mr. Payne, junior high school teacher), Richard Dillard (Frank Pickford), Kathleen Cunningham (Mrs. Pickford, Kevin's Mom), Katherine Asher (Mrs. Burnett, Carl's Mom), Zooey Greif (Pentico), Rick Moser (Assistant Coach), John Swasey (Beer Deliver Guy), Zach Taylor (Freshman Smartass), Jacob Jones (Freshman Smartass), Priscilla Kinser (Freshman Girl 1), Erika Geminder (Freshman Girl 2), Heidi Cole Trenbath (Freshman Girl 3), Zeke Mills (Old Timer), Michael Gillespie (Party Guy), Tom Hoeck (Chaparone), Fred Lerner (Guy with Pistol)

Before Sunrise (1995)

Production Companies: Castle Rock Entertainment, Detour Filmproduction, Filmhaus Wien Universa Filproduktions, Sunrise Production, Columbia Pictures Corporation Producer: Anne Walker-McBay

Co-Producers: Wolfgang Ramml, Gernot Schaffler, Ellen Winn Wendl

Associate Producer: Gregory Jacobs

Executive Producer: John Sloss

Director: Richard Linklater

Screenplay: Richard Linklater, Kim Krizan

Cinematography: Lee Daniel

Editor: Sandra Adair

Original Music: Fred Frith

Main Cast: Ethan Hawke (Jesse), Julie Delpy (Céline), Andrea Eckert (Wife on Train), Hanno Pöschl (Husband on Train), Karl Bruckschwaiger (Guy on Bridge), Tex Rubinowitz (Guy on Bridge), Erni Mangold (Palm Reader), Dominik Castell (Street Poet), Haymon Maria Buttinger (Bartender), Harald Waiglein (Guitarist in Club), Bilge Jeschim (Belly Dancer), Kurti (Percussionist), Hans Weingartner (Café Patron), Liese Lyon (Café Patron), Peter Ily Huemer (Café Patron), Otto Reiter (Café Patron), Hubert Fabian Kulterer (Café Patron), Branko Andric (Café Patron), Constanze Schweiger (Café Patron), John Sloss (Café Patron), Alexandra Seibel (Café Patron), Georg Schöllhammer (Café Patron), Christian Ankowitsch (Café Patron), Wilbirg Reiter (Café Patron), Barbara Klebel (Musician on Boat), Wolfgang Staribacher (Musician on Boat), Wolfgang Glüxam (Harpsichord Player), Adam Goldberg (Man Sleeping on Train), Paul Poet (Guy in Bar)

SubUrbia (1996)

Production Companies: Castle Rock Entertainment, Detour Filmproduction

Producers: Ginger Sledge, Anne Walker-McBay

Executive Producer: John Sloss

Director: Richard Linklater

Story: Eric Bogosian

Screenplay: Eric Bogosian

Cinematography: Lee Daniel

Editor: Sandra Adair

Main Cast: Jayce Bartok (Pony), Amie Carey (Sooze), Nicky Katt (Tim), Ajay Naidu (Nazeer Choudhury), Parker Posey (Erica), Giovanni Ribisi (Jeff), Samia Shoaib (Pakeesa Choudhury), Dina Spybey (Bee-Bee), Steve Zahn (Buff), Kitt Brophy (Sooze's Mom), Jonn Cherico

(Shopping Channel Host), Keith Preusse (Officer Chip), Eric Park (Officer Gary), William Martin Hayes (Scuff), Bill Wise (George the Limo Driver), M.J. Lin (Restaurant Hostess)

The Newton Boys (1998)
Production Companies: Twentieth Century-Fox Film Corporation, Detour Filmproduction
Producer: Anne Walker-McBay
Co-Producer: Clark Lee Walker
Associate Producer: Keith Fletcher
Executive Producer: John Sloss
Director: Richard Linklater
Story: Claude Stanush
Screenplay: Richard Linklater, Claude Stanush, Clark Lee Walker
Cinematography: Peter James
Editor: Sandra Adair
Original Music: Edward D. Barnes
Main Cast: Matthew McConaughey (Willis Newton), Skeet Ulrich (Joe Newton), Ethan Hawke (Jess Newton), Gail Cronauer (Ma Newton), Vincent D'Onofrio (Dock Newton), Jena Karam (Orphan Singer), Julianna Margulies (Louise Brown), Casey McAuliffe (Orphan Singer), Dwight Yoakam (Brentwood Glasscock), Charles Gunning (Slim), Regina Mae Matthews (Orphan Fiddler), Becket Gremmels (Lewis), Lew Temple (Waiter), Glynn Williams (Farmer Williams), Charles 'Chip' Bray (Bank Teller), Chloe Webb (Avis Glasscock), Gary Moody (Crooked Banker), Robert Iannaccone (Tailor), Jennifer Miriam (Catherine), Anne Stedman (Madeline), Marjorie Carroll (Old Woman), Katie Gratson (Young Hotel Clerk), Angie Chase (Kat), Lynn Mathis (Arthur Adams), Ed Dollison (Night Guard), Boots Southerland (Wagon Driver), Bo Hopkins (K.P. Aldrich), Tommy Townsend (Omaha Detective), Mary Love (Hotel Maid),

A.G. Zeke Mills (Old Usher), Abra Moore (Argosy Ballroom Singer), Lori Heuring (Flapper), Joe Stevens (Bank Association President), Eddie Matthews (Bank Messenger), Scott Roland (Bank Messenger (Steve)), J.P. Schwan (Bank Messenger), Rooster McConaughey (Tool Pusher), Bo Franks (Barker), Ali Nazary (Thug), Ron De Roxtra (Murray), David Jensen (William Fahy), Brad Arrington (Hobo), Richard A. Jones (Engineer), Randy Stripling (Fireman), Harold Suggs (Old Brakeman), Chamblee Ferguson (Head Postal Clerk), F.W. Post (Postal Turkey), Grant James (Gangland Doctor), Mark Fickert (Chicago Sergeant), Kerry Tartack (Chicago Detective), Luke Askew (Chief Schoemaker), Blue McDonnell (Nurse), Eduardo Cavazos Garza (Mexican Cab Driver), Ken Farmer (Frank Hamer), Daniel T. Kamin (District Attorney), Ross Sears (Judge)

Waking Life (2001)
Production Companies: Fox Searchlight Pictures, Independent Film Channel Productions, Thousand Words, Flat Black Films, Detour Filmproduction
Producers: Tommy Pallotta, Jonah Smith, Anne Walker-McBay, Palmer West
Executive Producers: Caroline Kaplan, Jonathan Sehring, John Sloss
Director: Richard Linklater
Screenplay: Richard Linklater
Cinematography: Richard Linklater, Tommy Pallotta
Editor: Sandra Adair
Original Music: Glover Gill
Main Cast: Trevor Jack Brooks (Young Boy Playing Paper Game), Lorelei Linklater (Young Girl Playing Paper Game), Wiley Wiggins (Main Character), Glover Gill (Accordion Player), Lara Hicks (Violin Player), Ames Asbell (Viola Player), Leigh Mahoney (Viola Player), Sara

Nelson (Cello Player), Jeanine Attaway (Piano Player), Erik Grostic (Bass Player), Bill Wise (Boat Car Guy), Robert C. Solomon (Philosophy Professor), Kim Krizan (Herself), Eamonn Healy (Shape-Shifting Man), J.C. Shakespeare (Burning Man), Ethan Hawke (Jesse), Julie Delpy (Céline), Charles Gunning (Angry Man in Jail), David Sosa (Himself), Alex Jones (Man in Car with P.A.), Otto Hofmann (Himself), Aklilu Gebrewold (Himself), Carol Dawson (Coffee Shop Chatter), Lisa Moore (Coffee Shop Chatter), Steve Fitch (Chimpanzee), Louis Mackey (Himself), Alex Nixon (Man Writing a Novel at the Bar), Violet Nichols (Woman Talking to the Novel Writer), Steven Prince (Man Talking to the Bartender), Ken Webster (Bartender), Mary McBay (Woman on TV), Kregg A. Foote (Man on TV), Jason T. Hodge (Man with the Long Hair), Guy Forsyth (Himself), John Christensen (Guy Talking about Turning the Light on in Dreams), Caveh Zahedi (Himself), David Jewell (Man Talking to Caveh), Adam Goldberg (One of Four Men), Nicky Katt (One of Four Men), E. Jason Liebrecht(One of Four Men), Brent Green (One of Four Men), RC Whittaker (Man on the Lamppost), Hymie Samuelson (Mr. Debord), David Martínez (Man on the Train), Ryan Power (Young Disappearing Guy), Tiana Hux (Soap Opera Woman), Speed Levitch (Himself), Steve Brudniak (Goatee Man), Marta Banda (Friendly Girl), Steven Soderbergh (Interviewed on Television), Charles Murdock (Old Man), Mona Lee (Quiet Woman at Restaurant), Edith Mannix (Older Artist in the Park), Bess Cox (Old Woman Sitting for a Portrait), Louis Black (Kierkegaard Disciple), Richard Linklater (Pinball Playing Man/Man on Back of Boat)

Tape (2001)
Production Companies: Detour Filmproduction, Independent Film Channel Productions, IFC Productions, InDigEnt (Independent Digital Entertainment), Tape Productions Inc.
Producers: Alexis Alexanian, Anne Walker-McBay, Gary Winick
Co-Producer: Robert Cole, David Richenthal
Executive Producers: Caroline Kaplan, Jonathan Sehring, John Sloss
Director: Richard Linklater
Story: Stephen Belber
Screenplay: Stephen Belber
Cinematography: Maryse Alberti
Editor: Sandra Adair
Main Cast: Ethan Hawke (Vince), Robert Sean Leonard (Jon Salter), Uma Thurman (Amy Randall)

Live from Shivas's Dance Floor (2003)
Production Companies: Detour Filmproduction, Giraffe Partners
Producers: David Holbrooke, Sarah Holbrooke, Perri Peltz
Associate Producer: Ian Grody
Director: Richard Linklater
Cinematography: Lee Daniel
Editor: Sandra Adair
Original Music: Golden Arm Trio
Main Cast: Timothy 'Speed' Levitch

The School of Rock (2003)
Production Companies: Paramount Pictures, Scott Rudin Productions, MFP Munich Film Partners Gmbh & Company/ Produktions KG, New Century, Sor Productions
Producer: Scott Rudin
Executive Producers: Scott Aversano, Steve Nicolaides
Director: Richard Linklater
Story: Mike White
Screenplay: Mike White
Cinematography: Rogier Stoffers

Editor: Sandra Adair

Original Music: Craig Wedren

Main Cast: Jack Black (Dewey Finn), Adam Pascal (Theo), Lucas Papaelias (Neil), Chris Stack (Doug), Sarah Silverman (Patty Di Marco), Mike White (Ned Schneebly), Lucas Babin (Spider), Joan Cusack (Rosalie Mullins), Jordan-Claire Green (Michelle), Veronica Afflerbach (Eleni), Miranda Cosgrove (Summer Hathaway), Joey Gaydos Jr. (Zack Mooneyham), Robert Tsai (Lawrence), Angelo Massagli (Frankie), Kevin Clark (Fred), Maryam Hassan (Tomika), Caitlin Hale (Marta), Cole Hawkins (Leonard), Brian Falduto (Billy), James Hosey (Marco), Aleisha Allen (Alicia), Zachary Infante (Gordon), Rebecca Brown (Katie), Jaclyn Neidenthal (Emily), Suzzanne Douglas (Tomika's Mother), Eron Otcasek (Musician), Carlos Velázquez (Musician), Kimberly Grigsby (Mrs. Sheinkopf), Lee Wilkof (Mr. Green), Kate McGregor-Stewart (Mrs. Lemmons), Wally Dunn (Gym Teacher), Tim Hopper (Zack's Father), Michael Domínguez-Rudolph (Art Student), Crash Cortez (Max), Nicky Katt (Razor), John E. Highsmith (Tony), Heather Goldenhersh (Sheila), Timothy 'Speed' Levitch (Waiter), Scott Graham (Punk Rock Guy), Sharon Washington (Alicia's Mother), Kim Brockington (Leonard's Mother), Marty Murphy (Concerned Father), Kathleen McNenny (Freddy's Mother), Joanna P. Adler (Summer's Mother), Robert Lin (Lawrence's Father), Barry Shurchin (Cop), MacIntyre Dixon (Bus Driver), Amy Sedaris (Mrs. Haynish), Mary Fortune (Teacher's Assistant), Mandy Siegfried (Female Employee), Carlos J. Da Silva (Security Guard), Ian O'Malley (Radio Exec), Chris Line (Radio DJ), Kyle Meaney (Toby)

Before Sunset (2004)

Production Companies: Castle Rock Entertainment, Detour Filmproduction, Warner Independent Pictures

Producers: Richard Linklater, Anne Walker-McBay

Co-Producer: Isabelle Coulet

Executive Producer: John Sloss

Director: Richard Linklater

Story: Richard Linklater, Kim Krizan

Screenplay: Richard Linklater, Julie Delpy, Ethan Hawke

Cinematography: Lee Daniel

Editor: Sandra Adair

Main Cast: Ethan Hawke (Jesse), Julie Delpy (Celine), Vernon Dobtcheff (Bookstore Manager), Louise Lemoine Torres (Journalist #1), Rodolphe Pauly (Journalist #2), Mariane Plasteig (Waitress), Diabolo (Philippe), Denis Evrard (Boat Attendant), Albert Delpy (Man at Grill), Marie Pillet (Woman in Courtyard)

$5.15/Hr (2004)

Production Company: Home Box Office (HBO)

Producers: Richard Linklater, David Miner, Erwin Stoff, Anne Walker-McBay

Executive Producer: Rodney Rothman

Director: Richard Linklater

Screenplay: Richard Linklater

Editor: Sandra Adair

Main Cast: Peter Atherton (Customer #1), Mitch Baker (Mitch), Johnny Bartee (Trucker), David Bewley (Vice President), Frank Brantley (Restaurant Patron), Chamblee Ferguson (Vice President), América Ferrera (Brianna), Erick Garibay (Convenience Store Customer), Eric Hernández (Focus Group Extra), Preston Jones (Frat Daddy), Kathy Lamkin (Customer #2), Clark Middleton (Vince), Patricia Miller (Dishwasher), Angela Rawna (Vice President), Retta (Joy), Brenna Rivas (Driver), Christopher

Ryan (Quick Cash Clerk), Keri Safran
(Brandy), Spencer Scott (Brian Watson),
William Lee Scott (Bobby), Nicole Lin
Taylor (Waitress), Bill Wise (Edgar),
Missy Yager (Wing)

Bad News Bears (2005)
Production Companies: Detour
    Filmproduction, Geyer Kosinski, Media
    Talent Group
Producers: J. Geyer Kosinski, Richard
    Linklater
Co-Producer: Bruce Heller
Associate Producers: Adam Ellison, Sara
    Greene, Brad Marks
Executive Producer: Marcus Viscidi
Director: Richard Linklater
Screenplay: Bill Lancasterand, Glenn
    Ficarra, John Requa
Cinematography: Rogier Stoffers
Editor: Sandra Adair
Original Music: Ed Shearmur
Main Cast: Billy Bob Thornton (Morris
    Buttermaker), Greg Kinnear (Roy
    Bullock), Marcia Gay Harden (Liz
    Whitewood), Sammi Kane Kraft
    (Amanda Whurlitzer), Ridge Canipe
    (Toby Whitewood), Brandon Craggs
    (Mike Engelberg), Jeffrey Davies
    (Kelly Leak), Timmy Deters (Tanner
    Boyle), Carlos Estrada (Miguel Agilar),
    Emmanuel Estrada (José Agilar), Troy
    Gentile (Matthew Hooper), Kenneth
    'K.C.' Harris (Ahmad Abdul Rahim),
    Aman Johal (Prem Lahiri), Tyler
    Patrick Jones (Timmy Lupus), Jeffrey
    Tedmori (Garo Daragabrigadien), Carter
    Jenkins (Joey Bullock), Seth Adkins
    (Jimmy), Chase Winton (Ms. Cleveland),
    Arabella Holzbog (Shari Bullock), Nectar
    Rose (Paradise), Lisa Arturo (Peaches),
    Elizabeth Carter (Chandalier), Monique
    Cooper (Lolita), Candace Kita (China),
    Kate Luyben (Daisy), Shamron Moore
    (Cherry Pie), Jeffrey Hutchinson
    (Baseball Official), Sonya Eddy

(Saleslady), Karen Gordon (Saleslady),
Maura Vincent (Shopper), Jennifer Carta
(Softball Player Suzy), Dennis LaValle
(Deaver Dad), Robert Peters (Yankee
Dad), Kevin R. Kelly (Yankee Dad),
Shannon O'Hurley (All American Mom),
Hunter Cole (All American Boy), Wil
Myer (All American Boy), Pancho Moler
(Kevin), Jack Acampora (Yankee Player),
Bretton Bowman (Yankee Player), Ryan
Cruz (Yankee Player), Nick Lovullo
(Yankee Player), Richard Martínez
(Yankee Player), Payton Milone (Yankee
Player), Ernesto Junior Prado (Yankee
Player), Kirby James Shaw (Yankee
Player), Cody Thompson (Yankee
Player), Hayden Tsutsui (Yankee Player),
Matthew Walker (Yankee Player), Darin
Rossi (Umpire), Gary A. Rodríguez
(Umpire), Scott Adsit (Umpire), Kevin
Makely (Umpire), Robert Matthew
Wagner (Umpire), Ken Medlock
(Umpire), Josh M. Goldfield (Umpire),
Mike Paciorek (Umpire), Jeff Conrad
(State Band Member), Sam Farrar (State
Band Member), Alex Greenwald (State
Band Member), Darren Robinson (State
Band Member)

Fast Food Nation (2006)
Production Companies: Recorded Picture
    Company, Participant Productions, Fuzzy
    Bunny Films, BBC Films
Producers: Malcolm McLaren, Jeremy
    Thomas
Co-Producer: Ann Carli, Alexandra Stone
Associate Producer: Sara Greene
Executive Producers: Chris Salvaterra, Ed
    Saxon, Eric Schlosser, Jeff Skoll, Ricky
    Strauss, David Peter, Watson M.
    Thompson
Director: Richard Linklater
Story: Eric Schlosser
Screenplay: Eric Schlosser, Richard
    Linklater
Cinematography: Lee Daniel

Editor: Sandra Adair

Original Music: Friends of Dean Martínez

Main Cast: Wilmer Valderrama (Raúl), Catalina Sandino Moreno (Sylvia), Ana Claudia Talancón (Coco), Juan Carlos Serran (Esteban), Armando Hernández (Roberto), Greg Kinnear (Don Anderson), Frank Ertl (Jack), Michael Conway (Phil), Mitch Baker (Dave), Ellar Salmon (Jay Anderson), Dakota Edwards (Stevie Anderson), Dana Wheeler-Nicholson (Debi Anderson), Luis Guzmán (Benny), Bobby Cannavale (Mike), Francisco Rosales (Jorge), Ashley Johnson (Amber), Paul Dano (Brian), Patricia Arquette (Cindy), Roger Cudney (Terry), Glen Powell (Steve), Cherami Leigh (Kim), Esai Morales (Tony), Yareli Arizmendi (Gloria), Matt Hensarling (Kevin), Mileidy Moron Marchant (Vicky), Kris Kristofferson (Rudy Martin), Raquel Gavia (Rita), Hugo Pérez (Francisco), Bruce Willis (Harry Rydell), Helen Merino (Lisa), Erinn Allison (Hotel Desk Clerk), Barbara Chisholm (Waitress), Larizza Salcido Gameros (María), Lana Dieterich (UMP Nurse), John Scott Horton (Greg), Ethan Hawke (Pete), Aaron Himelstein (Andrew), Avril Lavigne (Alice), Marco Perella (Tom Watson), Lou Taylor Pucci (Gerald 'Paco'), Mónica Cano Mascorro (Magdalene), Carlos Adrian Romero Ayala (Tino), Humberto E. Vélez Sánchez (Cesar), Cora Cardona (Kristen – UMP Translator)

A Scanner Darkly (2006)

Production Companies: Thousand Words, Warner Independent Pictures (WIP, Section Eight, Arts Entertainment, Detour Filmproduction

Producers: Tommy Pallotta, Jonah Smith, Erwin Stoff, Anne Walker-McBay, Palmer West

Co-Producer: Erin Ferguson

Associate Producer: Sara Greene

Executive Producers: George Clooney, Ben Cosgrove, Jennifer Fox, John Sloss, Steven Soderbergh

Director: Richard Linklater

Story: Philip K. Dick

Screenplay: Richard Linklater

Cinematography: Shane F. Kelly

Editor: Sandra Adair

Original Music: Graham Reynolds

Main Cast: Rory Cochrane (Charles Freck), Robert Downey Jr. (James Barris), Mitch Baker (Brown Bear Lodge Host), Keanu Reeves (Bob Arctor), Sean Allen (Additional Fred Scramble Suit Voice), Cliff Haby (Voice from Headquarters), Steven Chester Prince (Cop), Winona Ryder (Donna Hawthorne), Natasha Valdez (Waitress), Mark Turner (Additional Hank Scramble Suit Voice), Woody Harrelson (Ernie Luckman), Chamblee Ferguson (Medical Deputy #2), Angela Rawna (Medical Deputy #1), Eliza Stevens (Arctor's Daughter #1), Sarah Menchaca (Arctor's Daughter #2), Melody Chase (Arctor's Wife), Leif Anders (Freck Suicide Narrator), Turk Pipkin (Creature), Alex Jones (Street Prophet), Lisa Marie Newmyer (Connie), Wilbur Penn (Medical Officer #1), Ken Webster (Medical Officer #2), Hugo Pérez (New Path Staff Member #1), Rommel Sulit (New Path Staff Member #2), Dameon Clarke (Mike), Christopher Ryan (New Path Resident #1), Leila Plummer (New Path Resident #2), Jason Douglas (New Path Farm Manager), Marco Perella (Donald)

Inning by Inning: A Portrait of a Coach (2008)

Production Company: Detour Filmproduction

Producer: Brian Franklin

Senior Producer: Daniel Silver

Associate Producers: Sandra Adair, Sara Greene

Executive Producers: Connor Schell, John Sloss

Director: Richard Linklater

Cinematography: Brian Franklin

Editor: Sandra Adair

Original Music: Michael McLeod

Main Cast: Cathy Clark, Roger Clemens, Buck Cody, J.Brent Cox, Deloss Dodds, Pete Donovan, Augie Garrido, George Horton, Joe Jamail, Seth Johnston, William Kernen, Mark Kotsay, Bill Little, Dustin Majewski, Jose Mota, Phil Nevin, Darrell Royal, Tom Sommers, Neale Stoner, Huston Street, Taylor Teagarden, Curtis Thigpen, Tim Wallach, Dave Weatherman, Kevin Costner

Me and Orson Welles (2008)

Production Companies: CinemaNX, Cinetic Media, Detour Filmproduction, Framestore, Fuzzy Bunny Films, Hart-Lunsford Pictures, Isle of Man Film Commission

Producers: Ann Carli, Richard Linklater, Marc Samuelson

Co-Producers: Vincent Palmo Jr., Holly Gent Palmo

Associate Producers: Sara Greene, Jessica Parker

Executive Producers: Steve Christian, Steve Norris, John Sloss

Line Producer: Richard Hewitt

Director: Richard Linklater

Story: Robert Kaplow

Screenplay: Holly Gent Palmo, Vincent Palmo Jr.

Cinematography: Dick Pope

Editor: Sandra Adair

Original Music: Michael J. McEvoy

Main Cast: Zac Efron (Richard Samuels), Claire Danes (Sonja Jones), Christian McKay (Orson Welles), Ben Chaplin (George Coulouris), Zoe Kazan (Gretta Adler), Eddie Marsan (John Houseman), Kelly Reilly (Muriel Brassler), James Tupper (Joseph Cotten), Leo Bill (Norman Lloyd), Al Weaver (Sam Leve), Iain McKee (Vakhtangov), Simon Lee Phillips (Walter Ash), Simon Nehan (Joe Holland), Imogen Poots (Lorelei Lathrop), Patrick Kennedy (Grover Burgess), Janie Dee (Mrs. Samuels), Marlene Sidaway (Grandmother Samuels), Garrick Hagon (Dr. Mewling), Megan Maczko (Evelyn Allen), Aaron Brown (Longchamps Kid #1), Travis Oliver (John Hoyt), Nathan Osgood (Radio Announcer), Robert Wilfort (Radio Director), Michael Brandon (Les Tremayne), Saskia Reeves (Barbara Luddy), Aidan McArdle (Martin Gabel), Michael J. McEvoy (I.L. Epstein), Thomas Arnold (George Duthie), Jo McInnes (Jeannie Rosenthal), Daniel Tuite (William Mowry), Emily Allen (Virginia Welles), John Young (Longchamps Kid #2), Eddi Reader (Singer), Jools Holland (Band Leader), Steven Parry (Mercury Trumpet Player), Jay Irving (Mercury Percussion Player), David Garbutt (Mercury French Horn Player), Shane James Bordas (Conspirator), Alessandro Giuggioli (Conspirator)

Bernie (2011)

Producers: Liz Glotzer, Judd Payne, Celine Rattray, Martin Shafer, Ginger Sledge

Associate Producers: Todd J. Labarowski, Sean McEwen, Shane Stranger

Executive Producers: Michael Bassick, William T. Conway, Don Fox, Jack Gilardi Jr., Johnny Lin, Duncan Montgomery, Darby Parker, Jack Selby

Director: Richard Linklater

Screenplay: Skip Hollandsworth, Richard Linklater

Cinematography: Dick Pope

Main Cast: Jack Black (Bernie Tiede), Matthew McConaughey (Danny

Buck Davidson), Rip Torn (Clifton L. 'Scrappy' Holmes), Shirley MacLaine (Marjorie Nugent), Rick Dial (Don Leggett), Wendy Crouse (Prison Visitor), Gary Teague (Neighborhood Onlooker), Grant James Mr. Estes), Mona Lee Fultz (Cashier), David Blackwell (Mel), Juli Erickson (Mrs Estes), Kevin Machate (Federal Agent), Dale Dudley (Jerry), Brady Coleman, (Scrappy Holmes), Jerry Biggs (The Judge)

Up to Speed (2012)
Production Company: Cinetic Media, Hulu (distributor)
Producers: Joe Cacciotti, Richard Linklater, Alex Lipschultz, Kirsten McMurray
Executive Producer: Dana O'Keefe, John Sloss
Director: Richard Linklater (Series 1, Episode 5: 'Chicago')
Cinematography: Shane F. Kelly (1 episode)
Editor: Mike Saenz (2 episodes)
Main Cast: Timothy 'Speed' Levitch, John C. McDonnell (various)

Before Midnight (2013)
Producers: Christos V. Konstantakopoulos, Richard Linklater, Sara Woodhatch
Co-producer: Vincent Palmo Jr.
Associate Producer: Lelia Andronikou
Executive Producers: Liz Glotzer, Jacob Pechenik, Martin Shafer, John Sloss
Line producer: Kostas Kefalas
Director: Richard Linklater
Screenplay: Richard Linklater, Ethan Hawke, Julie Delpy
Cinematography: Christos Voudouris
Editor: Sandra Adair
Assistant Editor: Mike Saenz
Costume Design: Vasileia Rozana
Make-up Department: Kyriaky Melidou, Ioulia Sygrimi, Hronis Tzimos, Evi Zafiropoulou
Production Management: Maria Hatzakou, Laura Yates

Second Unit Director; Emmanuela Fragiadaki, Anna Nikoloaou, Vincent Palmo Jr.
Art Department: Fiannis Mylonas
Sound Department: Colin Gregory, Colin Nicholson
Main Cast: Ethan Hawke (Jesse), Julie Delpy (Celine), Seamus Davey-Fitzpatrick (Hank), Athina Rachel Tsangari (Ariadni), Ariane Labed (Anna), Yota Argyropoulou (Natalia)), Walter Lassally (Patrick), Jennifer Prior (Ella), Yannis Papadopoulos (Achilleas), Panos Koronis (Stefanos), Charlotte Prior (Nina), Enrico Focardi (Kid 1), Manolis Goussias (Kid 2), Anouk Servera (Kid 3)

Boyhood (aka *Untitled 12-Year Richard Linklater Project*, estimated release 2015)
Producers: Anne Walker-McBay
Executive Producer: John Sloss
Director: Richard Linklater
Screenplay: Richard Linklater
Cinematography: Lee Daniel
Main Cast: Ellar Salmon (Mason), Patricia Arquette (Mason's mother), Ethan Hawke (Mason's father), Jordan Howard (Tony), Tamara Jolaine (Tammy), Tyler Strother (Bully's friend), Evie Thompson (Jill), Angela Rawna (Professor Douglas), Cambell Westmoreland (Kenny), Jordan Strassner (College Student), Shane Graham (Stanley), Nick Krause (Charlie), Cassidy Johnson (Abby), Kristen Devine (Middle School Student), Tabatha Paige Beustring (Girl in Car), Derek Chase Hickey (Steve), Alec Van Beustring (College Student), Amber A. Wood (Middle school student), Erika Ganey (College Student), Micaela Phillips (Hero Girl), Laurel Elm (Middle School Student)

BIBLIOGRAPHY

Anderson, Benedict (1983) *Imagined Communities: Reflections on the Origin and Spread of Nationalism*. London: Verso.

Anderson, Sherwood (2008) *Winesburg, Ohio*. Oxford: Oxford University Press.

Anon. (1994) 'Conversations: Richard Linklater', *The Idler*, 6 September. On-line. http://idler.co.uk/conversations/conversations-richard-linklater/ (accessed 10 March 2009).

Anon. (2008) 'Toronto: Richard Linklater premieres "Me and Orson Welles"', *The Los Angeles Times*, 5 September. On-line. http://latimesblogs.latimes.com/the_big_picture/2008/09/richard-linklat.html (accessed 10 January 2010).

Anon. (2009a) http://www.austinfilm.org (accessed 10 November 2009).

Anon. (2009b) 'Texas Legislators See Red at TXMPA Lobby Day', 4 March. On-line. http://txactor.com/2009/03/04/texas-legislators-see-red-at-txmpa-lobby-day-2009.html (accessed 14 June 2009).

Anon. (2009c) 'Texas Governor Rick Perry Signs Film Incentives Bill to Entice Movie, Television and Video Gaming', 4 May. On-line. http://www.clickpress.com/releases/Detailed/127304005cp.shtml (accessed 14 June 2009).

Anon. (2009d) 'Nobody got anywhere by slacking. Except director Richard Linklater, obviously', BBC, no date of publication given. On-line. http://ww.bbc.co.uk/dna/collective/A818778 (accessed 12 June 2009).

Anon. (2009e) http://www.gov.im/dti/iomfilm/mediadevfund.xml (accessed 16 April 2009).

Anon. (2009f) http://www.boxofficemojo.com/people/chart/?id=richardlinklater.htm (accessed 25 May 2009).

Anon. (2009g) http://www.census.gov/hhes/www/poverty/threshld/thresh92.html (accessed 12 June 2009).

Anon. (2009h) http://www.national911memorial.org/site/PageServer?pagename=New_Home (accessed 4 December 2009).

Anon. (2009i) http://www.globalsecurity.org/eye/wtc.htm (accessed 15 December 2009).

Anon. (2009j) http://hungerreport.org/2009/chapters/us-poverty/62-current-reform (accessed 12 January 2010).

Anon. (2010a) Encyclopaedia Britannica. On-line. http://www.britannica.com/EBchecked/topic/145744/Cubism (accessed 10 January 2010).

Anon. (2010b) http://www.moveon.org/about.html (accessed 10 January 2010).

Anon. (2010c) http://www.upgradedemocracy.com (accessed 10 January 2010).

Anshen, David (2007) 'Alphaville: A Neorealist Science Fiction Fable about Hollywood', in Laura E. Ruberto and Kristi M. Wilson (eds) *Italian Neorealism and Global Cinema*. Detroit: Wayne State University Press, 91- 110.

Antliff, Mark and Patrice Leighten (2001) *Cubism and Culture*. London: Thames and Hudson.

Aristotle (2009) *Metaphysics*. On-line. http://ebooks.adelaide.edu.au/a/aristotle/metaphysics/ (accessed 19 December 2009).

Ashraf, Irshad (2004) *Linklater: St. Richard of Austin*. Documentary produced by World of Wonder (www.worldofwonder.net.) presented by Ben Lewis and directed by Irshad Ashraf. Broadcast on *The Art Show*, Channel 4 in December 2004.

Atkinson, Mike (2007) 'That's Entertainment', *Sight & Sound*, 17, 4, 18–22.

Auden, W. H. (1970) *Collected Poems*. London: Random House.

Badt, Karin Luisa (2006) 'What's Wrong with Fast Food?: A Conversation with Richard Linklater and Eric Schlosser on "Fast Food Nation" with additional comments by Catalina Sandino Moreno and Ethan Hawke', *Bright Lights Film Journal*, November. On-line. http://www.brightlightsfilm.com/54/fastfood.htm (accessed 25 May 2009).

Bakhtin, Mikhail M. (1984a [1965]) *Rabelais and His World* (trans. Hélène Iswolsky). Bloomington: Indiana University Press.

_____ (1984b [1929]) Caryl Emerson (ed.) *Problems of Dostoevsky's Poetics*. Minneapolis: University of Minnesota Press.

_____ (2006a [1975]) Michael Holquist (ed.) *The Dialogic Imagination: Four Essays by M. M. Bakhtin* (trans. Caryl Emerson and Michael Holquist). Austin: University of Texas Press.

_____ (2006b [1940]) 'From the Prehisory of Novelistic Discourse', Michael Holquist (ed.) *The Dialogic Imagination: Four Essays by M. M. Bakhtin* (trans. Caryl Emerson and Michael Holquist). Austin: University of Texas Press, 41–83.

_____ (2006c [1937–38]) 'Forms of Time and of the Chronotope in the Novel: Notes Towards a Historical Poetics', Michael Holquist (ed.) *The Dialogic Imagination: Four Essays by M. M. Bakhtin* (trans. Caryl Emerson and Michael Holquist). Austin: University of Texas Press, 84–258.

_____ (2006d [1934–35]) 'Discourse in the Novel', Michael Holquist (ed.) *The Dialogic Imagination: Four Essays by M. M. Bakhtin* (trans. Caryl Emerson and Michael Holquist). Austin: University of Texas Press, 259–422.

Barthes, Roland (1982) 'The Death of the Author', *Image, Music, Text*. London: Flamingo, 142–48.

Bartyzel, Monika (2009) 'Richard Linklater Script Gets Shelved', *Cinematical*, 5 June. On-line. http://www.cinematical.com/2009/06/05/richard-linklater-script-gets-shelved/ (accessed 8 June 2009).

Baudrillard, Jean (2003 [2001]) *The Spirit of Terrorism* (trans. Chris Turner). London: Verso.

_____ (2001) 'The Gulf War Did Not Take Place', Mark Poster (ed.) *Jean Baudrillard: Selected Writings*. Cambridge: Polity Press, 231–53.

_____ (2009 [2001]) 'The Spirit of Terrorism' (trans. Rachel Bloul), reprinted from *Le Monde*, 2 November 2001. On-line. http://www.egs.edu/faculty/baudrillard/baudrillard-the-spirit-of-terrorism.html (accessed 10 November 2009).

Bazin, André (2009) *What is Cinema?* (trans. Timothy Barnard). Montreal: Caboose.

Bergson, Henri (1992a) *The Creative Mind: An Introduction to Metaphysics*. Secausus, NJ: Citadel Press.

_____ (1992b) 'Introduction 1', *The Creative Mind: An Introduction to Metaphysics*. Secausus, NJ: Citadel Press, 11–29.

_____ (1992c) 'Introduction 2', *The Creative Mind: An Introduction to Metaphysics*. Secausus, NJ: Citadel Press, 30–90.

_____ (1992d) 'The Possible and the Real', *The Creative Mind: An Introduction to Metaphysics*. Secausus, NJ: Citadel Press, 91–106.

_____ (1992e) 'The Perception of Change', *The Creative Mind: An Introduction to Metaphysics*. Secausus, NJ: Citadel Press, 130–58.

_____ (1992f) 'Introduction to Metaphysics', *The Creative Mind: An Introduction to Metaphysics*. Secausus, NJ: Citadel Press, 159–208.

_____ (1998) *Creative Evolution* (trans. Arthur Mitchell). Mineola, New York: Dover Publications.

_____ (2003) *Time and Free Will: An Essay on the Immediate Data of Consciousness*. Mineola, NY: Dover Publications.

Berra, John (2008) *Declarations of Independence: American Cinema and the Partiality of Independent Production*. Bristol: Intellect.

Best, Steven and Douglas Kellner (1977) *The Postmodern Turn*. New York: Guilford Press.

Biskind, Peter (1998) *Easy Riders, Raging Bulls*. London: Bloomsbury.

_____ (2004) *Down and Dirty Pictures*. London: Bloomsbury.

Bordwell, David (1985) *Narration in the Fiction Film*. Madison: University of Wisconsin Press.

_____ (2006) *The Way Hollywood Tells It: Story and Style in Modern Movies*. Berkeley: University of California Press.

Bould, Mark (2009) *The Cinema of John Sayles: A Lone Star*. London: Wallflower Press.

Bozelka, Kevin John (2008) 'An Interview with Richard Linklater', *The Velvet Light Trap* 61, 55–6.

Bradshaw, Nick (2006) 'Lost in the Loop', *Sight and Sound*, 16, 8, 40–3.

Bresson, Robert (1997) *Notes on the Cinematographer*. Copenhagen: Green Integer 2.

Brian, T. T. (2009) 'Interview: Managing Expectations of Life, Love With "Management" Director Stephen Belber', *HollywoodChicago*, 14 May. On-line. http://www. hollywoodchicago.com/news/7747/interview-managing-expectations-of-life-and-love-with-writer-director-stephen-belber (accessed 18 May 2009).

Brody, Richard (2008) *Everything is Cinema: The Working Life of Jean-Luc Godard*. London: Faber & Faber.

Brooks, Xan (2006) 'I've never been in the firing line like this before', *The Guardian*, 22 May. On-line. http://www.guardian.co.uk/news/2006/may/22/food.film (accessed 10 June 2009).

Bruni, Frank (1998) 'Manhattan Through a Warped Window; Featured in a Film: A Homeless Tour Guide's Offbeat City View', *The New York Times*, 1 October. On-line. http://www.nytimes.com/1998/10/01/nyregion/manhattan-through-warped-window-featured-film-homeless-tour-guide-s-offbeat-city. html?sec=&spon=&pagewanted=2 (accessed 13 November 2009).

Buchanan, Kyle (2009) 'Downsized Miramax Claims its First Casualty, Richard Linklater's Liars (A to E)', *Movieline*, 16 November. On-line. http://movieline. com/2009/11/16/exclusive-downsized-miramax-claims-its-first-casualty-richard-linklaters-liars-a-e/ (accessed 16 March 2013).

Buñuel, Luis (1985) *My Last Breath*. Glasgow: Flamingo.

Burch, Noël (1992) *Theory of Film Practice*. Princeton, NJ: Princeton University Press.

Calderón de la Barca, Don Pedro (1961) Albert B. Sloman (ed.) *La vida es sueño*. Manchester: Manchester University Press.

Camus, Albert (1991) *The Myth of Sisyphus and Other Essays*. London: Vintage.

Charity, Tom (2001) *John Cassavetes: Life Works*. London: Omnibus Press.

_____ (2007) 'Richard Linklater', *The Rough Guide to Film*. London: Rough Guides Ltd., 321.

Chomsky, Noam (2001) *9–11*. New York: Seven Stories Press.

Ciampa, Su (2003) 'Ground Zero: Where the Buffalo Roam?', *Salon*, 21 January. On-line. http://www.salon.com/ent/movies/feature/2003/01/21/linklater_wtc/ index.html (accessed 15 November 2009).

Connelly, Brendon (2010) 'Richard Linklater Casting "Bernie", Fargo-Like Crime Story', 6 August. On-line. http://www.bleedingcool.com/2010/08/06/richard-linklater-casting-bernie-fargo-like-crime-story/ (accessed 10 January 2011).

Cooke, Paul (2007) 'Introduction: World Cinema's "Dialogues" with Hollywood', in Paul Cooke (ed.) *World Cinema's 'Dialogues' with Hollywood*. Basingstoke: Palgrave Macmillan, 1–16.

Cooper, Douglas (1999) *The Cubist Epoch*. London: Phaidon Press.

Corliss, Richard and Mary Corliss (2006) 'Getting Indigestion Over "Fast Food Nation"', *Time*, 19 May. On-line. http://www.time.com/time/arts/ article/0,8599,1620667,00.html (accessed 8 June 2009).

Corn, Kahane (2006) 'Making "Dazed". Documentary on the making of *Dazed and Confused* included as extra feature on the Criterion Collection edition of *Dazed and Confused*.

Corrigan, Timothy (1991) *A Cinema without Walls: Movies and Culture after Vietnam*. New Brunswick, New Jersey: Rutgers University Press.

Coupland, Douglas (1996) *Generation X*. London: Abacus.

_____ (1998) *Girlfriend in a Coma*. London: Harper Collins.

_____ (2004) *Microserfs*. London: Harper Collins.

Cullum, Paul (2009) 'The Eagle Has Landed', *Eagle Pennell & The Whole Shootin' Match* booklet, *The Whole Shootin' Match* DVD. London: Watchmaker Films, 23–7.

Daniel, Lee (2000) 'Where The Magic Takes Place', *Austin Film Society: 20th Anniversary Retrospective 1985–2000*.

Dashevsky, Evan (2003) 'War Correspondence from the Present Tense. An Interview with Timothy "Speed" Levitch', *Hybrid Magazine*, April. On-line. http://www.hybridmagazine.com/culture/0403/dashevsky.shtml (accessed 29 November 2009).

Davis, Lennard (1987) *Resisting Novels: Ideology and Fiction*. New York: Methuen.

Debord, Guy (1983) *Society of the Spectacle*. Detroit: Black & Red.

_____ (2006) 'Theory of the Dérive', Ken Knabb (ed.) *Situationist International Anthology*. Berkley: Bureau of Public Secrets, 50–54.

Deleuze, Gilles (2005a) *Cinema 1*. London: Continuum.

_____ (2005b) *Cinema 2*. London: Continuum.

Deleuze, Gilles and Pierre-Félix Guattari (1983) *Anti-Oedipus: Capitalism and Schizophrenia*. Minnesota: University of Minnesota Press.

Descartes, René (1996) *Meditations on First Philosophy with Selections from the Objections and Replies*, John Cottingham (ed.) Cambridge: Cambridge Texts in the History of Philosophy.

Dick, Philip K. (1995) 'The Android and the Human', Lawrence Sutin (ed.) *The Shifting Realities of Philip K. Dick: Selected Literary and Philosophical Writings*. USA: Vintage Books, 183–210.

_____ (2006) *A Scanner Darkly*. London: Gollancz.

Dickenson, Ben (2006) *Hollywood's New Radicalism: War, Globalisation and the Movies from Reagan to George W. Bush*. London: I. B. Tauris

Durkheim, Emile (2003) 'Note on Social Morphology', Mustafa Emirbayer (ed.) *Emile Durkheim: Sociologist of Modernity*. London: Wiley-Blackwell, 77–78.

Ebert, Roger (1980) 'The Whole Shootin' Match', *The Chicago Sun-Times*, 9 April. On-line. http://rogerebert.suntimes.com/apps/pbcs.dll/article?AID=/19800409/REVIEWS/4090301/1023 (accessed 3 July 2009).

_____ (1993) 'Dazed and Confused', *The Chicago Sun-Times*, 24 September. On-line. http://rogerebert.suntimes.com/apps/pbcs.dll/article?AID=/19930924/REVIEWS/309240302/1023 (24 (accessed 15 April 2009).

_____ (2001) *Tape*, *The Chicago Sun-Times*, 16 November. On-line. http://rogerebert.suntimes.com/apps/pbcs.dll/article?AID=/20011116/REVIEWS/111160303/1023 (accessed 14 August 2009).

_____ (2008) 'In Search of A Midnight Kiss', *The Chicago Sun-Times*, 21 August. On-line. http://rogerebert.suntimes.com/apps/pbcs.dll/article?AID=/20080821/REVIEWS/327/1023 (accessed 4 August 2009).

Elsaesser, Thomas (2003) *European Cinema: Face to Face with Hollywood*. Amsterdam: Amsterdam University Press.

Evans, Peter William (2007) 'An *Amour* Still *Fou*: Late Buñuel', in Graeme Harper and Rob Stone (eds) *The Unsilvered Screen: Surealism on Film*. London: Wallflower Press, 38–47.

Farrell, John Aloysius (1994) 'UCLA students cheer Clinton's portrait of them', *The Boston Globe*, 21 May. On-line. http://www.encyclopedia.com/doc/1P2–8280275. html (accessed 10 July 2009).

Feinstein, Howard (2006) 'Happy Meals', *Filmmaker*, Fall. On-line. http://www. filmmakermagazine.com/fall2006/features/happy_meals.php (accessed 3 June 2009).

Feuer, Jane (1993) *The Hollywood Musical*. Hong Kong: Macmillan.

Fishman, Daniel B. (1999) *The Case for Pragmatic Psychology*. New York: New York University Press.

Fiske, John (1989) *Understanding Popular Culture*. London: Routledge.

Fowler, Bridget (1977) *Pierre Bourdieu and Cultural Theory: Critical Investigations*. London: Sage.

French, Philip (2008) 'In Search of a Midnight Kiss', *The Guardian*, 15 June. On-line. http://www.guardian.co.uk/film/2008/jun/15/culture.filmandmusic (accessed 4 August 2009).

García, Chris (2009) 'Come film with Austin: In its first few years, moviemaking has taken off at the old airport's leftover hangars', *Austin 360*, 28 January. On-line. http://www.austin360.com/movies/content/movies/stories/2009/01/0130austist udios.html (accessed 23 June 2009).

Gellert, Michael (2002) *The Fate of America*. Washington D.C.: Potomac Books.

Geuens, Jean-Pierre (2002) *Film Production Theory*. Albany: State University of New York Press.

Gilbey, Ryan (2004) 'Before Sunset', *Sight & Sound*, 14, 8, 44.

Girgus, Sam B. (2007) 'The Modernism of Frank Capra and European Ethical Thought', in Paul Cooke (ed.) *World Cinema's 'Dialogues' with Hollywood*. Basingstoke: Palgrave Macmillan, 86–102.

Gleiberman, Owen (1994) 'Dazed and Confused', *Entertainment Weekly*, 24 September. On-line. http://www.ew.com/ew/article/0,,308072,00.html (accessed 2 June 2009).

Graham, Mark (2009) 'Richard Linklater Working On "Spiritual Sequel" to "Dazed and Confused"', *New York Entertainment*, 27 March. On-line. http://nymag.com/ daily/entertainment/2009/03/richard_linklater_working_on_s.html (accessed 14 April 2009).

Grant, Barry Keith (2007) *Film Genres: From Iconography to Ideology*. London: Wallflower Press.

Gross, David M. and Sophfronia Scott (1990) 'Proceeding with Caution', *Time*, 16 July. On-line. http://www.time.com/time/magazine/article/0,9171,970634,00. html (accessed 16 September 2009).

Gross, Michael Joseph (2005) 'Want Stealth with That?: The "Fast Food Nation" Film Goes Undercover', *The New York Times*, 30 October. On-line. http://www.nytimes.com/2005/10/30/movies/30gros.html (accessed 8 June 2009).

Harris, Mark (2008) *Scenes from a Revolution*. Edinburgh: Canongate.

Hermann Hesse (2009). On-line. http://maverickphilosopher.powerblogs.com/posts/1211851545.shtml (accessed 4 September 2009).

Hewitt, Chris (2004) '"Before Sunset" director puts his life's lessons on film', *Saint Paul Pioneer Press*, 15 July. On-line. http://www.Highbeam.com/doc/1G1–119516648.html (accessed 4 December 2005).

Hickman, Jonathan W. (2001) 'Tracking the Tale of the TAPE with screenwriter Stephen Belber', 10 December. On-line. http://www.einsiders.com/features/interviews/stephenbelber.php (accessed 18 May 2009).

Hicks, Alice M. (1995) 'Richard Linklater's All-Nighter', *Moviemaker*, 12 April. On-line. http://www.moviemaker.com/directing/article/richard_linklaters_allnighter_3122/ (accessed 12 January 2009).

Hillier, Jim (1993) *The New Hollywood*. London: Studio Vista.

_____ (ed.) (2006) *American Independent Cinema: A Sight & Sound Reader*. London: British Film Institute.

Hoffman, Michael J. and Patrick D. Murphy (1992) *Critical Essays on American Modernism*. New York: G. K. Hall & Co.

Holquist, Michael (1984) 'Prologue', Mikhail M. Bakhtin, *Rabelais and His World* (trans. Hélène Iswolsky). Bloomington: Indiana University Press, xiii-xxiii.

Hughes, Robert (1989) 'Art: Goya: a Despairing Assault on Terminal Evil', *Time*, 30 January. On-line. http://www.time.com/time/magazine/article/0,9171,956813,00.html (accessed 10 December 2009).

Jacobs, Diane (1977) *Hollywood Renaissance*. South Brunswick and New York: A. S. Barnes and Company.

James, Nick (2004) 'Debrief Encounter', *Sight & Sound*, 14, 8, 12–15.

Jiménez Blanco, María Dolores (2009) 'The Perception of Spanish Art in America'. Keynote address at Conference on Hispanic Visual Cultures: Fractured Identities, Cardiff University, 3 July 2009.

Johnson, Allan G. (2000) *The Blackwell Dictionary of Sociology: A User's Guide to Sociological Language*. London:Wiley-Blackwell.

Johnson, Jeri (1993) 'Introduction', *Ulysses*. Oxford: Oxford University Press, ix–xxxvii.

Jones, Jonathan (2007) 'Pablo's Punks', *The Guardian*, 9 January. On-line. http://www.guardian.co.uk/culture/2007/jan/09/2 (accessed 3 July 2009).

Jones, Kent (2002) 'To Live or Clarify the Moment: Rick Linklater's "Waking Life"', *Senses of Cinema*, March. On-line. http://archive.sensesofcinema.com/contents/01/19/waking.html (accessed 12 August 2009).

Joyce, James (1993) *Ulysses*. Oxford: Oxford University Press.

_____ (2000) *Finnegans Wake*. London: Penguin Modern Classics.

Kaplow, Robert (2008) *Me and Orson Welles*. London: Vintage Books.

Kaufman, Anthony (2001) 'Dazed and Enthused; Richard Linklater Proves He's No Slacker', *Indiewire*, October 18. On-line. http://www.indiewire.com/article/interview_dazed_and_enthused_richard_linklater_proves_hes_no_slacker/ (accessed 10 August 2009).

Kemp, Philip (2006) 'Slacker', in Jim Hillier (ed.) *American Independent Cinema: A Sight and Sound Reader*. London: British Film Institute, 130–1.

Kinder, Marsha (1993) *Blood Cinema: The Reconstruction of National Identity in Spain*. Berkeley: University of California Press.

King, Geoff (2005) *American Independent Cinema*. London: I. B. Tauris.

_____ (2009) *Indiewood, USA*. London: I. B. Tauris.

Koresky, Michael (2004a) 'Mind The Gap', *Reverse Shot*, Summer. On-line. http://www.reverseshot.com/legacy/summer04/shivas.html (accessed 12 March 2009).

_____ (2004b) 'Thanks for the Memory', *Reverse Shot*, Summer. On-line. http://www.reverseshot.com/legacy/summer04/tape.html (accessed 1 March 2009).

_____ (2006) 'Review: Raw Meat: Richard Linklater's "Fast Food Nation"', *Indiewire*, 16 November. On-line. http://www.indiewire.com/article/review_raw_meat_richard_linklaters_fast_food_nation/ (accessed 13 July 2009).

Kracauer, Siegfried (1960) *Theory of Film: The Redemption of Physical Reality*. Oxford: Oxford University Press.

Kristeva, Julia (1984) *Revolution in Poetic Language* (trans. Léon Roudiez). New York, Columbia University Press.

Krizan, Kim (1995) 'Love … it's a bitch', Richard Linklater and Kim Krizan (eds) *Before Sunrise*. New York: St. Martin's Griffin Press, 6.

La Franco, Robert (2006) 'Trouble in Toontown', *Wired*, 14, 3. On-line. http://www.wired.com/wired/archive/14.03/scanner.html (accessed 14 December 2009).

Lefebvre, Henri (1991) *The Production of Space*. London: Blackwell.

Levitch, Timothy (2009) 'Speed Levitch Explains It All', *The Austin Chronicle*, 18, 13. No date of publication given. On-line. http://www.austinchronicle.com/issues/vol18/issue13/screens.cruise.side.html (accessed 13 November 2009).

Levy, Emanuel (2001) *Cinema of Outsiders: The Rise of American Independent Film*. New York: New York University Press.

Linklater, Richard (1993) 'Still Dazed after All These Years', *Dazed and Confused*. New York: St. Martin's Press, 5.

_____ (1995) 'Introduction', Richard Linklater and Kim Krizan (eds) *Before Sunrise*. New York: St. Martin's Griffin Press, 5.

_____ (2003) 'Director's Statement', *Live from Shiva's Dance Floor* booklet with DVD. USA: Aspyr Media Inc.

_____ (2004) 'Slacker Culture', *Slacker* booklet with DVD. USA: Criterion Collection.

_____ (2006a) 'Dear Cast', *Dazed and Confused* booklet with DVD. USA: Criterion Collection, 52.

_____ (2006b) 'To The Filmmakers', *Dazed and Confused* booklet with DVD. USA: Criterion Collection, 53.

_____ (2006c) _Dazed and Confused_ DVD Commentary. USA: Criterion Collection.

_____ (2009) Untitled article, _Eagle Pennell & The Whole Shootin' Match_ booklet with _The Whole Shootin' Match_ DVD Special Edition. London: Watchmaker Films, 15.

Linklater, Richard and Kim Krizan (2005) 'Before Sunrise', Richard Linklater, Kim Krizan, Ethan Hawke and Julie Delpy (eds) (2005) _Before Sunrise and Before Sunset_. New York: Vintage Books.

Lowenstein, Stephen (2009) _My First Movie: Take Two_. London: Vintage Books.

Lyotard, Jean-François (1999) _The Postmodern Condition: A Report on Knowledge_. Manchester: Manchester University Press.

MacCabe, Colin (2003) _Godard: A Portrait of the Artist at Seventy_. New York: Farrar, Strauss & Giroux.

MacDowell, James (2008) 'Love and Fate in "The Clock" and "Before Sunrise"', _Alternate Takes_, 3 January. On-line. http://www.alternatetakes.co.uk/?2008,1,194 (accessed 14 June 2009).

Martin-Jones, David (2006) _Cinema and National Identity_. Edinburgh: Edinburgh University Press.

Mendik, Xavier and Steven Jay Schneider (eds) (2002) _Underground USA: Filmmaking Beyond the Hollywood Canon_. London: Wallflower Press.

Merritt, Greg (2000) _Celluloid Mavericks: A History of American Independent Film_. New York: Thunder's Mouth Press.

Milovanovic, Dragan (1995) 'Dueling Paradigms: Modernist v. Postmodernist Thought', _Humanity and Society_, 19, 1, 1–22. On-line. http://www.critcrim.org/critpapers/milovanovic_postmod.htm (accessed 27 June 2009).

Monaco, James (2000) _How to Read a Film_. Oxford: Oxford University Press.

Moreno, Ashley (2008) 'Zen and the Art of Winning Championships', _The Austin Chronicle_, 30 May. On-line. http://www.austinchronicle.com/gyrobase/Issue/story?oid=629432 (accessed 12 December 2009).

Morrey, Douglas (2005) _Jean-Luc Godard_. Manchester: Manchester University Press.

Mottram, James (2006) _The Sundance Kids: How the Mavericks Took Back Hollywood_. New York: Faber & Faber.

Naficy, Hamid (2001) _An Accented Cinema: Exilic and Diasporic Filmmaking_. Princeton, NJ: Princeton University Press.

Neale, Steve (2000) _Genre and Hollywood_. London: Routledge.

Norton, Glen (2000) 'The Seductive Slack of "Before Sunrise"', _Post Script – Essays in Film and the Humanities_, 19, 2, 62–72.

O'Connell, Joe (2009) 'New Texas film-industry incentives could bring Fox TV series to Dallas', _The Dallas Morning News_, 24 April. On-line. http://www.dallasnews.com/sharedcontent/dws/news/city/dallas/stories/042409gdshotintexas_hp.107514a2a.html (accessed 12 June 2009).

Odintz, Mark (2009) '"The Whole Shootin' Match" as Southern Culture', _Eagle Pennell & The Whole Shootin' Match_ booklet, _The Whole Shootin' Match_ Special Edition DVD. London: Watchmaker Films, 18–19.

Peary, Gerald (2004) 'Richard Linklater & Julie Delpy', *Boston Phoenix*, June. On-line. http://www.geraldpeary.com/interviews/jkl/linklater.html (accessed 28 August 2009).

Pedraja, Luis G. (1999) 'Whitehead, Deconstruction and Postmodernism', *Process Studies*, 28, 1/2, 68–84. On-line. http://www.religion-online.org/showarticle. asp?title=2986 (accessed 12 June 2009).

Pierson, John (1996) *Spike, Mike, Slackers & Dykes: A Guided Tour across a Decade of Independent American Cinema*. London: Faber & Faber.

Powell, Anna (2008) 'Off Your Face: Schizoanalysis, Faciality and Film', in Ian Buchanan and Patricia MacCormack (eds) *Deleuze and the Schizoanalysis of Cinema*. London and New York: Continuum, 116–29.

Price, Brian (2003) 'Richard Linklater', *Senses of Cinema*. On-line. http://www. sensesofcinema.com/2003/great-directors/linklater/ (accessed 29 January 2006).

Richards, David (1994) 'Review/Theater: Suburbia: Aimless Youth, Shouting Out Its Angst', *New York Times*, 23 May. On-line. http://theater2.nytimes.com/mem/ theater/treview.html?pagewanted=print&res=9A05E6DF1E38F930A15756C0A 962958260 (accessed 14 June 2009).

Robey, Tim (2007) 'The Best Years in the Life of Richard Linklater', *Sight & Sound*, 17, 4, 24–27.

Rodríguez, Robert (2006) *Rebel Without A Crew*. New York: Plume.

Rosenbaum, Jon (2001) '"Slacker"'s Oblique Strategy', reprinted from *The New York Observer*, 13 August 2001, in *Slacker* booklet, *Slacker* DVD (2004). USA: Criterion Collection.

_____ (2004) 'Spur of the Moment', *The Chicago Reader*, 4 July. On-line. http:// www.chicagoreader.com/chicago/spur-of-the-moment/Content?oid=915922, (accessed 24 September 2009).

Rosenthal, Edna (2008) *Aristotle and Modernism: Aesthetic Affinities of T. S. Eliot, Wallace Stevens and Virginia Woolf*. Brighton: Sussex Academic Press.

Roud, Richard (1980) *Cinema: A Critical Dictionary: The Major Filmmakers*. New York: Viking.

Russell, Mike (2006) 'The Culturepulp Q&A: Richard Linklater', *CulturePulp*, 1 July. On-line. http://homepage.mac.com/merussell/iblog/B835531044/ C1592678312/E20060701140745/index.html (accessed 23 October 2009).

Ryan, Michael and Douglas Kellner (1990) *Camera Politica: The Politics and Ideology of Contemporary Hollywood Film*. Bloomington: Indiana University Press.

Sabiston, Bob (2009a) 'God's Little Monkey'. On-line. http://www.flatblackfilms. com/Flat_Black_Films/Films/Pages/Gods_Little_Monkey.html (accessed 26 June 2009).

_____ (2009b) 'Project Incognito'. On-line. http://www.flatblackfilms.com/Flat_ Black_Films/Films/Pages/Project_Incognito.html (accessed 26 June 2009).

_____ (2009c) 'Rotoshop'. On-line. http://www.flatblackfilms.com/Flat_Black_ Films/Rotoshop.html (accessed 26 June 2009).

_____ (2009d) 'RoadHead'. On-line. http://www.flatblackfilms.com/Flat_Black_Films/Films/Pages/Roadhead.html (accessed 26 June 2009).

_____ (2009e) 'Snack and Drink'. On-line. http://www.flatblackfilms.com/Flat_Black_Films/Films/Pages/Snack_and_Drink.html(accessed 26 June 2009).

_____ (2009f) 'Figures of Speech'. On-line. http://www.flatbla.ckfilms.com/Flat_Black_Films/Films/Pages/Figures_of_Speech.html (accessed 26 June 2009).

_____ (2009g) 'Yard'. On-line. http://www.flatblackfilms.com/Flat_Black_Films/Films/Pages/Yard.html (accessed 26 June 2009).

_____ (2009h) 'Fourth Obstruction'. On-line. http://www.flatblackfilms.com/Flat_Black_Films/Films/Pages/Fourth_Obstruction.html (accessed 26 June 2009).

_____ (2009i) 'A Scanner Darkly'. On-line. http://www.flatblackfilms.com/Flat_Black_Films/Films/Pages/A_Scanner_Darkly.html (accessed 26 June 2009).

Saint John of the Cross (2003) *Dark Night of the Soul*. Mineola, NY: Dover Publications.

Saint Teresa of Avila (2007) *Interior Castle*. Mineola, NY: Dover Publications.

Sarris, Andrew (1985 [1962]) 'Notes on the Auteur Theory in 1962', in Gerald Mast and Marshall Cohen (eds) *Film Theory and Criticism*, 3rd edition. New York: Oxford University Press, 527–40.

Savlov, Marc (2009) 'What Would Jean-Luc Do?', *The Austin Chronicle*, 24 July 2009, 41–42.

Schlosser, Eric (2001) *Fast Food Nation*. New York: Allen Lane/Penguin Press.

_____ (2004) *Reefer Madness*. England: Penguin Books.

Schwartz, David (2004) 'The Daily Show or "It's Impossible to Learn to Plow by Reading Books"', *Reverse Shot*, Summer. On-line. http://www.reverseshot.com/legacy/summer04/plow.html (accessed 12 September 2009).

Self, Will (2009) Interviewed on *Today*, Radio 4, BBC, 4 November 2009.

Sheldrake, Rupert (2009). On-line. http://www.sheldrake.org/homepage.html (accessed 12 November 2009).

Sklar, Robert (1993) *Film: An International History of the Medium*. New York: Prentice Hall.

Sloman, Albert B. (1961) 'Introduction', in Calderón de la Barca, Don Pedro, Albert B. Sloman (eds) *La vida es sueño*. Manchester: Manchester University Press, ix–xxxix.

Smith, Gavin (2006) 'Lost in America: Interview with Richard Linklater', *Film Comment*, July–August. On-line. http://www.newyorkfilmfestival.com/fcm/ja06/richardlinklater2.htm (accessed 14 April 2009).

Smith, Kevin (2008) '"Slacker" Now on Hulu', 9 October. On-line. http://blog.hulu.com/2008/10/9/slacker (accessed 3 November 2009).

Sontag, Susan (1969) *Styles of Radical Will*. New York: Farrar, Straus and Giroux.

_____ (2001) 'The Talk of the Town', *The New Yorker*, 24 September. On-line: http://www.newyorker.com/archive/2001/09/24/010924ta_talk_wtc (accessed 5 January 2010).

Sørensen, Georg (2003) *The Transformation of the State: Beyond the Myth of Retreat.* Basingstoke: Palgrave Macmillan.

Southgate, Beverley (2003) *History in Postmodernity: Fear or Freedom?.* London and New York: Routledge.

Speed, Lesley (1998) 'Tuesday's Gone: The Nostalgic Teen Film', *Journal of Popular Film and Television* 26, 1, 24–32.

_____ (2007) 'The Possibilities of Roads Not Taken: Intellect and Utopia in the Films of Richard Linklater', *Journal of Popular Film & Television*, 35, 3, 98–106.

Spong, John (2006) 'The Spirit of '76' in *Dazed and Confused* DVD booklet, Criterion Collection, 33–47.

Stam, Robert (2000) *Film Theory: An Introduction.* London: Blackwell.

Sternbergh, Adam (2010) 'The Ethan Hawke Actors Studio', *New York*, 31 January. On-line. http://nymag.com/arts/theater/profiles/63419/ (accessed 6 February 2010).

Stevenson, Robert Louis (2009) 'An Apology for Idlers' in *An Apology for Idlers.* London: Penguin. First printed 1877, 'An Apology for Idlers' in *Cornhill Magazine*, July 1877, XXXVI, 80–6.

Stone, Rob (2007) 'Between Sunrise and Sunset: An Elliptical Dialogue between American and European Cinema', in Paul Cooke (ed.) *World Cinema's 'Dialogues' with Hollywood.* Basingstoke: Palgrave Macmillan, 218–37.

_____ (2010) 'Ambition's Debt', *Sight & Sound*, 20, 1, 34–6.

Suárez, Juan A. (2007) *Jim Jarmusch.* Urbana and Chicago: University of Illinois Press.

Tarkovsky, Andrei (1989) *Sculpting in Time: Tarkovsky the Great Russian Filmmaker Discusses his Art.* Austin: University of Texas Press.

Tracy, Andrew (2004) 'Up a Lazy River', *Reverse Shot*, Summer. On-line. http://www.reverseshot.com/legacy/summer04/newton.html (accessed 5 May 2008).

Travers, Peter (2000) 'Dazed and Confused', *Rolling Stone*, 8 December. On-line. http://www.rollingstone.com/reviews/movie/5947243/review/5947244/dazed_and_confused (accessed 15 April 2009).

Tzioumakis, Yannis (2006) *American Independent Cinema: An Introduction.* Edinburgh: Edinburgh University Press.

Walsh, David (1998) 'You Can't Hold Back the Human Spirit', March. On-line. http://www.wsws.org/arts/1998/mar1998/link-m27.shtml (accessed 27 March 1998).

Ward, David (1995) 'A Poetics of Resistance', in David Ward (ed.) *A Poetics of Resistance: Narrative and the Writings of Pier Paolo Pasolini.* Madison: Fairleigh Dickinson University Press, 19–25.

Ward, Mike (2007) '$20 million incentive package proposed for filmmakers', *Statesman*, 30 January. On-line. http://www.statesman.com/news/content/region/legislature/stories/01/30/30film.html (accessed 14 June 2009).

Ward, Paul (2006) 'Shape-Shifting Realism', *Sight & Sound* 16, 8, 42.

Waxman, Sharon (2006) *Rebels on the Backlot.* New York: Harper Perennial.

Weidner, Chris (2010) 'Open Casting Call For Richard Linklater's Texas Feature Film "Bernie"', 5 August. On-line. http://www.shortfilmtexas.com/2010/open-casting-call-for-richard-linklaters-texas-feature-film-bernie/ (accessed 21 December 2010).

Wilinsky, Barbara (2001) *Sure Seaters: The Emergence of the Art House Cinema*. Minneapolis & London: University of Minnesota Press.

Wood, Jason (2006) 'Richard Linklater', *Talking Movies: Contemporary World Filmmakers in Interview*. London: Wallflower Press, 150–5.

Wood, Robin (1986) *Hollywood from Vietnam to Reagan*. New York: Columbia University Press.

_____ (1988) *Sexual Politics and Narrative Film: Hollywood and Beyond*. New York: Columbia University Press.

Wyatt, Edward (2003) 'New Trade Center Site Plans Draw Some Old Complaints', *The New York Times*, 14 January. On-line. http://www.nytimes.com/2003/01/14/nyregion/new-trade-center-site-plans-draw-some-old-complaints.html?scp=1&sq=&st=nyt&pagewanted=1 (accessed 5 January 2010).

Wyatt, Justin (1994) *High Concept: Movies and Marketing in Hollywood*. Austin: University of Texas Press.

_____ (1998) 'The Formation of the "Major Independents": Miramax, New Line and the New Hollywood', in Steve Neale and Murray Smith (eds) *Contemporary Hollywood Cinema*. London: Routledge, 74–90.

Žižek, Slavoj (1992) *Looking Awry: An Introduction to Jacques Lacan through Popular Culture*. Cambridge, MA: MIT Press.

INDEX

Literary and artistic works are listed under authors; *italic* numbers refer to illustrations; n. indicates an endnote.